Languages of Belief and Early Sociology in Nineteenth-Century France

Michiel Van Dam

Languages of Belief and Early Sociology in Nineteenth-Century France

The Elementary Forms of Sociological Life

palgrave
macmillan

Michiel Van Dam
University of Antwerp
Antwerpen, Belgium

ISBN 978-3-031-70022-4   ISBN 978-3-031-70023-1   (eBook)
https://doi.org/10.1007/978-3-031-70023-1

© The Editor(s) (if applicable) and The Author(s), under exclusive license to Springer Nature Switzerland AG 2024

This work is subject to copyright. All rights are solely and exclusively licensed by the Publisher, whether the whole or part of the material is concerned, specifically the rights of translation, reprinting, reuse of illustrations, recitation, broadcasting, reproduction on microfilms or in any other physical way, and transmission or information storage and retrieval, electronic adaptation, computer software, or by similar or dissimilar methodology now known or hereafter developed.
The use of general descriptive names, registered names, trademarks, service marks, etc. in this publication does not imply, even in the absence of a specific statement, that such names are exempt from the relevant protective laws and regulations and therefore free for general use.
The publisher, the authors and the editors are safe to assume that the advice and information in this book are believed to be true and accurate at the date of publication. Neither the publisher nor the authors or the editors give a warranty, expressed or implied, with respect to the material contained herein or for any errors or omissions that may have been made. The publisher remains neutral with regard to jurisdictional claims in published maps and institutional affiliations.

This Palgrave Macmillan imprint is published by the registered company Springer Nature Switzerland AG.
The registered company address is: Gewerbestrasse 11, 6330 Cham, Switzerland

If disposing of this product, please recycle the paper.

Acknowledgements

This book has come about as the result of four years of research as part of an interdisciplinary project on solidarity, social science and religion at the University of Antwerp, generously funded by the university's Special Research Fund (BOF). It is the product of a fruitful encounter, a rare research opportunity and my own, now more than decade-long obsession with the so-called weakness of believing. First and foremost, then, I am indebted to the creators and supervisors of the project, Bert De Munck, Stijn Oosterlynck and Patrick Loobuyck, for their faith in me. As I tend to write with the fullness of my person, it is difficult to draw the lines between professional and personal indebtedness. I simply wish to thank these people for their thoughts, their words, their friendship, their kindness and their profound influence on me during the time of writing this book: Lise Dheedene, Hannah Fluit, Josine Buggenhout, Gena Kagermanov, Anita Kafka, Jochem De Schutter. A special mention should also go to Steven Vanden Broecke, my *Doktorvater*, who instilled in me a passion for close yet charitable reading. I am still greatly indebted to his readings of Michel de Certeau and the history of belief-narrations. Thank you also to Sharla Plant, my editor at Palgrave Macmillan, for her willingness to take on what is and remains a quite peculiar book project.

And finally, this book is dedicated to my wife, Priscella Mekenkamp and our son, Ezra. Your love and affection radiate throughout the pages of this book.

Contents

1 **Introduction**   1
   The Secularity of Classical Sociology in Question   1
   An Intellectual History of Social Science: Ideas Versus Languages as Sites of Intervention   4
   On Matters of Translation, or: What Does It Mean to Speak and Think Belief?   12
   Epistemology, Genealogy, Archaeology: Approaching the History of Social Science and Religion   18
   The Elementary Forms of Sociological Life   29
   Structure of the Book   31
   Concluding Remarks   34

2 **On the Possibility of a Sociological Mode of Existence. Bruno Latour and the Post-Secular Critiques of Belief**   35
   Introduction   35
   Post-Secular Critiques of Belief   38
   The Post-Secular Critique of Belief as an Act and Intervention: Bruno Latour   44
   The Limits of Conceptual Clarity   49
   The Critique of Belief as an Echo of Sociological Modernity   55
   Conclusion   60

3 Historicizing the Sociological Belief/Knowledge-Composition: Theories and Method ... 63
Introduction ... 63
The Advantages of History: Belief as Modality and Historical Language ... 64
A Historical Anthropology of Belief and Its Languages: Michel de Certeau ... 69
The Anthropology of Sociological Belief ... 73
Conclusion ... 81

4 Early Experiments in the Sociological Operation I: Languages of Belief Within the French Eighteenth-Century Knowledge Culture ... 83
Introduction ... 83
The Formality of Belief: From an Ethics of Enlightenment to the Social Facts of Societal Structures ... 85
Belief and the Birth of the Social Sciences in the Early Nineteenth Century ... 92
Conclusion ... 96

5 Early Experiments in the Sociological Operation II. The Christian Sociologism of Louis de Bonald ... 99
Introduction ... 99
Situating Louis de Bonald: Catholic Reactionary, Philosopher, Thinker of Society ... 102
Making Solidarity Between the Philosophical and Religious Classes: Belief in the Work of Louis de Bonald ... 105
Narrating Belief and Natural Society into Existence: Bonaldian Techniques of Self-Historicization ... 115
Conclusion ... 129

6 Early Experiments in the Sociological Operation III. The Socialist Sociologisms of Saint-Simon and the Saint-Simonists ... 133
Introduction ... 133
Saint-Simon: Between Sociology, Socialism and Religion ... 135

A Case of mentir-vrai? *Historiographical Interpretations of the Saint-Simonists and Belief*	139
A Saint-Simonist Philosophy of the Present: Modernity and the Arrival of the Cartesian Regime of Belief	141
From Philosophy to Prescriptive Ethic: Believing Alternatively as a Saint-Simonist Moral Practice	149
Towards a Hidden Knowledge of the Social: Belief and Experience in Saint-Simonist Thought	161
Conclusion	167

7 Sociology as Institution and as Spiritual Authority: Languages of Belief in the Work of Auguste Comte — 171

Introduction: The Advent of Positivism — 171
The Peculiar Case of Auguste Comte — 175
The Comtean Passage: Moving Sociology Beyond the Reactionary Debates of the Early Nineteenth Century — 180
Narrating the Sociological Government of Beliefs: Aristotle, St. Paul, Gall — 185
The Institutionalization of Beliefs: Cult and Education — 190
Keeping Beliefs Alive Within a Positivist Knowledge Culture: Comte on Prayer — 195
Conclusion — 199

8 Narrating Solidarity Through the Division of Belief: Durkheim and the History of Belief Systems — 203

Introduction — 203
Prologue. On Belief as a Category of Historical and Sociological Analysis: Durkheim and Seignobos — 205
Critiques of Durkheimian Approaches to Belief — 211
Orienting Durkheim Within the History of Belief: Thinking Society Through the Division of Belief with Comte and Fustel de Coulanges — 218
From an Organic to a Mechanical Government of Beliefs: Sociological Faith in the Function of Solidarity — 224
Conclusion — 232

9 The Varieties of Sociological Experience. Durkheimian Belief/Knowledge-Compositions 235
Introduction 235
Beliefs as Representations: Durkheim and the Neo-Kantian Theory of Belief 237
Thinking Sociology as a Positivist Institution: Durkheim on Pragmatism 244
Pragmatism and Sociological Positivism on the Poetic Function of Belief 251
Conclusion 262

10 Epilogue: Sociology and Belief Beyond Positivism 269
Introduction 269
Speaking Belief Sociologically, After Durkheim: Mauss, Parsons and Beyond 269
Conceptualizing the Belief-Relation in Mauss: Giving, Praying, Sacrificing 270
Productive Typologies: Parsons on Systems of Belief 276
Conclusion 279

11 Concluding Remarks: Returning to the Post-Secular 281
Introduction 281
The Institution of Sociology and the Performativity of the Sociological Belief-Language 283
Returning to the Post-Secular and the Conditions of Sociological Modernity 290

Bibliography 297

Index 325

CHAPTER 1

Introduction

THE SECULARITY OF CLASSICAL SOCIOLOGY IN QUESTION

The current debate on the discipline of sociology, its historical legacy as a modernist science and its relation to religion is predominantly framed through the lens of the 'post-secular': whereas nineteenth- and twentieth-century sociologists, so it is argued, took the gradual disappearance of religion in civil life as both empirically and normatively given, contemporary researchers are no longer convinced that this is the case and therefore seek to question, critique and reorient the typical secularization theories as put forward by early sociologists like Henri de Saint-Simon, Auguste Comte, Émile Durkheim and Max Weber. The 'post' in post-secular refers to the increased questioning by contemporary scholars of both the empirical and normative premises of classical secularization theories. Empirically, several social scientists point out that, rather than simply declining, religious movements and institutions are flourishing and even growing in several parts of the world.[1] Also, in a more normative sense, social and

---

[1] Peter L. Berger, "The Desecularization of the World: A Global Overview", in: *The Desecularization of the World: Resurgent Religion and World Politics*, ed. Peter L. Berger (Grand Rapids, MI: William B. Eerdmans Publishing Company, 1999), 1–18; Paul Cloke & Justin Beaumont, "Geographies of postsecular rapprochement in the city", *Progress in Human Geography* 37, no. 1 (2012): 27–51.

political philosophers have started to argue, from within the post-secular framework, that religion is not *a priori* antithetical to a rationalizing society, meaning that moral and social progress and religious devotion are processes which, potentially, can still go hand in hand, even function as possible mutual beneficiaries.[2]

The post-secular paradigm has, then, unearthed several fruitful and sociologically important avenues of research through its self-declared rupture with its own modernist and secularist past, opening up central themes of the discipline—solidarity, community-formation, social change, public opinion—to include religious traditions, actors and objects as potential sources of social agency, identification and transformation.[3] In essence, it has sought to remove 'being secular' as a form of institutional and epistemological gatekeeping, nurturing instead an attitude of openness and reciprocity towards the religious other and their own conceptual instruments of interpretation and meaning-giving.

There is one aspect, within this analytical framework, which has, however, remained unexplored and that is the question of the genuine *secularity* of the nineteenth- and twentieth-century social science itself. Often, post-secular scholars frame their own interventions as originating in the explicit critique that the methodological and theoretical toolsets of the sociological moderns were in themselves biased towards more rationalist versions of religious traditions, with exclusionary effects and misleading societal prognostications as a result.[4] It is the claim, in other words, that these moderns imposed categories and demarcations onto the religious domain foreign to the latter (the "Western-style objectifications of religion", in the words of Arvind-Pal S. Mandair and Markus Dressler) and, as such, repopulated and ultimately exiled religious believers from their

---

[2] Jürgen Habermas, "Notes on Post-Secular Society", *New Perspectives Quarterly* 25, no. 4 (2008): 17–29.

[3] Timothy Stacey, "Imagining solidarity in the twenty-first century: towards a performative postsecularism", *Religion, State and Society* 45, no. 2 (2017): 141–158; Paul Cloke, Christopher Baker, Callum Sutherland, & Andrew Williams (eds.), *Geographies of Postsecularity: Re-envisioning Politics, Subjectivity and Ethics* (London: Routledge, 2019); David Herbert & Josh Bullock, "The Diversity of Nonreligion: Meaning-Making, Activism and Towards a Theory of Nonreligious Identity and Group Formation", in: *Non-Religion in Late Modern Societies: Institutional and Legal Perspectives*, eds. Anne-Laure Zwilling & Helge Årsheim (Cham: Springer, 2022), 151–171.

[4] The most famous exponent of this critique being Talal Asad, cf. Talal Asad, *Formations of the Secular: Christianity, Islam, Modernity* (Stanford: Stanford University Press, 2003).

own previously privileged spaces.[5] Such an intervention, however, is paired with another, more implicit claim which is understood as a given rather than anything to question in itself: that these secularizing toolsets, while foreign to religious believers, fully encapsulated the identities and desires of the sociological moderns on the other hand.

The question remains, however, whether the sociological moderns can be approached as a homogenous bloc of secularists and whether classical sociology was as secular as it is made out to be. If modernity transformed the possible experience of religion in civil society, should we not ask ourselves in what ways the pendulum swung back the other way? Was sociology itself also not susceptible to historical transformations, influences and reorientations in its shifting engagements with historical religions in transition? In other words, we still need to investigate whether nineteenth- and twentieth-century social science was self-secularizing, how these modernist social scientists formed relationships to their own secularizing theories and what these relationships exactly looked like. It is by investigating the secularity of social science itself, tracing its historical development in relation to both its religious object and its own discourses of secularization that we can gain a better understanding of the kind of problems we face today as well as the ways in which we can respond. Without understanding the history of secularity and non-secularity within the sociological discipline itself, it is impossible to convincingly analyse the state of our current post-secular condition. To go forward, in other words, it is imperative that the sociological discipline first looks back at its own contexts of becoming.

It is my claim here that such an historical anthropology of the sociological moderns and their complex engagements with religion then has been insufficiently undertaken and when it has been done, for example in Bruno Latour's anthropology of the moderns, it has failed to effectively historicize the sociology/religion-relation. In the case of the latter, rather than investigating the different compositions sprouting from the interactions between sociology and religion, it has instead simply continued the incessant boundary work which has been occurring between the two domains since the inception of the social sciences in the early nineteenth

---

[5] Arvind-Pal S. Mandair and Markus Dressler, "Introduction: Modernity, Religion-Making, and the Post-Secular", in: *Secularism and Religion-Making*, eds. Markus Dressler & Arvind-Pal S. Mandair (Oxford: Oxford University Press, 2011), 3–36.

century.⁶ Throughout this work, I will try to circumvent this tradition of boundary work and contestation by imposing my own framework, that of historical belief-languages. I consider 'belief' to be a uniquely suitable interpretative prism because of its migratory status as a concept, as something that was continuously appropriated and reshaped by both sociological and religious actors, as it was used for defining and giving shape to religious and non-rational practices. Instead of taking the standard opposition between a social *science* and a religious *worldview*, I will focus on how both domains navigated languages of belief to think and govern themselves, thus avoiding a more teleological approach.

Beliefs, for the sociological moderns, were highly functional and performative instruments: they were not merely categories of (scientific) analysis, they were also ways of giving meaning to what *being a sociologist* and *doing sociology* was. It is with these techniques of self-historicization via languages of belief that I am here concerned, as they can paint a better picture of what 'being secular' actually meant within the sociological discipline. It allows me to draw an innovative trajectory throughout the history of sociology and religion, one where Bonaldian social constitutionalism, Comtean altruism and Durkheimian solidarity can be approached as highly contextualized interventions, not merely epistemological instruments but conceptual explorations and compositions within the field of historical belief-languages. Such a reading of sociological belief-languages as a means of bringing the fields of sociology and religion into dialogue is informed and inspired by the work of French historian and anthropologist Michel de Certeau and is, as such, intended as a historical application of the Jesuit's project of an anthropology of believing as imagined in the final years of his life.⁷

An Intellectual History of Social Science: Ideas Versus Languages as Sites of Intervention

This book seeks to provide an intellectual history on the different languages of belief existing in the nineteenth and early twentieth century, specifically as a tool for navigating the domain of 'society', a concept which was becoming increasingly prevalent in the seventeenth and eighteenth

---

⁶ Cf. infra Chap. 2.

⁷ Cf. Michel de Certeau, "L'institution du croire. Note de travail", *Recherches de science religieuse* 71 (1983): 61–80. I expand on this approach in Chap. 3.

centuries as a way of framing and thinking communal life.⁸ Taking up a historical-constructivist perspective, I start out from the premise that something like 'society' did not always exist, at least not in the way it has come to be understood today.⁹ Rather, I emphasize the line of thought which approaches society as a category and concept that was constructed through all kinds of virtual, material, philosophical and reflective practices, eventually transforming into a particular kind of habitable space, both materially and virtually, through which communities, ideologies and collective struggles could be formed, articulated and experienced.¹⁰ In the case of France, this process took place in the seventeenth and eighteenth centuries and played a central role in making possible the idea that social life was populated by individuals who could shape the forms and conditions of this life, through such instruments as reason, philosophy, historical understanding and the sciences.¹¹

While it can be debated to what degree the self-reflexive awareness of something like a 'society' existing in an independent and autonomous fashion impacted the everyday social conditions and interactions, here I will limit myself to the claim that the foundation of the social sciences in the late eighteenth and early nineteenth century was thoroughly influenced by the invention of this category, as the domain of society came to function as the primary imaginary space for explaining and exploring the question of why people lived together in a collective manner and what it was that propelled them to act in a socially desirable and collaborative

---

⁸ On the history of this terminology, cf. David A. Bell, "Nation et patrie, société et civilisation: Transformations du vocabulaire social français, 1700–1789", in: *L'invention de la société. Nominalisme politique et science sociale au XVIIIᵉ siècle*, eds. Laurence Kaufmann & Jacques Guilhaumou (Paris: Éditions de l'École des hautes études en sciences sociales, 2003), 99–122.

⁹ The standard account of such an approach is still: Ian Hacking, *The Social Construction of What?* (Cambridge, MA: Harvard University Press, 1999). Hacking also discussed the invention of this category, cf. Ian Hacking, "L'ontologie historique", in: *L'invention de la société. Nominalisme politique et science sociale au XVIIIᵉ siècle*, eds. Laurence Kaufmann & Jacques Guilhaumou (Paris: Éditions de l'École des hautes études en sciences sociales, 2003), 287–310.

¹⁰ For its political history, cf. Jacques Donzelot, *L'invention du social. Essai sur le déclin des passions politiques* (Paris: Fayard, 1984).

¹¹ Laurence Kaufmann & Jacques Guilhaumou, "Présentation", in: *L'invention de la société. Nominalisme politique et science sociale au XVIIIᵉ siècle*, eds. Laurence Kaufmann & Jacques Guilhaumou (Paris: Éditions de l'École des hautes études en sciences sociales, 2003), 9–20.

fashion.[12] This was a point of historical transition, furthermore, which coalesced with both a crisis of religion as a self-evident category for interpreting communal living, and with a philosophical revolution rooted in the question of what it meant to believe.[13] It is my argument that this historical coalescence has, in many ways, shaped the discipline of sociology in a way that can still be experienced today.

It is not, however, a history of the social sciences, at least not in the typical sense. My goal is not to explain or contextualize the birth of a specific, sociological way of *thinking*, as put forward in some classics of the genre, such as Robert Nisbet's *The Sociological Tradition* (1966), Johan Heilbron's *The Rise of Social Theory* (1995) or Marc Joly's recent book, *La révolution sociologique* (2017).[14] Rather, the domain of the 'unfolding' social sciences of the nineteenth and early twentieth centuries serves as the material landscape for investigating the ways these languages of belief were appropriated, reconstructed and reimagined by the sociological moderns, acting as the terrain for a series of historical meetings. The explorers and administrators of this new place called society—social scientists, bureaucrats, clergy, urban planners, industrialists, political economists, poets, artists, union organizers, revolutionaries—all of these required a grammar and language to successfully enter, explore and cultivate the social domain, one of which, so I will argue, was the language of belief, a language with a rich and diverse history of its own.[15]

But what do I exactly mean when I speak of something like a 'language of belief'? Such a question requires us to, first, expand on the notion of

---

[12] On this process, cf. infra ch. 4. A good summary is provided by Johan Heilbron, "The Emergence of Social Theory", in: *The Cambridge Handbook of Social Theory, vol. I: A Contested Canon*, ed. Peter Kivisto (Cambridge: Cambridge University Press, 2021), 1–23.

[13] This transition is nicely captured by Paul Veyne: "People hardly believe anymore that there is such a thing as human nature, and they leave to political philosophers the idea that a truth of things exists. But they believe in society, and this enables them to account for the area between what is called economics and what can be put under the heading of ideology." Cf. Paul Veyne, *Did the Greeks Believe in their Myths? An Essay on the Constitutive Imagination*, transl. by Paula Wissing (Chicago: University of Chicago Press, 1988), 120.

[14] Robert A. Nisbet, *The Sociological Tradition* (New Brunswick: Transaction Publishers, 1993 [1st ed. 1966]); Johan Heilbron, *The Rise of Social Theory*, transl. by Sheila Gogol (Minneapolis, MN: University of Minnesota Press, 1995); Marc Joly, *La révolution sociologique. De la naissance d'un régime de pensée scientifique à la crise de la philosophie (XIXe-XXe siècle)* (Paris: Éditions La Découverte, 2017).

[15] On this history, cf. Ethan H. Shagan, *The Birth of Modern Belief: Faith and Judgment from the Middle Ages to the Enlightenment* (Princeton: Princeton University Press, 2018).

'language' as an avenue for the study of intellectual history, and we can do this by briefly reflecting on the tradition of the history of ideas and how it has evolved in recent decades. Typical intellectual history (it gradually crystallized into its own distinct field of inquiry around the middle of the twentieth century) focused on ideas, concepts, categories and ideologies, uttered by such authorial actors as philosophers, political theorists and the likes.[16] The main point of reference in this kind of framework can best be described by what early twentieth-century American philosopher and historian Arthur O. Lovejoy termed "unit-ideas", a series of primal, simple ideas which are broadly shared between cultures and which are subsequently adapted, mixed and compounded into new philosophies and doctrines.[17] And while Lovejoy received his fair share of critique in the subsequent decades for what seemed to be a rather structuralist and essentialist kind of historiography, his general vision of a historical investigation of the formation and development of systems of ideas, beyond the immediate scope of the historical author, remained thoroughly formative of the discipline itself.[18]

The second half of the twentieth century witnessed a further intensification of this perspective, with the 'death of the author' associated with such postmodern thinkers as Michel Foucault and Jacques Derrida a prime example of this. At the same time, such attempts at moving beyond the author stimulated further critical reflections on the status of the 'idea' and 'concept' as the main referential units of such a history, often inspired by novel engagements with Marxist historiography and/or the philosophy of language.[19] A number of intellectual-historical traditions were born out of this desire to think intellectual life beyond a 'mere' discussion of ideas and its contents: the Cambridge School emphasized the importance of context, German *Begriffsgeschichte* aimed to point out the social origins of certain ideas and its influence in the historical trajectories of such ideas,

---

[16] For a more extensive historical overview of the discipline's development, especially within an American context, cf. Anthony Grafton, "The History of Ideas: Precept and Practice, 1950–2000 and Beyond", *Journal of the History of Ideas* 67, no. 1 (2006): 1–32.

[17] Arthur O. Lovejoy, *The Great Chain of Being: A Study of the History of An Idea* (Cambridge, MA: Harvard University Press, 1936), 3–23.

[18] Nico Mouton, "An Apologia for Arthur Lovejoy's Long-Range Approach to the History of Ideas", *History & Theory* 62, no. 2 (2023): 272–295.

[19] Quentin Skinner, "Meaning and Understanding in the History of Ideas", *History and Theory* 8, no. 1 (1969): 3–53.

and French intellectual historians were fascinated by how ideas spawned entire mechanisms of discourse beyond their original meanings.[20]

Recently, certain intellectual historians, like Elías José Palti, have started looking for ways of synthesizing these shared goals across different historiographical traditions in order to better understand the complex interaction between ideas and its environment in a more concise and cohesive manner.[21] One way of exploring such a pathway, according to Palti, is to think intellectual history, not as a study of particular ideas per se, but as a study of entire intellectual languages. The main difference between these two approaches is the concrete site which serves as a locus of investigation: whereas the study of ideas is mainly located in that space which exists between the objective existence of the idea and the subjective mind of the historical actor, an inquiry into intellectual languages finds itself limited to the material landscape populated by ideas and the discursive conditions of possibility enabling the imagination and articulation of these ideas. Or as Palti formulates it:

> In sum, a history of political languages leads us beyond the frameworks of the *philosophies of consciousness*, which are at the basis of the history of ideas. It takes us away from the subjective plane, the representations that subjects have of reality, and reorients our focus to the objective plane of actual practices: more precisely, to the symbolic dimension that is built into them, and that is set into motion in the very performance of them.[22]

Whether the individual subject has the right 'understanding' of a particular idea, whether they correctly capture its meaning given to it by others, whether there even is such a thing as the objective and correct substance of an idea (e.g. the perfect encapsulation of something such as 'democracy' or 'God'), these questions are fully parked to the side in a history of intellectual languages. Instead, what is attempted in such an approach is to bring into view how certain ideas in history have enabled the construction of an incredibly rich system of intersubjective communication, through the practicing, performing, formalizing and institutionalizing of these

---

[20] Melvin Richter, "Reconstructing the History of Political Languages: Pocock, Skinner, and the Geschichtliche Grundbegriffe", *History and Theory* 29, no. 1 (1990): 38–70.

[21] Elías José Palti, "The 'Theoretical Revolution' in Intellectual History: From the History of Political Ideas to the History of Political Languages", *History and Theory* 53 (October 2014): 387–405.

[22] Ibid., 396.

ideas.²³ To think something like 'virtue', for example, has not only intellectual consequences (e.g. a reinvigoration of the debate, an addition to a previously lacking theory, an opening of a novel conceptual horizon) but also real-life, historical effects, such as the creation of a discursive lifeworld which can be inhabited, a community of so-called virtue-speakers and an ever-changing network of actors bound by all sorts of factors (ideological, socio-economic, cultural, etc.).

An intellectual *language*, furthermore, cannot be equated to something like an intellectual *tradition*. In his article, Palti focuses on the domain of politics and makes the distinction between political traditions (e.g. republicanism, liberalism, socialism, and so on), and something like a political-intellectual language. While political-intellectual traditions are bound by a particular proposition's relation to a set of maxims and principles ('is this idea genuinely republican?'), an intellectual language, on the other hand, is marked by a particular type of "mode of production", which, in the case of political-intellectual languages, is defined by its status as *"semantically indeterminate*, that is, they accept the most diverse and indeed contradictory forms of articulation on the level of the ideological contents of speech".²⁴ A single political-intellectual language, in other words, can allow the production of republican, liberal and socialist statements, much in the same way that a language like English can sustain all kinds of propositions which are semantically contradictory but syntactically compatible (e.g. 'The Earth is an oblate spheroid'; 'The Earth is a flat disk').²⁵

The advantage of such an approach, of course, is that all these different intellectual traditions are engaged simultaneously as speaking the same *language*, rather than being divided into separate, historically bordered entities. In contrast to the horizontal scheme of the classical history of ideas—where an idea is extracted and traced across the historical timeline—Palti suggests an alternative:

> But if intellectual history is conceived as unearthing political languages, the old approach won't do because political languages cannot be discovered except by vertically cutting through the entire ideological spectrum. The different currents of thought now become relevant only insofar as, in their

---

²³ Ibid., 400.
²⁴ Ibid., 395.
²⁵ Ibid.

mutual interaction, they reveal the set of shared premises on which the public discourse of an epoch hinged, and how these premises shifted over time.[26]

A second advantage of this type of framework is that it provides a novel and convincing account of conceptual change. Whereas the history of ideas was typically dependent on either individual authors (the 'genius' who transcends the rigours of historical time) or external material processes (culture as shaped by shifts in the economy) in order to explain such change, a history of intellectual languages attributes a certain kind of materiality to intellectual life itself, with this materialistic nature of languages constitutive for the understanding of intellectual life's historical trajectories. In the latter approach, intellectual life is considered as a linguistic field, a textual surface which is littered with semantic gaps and troughs, with conceptual change occurring through the exploitation of these aporias by different kinds of actors.[27]

Palti again turns to the realm of the political in order to further clarify this state of affairs, explaining this concrete material composition through the nature of political interaction itself: according to him, what characterizes an exchange as a *political* exchange is the fact that this exchange is, in many ways, unresolvable.[28] There is no final horizon of a complete and collective agreement on the meaning of a political concept (echoing the thought of French political theorist Pierre Rosanvallon), because this collective agreement would constitute the end of politics itself: "Political debate thus at once presupposes and excludes the possibility of fixing the meaning of political concepts. It is the simultaneous necessity and impossibility of defining concepts that opens the field of politics, that makes concepts *political* concepts."[29] A political language is always, by definition, semantically indeterminate. It can always be contested and, as a result, give way to new sorts of intellectual formations, new meanings and new alliances of actors reorganizing its linguistic field.

Any sort of change to a political-intellectual language, then, does not arise from the actions of a single author or the (political, socio-economic,

[26] Ibid., 401.
[27] Ibid., 404.
[28] Ibid., 398.
[29] Ibid.

institutional, ...) context surrounding it, but the concrete discursive-material composition of the language itself, with the latter being infused with its own temporality and historicity. This composition, as discussed in previous paragraphs, contains both contiguous (e.g. allowing multiple ideological positions) and aporetic (e.g. conceptual contradictions which cannot be resolved) elements at the same time, with the task of the historian to investigate how the balance of these two elements was synchronically constructed in concrete political languages, and how this balance eventually evolved and developed in a diachronic manner.[30]

But this leaves us with the question whether other, non-political intellectual languages are also infused with such qualities as historicity, temporality and semantic indeterminacy, or whether this exclusively belongs to the realm of politics? While I cannot answer this question in any sort of general manner, I would like to briefly make the case in the next section that these qualities are also upheld in those intellectual languages with which we are concerned here, those of 'belief'. The core of the argument made in this section will consist of the claim that 'belief' can not only be considered in the way that it is typically done—i.e. as a concept, category or mental state—but as a language as well: it can be used to describe a particular mode of communication, as a signifier for a particular kind of semiotic relation between actors. 'Belief', in other words, will be used throughout the book in a manner similar to the way someone like Palti approaches the notion of 'political': as an adjective which characterizes a unique sort of communicative bond, practice and semantic field, the main characteristic of which can best be described as the navigation and negotiation of alterity.[31] Furthermore, I contend that this kind of language—both its historical variants as well as its contemporary variant in the nineteenth century—played a crucial role in the early formation of sociology, both as a means of differentiation (from religion and theological discourses) and as a means of self-imagination.

---

[30] Ibid., 404.

[31] Ibid., 400: "One fundamental reason is that political languages actually do not consist of *statements* (contents of discourse), which could be listed, but of a characteristic *form* of producing them." On this characterization of a belief-language, cf. Michel de Certeau, "Une pratique sociale de la différence: croire", *Faire croire. Modalités de la diffusion et de la réception des messages religieux du xiie au xve siècle, École française de Rome*, no. 303 (1981): 363.

On Matters of Translation, or: What Does It Mean to Speak and Think Belief?

Reflecting on the question of belief and its role within the history of the social sciences is not a particularly innovative stance to take. The practice of believing as a social phenomenon constituted a crucial site of interest for the social sciences from its very beginning, and this for a number of reasons. First of all, there were practical, historical reasons: some of the foremost influences of the early social sciences examined and reflected on this practice, such as Rousseau, Montesquieu, Condorcet, Hume and Smith.[32] Their research interests were very much continued by their nineteenth-century successors, including their reflections on belief as a cultural practice.[33] Another reason can be found in the concrete context of the early social sciences' formation in nineteenth-century France, where the theme of religion, religious practices and the importance of spiritual meaning in the foundation of communities was a central object of investigation for the burgeoning discipline.[34] 'Belief', considered at the time as a typical tenet of any organized religion, was a fruitful avenue for engaging with this theme, especially because of its ambiguous status as something that was connected to both mechanisms of dogmatic faith and empirical knowledge as already articulated in the Aristotelian tradition.[35]

And finally, the practice of belief was one of those practices which came to represent the unique qualities of the social domain, as it constituted a practice which defied an explanation from those other typical interpretative disciplines of societal life, economy and jurisprudence.[36] Neither a practice typified by self-interest nor one which was stipulated by contractual terms, 'to believe' signalled a kind of practice—alongside others such as sacrifice, prayer, altruism, gift-giving, suicide, ...—which was both

---

[32] Shagan, *The Birth of Modern Belief*, 250–281; Christopher J. Berry, *Essays on Hume, Smith and the Scottish Enlightenment* (Edinburgh: Edinburgh University Press, 2018), 89–109.

[33] On the relation between eighteenth-century enlightened philosophy and the early nineteenth-century social sciences, cf. ch. 4.

[34] François-André Isambert, "The early days of French sociology of religion", *Social Compass* 16, no. 4 (1969): 435–452.

[35] This connection is explicitly articulated in Durkheim and other sociological moderns, cf. infra and: Anne Warfield Rawls, *Epistemology and Practice: Durkheim's The Elementary Forms of Religious Life* (Cambridge: Cambridge University Press, 2004), 2n3.

[36] de Certeau, "Une pratique sociale de la différence: croire", 363–364.

societally commonplace and seemingly irrational. The strange nature of such practices—*made* strange, furthermore, through the institutional and existential crises experienced by organized religion in modernity—further necessitated, in a sense, the birth of a discipline such as sociology, which aimed to fully explain the complex and at times paradoxical nature of what came to be seen as 'social life'.[37] From the very start of the discipline, in other words, 'belief' was both an object which needed to be investigated and explained, and a peculiar phenomenon which enabled theoretical and methodological reflections on the nature of 'the social' and the discipline examining it.

Today, such reflections on the role of belief in the social science are still commonplace. Bruno Latour, who I will discuss more extensively in the next chapter, took central aim at the notion and its employment by the sociological moderns in his famous book *Sur le culte des dieux faitiches* (2010), and countless others, sociologists and non-sociologists, have done so as well, both before and after him. Another well-known example is Christian Smith's 2014 book *The Sacred Project of American Sociology*, in which the American sociologist of religion sought to uncover "the shared beliefs and commitments" fuelling the American sociological project, a project furthermore which was, despite the secular rhetoric of the sociological community, deeply imbued with spiritual meaning and practices according to Smith.[38] 'Belief' was not something that the science of sociology could shed from its practices and institutions, according to these commentators, and, as such, needed to be studied and investigated in order to gain a better understanding of the discipline and its workings.[39]

At the same time, however, what equally marks these different interventions into the question of sociology and belief is a shared premise: that 'belief' is a thing in itself which can be located (either individually or collectively), uncovered and described in order to gain further insight into a, most often hidden, state of things.[40] But such a premise carries a certain risk with it in its own right, and that is the dual risk of arbitrary demarcation and generalization. Christian Smith's argument—that

---

[37] Philippe Steiner, "Religion and the sociological critique of political economy: Altruism and gift", *European Journal for the History of Economic Thought* 24, no. 4 (2017): 876–906.
[38] Christian Smith, *The Sacred Project of American Sociology* (Oxford: Oxford University Press, 2014), 117.
[39] Ibid., 26.
[40] Ibid., 147.

American sociology is founded on a spiritual commitment to a series of sacred principles—is a good example of this. For this argument to make sense, Smith first needs to set out what exactly constitutes 'American sociology' before ascribing to it a set of principles which are universally applicable to this project. But this quickly starts to unravel, as American sociology is a thoroughly historical, ambiguous, complex and self-contradictory entity, an uncomfortable fact which leads to a quite remarkable characterization:

> If we had to characterize American sociology's sacred project in brief, therefore, we might say that it stands in the *modern liberal-Enlightenment-Marxist-social-reformist-pragmatist-therapeutic sexually liberated-civil rights-feminist-GLBTQ-social constructionist-poststructuralist/postmodernist* "tradition." That odd conglomeration, I suggest, conveys much of the lineage, interest, and energy propelling the spiritual project of American sociology. Again, it does not matter that this or that particular important sociologist is or is not aware of or does or does not believe in or endorse all of the elements of or influences on this spiritual project. What matters is that it in fact animates, though not necessarily consciously and explicitly, the working beliefs and activities of many if not most American sociologists, especially those who are most vocal and activist, and so has come to define the presupposed, default, "obvious" purpose, culture, and institutional orientation of the discipline.[41]

Smith brings together, correctly I would argue, all kinds of diffuse and aporetic elements belonging to the sociological landscape under a single header, again rightly presuming that these contradictory factions share a broader framework and conditions of possibility for their enunciation.[42] Where Smith goes wrong, however, is his confusion of 'traditions' and 'languages': the American sociological project cannot be considered, as Palti has convincingly argued, semantically cohesive (i.e. as sharing a singular set of ideals, principles and beliefs, hidden or not), as this would demand of the historian that they completely ignore the self-articulated ideals, principles and beliefs of particular traditions within the project (e.g. liberal vs. Marxist sociological traditions).[43] Rather, such an eclectic collection of viewpoints and arguments only makes sense if we approach it as a

---

[41] Ibid., 11.
[42] Ibid., 25–27.
[43] Palti, "The 'Theoretical Revolution' in Intellectual History", 395.

syntactical framework, in which these different traditions share certain "objective conditions of their public utterance", those conditions which, while allowing for semantically contradictory statements, still make all of them *sociological*.[44]

What is still needed, in other words, is an approach of 'belief' within the history of the social sciences which is able to both preserve the individual complexity and difference among sociological traditions, and locate the shared conditions of possibility enabling these individual traditions to produce sociological statements. This is where an intellectual-historical language-approach proves its value. But how exactly can we think of 'belief', not as a category, concept or mental state, but as something which characterizes an entire form of interaction? Two facets of the act of believing are key for this understanding: its social nature and its lack of tangible object. First of all, its social nature: in his phenomenological anthropology on the act of believing, Michel de Certeau pointed out how this practice often depends on the existence of other believers. As there is no certainty to be found in a belief, the believer, the French Jesuit argued, finds reassurance that the believed thing might genuinely exist since there are others who act on the same presupposition.[45] Individual acts of belief, then, are very often underpinned by networks of believers, who function as a kind of supplementary warranty on the thing believed.

Secondly, and as an extension on this first facet, it is a characteristic of certain beliefs—especially religious ones, e.g. 'The nature of God is trinitarian in form' but many others as well—that they can never be made fully tangible. These are beliefs which anthropologist and cognitive scientist Dan Sperber has categorized as semi-propositional, meaning that they allow for a number of interpretations to be made (e.g. 'God is made up of God the Father, Jesus Christ and the Holy Spirit') rather than a singular corresponding proposition (e.g. 'It is raining outside').[46] And while such beliefs undoubtedly contribute to the dissemination of misinformation in society, Sperber, at the same time, emphasizes the social success of such semi-propositional belief systems, exactly because of their vagueness and ability to integrate multiple, aporetic points of view.[47] This particular

---

[44] Ibid., 402.

[45] de Certeau, "Une pratique sociale de la différence: croire", 374.

[46] Dan Sperber, *On Anthropological Knowledge: Three Essays* (Cambridge: Cambridge University Press, 1985), 51–53.

[47] Dan Sperber, "Culturally transmitted misbeliefs", *Behavioral and Brain Sciences* 32, no. 6 (2009): 534–535.

nature of semi-propositional beliefs is also interesting from an intellectual-historical point of view: it means that the space of belief, much like the space of politics, is a thoroughly historicized one, one which can always be challenged and contested.

To speak a language of belief, then, one is in the process of articulating a disposition, both towards the other (non-)believer and towards the (empty) object believed. A belief-language refers less to the content of the words spoken—i.e. the communication of beliefs rather than any form of knowledge—than to the type of interaction—in which a kind of ineradicable form of otherness is navigated. Speaking such a language, as a result, does not equate to being in possession of certain beliefs.[48] While the latter is concerned with the precise mental state of a 'believer', the former is exclusively concerned with the social-discursive mechanisms undergirding such psychological formations. To investigate the former does not result into any sort of insight into the latter. In other words, examining the mechanisms of belief-language(s) within early sociology and the different narrative techniques employed by sociological moderns for navigating such a language does not produce any understanding of the 'beliefs' possessed by these sociological moderns themselves.

What we are concerned with, then, are languages of belief understood and approached as historical formations. These formations consist of the belief-concepts discussed and contested, the speakers and their broader communities, and the institutions (political, cultural, intellectual) which attempt to tie down these belief-signifiers in order to make them employable towards a particular social rationality.[49] The many concrete signifiers of belief—'croyance', 'croire', 'foi', 'credo', 'conviction', 'crédit', 'fidélité'—are then less considered as representing any positive content on their own than functioning as "indexes of problems", in the words of Palti.[50] They are narrative interventions, semantic attempts at articulating and giving meaning to a practice which cannot be defined once and for all, which cannot evade its continuous contestability. At the same time, this inability to close the semantic space allows for the creation of a community of speakers, as they discuss and contest the meanings allocated to the

---

[48] On what it means to possess such beliefs, cf. W. V. Quine & J. S. Ullian, *The Web of Belief* (New York: Random House, 1970), 3–19.
[49] de Certeau, "L'institution du croire", 61–80.
[50] Palti, "The 'Theoretical Revolution' in Intellectual History", 398.

practice by others.⁵¹ The history of belief-languages consists of an endless proliferation of such communities, their attempted institutionalizations (Christian dogma, philosophical naturalism, …) and the complex encounters and entanglements of such institutionalized discourses.

The central purpose of the book is to focus on one of these meetings—the French classical sociologists, their attempts at constructing their own historical formations of a belief-language, and their encounters with other historical languages of belief—in order to further historicize the sociological composition of social knowledge, forms of believing and the religious object, as a means for cultivating techniques of self-government and -fashioning. Beyond this primary historiographical contribution, I also aim to respond to post-secular critiques of the sociological belief-category, by arguing that the engagement of the sociological moderns with the notion of 'belief' wasn't exclusively epistemological or political but deeply existential and authentic as well.⁵² I will focus on the French tradition because of its canonical stature as a context of sociological origin, its embeddedness within Enlightenment discussions on religion and secularity, and its political backdrop as a place of revolutionary unrest and a social crisis of belief.

My argument consists of the hypothesis that the ability to imagine oneself as a sociologist was intimately connected to certain historical processes taking place within the way the category of belief was understood and employed around the end of the eighteenth and the beginning of the nineteenth century.⁵³ Whereas 'society' was a relatively new concept within the eighteenth-century knowledge culture, 'belief', on the other hand, already had left a long historical path behind it, with this path being littered with a whole host of different meanings and contexts.⁵⁴ It was exactly this historical status, of meaning-accumulation and -proliferation, which made it into such a valuable resource for the early sociologists, its textual density and richness providing ample material for reflecting on and thinking both the particular condition of society as well as their own sociological identity and program. The modernist pluralization of belief-meanings—as articulated and performed in Enlightenment culture and

---

⁵¹ de Certeau, "L'institution du croire", 68–72.
⁵² Cf. infra ch. 2.
⁵³ Cf. infra ch. 4.
⁵⁴ For an overview of its different meanings within post-Reformation Catholicism, cf. Stefania Tutino, *The Many Faces of* Credulitas*: Credibility, Credulity, and Belief in Post-Reformation Catholicism* (Oxford: Oxford University Press, 2022).

contested by its Christian opponents—served, so I argue, as a creative instrument of self-articulation, -historicization, and -government for the sociological moderns, who sought to carve out a place for themselves in the chaotic landscape of a post-revolutionary France in spiritual crisis.

The book, in other words, seeks to offer a historical-anthropological account of the early interactions between sociological ways of self-historicization and languages of belief.[55] The hope is that such a historical picture can provide us with a better understanding of our own post-secular condition, one where the sociological use of the belief-category is, once again, questioned and problematized.[56] The preliminary conclusion to the book is that such a usage does not signal a fundamental problem for sociological modernity; rather, it should be seen as serving as its very condition of possibility.

Epistemology, Genealogy, Archaeology: Approaching the History of Social Science and Religion

To reflect on the category of 'belief' within the long history of social science also means to enter a complex and sensitive debate, which is the debate on the relationship between the projects of science and religion in modernity. In this section, I would like to take a brief look at the two main positions in this debate, focusing specifically on the case of social science, while simultaneously articulating the positioning of my own argument in this book and how it aims to add something new to this long-term discussion.

Stating that there are two main positions in the debate on science and religion can easily be considered as an oversimplification. As a response, however, I would argue that what I am concerned with here is only a small fragment of the debate, which is the question of how these two domains were *historically* related, specifically as it impacted the development of 'sociology' as a science *and* mode of existence. In other words, I am not particularly concerned with the universal-philosophical facets of the debate (e.g. 'what are all the different types of interactions between the two

---

[55] A similar method for investigating the history of sociology and the history of believing can be found in: Philippe Gonzalez & Laurence Kaufmann, "The Social Scientist, the Public and the Pragmatist Gaze: Exploring the Critical Conditions of Sociological Inquiry", *European Journal of Pragmatism and American Philosophy* 4, no. 1 (2012): 1–30.

[56] On this condition, cf. ch. 2, section "Post-secular critiques of belief".

domains and what does this mean for the domains in themselves?') nor am I making any arguments on its potential normative effects on different political and social contexts (e.g. 'how should these two domains relate to each other in a liberal-democratic context and civil law framework?'). Here, I am solely concerned with the historical event of the sociological tradition displacing the tradition of (positive) theology as the privileged discourse for thinking and communicating what constitutes a (good) society and community, and how later historians, sociologists, theologians and religious studies scholars have imagined and narrated this event.[57]

Bearing this in mind, I would argue that two main positions can indeed be discerned, which I will call the 'epistemological' and 'genealogical' positions. I understand the epistemological position as entailing the view that the displacement of theological discourses on society by social-scientific ones was the result of fundamental transformations taking place in the eighteenth- and nineteenth-century Western-European knowledge cultures. These transformations are often summarized and typecast as a series of intellectual revolutions, effecting the domains of politics (the return of democratic politics via the French and American Revolutions), economy (the Industrial Revolution and the development of capitalism), education (the proliferation of universities, professional schools and research centres), science (the differentiation and specialization of scientific disciplines), and culture (the enlightened idealization and governmental policy of tolerating distinct religious denominations).[58] As a result of these revolutions and the parallel breakdown of the so-called old order of feudalism and Christianity, a new space of social imagination and the proliferation of social ideas was opened.[59] Where once, so the (much simplified) story goes, the theological framework fuelled by different Christian dogmas had been primarily responsible for the understanding and

---

[57] In response to this displacement, Christian thinkers would increasingly voice their own worldviews in these more 'scientific registers', cf. Gilbert Faccarello, "A dance teacher for paralysed people? Charles de Coux and the dream of a Christian political economy", *The European Journal of the History of Economic Thought* 24, no. 4 (2017): 828–875.

[58] Björn Wittrock, Johan Heilbron & Lars Magnusson, "The Rise of the Social Sciences and the Formation of Modernity", in: *The Rise of the Social Sciences and the Formation of Modernity: Conceptual Change in Context, 1750–1850*, eds. Johan Heilbron, Lars Magnusson, & Björn Wittrock (Dordrecht: Springer Dordrecht, 1998), 1–4; Lynn Hunt, Margaret C. Jacob & Wijnand Mijnhardt, *The Book That Changed Europe: Picart & Bernard's Religious Ceremonies of the World* (Cambridge, MA: Harvard University Press, 2010), 1–21.

[59] Nisbet, *The Sociological Tradition*, 21–23.

interpretation of communal phenomena, now these social events and practices increasingly became the prerogative of the social and human sciences, who looked at these phenomena from a more abstract, comparative and scientific manner.[60] Theology, in this narrative, was understood to have made way for the social sciences as the privileged avenue for approaching and thinking this thing called society, with many 'modern' theologians and religious philosophers subsequently adopting sociological concepts and terminology for reflecting on the state of religion in modernity.[61]

In many ways, this view can be described as the classical stance, as it strongly mirrors the self-articulated narratives of those early modern and modern social theorists—like Montesquieu, Jean-Jacques Rousseau, David Hume, Adam Smith, to give just a few examples—who were in the very act of displacing such theological discourses and who legitimized their more secular and natural-historical visions of both society and religion via claims of universality and reasonableness.[62] Abstracting Christian, Judaic and Islamic dogmas represented a form of intellectual, social, cultural and political liberation to these theorists, allowing the enlightened thinker the genuine mental and cognitive space of imagination for rethinking and improving social life.[63] To be *modern*, in other words, required the abandonment of superstitions (religious or otherwise), the mental bracketing of religious truths (i.e. as not intrinsically superior to other kinds of truths) and the embrace of a scientific, comparative and critical form of thought.[64] This attitude, and the associated understanding of the modern social science/religion-relation as being (ideally) guided by a free marketplace of ideas, gradually evolved into the dominant narrative of the sociological tradition, where social science was seen as having won its place in this marketplace through the epistemological robustness of its scientific methods and the originality of its core ideas.[65]

[60] Heilbron, *The Rise of Social Theory*, 5–6.

[61] Johannes Zachhuber, "Individual and Community in Modern Debates about Religion and Secularism", in: *Religious Responses to Modernity*, eds. Yohanan Friedmann & Christoph Markschies (Berlin: Walter de Gruyter, 2021), 11–32.

[62] Heilbron, "The Emergence of Social Theory", 2–3; Christopher J. Berry, *Social Theory of the Scottish Enlightenment* (Edinburgh: Edinburgh University Press, 1997), 4–7.

[63] Heilbron, "The Emergence of Social Theory", 4–5.

[64] Berry, *Essays on Hume, Smith and the Scottish Enlightenment*, 247–263.

[65] See for example: Nisbet, *The Sociological Tradition*, 316: "And the visions and the ideas that were ignited! Would anyone deny that the sociological ideas which emerged in the brief period between Tocqueville and Weber have been other than determinative of the way we, a century later, continue to see the social world about us? Would anyone wish to estimate what

At the same time, these claims of universality and reasonableness were contested from the start by other theorists of social life and have since given rise to a number of scholarly traditions, a collection of traditions which I will categorize here as being fundamentally 'genealogical'.[66] Some examples of traditions falling within this category are those of 'critical religion', 'post-secularism', 'political anthropology', 'postcolonial sociology' and several others. What connects these different traditions, despite their many disagreements, is an alternative narrative on the historical bond between religion and the social sciences: rather than this bond being characterized by the supposedly natural interaction of ideas within an open intellectual marketplace, the story of social science and religion, according to the genealogical perspective, was and remains defined by relations of power. To take a genealogical approach of this historical bond, then, is to seek to uncover the mechanisms of power underlying the domains of social science and religion, displaying how positions of both authority and subservience were constructed between the two.[67]

Typically, these narrative schemes present the domain of 'religion' as *being made* subservient with the coming of modernity, with the domain of the social sciences playing an important role in this process as an epistemic instrument of, what scholars like George Steinmetz have considered to be, thoroughly imperialist and colonial contexts.[68] For critical religion scholars like Timothy Fitzgerald and others in his field, what is most interesting and crucial about the very idea and category of 'religion' in modernity was its "ideological function [...] in the formation of an imagined domain of

would be left in contemporary sociological analysis if we stripped from it such constitutive ideas as community, authority, status, the sacred, alienation – and all of the related ideas and perspectives that flow from them? How many of us even *perceive* the society around us – quite apart from interpreting it – except through the perceptual filters of these ideas and perspectives?"

[66] On the historical contestation of the liberal-epistemological narrative, cf. Carolina Armenteros, *The French Idea of History: Joseph de Maistre and His Heirs, 1794–1854* (Ithaca, NY: Cornell University Press, 2011), 217–254.

[67] The conceptual groundwork for such a genealogical tradition is typically viewed as being provided by Nietzsche: Michel Foucault, "Nietzsche, Genealogy, History", in: *Language, Counter-Memory, Practice: Selected Essays and Interviews*, ed. D.F. Bouchard (Ithaca: Cornell University Press, 1977), 139–164.

[68] George Steinmetz, *The Colonial Origins of Modern Social Thought: French Sociology and the Overseas Empire* (Princeton: Princeton University Press, 2023), 42–44.

non-religious politics, economics and the liberal capitalist ideology".[69] 'Religion', in other words, was not so much an accurate signifier for a collection of real-life practices and objects, than an invented category with a primary function of enabling the ideological government of others within the project of modernity.[70]

Furthermore, according to this critical-genealogical perspective on the historical bond between social science and religion, the nineteenth-century discipline of sociology played a constitutive role in this categorical invention of 'religion', artificially constructing the divide between rational, factual secularity and irrational, illusional religiosity.[71] As a result, sociological moderns were able to present themselves as impartial analysts of societal phenomena such as religion while simultaneously obscuring their own, what Christian Smith has termed, sacred project of sociology.[72] The ultimate purpose of this genealogical narrative, then, is to further uncover the irrational, illusional aspects, not of 'religion', but of modern social science itself, in order to approach the two domains of religion and social science in, what such scholars deem to be, a more genuinely symmetrical manner.

Where some scholarly fields are characterized by an eclectic mix of narrative traditions living relatively peacefully next to each other, the same cannot be said of the genealogical and epistemological positions on the history of religion and social science. Both narrative traditions are largely mutually exclusive and are often directly aimed against each other: whereas defenders of the epistemological viewpoint will criticize the relativism of the genealogical perspective, those emphasizing the importance of power in the history of religion and social science will lambast their opponents for being blind towards the many unarticulated effects of authority and

---

[69] Timothy Fitzgerald, "Introduction", in: *Religion and the Secular: Historical and Colonial Formations*, ed. Timothy Fitzgerald (London: Equinox, 2007), 20.

[70] Trevor Stack, Naomi Goldenberg & Timothy Fitzgerald (eds.) *Religion as a Category of Governance and Sovereignty* (Leiden: Brill, 2015); Daniel Dubuisson, *The Invention of Religions*, transl. by Martha Cunningham (Sheffield: Equinox Publishing Limited, 2019). My thanks goes to one of the anonymous reviewers of the book manuscript for suggesting an extended discussion of this literature.

[71] Mitsutoshii Horii, *'Religion' and 'Secular' Categories in Sociology: Decolonizing the Modern Myth* (Cham: Palgrave Macmillan, 2021), viii.

[72] Smith, *The Sacred Project of American Sociology*.

silencing within the scientific apparatus.[73] At the same time, such a polemic response is perhaps to be expected in the scenario where both camps, if we may call them that, are able to lay claim to generally robust and reasonable arguments. On the one hand, there can be little doubt that the ideas of the social sciences were, in many ways, innovative and ground-breaking and, furthermore, rooted in empirical and rational observations.[74] On the other hand, however, it is also true that, while the domains of religion and social science do not share an equal part in their ability to make scientific claims, they are equally susceptible to mechanisms of power, with the latter often failing to take these mechanisms into account in a self-reflexive manner.[75] Although, with regard to the final point, it should also be noted that this is not always the case, as several sociological moderns have attempted to erect programs integrating such self-reflexive practices.[76]

My intention here is not evaluate which narrative position is more right than the other or which should be preferred in an investigation of the historical bond between religion and social science. Rather, it is simply to suggest that, while both offer valuable perspectives and methods for thinking about this bond, they also share between them a similar limitation. This limitation manifests itself in their difficulty of explaining differentiation and agency among the sociological moderns at the level of the actor-as-author. This is, perhaps, not that surprising considering how both traditions focus less on the particular make-up of these domains on the level of individual authors (theologians, sociologists, administrators, activist priests, social reformists, revolutionaries, journalists, political economists, pamphleteers, and so on) and more on how both domains were concretely involved in the societal processes of modernization and secularization.

And while such focuses on the societal-procedural level are suited to questions of (non-)modernity, they also bring with them certain

---

[73] One typical example of this contestation can be found in the so-called science wars of the 1990s, which saw a prolonged and intense discussion between the exact and social sciences on the degree to which scientific truth was 'socially constructed': cf. Keith M. Ashman & Philip S. Baringer (eds.), *After the Science Wars* (London/New York: Routledge, 2001).

[74] Johan Heilbron, *French Sociology* (Ithaca: Cornell University Press, 2015), 12–15.

[75] Smith, *The Sacred Project of American Sociology*, 26.

[76] For example, Pierre Bourdieu and Loïc Wacquant, *An Invitation to Reflexive Sociology* (Chicago: University of Chicago Press, 1992).

conceptual and categorical tendencies. Tendencies such as the homogenization of domains as 'religion' and 'social sciences' as collective actors in themselves, and the generalization of certain historical processes—modernizing, secularizing, institutionalizing, de-institutionalizing, believing, spiritualizing, ritualizing, and so on—which emphasize historical transition rather than contemporary diversity and complexity. These are, in other words, macro-historical phenomena, beyond the level of the authorial actor as a point of differentiation. As a result, the many techniques, strategies and tactics of individual actors, residing both within and between these domains, are considered to be of little consequence. So a valuable historical question, such as 'what exactly did particular sociological moderns *do* and *not do* in relation to the domains of social science and religion?' becomes much more difficult to answer.[77] The modern, rather, is more or less exclusively understood in their degree of participation to the processes of modernization and secularization.

Here, however, I am not so much concerned with concrete attempts at defining, once and for all, the precise status and conditions of our historical era. Rather, I aim at problematizing its inverse: how should we understand this existential urge for perpetual historicization, and what does this urge mean for our ability to understand the different interactions between the domains of social science and religion? This is a much more straightforward and simple question, as it aims to bring into view a concrete kind of narrative practice among a particular group (the sociological moderns). In order to engage with this question, another narrative tradition needs to be brought in, one which is not so much directed at the evaluation of sociological truth-construction or its genealogical deconstruction, but rather at empirically contextualizing these practices of construction and deconstruction in their own right.[78]

This alternative tradition to those of epistemology and genealogy can be designated, I would argue, as 'archaeological'. A term typically associated with Foucaultian scholarship, I understand an archaeological narrative tradition to entail "the reconstitution of a historic field [...] in order to obtain the conditions of appearance for general knowledge discourses

---

[77] I elaborate on this problem more extensively in the next two chapters.

[78] The categories employed here—'truth', 'genealogy', 'deconstruction'—are the terms employed by the particular traditions themselves. My use of them is not meant as confirmation of their categorical accuracy.

within a given period".[79] The philosophy and hermeneutics of what exactly constitutes an 'archaeological approach' is too complex and long-winded to dwell upon for too long, so I will limit myself here to highlighting two facets of its nature which are of a particular interest to me for explaining the general approach I intend to take in this book: (1) its multidimensional understanding of the actor-as-author, and (2) its emphasis on the conditions of possibility structuring a historically given epistemic field.

First of all, concerning its understanding of the actor-as-author: the archaeological narrative has the benefit that it provides an alternative to the authorial models of both the epistemological and genealogical narratives. Whereas the dominant narratives can present the (sociological) author as either too strong (i.e. as the master thinker and sole inventor of sociological ideas) or as too weak (as being subservient to political institutions and class interests), the archaeological narrative aims to occupy a middle ground between these two positions, sketching out how the sociological modern inhabited a 'space of enunciation'.[80] As a result, the (typically modernist) self-imagination of the author as the master of the textual landscape transforms into one other type of enunciation within a sea of enunciations, all of which are shaping and impacting this landscape.[81] The figure of the author then also transforms, from someone extending absolute lordship across a text to someone who is searching for creative and original ways to meaningfully inhabit a chaotic and dynamic space through a series of techniques and tactics of writing.[82]

A second facet which can prove to be illuminating is the archaeological emphasis on the structures determining a historical context of knowledge discourses which, according to Judith Revel, is a strong departure from a typical history of ideas, with the latter more or less exclusively concerned with the historical evolution of these ideas themselves.[83] The same cannot be said of an archaeological approach. In the words of philosopher Joseph J. Tanke, the "point of archaeology is to describe how a statement functions with respect to the rules for the formation of discourse, that is, to determine if it confirms a set of existing rules or if it inaugurates a new set

---

[79] Judith Revel, *Dictionnaire Foucault* (Paris: Ellipses, 2008), 13 (my translation).
[80] Michel Foucault, *L'archéologie du savoir* (Paris: Gallimard, 1969), 109–172.
[81] Ibid., 127–132.
[82] Michel de Certeau, *The Practice of Everyday Life*, transl. by Steven Rendall (Berkeley: University of California Press, 1984), 134–136.
[83] Revel, *Dictionnaire Foucault* (Paris: Ellipses, 2008), 13.

of rules".[84] The historian, in other words, has the task of reconstructing both the discursive rules of a given context and the formation of a set of statements, looking at whether the enunciations conform to the paradigmatic rules or whether these statements aim to organize a novel framework of meaning.

Such a perspective is interesting when thinking about the sociological moderns and religion, how they navigated the construction of their own epistemic field around the beginning of the nineteenth century, and how they negotiated confrontations with other, non-sociological actors who were inhabiting similar spaces. An archaeological narrative frames these confrontations less as an open marketplace of ideas or as an ideological struggle for power and authority than as a historically contingent context, consisting of a whole host of discursive mechanisms.[85] This is not to say, of course, that ideas and/or power do not matter within such a narrative framework, but rather that the notions of productivity and contingency stand at the forefront.[86] "There is no prime mover behind historical causality", said Paul Veyne, the French historian, in his discussion of the method of archaeology, "everything acts upon everything else and everything reacts against everything else."[87] The purpose of an archaeological framework then, within the context of the early nineteenth-century emergence of the social sciences and its engagement with the religious domain, is to further enable an empirical tracing of these different textual meetings and exchanges without relying on an *a priori* categorical framework of modernization and secularization.

As such, it is an attempt to historically investigate what can be called 'the sociological operation'. What exactly do I mean by this term? In his classic work on the theory and practice of historiography, published in 1975 and titled *L'Écriture de l'histoire* (transl.: *The Writing of History*, 1988), Michel de Certeau spoke of the so-called historiographical operation.[88] With this, he meant to signal how writing history was not just a

---

[84] Joseph J. Tanke, "On the Powers of the False: Foucault's Engagements with the Arts", in: *A Companion to Foucault*, eds. Christopher Falzon, Timothy O'Leary & Jana Sawicki (Malden, MA: Wiley-Blackwell, 2013), 123.

[85] Foucault, *L'archéologie du savoir*, 183–190.

[86] Paul Veyne, *Foucault: His Thought, His Character*, transl. by Janet Lloyd (Malden, MA: Polity Press, 2010), 54–58.

[87] Ibid., 55.

[88] Michel de Certeau, "The Historiographical Operation", in: Ibid., *The Writing of History*, transl. by Tom Conley (New York: Columbia University Press, 1988), 56–113.

form of human science enacting and manifesting itself, but rather something that was socially and institutionally practised and bound to a given place.[89] This realization—of the historicized and relational nature of doing historiography—was represented by de Certeau as part of a broader "epistemological awakening" in 1970s French scholarship, with others like "Serge Moscovici, Michel Foucault, Paul Veyne and many others" reflecting on this socialized and contextually embedded nature of historical writing.[90] For de Certeau, to properly understand historical writing, we need to engage with the multifaceted reality of the historiographical operation:

> On a necessarily limited scale, envisaging history as an operation would be equivalent to understanding it as the relation between a *place* (a recruitment, a milieu, a profession or business, etc.), analytical *procedures* (a discipline), and the construction of a *text* (a literature). That would be to admit that it is part of the "reality" with which it deals, and that this reality can be grasped "as a human activity," or "as a practice." From this perspective I would like to show that the historical operation refers to the combination of a social *place*, "scientific" *practices*, and *writing*.[91]

To bring a scientific operation into full view, in other words, is to describe and reflect on a science's social situatedness, the way it is practised and its literary, narrative articulations of said practices. Furthermore, an archaeological view of such an operation aims to consider the kind and form of interactions between these different operational facets.

While such an account differs from the standard narratives on the historical bond between social science and religion, it is not the case that no scholarly traditions exist in a similar vein to this more archaeological approach. In Francophone academia, for example, recent trends in the history, sociology and anthropology of social sciences take up a similar perspective. Inspired by the work of Foucault and de Certeau, the work of such scholars as Jean-François Bert, Jérôme Lamy and Christian Jacob aims to lay bare the spatial and material conditions enabling scientific truth-production, the different techniques employed by social scientists to

---

[89] Ibid., 56.

[90] Ibid., 57. Similar "epistemological awakenings" were of course also taking place in other scholarly contexts. To give just one example, concerning the growth and development of the tradition of 'social epistemology' in the United States, cf. Tarcisio Zandonade, "Social Epistemology from Jesse Shera to Steve Fuller", *Library Trends* 52, no. 4 (2004): 810–832.

[91] de Certeau, "The Historiographical Operation", 57.

construct knowledge-claims, and the many networks carrying and disseminating such claims.[92] Similar to my reading of Foucault and de Certeau (cf. infra), they explicitly intend to take into account the way social-scientific actors-as-authors are always pluralistically constituted, meaning that they (e.g. sociological moderns) are mediated bodies in whole range of ways: institutionally, spatially, objectively, materially, textually and so on.[93] Unlike the epistemological or genealogical narratives, no site of constitution is particularly privileged in such an approach. Rather, the goal is to consider the authorial subject as a form in perpetual mediation, a process which needs to be empirically observed and described.

Furthermore, someone like Jean-François Bert has already alerted the reader to the possibilities this provides for an investigation of the historical bond between social sciences and religion: rather than approach these two as bordered domains, the 'social sciences' and 'religion' can also be engaged as a series of techniques and practices responsible for these acts of constitution, an engagement Bert ascribes to the work of, amongst others, Mauss and Foucault.[94] As such, the question of the historical bond between social sciences and religion moves away from its societal-procedural character typical of the epistemological and genealogical narratives, and rather becomes a question of everyday practices, acts and constitutions which can be observed, described and compared beyond their mere categorization as sacred or secular, religious or scientific.[95] It was a bond which needed to be continuously invented, re-invented and negotiated between all kinds of different actors, and which required the use of such categories as 'modernity', 'religion' and 'belief'. It is with these everyday acts and techniques—the different narrations of 'belief' by the nineteenth-century sociological modern—that I am here concerned.

---

[92] Cf. for example: Christian Jacob, *Qu'est-ce qu'un lieu de savoir?* (S.l.: Open Edition Press, 2014); Christian Jacob, *Des mondes lettrés aux lieux de savoir* (Paris: Les Belles Lettres, 2018); Jérôme Lamy, *Faire de la sociologie historique des sciences et des techniques* (Paris: Hermann, 2018); Jean-François Bert & Jérôme Lamy, *Voir les savoirs: Lieux, objets et gestes de la science* (Paris: Anamosa, 2021); Jean-François Bert, *Le corps qui pense: Une anthropologie historique des pratiques savantes* (Basel: Schwabe Verlag, 2023).

[93] Jean-François Bert, *Atelier de Marcel Mauss. Un anthropologue paradoxal* (Paris: CNRS Editions, 2012), 'Introduction'.

[94] Jean-François Bert, "Relire 'les techniques du corps'. Les enjeux d'un programme de recherche", in: *Lire Les techniques du corps. Relire Marcel Mauss*, ed. Jean-François Bert (Paris: Éditions de la Sorbonne, 2022), 5–43.

[95] Jean-François Bert, *Le courage de comparer. L'anthropologie subversive de Marcel Mauss* (Genève: Labor et fides, 2021), 63–66.

The Elementary Forms of Sociological Life

The title of the book, and its subtitle specifically, also deserves further elaboration. Despite being an obvious reference to one of the most famous books in the history of the sociology of religion—Durkheim's *Les formes élémentaires de la vie religieuse* (1912)—the book of the French sociologist also serves as a kind of model to my own.[96] In his seminal work, Durkheim aimed to bring his own time of philosophical modernity, best exemplified by Kantian apriorism and Humean empiricism, into direct communication with the oldest societies known to man, the Australian Aboriginals, and their systems of categorization, totemism.[97] His goal, as it had been throughout his oeuvre, was to transcribe the entire spectrum of social-cultural self-articulation and the different pathways of individual and collective agency it afforded to the forces of society.[98] In this way, he tried to capture the workings of society in its fullest, most historical form, searching for a language in which the real and the social could reach its closest approximation. The modern present and the distant, faraway past simply served as the bookends of possible human experience, the edges of the human fishbowl and the outer limits of the social scientist's laboratory.

My purpose here is similar, if not quite as outrageous in its ambition. I aim to create a historical line of communication between present-day sociology and its primitive (an "imprecise" yet "very useful" term, according to Durkheim, "when its meaning is carefully defined") other, the very first 'sociologists' of the eighteenth and nineteenth centuries.[99] Unlike Durkheim, however, I do not aim to present an exhaustive picture of potential sociological self-elaboration, but to trace the semiotic matrix of early sociology: the different strategies employed for conceptualizing its own interventions and historical positions, its borrowing and moulding of

---

[96] Émile Durkheim, *Les formes élémentaires de la vie religieuse: le système totémique en Australie* (Paris: Félix Alcan, 1912). Throughout the book I will make use of this edition, as well as several English translations, for when I am citing large blocks of text, to improve general readability. These are: Émile Durkheim, *The Elementary Forms of Religious Life*, transl. and with an introduction by Karen E. Fields (New York: The Free Press, 1995), and Émile Durkheim, *The Elementary Forms of Religious Life*, transl. by Carol Cosman, introduction by Mark S. Cladis (Oxford: Oxford University Press, 2001). I will add their date of publication, to delineate between the two English translations.

[97] Mark S. Cladis, "Introduction", in: Durkheim, *The Elementary Forms of Religious Life*, xxiv–xxvi.

[98] Cf. infra, ch. 8: "Narrating Solidarity through the Division of Belief".

[99] Durkheim, *The Elementary Forms of Religious Life* (2001), 3n1.

existing historical languages of belief, and the signifiers used to differentiate one position from the other.

A curious inversion takes place in this way: the modernist social scientist studying primitive societies himself transforms into a primitive, the looking glass turned right around in order to focus in on the unarticulated movements, techniques and 'beliefs' of the now-barbarized sociologist.[100] This is not to belittle Durkheim, as it had been neither for him when he juxtaposed the totemic practices with their Kantian successors. It merely represents a kind of phenomenological bracketing, a temporary and virtual marking of a beginning and an end, which is an unfortunate necessity for when one aims to trace the unfolding of a historical language through time.[101] The desired result is to bring the sociological present into dialogue, once again, with its notorious predecessors, not as a source of inspiration or as an original yet fundamentally different partner, but as speakers of a particular kind of language and as inventors of a certain mode of existence, that of sociological modernity. In this way, the present-day sociologist is also, once again, reminded of their own composition, as part autonomous selves, part contemporary primitives. To reflexively articulate, pinpoint and categorize 'beliefs' within society, as a sociologist, does not extract oneself from the broader history of believing, despite what the early sociologists claimed, arguing that such practices brought them to safely land into the historical territory of science, knowledge and reason. Reflexivity and categorization are means of bifurcation: it simply means that the sociologist is now speaking in two historical places at once, the land of reason and the land of belief. It is with the sociological cultivation of the second space, their role and form within the history of believing, that I am here mainly concerned with.

---

[100] I would defend my use of this (highly controversial) term, as it has genuine stylistic and narrative purpose: it is meant to further highlight how Durkheim's narrative scheme (the structural-conceptual entanglement of the indigenous Australians, the Western philosophers, and the sociological analysts) in *The Elementary Forms* is both mirrored *and* inverted here, where the Durkheimian sociologist—much like the indigenous Australians studied in *The Elementary Forms*—has both articulated and non-articulated facets in their experience and practice of their culture. In the same way that Durkheim imposed an external language of 'beliefs and rites' onto Aboriginal displays of religion, so do I intend to apply a historical excavation of the way material languages of belief impacted the Durkheimian textual landscape, at times beyond the reflexive articulation of these so-called sociological primitives themselves. As such, I would defend the usage of the term, despite its painful past as a tool for colonial suppression.

[101] Cf. infra ch. 8.

In this way, the canonical works of the early sociologists are made to become a part of the scholarly tradition of an anthropology of knowledge, rather than merely acting as a series of reflections and interventions on this tradition itself. Most of the scholars already working within this specific branch of the tradition, like Jean-François Bert and Jérôme Lamy, have mainly focused on the different techniques of these social scientists, such as their navigations of archival matter and their ways of making the social visible.[102] Others, like Joan Stavo-Debauge, have prioritized the materiality of the text itself as the level of analysis, entering the text in the way an anthropologist enters into the field, tracing the interactions between the sociological actor-author and the different, historical 'hantises' ("hauntings") stalking them.[103] It is in this latter manner that I will approach the texts of the early sociologists, looking at the way the sociological actor-authors acted and *were acted upon* by languages of belief in their exploration and articulations of society.

Structure of the Book

The book is made up of eleven chapters. These eleven chapters are divided into four main sections: a problematization of the sociological present and a theoretical discussion on the tools best suited for bringing this present and its past into communication for a shared analysis (Chaps. 1, 2, and 3); a historical anthropology of the different strategies of self-government and -historicization via languages of belief among the early sociologists in post-revolutionary France (Chaps. 4, 5, and 6); a reconstruction of the debates between positivists and anti-positivists in the second half of the nineteenth and first half of the twentieth centuries, and the role played by languages of belief as an instrument of navigation and differentiation (Chaps. 7, 8, and 9); and, finally, some concluding remarks, both on the further development of the sociological language of belief into the twentieth century as well as on its renewed problematization within the post-secular tradition (Chaps. 10 and 11).

---

[102] Cf. for example: Jean-François Bert & Jérôme Lamy, *Voir les savoirs: Lieux, objets et gestes de la science* (Paris: Anamosa, 2021).

[103] Cf. Audran Aulanier & Joan Stavo-Debauge, "La phénoménologie: méthode pour la sociologie ? Entretien avec Joan Stavo-Debauge", Implications Philosophiques, last consulted on the 13th of January 2023, https://www.implications-philosophiques.org/la-phenomenologie-methode-pour-la-sociologie-entretien-avec-joan-stavo-debauge-propos-recueillis-par-audran-aulanier-2/.

In the first chapter following this introduction, I will focus on the current climate of sociology and its relation to the category of belief. My main interlocutor in this chapter will be Bruno Latour, the famous French philosopher and sociologist, who I will approach as a kind of *compagnon de route*, although one with a different destination in the end. I will argue that Latour's project of reading modernity against the grain was rooted in his engagement with sociological modernity as a new belief-language, one where 'belief-in-belief' replaced more authentic, religious ways of believing while obscuring proper social-scientific readings of society, as imagined by Gabriel Tarde. For this, he thoroughly studied and assessed the work of Durkheim, accusing the latter of fundamentally misunderstanding the explanatory value of the social. In my discussion of Latour, I will separate his historicist-anthropological method from his normative-philosophical critique of sociology, seeking to preserve the former while problematizing the latter.

In the third chapter, I will seek to expand on Latour's historical-anthropological method, by discussing the work of Michel de Certeau and Pierre Bourdieu. I argue that these scholars form important complementary pieces to the Latourian method for investigating the history of social sciences and belief-languages, through their respective anthropologies of belief and their applications of these anthropologies to social-scientific methods. While they themselves wrote very little on the actual history of sociology and its interaction with the history of languages of belief—and if they did, it was rather critically—I will make the case that their symmetrical methods provide excellent tools for analysing these historical encounters, beyond the typical narratives of secularization, modernization and/or disenchantment.

Chapters 4, 5, and 6 centre upon a single context, the theoretical reflections on the domain of the social in post-revolutionary France, where the violence of the Terror had severely impacted the legacy of the Enlightenment's social philosophies and its potential recuperation in what was a society experienced as being increasingly divisive and selfish. In these chapters, I will investigate the first attempts at the construction of a sociological language of belief, and this in three different traditions: that of the Enlightenment, that of the Catholic-reactionary school and that of the early socialists. The latter two will be approached through the works of Louis de Bonald and Saint-Simon, two thinkers who are often considered as distant forefathers of the sociological discipline, but whose work is typically differentiated from the sociological canon. Here, I will show how the notion of 'belief' and its historical proliferation of meanings was instrumental for these thinkers in exploring society in new and dynamic ways, negotiating, at the same time, that other central domain of social self-government, religion.

Chapters 7, 8, and 9 will turn towards a second case study, the methodological debates between positivists and anti-positivists in the second half of the nineteenth century and first half of the twentieth century. The figures that I will discuss are Auguste Comte and Émile Durkheim, along with some of their main interlocutors such as Gabriel Tarde and Henri Bergson, looking at the way they used historical languages of belief to think both themselves and their sociological other. I will approach this context as an entry point into the history of sociology where 'belief' was transforming into a tool of sociological self-historicization and -differentiation, a malleable concept which could function as a way of explaining the proliferation of sociological readings and traditions itself. The religious object, which had still played a central role in the post-revolutionary context of Bonald and Saint-Simon, was gradually made into a sociological one, that of the sociologist-object and its integral proliferation within the boundaries of the sociological system. As such, this context will be approached as an example of sociological engagements with belief further cementing themselves as an autonomous mode of existence, which could be channelled as a tool for methodological and theoretical innovation and differentiation.

The book will conclude with an epilogue and a brief conclusion, starting with a commentary on the development of the Durkheimian school after Durkheim and how different sociological traditions, like Maussian anthropology and sociological action theory à la Parsons, were considerably shaped by their engagement with the belief-category. It will aim to give an example of disciplinary registers crossing borders, with the language of belief providing, once again, a way of giving such meetings a sense of historical meaning and understanding, while impacting the sociologist-actor's own space of action. And then, finally, I will end the book with a call, aimed at sociologists, philosophers, historians and others working on the intersection between modernity, religion and social science, for a more extensive and reflective investigation of the researchers' own techniques, language uses and practices, and a greater awareness of the complex historical backgrounds of these techniques and acts. It seeks to put forward the thought that the language and concepts one employs are not merely lifeless objects, only given life when taken up by the scientist of the social; they are actors in their own right, elusive and unpredictable, with whom a relationship needs to be built through mutual interaction and recognition.

Concluding Remarks

Before fully commencing my discussion of the historical languages of belief, their different employments by sociological actors and their original sociological iterations, I want to end this introduction with some clarifying remarks on the position of the book itself. Through its rather peculiar composition—an intellectual history without extensive archival research, its reproduction of the typical sociological canon and its occupants, and its very narrow and specific reading of a small part of the history of social sciences–it can present a potential source of frustration for different scholarly traditions: intellectual historians, sociologists of religion, social theorists and so on. Dependent on its angle of reception, it can be seen as both saying too much as well as doing too little.

This book, however, has not the pretence of being a definitive and exhaustive work on the history of sociology, as I have already alerted the reader to in the beginning of this introduction. Rather, it aims to take on the form of a series of creative readings, where the history of sociology is engaged with as a particularly rich material base, especially through its intersection with the histories of belief and religion. In this way, I take inspiration of the work of someone like Bruno Karsenti, who has also approached the sociological tradition as a handy tool "to think with" in his works *D'une philosophie à l'autre* (2013) and *La place de Dieu. Religion et politique chez les modernes* (2023).[104] This book tries to provide a similar 'service', starting out from the current state of sociological modernity and its religious other, in order to rethink the complex textual traditions left behind by some of the great explorers of society and their production of sociological languages.

---

[104] Bruno Karsenti, *D'une philosophie à l'autre. Les sciences sociales et la politique des Modernes* (Paris: Gallimard, 2013); Ibid., *La place de Dieu. Religion et politique chez les modernes* (Paris: Fayard, 2023).

CHAPTER 2

On the Possibility of a Sociological Mode of Existence. Bruno Latour and the Post-Secular Critiques of Belief

Introduction

It has become commonplace to claim that the classical-sociological explanations of religion and religious forms of social life have failed to foresee what is called our current post-secular condition.[1] Religion, instead of vanishing or, at the very least, rationalizing according to modernist standards, has persisted and in increasingly explosive and irrational fashion.[2] This failure, so it is claimed, is essentially a conceptual one. The tools which our sociological predecessors left us—thinking religion through the prism of beliefs, rites, symbolism, immanence and transcendence, modernity and its processes of individualization, rationalization and secularization—are more and more considered to be blunt, ineffective, and perhaps most importantly, *outdated*.[3] They no longer effectively capture the complexities we are facing in the superdiverse society of the twenty-first century, where religion itself is constantly transforming in dynamic,

---

[1] The classical work in this regard is still José Casanova, *Public Religions in the Modern World* (Chicago: The University of Chicago Press, 1994), esp. 17–39.

[2] Bruno Latour, "Beyond belief: Religion as the 'dynamite of the people'", in: *The Routledge Handbook of Postsecularity*, ed. Justin Beaumont (Abingdon: Routledge, 2019), 27–37.

[3] Jason Ānanda Josephson-Storm, "The Superstition, Secularism, and Religion Trinary: Or Re-Theorizing Secularism", *Method and Theory in the Study of Religion* 30 (2018): 1–20.

© The Author(s), under exclusive license to Springer Nature Switzerland AG 2024
M. Van Dam, *Languages of Belief and Early Sociology in Nineteenth-Century France*,
https://doi.org/10.1007/978-3-031-70023-1_2

multicultural environments.[4] As a result, sociologists are now forced to think religion anew, constructing post-secular methods of sociological research where religious manifestations are no longer filtered through a modernist, enlightened-liberal and anti-religious perspective.[5]

What then remains of the sociology of religion, and what should it do with its classical heritage of modernist thinkers? In other words, the sociology of religion has arrived, to quote David Smilde and Matthew May, at a moment of "critical paradigmatic reflection", which requires the sociologist to not just analyse its religious subjects and objects, but to also look in the mirror and decide "[w]hether the current situation appears as an opportunity, transition, or crisis".[6] In this sense, sociology is employing the social history of religion and sociology as a crux to think itself, creatively, in order to sustain its own historical survival as a legitimate undertaking for speaking and conceptualizing the religious dimensions of social life.[7] In this book, I will try to engage with this sociological moment of self-reflection, not by seeking to interpret the sociological present in my own way (as opportunity, transition or crisis), but by asking what such moments of self-narrating contemplation mean for our understanding of the historical relation between sociology and religion. I will argue that any future approximations of socio-religious phenomena cannot come exclusively through further conceptual clarification (i.e. to find the most suitable conceptual tools), but also needs to include a historical-anthropological examination of the sociological tradition and its different usages of these conceptual toolsets.

The key for this examination, then, is to be found in the ready to be abandoned toolset of the sociological moderns. What was belief, exactly, for classical sociologists like Comte, Durkheim and Mauss? Why were they committed to employing such an instrument in their own exploration of

---

[4] Irene Becci, "Religious Superdiversity and Gray Zones in Public Total Institutions", *Journal of Religion in Europe* 11, no. 2–3 (2018): 123–137.

[5] Manuel A. Vásquez, "Grappling with the Legacy of Modernity: Implications for the Sociology of Religion", in: *Religion on the Edge: De-centering and Re-centering the Sociology of Religion*, eds. Courtney Bender, Wendy Cadge, Peggy Levitt, & David Smilde (Oxford: Oxford University Press, 2013), 23–42.

[6] David Smilde and Matthew May, "The Emerging Strong Program in the Sociology of Religion", *SSRC Working Papers*, last consulted online on the 4th of May 2022: https://tif.ssrc.org/wp-content/uploads/2010/02/Emerging-Strong-Program-TIF.pdf.

[7] Véronique Altglas & Matthew Wood, "Introduction: An Epistemology for the Sociology of Religion", in: *Bringing Back the Social into the Sociology of Religion*, eds. Véronique Altglas & Matthew Wood (Leiden: Brill, 2018), 1–34.

phenomena of 'otherness': primitive cultures, religious traditions, folkloristic customs? And why has this category become so controversial in the post-secular tradition? The argument will be made here that these usages were not merely guided by conceptual factors, but by historical-contextual ones as well. 'Belief', during the historical time period of the birth of the social sciences, was not just a ready-made tool, a singular concept shared by a homogenous social-knowledge culture in a single meaning. Rather, it was a highly contested signifier with a complex history of its own, spawning different languages of belief, several of which shaped the sociological discipline. An understanding of sociological usages of the belief-category thus requires a reconstruction of these belief-languages as well, and their encounters with different sociological actors.

Furthermore, I will argue that these historical encounters persist into contemporary twenty-first-century social science, making the question of the ideal sociological engagement with religion not just a matter of a conceptual clarity, but one of hermeneutic self-examination as well. To gain a complete picture of what is at stake in the meeting between the scientific observer and the religious object, we need to make the different techniques and practices of navigation and negotiation performed by the sociologist, in the face of the multiple languages of belief, visible. The sociologist-actor consistently constructs their own belief/knowledge-composition, which, as Pierre Bourdieu has already argued, largely determines the potential relation with the socially observed objects. It is with these belief/knowledge-compositions in the post-secular tradition, and the different techniques of their construction, that I am concerned here.

The following two chapters aim to do two things, before I set off on my intellectual-historical investigation: first of all, I will show how the current, post-secular critiques of the classical-sociological language of beliefs represent less of a departure of sociological modernity than its presentist reiteration, as both traditions, of secular modernity and post-secular non-modernity, employed the category of belief as a way to think and conceptualize the historical place of the sociologist in society. The work of French philosopher and sociologist Bruno Latour will serve as the primary source for this claim, as I argue that his critique of the belief-category is still rooted in a broader language of belief and action, unable to fully abandon the belief-category as he distinctly intended and conceptualized throughout his work. While Latour himself seems to be well aware of this fact, he does not explicitly articulate this distinction, failing to separate his historical-anthropological method from his normative-philosophical claims.

And second, as a response to this, I want to introduce an alternative analytical framework for thinking sociology's relation to belief, one which doesn't advocate for its rejection but for its historicization, *as an assemblage of historical languages and meanings*. Turning to intellectual-historical anthropology as a privileged instrument for constructing such a framework, I will intend to make clear how such a method can help us better understand how the relation between the sociological discipline and languages of belief could be thought and investigated, both in its historical unfolding and in its present condition. As a result, we can gain a novel understanding of early sociology's usage of 'social beliefs' as a conceptual toolset, as well as present a broader and more nuanced framework of what the category can mean for the present, post-secular age. This I will further explore in the chapter following this one.

Post-Secular Critiques of Belief

What does it mean when sociologists and political philosophers claim that we are currently living in post-secular times? Several traditions of post-secularism exist, making it difficult to ascribe a singular meaning to the term.[8] Furthermore, the spectrum of post-secular traditions is characterized by a considerable degree of differentiation, both in terms of normative intent and descriptive extension, ranging from moderate pleas for mutual recognition of secular and religious voices in the public sphere (Taylor 2007; Habermas 2008) to more radical claims of a complete epistemic equality between the domains of faith and reason (Plantinga and Wolterstorff 1983). Taken at its most basic level, however, the different strands of post-secular thought can be brought together by their shared, conceptual critique of modernist conceptions of religion, accusing the latter of imposing an external, rationalist and propositional framework for evaluating religious experiences, rites, speech and meaning.[9] It is this external nature of modernity's understanding of religion, so it is argued, that has so often led to the latter's fundamental misunderstanding and

---

[8] For an up-to-date overview of the literature, cf. Justin Beaumont (ed.), *The Routledge Handbook of Postsecularity* (Abingdon: Routledge, 2019).

[9] Jonathan Z. Smith, "A Twice-Told Tale: The History of the History of Religion's History", in: Jonathan Z. Smith, *Relating Religion: Essays in the Study of Religion* (Chicago: Chicago University Press, 2004), 362–374; Timothy Larsen, *The Slain God: Anthropologists and the Christian Faith* (Oxford: Oxford University Press, 2014).

misrepresentation in secularization and modernization theories.[10] What is needed in our contemporary times—and this can be described as the shared project of post-secularism—is clearer and more authentic *communication* between the secular modernists and the religious practitioners, meaning not just an improvement in the usage of language, but also in the concrete work of understanding 'otherness'.[11] The *post-* in post-secularism, then, indicates that we have reached an epistemic threshold in time, signalling an (academic) era of theoretical and methodological reinvention. Through post-secular critiques (of modernity) and clarifications (of religion), we can take religion seriously again, making it more visible for scholarly attention.[12]

As a response to the invasive and external imposition executed by the moderns, post-secular approaches aim for an understanding of religion that is marked by such words as 'symmetry', 'inclusiveness', 'respect', 'understanding', 'learning processes', 'tolerance', 'mutual recognition', 'dialogue', and other such inherently charitable signifiers, in order to contest earlier reductionist methods applied by secular modernists.[13] The underlying assumption here is that the historical success of religion in our twenty-first-century multicultural society demands our respect, not just in a political and juridical sense, but also in an epistemological and methodological one. Someone like Habermas is therefore willing to concede the potential for religious traditions to assist in the collective search for shared truths in democratic societies (through their function as a source for moral intuitions), even if he is still adamant that this requires religious traditions to undergo their own processes of modernization.[14] All things considered,

---

[10] Eduardo Mendieta, "The postsecular condition and the genealogy of postmetaphysical thinking", in: *The Routledge Handbook of Postsecularity*, ed. Justin Beaumont (Abingdon: Routledge, 2019), 55.

[11] Cf. for example, Charles Taylor, "A Catholic Modernity?", in: *A Catholic Modernity? Charles Taylor's Marianist Award Lecture*, ed. James L. Heft, S.M. (Oxford: Oxford University Press, 1999), 13–37.

[12] Philip S. Gorski, David Kyuman Kim, John Torpey, and Jonathan VanAntwerpen, "The Post-Secular in Question", in: *The Post-Secular in Question: Religion in Contemporary Society*, eds. Philip S. Gorski, David Kyuman Kim, John Torpey, and Jonathan VanAntwerpen (New York & London: Social Science Research Council/New York University Press, 2012), 2.

[13] Jürgen Habermas, "Notes on Post-Secular Society", *New Perspectives Quarterly* 25, no. 4 (2008): 17–29, *passim*.

[14] Giorgi Areshidze, "Taking Religion Seriously? Habermas on Religious Translation and Cooperative Learning in Post-secular Society", *American Political Science Review* 111, no. 4 (2017): 724–737.

philosophers like Habermas and Taylor argue that previous models of democratic liberalism, secularism and modernity were too harsh towards the idea of religious devotion persisting into modernizing societies, making it the job for post-secular thought to broaden the social imaginaries of our potential futures.[15]

From this point of view, post-secular approaches show significant similarities to other, related trends in the social sciences and humanities, which are characterized by their anti- and/or post-modernism. These are, just to give a few examples, intellectual movements like the ontological turn in sociology (Latour 2005) and anthropology (Viveiros de Castro 2011; Holbraad and Pedersen 2017; Risjord 2020), the focus on ritual and performativity in religious studies (Lopez 1998; Orsi 2011), the integralist approach in the philosophy of religion (Milbank 1990 [2006]), and the increased emphasis on including postcolonial and subaltern perspectives in history and sociology (Kwame Anthony Appiah 1997; Chakrabarty 2000; J.G.A. Pocock 2009). While each of these traditions is distinct, with conflict and disagreement often prominent between these fields, all these disciplinary fields agree that a greater categorical sensibility is required towards religious and non-Western forms of knowledge and identification.

What these fields also share is the diagnosis of where the epistemological approach of modernity precisely failed. A sensibility towards non-Western otherness was made close to impossible within modernist thought, so it is argued, because of the latter's near exclusive emphasis on scientific reality and truth, and the universal validity of *propositional knowledge* as the measure of these truths.[16] The concept which encapsulated this more than any other was that of belief. Belief, according to post-secularists and their postmodern cousins, turns religion into a judgement on the state of the world and the forces which inhabit it, making it similar to other kinds of propositional judgement, such as scientific knowledge and ideological

---

[15] Jürgen Habermas & Charles Taylor, "Dialogue: Jürgen Habermas and Charles Taylor", in: *The Power of Religion in the Public Sphere*, eds. Eduardo Mendieta and Jonathan VanAntwerpen (New York: Columbia University Press, 2011), 60–69; Timothy Stacey, *Myth and Solidarity in the Modern World: Beyond Religious and Political Division* (Abingdon, Oxon: Routledge, 2018).

[16] Arvind-Pal S. Mandair and Markus Dressler, "Introduction: Modernity, Religion-Making, and the Post-Secular", in: *Secularism and Religion-Making*, eds. Markus Dressler & Arvind-Pal S. Mandair (Oxford: Oxford University Press, 2011), 9.

opinion.[17] According to Talal Asad, in his classic work *Genealogies of Religion: Discipline and Reasons of Power in Christianity and Islam* (1993), this understanding of religion as a collection of beliefs held by the individual believer is closely tied to specifically Christian and European historical trends, more precisely the burgeoning idea of a natural religion in the seventeenth century, which made 'religions' a universal and comparable entity.[18] This was for a long time considered to be the greatest strength of belief as a category, as it provided an instrument for thinking religion in a comparative manner, bringing religious practices into a broader framework of universal human action.[19] And yet, the result has often been the proliferation of asymmetries, between so-called superstitious primitive cultures and dispassionate, reasonable observers, with only the latter being successful in disposing themselves of non-rational opinions and sentiments through scientific means.[20]

This particular understanding of what a 'belief' is, is most often traced back to early modern enlightened thought, especially with philosophers like John Locke and David Hume, who were trying to construct an intellectual toolset which could simultaneously understand the psychological make-up of the individual human mind and its particular relation to collective socio-cultural phenomena like religion and other symbolic representations of the world, such as myth, folklore and magic.[21] Such a toolset, furthermore, would eventually lay the foundation of the human and social sciences in the nineteenth century, when the European intellectual class set itself the task of not only understanding the European pathway to industrial and economic supremacy, but also the historical relation of non-European cultures to modernity.[22] Beliefs, and a culture's ability to shed

---

[17] Talal Asad, *Genealogies of Religion: Discipline and Reasons of Power in Christianity and Islam* (Baltimore: The Johns Hopkins University Press, 1993), 39.

[18] Ibid., 40–43.

[19] Robert A. Orsi, *History and Presence* (Cambridge, MA: The Belknap Press of Harvard University Press, 2016), 63–64.

[20] Bruno Latour, *On the Modern Cult of the Factish Gods*, transl. by Catherine Porter and Heather MacLean (Durham: Duke University Press, 2010), ch. 1.

[21] The work of Canadian theologian Wilfred Cantwell Smith was seminal in this regard, through his investigations of the semantic history of 'belief', cf. W.C. Smith, *Belief and History* (Charlottesville: University of Virginia Press, 1977); Ibid., *Faith and Belief* (Princeton: Princeton University Press, 1987).

[22] Webb Keane, *Christian Moderns: Freedom and Fetish in the Mission Encounter* (Berkeley: University of California Press, 2007), 7.

its non-desirable beliefs (i.e. superstitions), came to play a central role in the earliest manifestations of these sciences, further paving the way for the power-structures which seemingly inevitably followed them.[23]

These kinds of psychological-cognitive readings of human culture became increasingly contested in the twentieth century, impelled by the anti-representational philosophies of two key figures, Ludwig Wittgenstein and Martin Heidegger.[24] The crux of Wittgenstein's argument against belief can be found in his critique of James George Frazer's *The Golden Bough: A Study in Comparative Religion* (1890), one of the most important and formative works of nineteenth-century social anthropology. The failure of Frazer's explanatory model for the belief systems of primitive religions, according to Wittgenstein, lay in its continuous interpretation of religious actions as being guided by opinions on the state of the world, and foolish ones at that.[25] Throughout his work in the philosophy of language, Wittgenstein aimed to show how human practices—religious and otherwise—cannot be understood properly if we only think of them in terms of 'true and false', in terms of an explanation via knowledge.

Rather, these practices should be approached as particular ways of being in the world, of giving expression to certain desires which are subsequently *satisfied* by the performance of certain rituals (e.g. burning in effigy or kissing a picture).[26] The explanatory value inherent within such rituals is limited for the anthropologist. The only way in which we can be brought closer to understanding such rituals is through description, eventually allowing us to accept such acts as manifestations of humanity: "One can only resort to *description* here, and say: such is human life."[27] The success

---

[23] Jacques Revel, "Forms of Expertise: Intellectuals and 'Popular' Culture in France (1650–1800)", in: *Understanding Popular Culture. Europe from the Middle Ages to the Nineteenth Century*, ed. Steven Kaplan (Berlin: Mouton Publishers, 1984), 255–273; Euan Cameron, *Enchanted Europe: Superstition, Reason, and Religion 1250–1750* (Oxford: Oxford University Press, 2010).

[24] Mark Risjord, "Anthropology Without Belief: An Anti-representationalist Ontological Turn", *Philosophy of the Social Sciences* 50, no. 5 (2020): 604. Cf. also Charles Guignon, "Philosophy after Heidegger and Wittgenstein", *Philosophy and Phenomenological Research* 50, no. 4 (1990): 649–672.

[25] Ludwig Wittgenstein, "Remarks on Frazer's *The Golden Bough*", in: *The Mythology in Our Language: Remarks on Frazer's Golden Bough*, transl. by Stephan Palmié, preface by Giovanni da Col, ed. by Giovanni da Col & Stephan Palmié (Chicago: Hau Books, 2018), 32.

[26] Ibid., 36.

[27] Ibid., 34; Michael Puett, "Wittgenstein on Frazer", in: *The Mythology in Our Language: Remarks on Frazer's Golden Bough*, transl. by Stephan Palmié, preface by Giovanni da Col, ed. by Giovanni da Col & Stephan Palmié (Chicago: Hau Books, 2018), 146–48.

of such a ritual, from a Wittgensteinian perspective, is no longer marked by its accurate representation of reality, by the truthfulness of the beliefs underlying it, but by its satisfaction of its own conditions of felicity, as J.L. Austin would later come to designate them.[28] Wittgenstein's problematization of belief through linguistic reflection was influential in anthropology, leading other prominent theorists such as Rodney Needham, Talal Asad and Malcolm Ruel to question the validity of the concept for understanding religious phenomena.[29]

Another important impetus was provided by German philosopher Martin Heidegger, whose object-oriented and externalist approach to being and knowledge stood diametrically opposed to the Enlightenment's philosophical tradition of internal, psychological beliefs.[30] Rather than considering objects as mere vehicles given meaning through their internal processing in human cognitive frameworks, Heidegger took on a realist approach to tool-being (a term later coined by object-oriented philosopher Graham Harman), granting objects their own force of agency in the construction of relations.[31] The things that move us and allow us to think and express ourselves—"floorboards, bolts, ventilators, gravity, and atmospheric oxygen"—do not simply come to life from the moment where we have internalized them in our minds through representations, they already exist, act and interact with each other beyond our own limited cognitive realms.[32] Heidegger's externalist realism has been a formative influence with many thinkers associated with post-secular thought, in philosophy (Charles Taylor 2007, 2016), anthropology (Tim Ingold 2000; Risjord 2020), and theology (John Milbank 1990 [2006]), further stimulating calls for an integralist approach to religion as opposed to one directed by the universalist validity of propositional knowledge and beliefs.

---

[28] Ibid., 44. Cf. also, J.L. Austin, *How To Do Things with Words: The William James Lectures delivered at Harvard University in 1955* (Oxford: Clarendon Press, 1962).

[29] Bosco Byungeun Bae, "The Textures of 'Belief': An interdisciplinary study towards a social scientific epistemology" (PhD diss., Durham University, 2015), 20–21.

[30] Risjord, "Anthropology Without Belief", 603.

[31] Graham Harman, *Tool-Being: Heidegger and the Metaphysics of Objects* (Chicago & La Salle: Open Court Publishing, 2002); Graham Harman, *Heidegger Explained: From Phenomenon to Thing* (Chicago & La Salle: Open Court Publishing, 2007).

[32] Harman, *Tool-Being*, 18.

The Post-Secular Critique of Belief as an Act and Intervention: Bruno Latour

The importance of these two thinkers for my purposes here is further underlined by the fact that their ideas are brought together by French philosopher and sociologist Bruno Latour, in what I consider to be the exemplary account of the post-secular critique of belief. While Latour is by no means the conventional flagbearer for post-secularism (in fact, he retains a somewhat hesitant attitude towards the term and the tradition),[33] it can be argued that it is he, rather than Habermas, Taylor or Casanova, who has been consistently conceptualizing and problematizing modernity's scientific apparatus for the past five decades, particularly in its organization and processing of non-human objects, which includes phenomena as diverse as bacteria and the divine.[34] Furthermore, Latour's ideal positioning is further given weight by his scholarly background as both a sociologist and anthropologist, two disciplines which, in their moment of origin, were heavily influenced by modernity's ambiguous relation to religion and non-modern beliefs.[35] In other words, Latour's work is located at the very crossroads of sacred-secular interaction, and, as a result, he has given serious reflection not only on these interactions, but also how this relation shapes the position and actions of the scientific investigator itself.[36] In many ways, his concern with speaking religiously, and how scientific discourse impacts and (mis)shapes such speech, has been consistently present in all of his work, starting from Latour's early studies in theology during the 1970s up until his final work on the politics of the Anthropocene.[37]

---

[33] Latour, "Beyond belief", 36.

[34] On the trio of Taylor, Habermas and Casanova as the typical flagbearers of post-secularism, cf. Justin Beaumont & Klaus Eder, "Concepts, processes, and antagonisms of postsecularity", in: *The Routledge Handbook of Postsecularity*, ed. Justin Beaumont (Abingdon: Routledge, 2019), 7.

[35] On these mutual influences, cf. Philippe Steiner, "Altruism, sociology and the history of economic thought", *European Journal for the History of Economic Thought* 26, no. 6 (2019): 1252–1274; Andrew Zimmerman, "German sociology and empire: From internal colonization to overseas colonization and back again", in: *Sociology & Empire: The Imperial Entanglement of a Discipline*, ed. George Steinmetz (London: Duke University Press, 2013), 166–187.

[36] Tim Howles, "The Political Theology of Bruno Latour" (PhD diss., University of Oxford, 2018), esp. 118–187.

[37] Henning Schmidgen, *Bruno Latour in Pieces: An Intellectual Biography*, transl. by Gloria Custance (New York: Fordham University Press, 2015), 11–19.

It is for these reasons that I will use the work of Latour as an exemplar for discussing the post-secular problematization of belief as a category, functioning as a springboard for broader reflections on the history of sociology and religion.

So what is the crux of Latour's post-secular critique of belief? In the eyes of Latour, the notion of belief, as employed by the moderns, was not just any category in their conceptual toolset. Rather, it represents the key instrument in the organization of their worldview. The informative mode of scientific exchange—'is it true? Is it real?'—has been the central marker of how to categorize religious phenomena, how to organize people into groups, those of believers and non-believers.[38] Belief, for the moderns, is less a descriptor of a certain conviction, than the assertion of a historical fact: there are people who believe and there are those who know. Belief, in other words, divides the world into a particular state of affairs, establishing the distinction between fetishists (i.e. those who are under the illusion of being moved by non-constructed agents) and factists (i.e. those who allow themselves to be guided by factual truth).[39] This is what Latour has termed as "belief in belief" and which he considers to be little more than a tool for control and domination used by the moderns in their encounter with the non-moderns.[40] The moderns perceive themselves to have reached a degree of manufacturability and self-awareness which gives them access to another plane, that of objectivity and philosophical robustness.[41]

This instrument of belief in belief did not limit itself to the epistemological colonization of non-Western cultures, but manifested itself in other areas as well. In the area of religious speech, for example, discussed by Latour in his book *Rejoicing, Or the Torments of Religious Speech* (2013), the French philosopher considers the notion of belief to be a foreign imposition in the realm of religion. A historical result of the modernist obsession with clear analytical language, the category of belief has turned the question of religion into a kind of metaphysical battlefield, with two camps, the believers and the non-believers, opposed on the question of God and whether He really exists or not.[42] The truth of religion, then,

---

[38] Bruno Latour, *Rejoicing, Or the Torments of Religious Speech*, transl. by Julia Rose (Malden, MA: Polity Press, 2013), 2–3.
[39] Latour, *On the Modern Cult*, 11–13.
[40] Ibid., 14–15.
[41] Ibid., 29–30.
[42] Latour, *Rejoicing*, 4.

comes to depend on a propositional scheme: "If God is real, then my belief in Him is validated, as are my dispositions and judgments tied to this belief."

The matter of speaking religiously thus transforms into an exclusive register on the reality of the world, competing with scientific propositions, both functioning as a type of information that describes and makes visible.[43] This is what Latour refers to as double-click communication, a reference to how information functions on a computer, where everything becomes immediately present through a simple click on the computer mouse.[44] Yet it would be a profound misunderstanding, says Latour, to expect religious transactions to function in a similar way. It is *transformation* that is the core business of religion, according to Latour, not information about how to navigate the world efficaciously: "there is no information in matters of religion, no maintenance of constants, no transfers of relationships intact throughout the stream of transformations. [...] [T]he connection between a religious text and the thing it talks about is not the same as the connection between a map and its territory."[45]

And this is why belief is such a problematic term for Latour, as it represents a complete distortion of what religion is, and more importantly, does. First, it misrepresents religion as somehow being informational in the same way scientific propositions are, making a revival of religious speech *a priori* impossible:

> Why does belief in belief make any revival of religious speech impossible? Because it leads thinking astray into a virtual world, one to which we 'could' have access 'if only' we had the means available to chains of information but of which belief actually remains forever deprived. It is this sleight of hand and nothing else that engenders the illusion of another world to which religious discourse, by some miraculous somersault, would provide exclusive access. People have even dared imagine a race, a competition, a sort of championship between informational speech and religious speech to see which of them went further, took us further. As if this hare and that tortoise could be pitted against each other on the same grounds – of speed and access to the far distant![46]

---

[43] Ibid., 18–22.
[44] Ibid., 21. Cf. also Michel Serres, *Petite Poucette* (Paris: Le Pommier, 2012).
[45] Latour, *Rejoicing*, 20.
[46] Ibid., 30.

And secondly, belief turns religious phenomena into representations, internal figments of the imagination. But for Latour, religious beings and objects—relics, angels, hymns and shared prayers—are not cognitive instruments to understand reality; they are real, external actors in their own right, carrying not informative content with them, but bringing transformation from the outside.[47]

In order to make clear this performativity of religious speech, Latour gives the example of two lovers, one asking the other whether they still loved them. To answer in a purely informational manner—'Yes, but you already know that, I told you so last year'—would be to completely misunderstand the question. The truth of love's expression, according to Latour, lies not in the accurate representation of the lover's internal sentiments. Instead, it lies in its efficaciousness in bringing the two together through such utterances, the *satisfaction* experienced by both in their shared reinvention of their love. "And so it isn't the sentence itself that the woman will closely follow, or the resemblance or dissimilitude between the two instances, but the *tone*, the manner, the way in which he, her lover, will revive that old, worn-out theme."[48] The truth of the speech, then, manifests itself afterwards: it is embodied in the strengthened bond that comes to exist between the two separate individuals, choosing to live together furthermore in the fragile yet sturdy house that their love has built.[49]

It is this kind of act, this kind of transformation that religious speech contains within itself. Its conditions of felicity are much better understood if we compare them to those directing love-speech, than to those which validate a scientific utterance. Just as the lover would be a fool to answer in an informative manner to the question 'Do you love me?', so is it besides the question to ask of an angel whether he is real or what kind of information he brings.[50] Rather, to encounter religious beings and to speak in a religious way is to bring others into presence, to enter into a new and shared world which is brought to life, be it through a warm gesture given

---

[47] Bruno Latour, *An Inquiry into Modes of Existence: An Anthropology of the Moderns*, transl. by Catherine Porter (Cambridge, MA: Harvard University Press, 2013), 303; Howles, "The Political Theology", 205–206.
[48] Latour, *Rejoicing*, 26.
[49] Ibid., 26.
[50] Latour, "Beyond belief", 31.

to a stranger, a song sung together or a prayer spoken in ritual devotion.[51] This is what is known in linguistics as the phatic function, the very act of establishing communication.[52] In this regard, religion is less about understanding the world through individual and collective beliefs, than about creating relations with others, experiencing the other as present in a shared imagined space, gaining access to the other as a fellow human being.[53] Religious beings, like God, angels and their many incarnated symbols, act as mediators, vessels which allow strangers to become neighbours.[54]

According to Latour, this phatic function of religion wasn't always misrecognized. Latour, walking into a small church in Montcombroux, recollects the image of medieval Bourbonnais peasants, who were deeply stirred by the same prayer that now leaves Latour, alone and hundreds of years later, seemingly unmoved.[55] It was apparent to Italian painter Fra Angelico (1395–1455) as well, the Early Renaissance artist, who was able to capture the nature of religious speech in his fresco at the Dominican Convent of San Marco, as it displays the demand of Christ *to be made* continuously present by his flock. Not to be represented, not to be rationally explained, but to be perennially reinvented, as the metaphorical nourishment of the *corpus mysticum* which comes together again and again in performative remembrance.[56] Using a Wittgensteinian philosophy of language and a Heidegger-inspired object-oriented ontology, Latour uncovers a religious mode of existence which is allergic to the question of belief, and which characterizes the latter as a historical and philosophical misstep, an unfortunate by-product of modernity's tendency to simplify its surroundings in order to categorize and dominate them. The moderns, in their ambition to find a rational theory of everything, forgot the pluralist character of the particular.

While many in the tradition of post-secularism would undoubtedly feel uncomfortable with some of Latour's more mystical formulations, the core of its qualms with modernity, secularism and the category of belief are articulated by Latour to its most thorough extent. The horizon of

---

[51] Howles, "The Political Theology", 258.
[52] Latour, *Rejoicing*, 33.
[53] Cf. for example, Orsi, *History and Presence*.
[54] Latour, *An Inquiry*, 320–323.
[55] Latour, *Rejoicing*, 11–12.
[56] Ibid., 106–108. Cf. also the work of Henri de Lubac, *Corpus Mysticum: The Eucharist and the Church in the Middle Ages*, trans. Gemma Simmonds, with Richard Price and Christopher Stephens (Notre Dame, IN: Notre Dame Press, 2007 [1944]).

post-secularism is to be found here, encapsulated in a reflection on religion that resembles a line drawn in the sand. The moderns, the classical sociologists and anthropologists who put their faith in the unlimited expansion of rational and representational understanding, are fundamentally mistaken in their double-click communication on God and religious phenomena, in their speculation on the informative nature of religious belief.

The Limits of Conceptual Clarity

The problem with belief then, according to Latour, is its conceptual inaccuracy: it inadequately conveys the meaning of religious speech, mistaking it for something it is not. As such, Latour labels belief a "category mistake".[57] While the consequences of this mistake are severe—Latour speaks of increasing levels of religious violence *as a result* of the moderns' "poisonous notion of belief"—the major fault of the moderns, from a post-secular perspective, lies in the realm of the epistemological, and more specifically, modernity's overreach in trying to grasp the essence of religious transformation through informational and propositional means.[58] The solution, for Latour, is relatively straightforward: an understanding of religious speech requires us to recognize its self-explanatory and self-sufficient nature as an autonomous mode of existence, a mode that is exclusively accessible through its repeated performance. In other words, we need to understand religion for what it truly is, not what we desire it to be, Latour echoing a critique already levelled by Wittgenstein at Frazer for his simplistic interpretation of primitive religion.[59]

Latour sees a way forward, for the non-religious, by turning to a new form of agnosticism, one that abandons belief as a potential entry point into the religious domain and which recognizes the impossibility of knowing otherness through a singular template of double-click communication.[60] This would result in what Latour considers to be a true pluralism, a plurality of templates. It is by respecting the reality and borders of these templates that we can end the conflict between secular and religious perspectives: "The only solution to the present religious wars indeed is in insisting on plurality, but not plurality of knowledge—we rather need

[57] Latour, "Beyond belief", 30.
[58] Ibid., 32.
[59] Cf. supra.
[60] Latour, "Beyond belief", 34.

more unity of knowledge!—but plurality of templates with which to measure the beings that are making us act and are thus holding us—be they law, love, politics, religion or many others. The idea of plurality or multiplicity of templates is how I embrace the notion of postsecularity."[61]

The seemingly modest request of a true pluralism, combined with Latour's self-presentation as an amicable peacemaker seeking to escape an escalation of *unnecessary* religious violence, can give the reader the idea that this whole discussion can be resolved in a scholarly and diplomatic fashion. It is a plea for a reasonable resolution to rationalistic excesses. The moderns, enthused by their many successes, succumbed to an analytical mistake, which we need to admit, correct and simply move on. Latour himself further emphasizes this sentiment by ending his discussion in his text "Beyond belief" with a reference to what he considers to be the true crisis of our age, global warming: "What we cannot afford is to have a war of gods just at the time when we have to also deal with the war of the world imposed by the intrusion of this strangest goddess of all, Gaia."[62] But the question remains, however, whether the pluralist adjustment of post-secular understandings of religion is an effective correction to earlier modernist failures, and whether it is through reason, and reason alone, that we can avoid this so-called war of gods.

The first thing to evaluate, then, is the precise nature of post-secularism's reasonableness. Is the renewed approach to religion, proposed not just by Latour but by Habermas and a whole host of other social theorists, able to avoid the categorical mistakes of the moderns? As I already discussed above, these mistakes were twofold: an epistemological asymmetry and a representationalist understanding of beliefs. By abandoning the category of belief and taking an object-oriented stance on the existence of religious beings, Latour claimed that he was simply putting all actors on the same playing field, by piercing the dual myths of barbarism and modernity:

> There have never been any Barbarians; we have never been Modern [...]! If I am putting amulet-covered Portuguese on the same level as amulet-covered Guineans, fetishists on the same level as anti-fetishists, saligram worshippers on the same level as iconoclastic Brahmans, I am not dragging them all down, *I am pulling them all up*.[63]

---

[61] Ibid., 36.
[62] Ibid., 36.
[63] Latour, *On the Modern Cult*, 33.

Such a call for symmetry, or at the very least, equal respectability between fetishists and anti-fetishists is a staple of post-secularist literature.[64] The story of modernist superiority, a result of a unique teleological pathway paved by reason and disenchantment, is generally considered to be little more than a myth within this literature.[65] A myth, furthermore, which has lent itself all too easily to a history of abuse and mistreatment of those who fell by modernity's wayside.[66] The logical conclusion it would seem, both epistemologically as well as morally, would be then to abandon such claims, and start over in our categorization of the world and its occupants. "We are like everyone else", exclaims Latour, quickly followed by three bracketed questions: "Where is the problem? where is the loss? where is the danger?"[67] While these are obviously rhetorical, Latour, at the same time, seems to take delight in turning the moderns' typical game against them, *imposing* a seemingly infallible logic and emphasizing its reasonableness, its naturalness and its beneficial facets to all concerned parties. But, as Latour himself has so often made clear, such modernist games are almost always accompanied by mechanisms of blackboxing, ways of hiding the process of construction underlying such logics.[68] To put it differently, Latour's rhetorical questions are not rhetorical at all—a fact I think he is more than well aware of himself—they are valid questions which still need answering. The blackbox of Latour's reasonable post-secularism still needs to be opened.

A good place to start would be to return, once again, to the question of belief. What do we lose when we abandon the idea that religion in some sense is concerned with the belief in religious beings? Why did the moderns place such emphasis on an apparently unnecessary and confusing category? These questions are difficult to answer from a Latourian framework, as the moderns are placed outside the scope of his social-constructivist anthropology. This shouldn't really come as a surprise, as the entire premise of Latour's project is built on the idea that the moderns are guilty

---

[64] Cloke & Beaumont, "Geographies of postsecular", 36.

[65] Jason Ā. Josephson-Storm, *The Myth of Disenchantment: Magic, Modernity, and The Birth of The Human Sciences* (Chicago and London: The University of Chicago Press, 2017).

[66] Talal Asad, "Anthropology and the Colonial Encounter", in: *The Politics of Antropology: From Colonialism and Sexism Toward a View from Below*, eds. Gerrit Huizer & Bruce Mannheim (Berlin: De Gruyter, 1973), 85–94.

[67] Latour, *On the Modern Cult*, 34.

[68] Bruno Latour, *Pandora's Hope: Essays on the Reality of Science Studies* (Cambridge, MA: Harvard University Press, 1999), 304.

of making a *category* mistake. Their self-articulations—theories, descriptions, categorizations—are not so much seen by Latour as meaningful actions in their own right, as they are added mechanisms concealing their true actions.[69] The moderns are just like everyone else, they only *pretend* to do something different, in order to achieve their goal of distinguishing themselves from non-Modern others.[70] In other words, their self-narrated identities as modern are superadditions, discursive strategies meant to perform a particular effect and create a hierarchical power-structure through differentiation (Latour terms this purification, which he distinguishes from and contrasts with productive forms of mediation and translation).[71] Even though the moderns construct fetishes and factishes, just like everyone else, they obfuscate their constructions underneath a discourse of objectivity, representation and discovery.[72]

An important side-effect of this critique becomes apparent here, which is that Latour's critique of the moderns still in large part depends on the reality of this self-categorization, the same reality Latour attempts to uncover as ultimately little effective. There really are such things as moderns. They are simply not what they say they are, or at least, not because of the reasons they themselves express. But if that's the case, what are we to do with them and their everyday, historical actions, their constructions, their built relations? For Latour, this is simple: we merely need to make the distinction between those articulations that are clarifying (the metamodernist schematical categories of 'purification', 'translation' and 'mediation') and those that are obfuscating (the modernist schematical categories of 'society', 'nature/culture', and 'social facts'), with the category of belief firmly being on the side of the latter.[73] But this division irks in its own manner as it seems to recreate the earlier modernist mistakes, only inverted: the Other—no longer the religious or primitive being, but the modern one—belongs, in the Latourian scheme, to a monolithic culture dominated by a set of orthodoxies (the so-called Constitution of the moderns), which is primarily designed to function as a totalizing discourse while distributing power and authority to those identifying as modern.[74]

---

[69] Latour, *On the Modern Cult*, 12–13.
[70] Bruno Latour, *We Have Never Been Modern*, transl. by Catherine Porter (Cambridge, MA: Harvard University Press, 1993), 37–39.
[71] Latour, *On the Modern Cult*, 15; Latour, *We Have Never Been Modern*, 38–39.
[72] Ibid., 17.
[73] Ibid., 30–34; Latour, *We Have Never Been Modern*, 10–12.
[74] Latour, *We Have Never Been Modern*, 14–48.

There is only one way of being modern, and once those conditions of felicity are left unsatisfied, the shroud of modernity simultaneously fades into nothingness.[75] The moderns are left in limbo, partly real and partly illusory.

Interestingly enough, this shows a remarkable similarity to how enlightened moderns themselves for a long time conceptualized ancient and mediaeval Christianity, as a dogmatic and totalizing orthodoxy, where the meaning of belief was singular and imposed from above, and which could only be accepted or rejected by the Christian body, the believers themselves.[76] To be Christian was, in other words, to believe in a certain kind of way, with any digression being either heretic or simply non-existent, without meaning.[77] This was, of course, not the case. The Christian orthodoxy of a theologically sound faith articulated by its class of philosophers and theologians was an ideal, but this ideal needed not only top-down articulation, but shared construction throughout the community of believers as well. The Jesuit historian Michael C. McCarthy has shown how Christian belief was permanently being negotiated, something that only came to life through the formation of networks and relationships, and experienced together with others.[78]

McCarthy takes the example of the Pelagian debates—a theological controversy in the fourth and fifth century CE on the matters of original sin and free will—to make clear how someone like Augustine not only formulated what belief should look like, but also sought to actively *construct* the story of a Christian community "united in belief" through practices of letter-writing and network-formation. The language of belief then functioned as a placeholder for the enactment of multiple modalities of believing: the bishop of Hippo was then able to combine the notion of belief as an individual judgement conforming to proper doctrine, with its understanding as something that is collectively and concretely realized, as something a group of believers agrees and acts upon together.[79] To believe, then, meant to both adhere to orthodox dogma and to perform certain social bonds in shared declarations. Latour himself, as we saw above, also emphasizes this, with his echoes of agrarian parish communities huddled

---

[75] Ibid., 47.
[76] Michael C. McCarthy, S.J., "Modalities of Belief in Ancient Christian Debate", *Journal of Early Christian Studies* 17, no. 4 (2009): 606–607.
[77] Ibid., 607.
[78] Ibid., 626.
[79] Ibid., 626–627.

together in small churches during the Middle Ages functioning as the very model for what he considers to be the religious mode of existence.

Yet at the same time, this idea of a monolithic orthodoxy of beliefs remains present in Latour, but in its inverse form, as noted by the prominent historian of belief, John H. Arnold.[80] According to Latour, it is with the enlightened moderns, like Edward Gibbon, Auguste Comte and Émile Durkheim, that such monolithic orthodoxies are instead to be found, exemplified by the singular template *par excellence*, the template of universal rationality.[81] But why should we go along with this same story on the authoritarian orthodoxy of modernist understandings of belief, if the history of Christianity and its diverse practices of belief has shown us the limits of such singular explanations? Was the modernist regime of belief itself not also susceptible to processes of construction, to different types of performance, to differing imaginations of our relation to others? It seems only reasonable to think that they were. The negotiation of what belief entailed, was undoubtedly different amongst the moderns, whether it be Immanuel Kant or David Hume, Edward Burnett Tylor or James George Frazer, Émile Durkheim or Max Weber. While it is true that it were the moderns who created the so-called category mistakes of 'society', 'nature/culture' and 'belief' and who aimed to make belief into a cognitive proposition, it is also true that we need to distinguish between the modernist *desire* for a rationalist-scientific orthodoxy and its concrete, historical practices of constructing such a belief/knowledge-composition. After all, there is a clear difference between proposing a self-articulated ideal of belief and actually applying the category of belief to the socially real, as the sociologist is then confronted with the inevitable dynamism and historicism of the very belief-practices they are trying to describe.[82]

It is only in the case of the latter, in the concrete applications of the category and its inevitable looping effects, that belief transforms into a creative category, as the sociologist herself is becoming, once again, an

---

[80] John H. Arnold, "Believing in Belief: Gibbon, Latour, and the Social History of Religion", *Past & Present* 260, no. 1 (2023): 236–268.

[81] Bruno Latour, "Formes élémentaires de la sociologie: Formes avancées de la théologie", *Archives de sciences sociales des religions* 167, juillet-septembre (2014), last consulted on the 7th of February 2022. URL: http://journals.openedition.org/assr/26199; Arnold, "Believing in Belief", 250.

[82] Cf. Bourdieu and Wacquant, *An Invitation to Reflexive Sociology*.

active participant in the making up of the so-called belief-practices.[83] Modernist sociological engagement with languages of belief, then, is something that comes alive as it is discussed and given shape in many different ways, reflexively impacting and influencing the very social domain it is describing as well.[84] To think belief, in a modernist and sociological-anthropological manner, is to intervene in a unique way in the social world, not just imposing a singular vision onto the social world, but allowing societal life to express itself in unpredictable ways, to let it speak through the construction of a narrative space where it can unfold itself.[85] Each sociological modern, in their own way, had to give shape to this complex relationship, between a static conceptual description of a belief-practice and its dynamic reality. This is what I propose to call classical sociology's own mode of existence, rather than describe it as a distortion of other such *sui generis* modes.

Latour, and other post-secular representatives of the critique of belief, typically fail to consider the complexity and multi-polarity of modernist, classical-sociological discourses of belief, taking them at their self-imposed normative value rather than considering these from a social-constructivist perspective, similar to religious, juridical and political beings. Their conceptual reproach of the category is unable to avoid the same pitfalls already experienced by the moderns, as the post-secular critique of belief falls victim to a reductionist framing of modernist engagements with the belief-category.

THE CRITIQUE OF BELIEF AS AN ECHO OF SOCIOLOGICAL MODERNITY

Latour, who explicitly rejects the modernist definition of 'belief', aims to revive another, alternative modality of thinking otherness, articulating it, for example, as love speech and as neighbourly love. The French philosopher-sociologist considers love as something that *must necessarily*

---

[83] On the notion of looping effects, cf. Ian Hacking, "Making Up People", in: *Forms of Desire: Sexual Orientation and the Social Constructionist Controversy*, ed. Edward Stein (New York: Routledge, 1992), 69–88.

[84] Ulrich Beck, Anthony Giddens, and Scott Lash, *Reflexive Modernization: Politics, Tradition and Aesthetics in the Modern Social Order* (Oxford: Polity Press, 1994).

[85] Bruno Karsenti, *L'homme total: sociologie, anthropologie et philosophie chez Marcel Mauss* (Paris: Presses Universitaires de France, 1997), 99–103.

be articulated, the construction of a fragile relationship, marked by risk and uncertainty, which requires to be reinvented between two (what can be called) 'believers' again and again.[86] His abandonment of the term 'belief' is then less a rejection of its realness as a social phenomenon than a pragmatic choice, further minimizing the chance for the practice to continue to be misunderstood and misrepresented:

> If there is such a thing as belief at all, it is the most complex, sophisticated, critical, subtle, reflective activity there is. But this subtlety can never unfold if one first attempts to break it down into cause-objects, source-subjects, and representations. To take away the ontology of belief, on the pretext that it occurs inside the subject, is to misunderstand objects and human actors alike.[87]

To truly understand belief, in other words, we must go beyond a concept which has been irretrievably tainted and contaminated by its modernist meanings. Perhaps more by accident than by intention, Latour is showing the historical intricacies of the term and its many different meanings, as well as its ability to function as a narrative vessel through which new projects of believing can be articulated. To look beyond 'belief', as Latour tries to do for its modernist variant, is not just a conceptual move in the philosophical history of truth-finding. It can also be approached as a practice which belongs to what can be called the *longue durée* history of believing, which is characterized by continuous attempts at capturing, in life-giving and -affirming language, the human act of being social, of committing and binding oneself to another.[88] Latour, in other words, is actively engaging with and intervening in the register of belief as a historical *language*, through his own writings from a sociological as well as Catholic starting point.[89] One example of this is how the French philosopher aims to restore our earthly bonds of believing through his philosophical work on the imagination of the Anthropocene as a material manifestation of

---

[86] Latour, *Rejoicing*, 53.

[87] Latour, *On the Modern Cult*, 42.

[88] Michel de Certeau, "Une pratique sociale de la différence: croire", *Faire croire. Modalités de la diffusion et de la réception des messages religieux du xiie au xve siècle*, École française de Rome, no. 303 (1981): 367–71.

[89] Howles, "The Political Theology", 310–311.

contemporary human solidarity and interdependence in the face of ecological disaster.[90]

It is in this paradoxical scheme—where belief reinvents itself through the negation of other modalities of belief—where many confusions arise. Is Latour for or against the notion of belief as a way of representing a religious mode of existence? The origin of this confusion lies in the idea that there is one, true understanding of what belief is, irrespective of the historical context and conditions giving the term its meaning. This is where Latour follows in the footsteps of the moderns.[91] While Latour is correct that the modernist understanding of 'belief' does not capture the full extent of its sophisticated and subtle activities, his own particular version of what the practice of believing constitutes (the medieval Bourbonnais peasants praying together) does not satisfy any degree of subtlety or complexity any more than the moderns do.[92] It is a singular composition of a belief-relation, partially descriptive and partially normative, with the explicit goal of demarcating the dual fields of religion and sociology.

Furthermore, its idealization of Catholic ritualistic performances of communion and togetherness strongly echoes similar sociological-narrative interventions from the nineteenth century, such as those of François-René de Chateaubriand, Felicité de la Mennais, Joseph de Maistre and Louis de Bonald, who coupled a reactionary and proto-sociological analysis of post-revolutionary France's social predicaments with an ideal of medieval Catholic social harmony.[93] Like Latour, these reactionaries were involved in an intellectual struggle for the hegemonic definition of what constitutes a good society, proper self-government, the social ties founding a living, well-ordered community and the role of religion as well as knowledge of the social in reaching these ideals.[94] Negating

---

[90] On this, cf. Bruno Latour, *Down to Earth: Politics in the New Climatic Regime*, transl. by Catherine Porter (Cambridge, MA: Polity Press, 2018).

[91] Graham Harman, "Entanglement and Relation: A Response to Bruno Latour and Ian Hodder", *New Literary History* 45, no. 1 (2014): 37–49.

[92] Arnold, "Believing in Belief", 265–266. On the different modalities of believing, cf. infra chapter 3.

[93] François-René de Chateaubriand, *Génie du christianisme, ou Beautés de la religion chrétienne* (Paris: chez Migneret, 1802); Felicité de la Mennais, *Essai sur l'indifférence en matière de religion* (Paris: Tournachon-Molin et H. Seguin, 1817), vol. I; Louis de Bonald, *De la Chrétienté et du Christianisme* (Paris: impr. de Lachevardière fils, 1825); Joseph de Maistre, *Du Pape* (Lyon: Chez Rusand, 1819), 2 vol.

[94] Dominique Iogna-Prat & Alain Rauwel, "Introduction: Reconfigurations socio-religieuses post-révolutionnaires", *Archives de sciences sociales des religions* 190 (2020): 11–26.

the truthfulness of other employments of 'belief' (such as those of the moderns) should then be understood as a crucial technique for further legitimizing one's own model of ideal community-formation.[95] This does not make it an illegitimate practice; defining what sociology should be is a crucial part of the sociological operation. This does mean, however, that it is not particularly suited to self-reflectively understand the sociological operation in its own right.

To understand these practices of imagining belief, on an intellectual-historical level, we should not evaluate different modalities of belief according to the level of their accuracy in approximating their 'belief-object', but rather we should historicize and contextualize said practices in their multiple forms and meanings.[96] It is, in other words, only by thinking belief as both a multimodal practice as well as a symbolic discursive space for self-historicization and reinvention, that it becomes possible to move beyond some of these confusions. Belief, from this perspective, is never just a singular category, with certain properties and qualities which can be defined in an ahistorical and objective manner. Rather, it should be thought of, in this context, as a collection of different, historical languages, each with their own particular grammar, discursive rules, and conditions of felicity, which can be reconstructed and investigated.[97]

These languages of belief, together with its categorical opposites (science/knowledge/theology), its unhappy cousins (pseudoscience/superstition), as well as its internal variations (faith/trust/altruism/...), form a historical network, which needs to be analysed as such in order to make sense of its endless contestations and problematizations within sociology.[98] This is something Pierre Bourdieu already referred to, when he remarked how the sociology of religion often found it difficult to control and translate the many different layers of what belief actually constituted for certain religious groups or institutions, as its own sociological language was itself inflected by the many pathways that it shared with certain branches of

---

[95] de Certeau, "L'institution du croire", 74–75.
[96] Patrick Royannais, "Michel de Certeau: l'anthropologie du croire et la théologie de la faiblesse de croire", *Recherches de Science Religieuse* 91, no. 4 (2003): 507.
[97] Palti, "The 'Theoretical Revolution' in Intellectual History", 387–405.
[98] Josephson-Storm, "The Superstition, Secularism, and Religion Trinary", 14.

Christian religion.[99] The borders of materiality and virtuality, theory and practice, slowly become blurred in a notion such as belief and the reflective engagements with it.

For example, when Auguste Comte described (Christian) faith in the fourth volume of his *Système de politique positive* (1854) as "the disposition to believe spontaneously, without earlier demonstration, the proclaimed dogmas by a competent authority [my translation]", this description did not stand alone, aimed just at accurately articulating what faith is from an early sociological perspective.[100] It was also part of a larger narrative philosophy of history, and was as such, throughout the *Système de politique positive*, systematically connected to (1) the history of Christianity as a socio-governmental organization based on spontaneous beliefs, (2) Comte's project of sociological faith as a renewed and *contemporary* system of government based on a reflective study of such historical systems, and (3) their shared role in the story of human collective government, as something that gradually unfolded itself.[101] Understood in this manner, the moderns' employment of the belief-category was not merely a discursive means of Latourian purification, but a narrative technique for imagining and governing the self. By giving meaning to what belief and faith was, as well as its role in creating a well-governed society, Comte was also able to articulate a relation to his own sociological self, excavating a place for himself in the long history of imagining and narrating belief.[102] The languages of belief formed a crucial tool, so I will argue, for the early sociologists to think sociology, not only as a science, but as a new mode of existence.

It is this interaction which needs to be analysed and described in a historical and anthropological fashion, in order to reconstruct this complex

---

[99] Pierre Bourdieu, "Sociologues de la croyance et croyances de sociologues", *Archives de sciences sociales des religions* 32, no. 63.1 (1987): 160.

[100] Auguste Comte, "Considérations sur le pouvoir spirituel (Mars 1826)", in: Auguste Comte, *Système de politique positive, ou Traité de sociologie, Instituant la Religion de l'Humanité*, Vol. IV: Appendice général du système de politique positive (Paris: Chez Carilian-Goeury et V^{or} Dalmont, 1854), 207: "la foi, c'est-à-dire la disposition à croire spontanément, sans démonstration préalable, aux dogmes proclamés par une autorité compétente".

[101] Ibid., 207–208.

[102] Michel Bourdeau, "Pouvoir spirituel et fixation des croyances", *Commentaire* 136, no. 4 (2011): 1096.

history of sociology and belief, without reducing it to a side-effect of the history of knowledge-accumulation or considering it as a unique phenomenon limited to the domain of the symbolic, such as religion.[103]

Conclusion

Throughout this chapter, I have tried to tackle the claim made by Bruno Latour and the broader post-secular tradition that the category of belief is one of the main obstacles for properly understanding both the societal-cultural practice of religion *and* the power-mechanisms undergirding the institutional and rhetorical structures of (sociological) modernity. Abandoning the category, so the argument goes, would free us from our perpetual misunderstanding of what religion is and does, and allow us to gain a clearer picture of what speaking religiously actually means. Furthermore, it would enable us to break free from the illusion that we were ever modern and secular, as it supposedly makes clear how secular modernity—including its employment of the belief-category—depended entirely on its (mistaken) system of categorization rather than on its effective representation of reality.

My response to this claim was two-fold: first of all, I made the argument that such a strategy does not so much constitute a breakaway from the sociological moderns, as claimed by Latour and other post-secular thinkers, as representing its very continuation. As I have tried to make apparent in both the introduction and the chapters following this, the sociological moderns used the belief-category as a narrative instrument of self-historicization, using it to simultaneously conceptualize both non-rational cultural practices as well as a novel social-scientific methodology. Latour and the post-secular critics of the belief-category continue this practice, criticizing the scientific methods of the sociological moderns while using the category as a narrative tool to make the conceptual distinction between the moderns and the post-secular non-moderns. Rather than escaping from the moderns' domain, Latour remains embedded within it, employing a language of belief as an instrument of critique without being able to escape its clutches altogether.

In the second part of my response, I argued that the abandonment of the belief-category does not bring us any closer to a better understanding

---

[103] For another attempt at this, cf. Douglas J. Davies & Michael J. Thate (eds.), *Religion and the Individual: Belief, Practice, and Identity* (Basel: MDPI, 2017).

of either something like religion nor the sociological moderns themselves. Rather, it simply constitutes an attempt at burying two centuries of history—of sociology of religion, and of religious engagements with the category—where our motivation should be to return to these many historical practices of narrating belief (religious and sociological), and understand how and why these practices took the form that they did. Again, Latour and the post-secular tradition share here a peculiar trait already possessed by their modernist opponents, which was the preference for an idealist understanding of language and history. The category of 'belief', as a result of its ambiguous propositional content and its usage across a whole host of disciplines, domains, vocabularies and interests, is a particularly muddy object. It is perpetually borrowed, reshaped, misunderstood and poorly applied, making it unappealing for those who call for conceptual clarity and, most of all, for a halt of interaction between the domains of science and religion, in the way that Latour does. A realist disposition, however, will concede that the proliferation of uses and narrations of the belief-category is simply a fact of history. A historical fact, moreover, which needs to be properly understood and historicized.

As a response to this Latourian, post-secular impasse, I will argue in the next chapter for a more reflective and historicist approach to the moderns' engagement with the belief-category. With this approach, the category of belief does not so much function as an obstacle to our proper understanding of religion, than as a historical gateway to understanding what makes the coexistence of secular-modernist and religious-spiritual languages such a confusing yet fascinating and productive enterprise. To abandon belief, not only as a category but as a language of self-historicization full-stop, would then be to abandon a very particular kind of relationship, one characterized by uncertainty, fragility and permanent negotiation. Its value lies in its malleability, allowing the actor to move freely from one domain to the other: it is a mode of expression that forms a central part of what it means to be religious (or at least, in a Christian way), and it is the social relationship that acts as an important condition of possibility for sociology as we know it.[104]

It is not something that can be abandoned on a whim. At the same time, Latour is right to admonish the poor results of our modernist predecessors and the excesses of rationalization that they have left behind. But rather than admonishing the classical sociologists for their failures, I

---

[104] Royannais, "Michel de Certeau: l'anthropologie du croire", 507.

believe it to be more productive to thoroughly investigate their concrete engagements with the historical languages of belief, that which Michel de Certeau would term the sociological operation and Pierre Bourdieu would see as the sociology of sociology, in a historical-anthropological fashion. This would then constitute a return to the moderns, with a historicist perspective, to gain a better understanding of how we can start to think of speaking religion, sociologically, without falling into reductionist traps or without leaving it to its own devices, uncriticized.

CHAPTER 3

Historicizing the Sociological Belief/Knowledge-Composition: Theories and Method

Introduction

In this chapter, I will aim to further flesh out the historical-anthropological method for studying the historical entanglement of the new sociological program in the nineteenth century, its relations with its religious other, and the languages of belief navigated by actors from both domains in order to balance these relations. This method is further meant to complement the work done of Bruno Latour which, so I argued in the previous chapter, left certain areas of this history unarticulated, namely a critical discussion of the historical entanglement which existed between the domains of sociology and religion in the nineteenth and twentieth centuries (and the role played by the belief-category within this entanglement), and the precise accordance of normative and empirical interpretations which is required for the sociological toolset. As such, I will try to set out a new analytical framework for investigating the relation between the social sciences, practices of belief and religious phenomena, in an attempt at fixing some of these broken channels of communication between the moderns and post-secularists.

The chapter will consist of three sections: in the first section, I will discuss two authors who I consider to have laid some important foundations for approaching belief as a historical language, Sebastiano Vecchio and

© The Author(s), under exclusive license to Springer Nature Switzerland AG 2024
M. Van Dam, *Languages of Belief and Early Sociology in Nineteenth-Century France*,
https://doi.org/10.1007/978-3-031-70023-1_3

Ethan H. Shagan. Thereafter, I will look at how the French historian and anthropologist, Michel de Certeau, sought to construct a historical anthropology of belief. And, finally, I will end the chapter by sketching out how such an anthropology of belief-languages could be applied to the shared history of the social sciences and religion, reflecting on the work of Pierre Bourdieu.

The Advantages of History: Belief as Modality and Historical Language

In a recent article, titled "Modi e questioni del credere" (2020), Italian philosopher Sebastiano Vecchio tries to give a schematic overview of the different meanings of 'believing' given throughout Western history, distinguishing five separate yet interconnected modalities: (1) cognitive-inferential; (2) socio-cultural; (3) linguistic-pragmatic; (4) rhetorical-narrative; and (5) dynamic-fiduciary.[1] These are all, in other words, practices, habits, and dispositions which have, at a certain point in time, been labelled as what the act of believing constitutes, in the attempts, by theologians, philosophers, historians and anthropologists, at semantically and philosophically capturing what this elusive kind of being and doing actually entails. Very briefly summarized, according to Vecchio, these modalities could be summed up as (1) an internalized, cognitive habit which regulates our everyday behaviour; (2) a relational bond between multiple actors through an acceptance of the other's belief; (3) a common-sense attitude towards generally accepted truths undergirding our social structures; (4) a particular kind of speech act which allows for the production of a communal space through articulation and recitation; and (5) a form of trust and loyalty in obedient devotion urged on by other displays of believing, often referred to as 'faith'.[2] While these five modalities have many distinctions, the one constant factor, Vecchio claims, is the aspect of alterity, of otherness.[3] The desire to understand and categorize 'belief', in other words, is rooted in our wish to give shape to a very concrete sort of relationship to others, a relationship which isn't explained fully by our

---

[1] Sebastiano Vecchio, "Modi e questioni del credere", *Rivista Italiana di Filosofia del linguaggio* 14, no. 1 (2020): 181–193.
[2] Ibid., *passim*.
[3] Ibid., 189.

self-interest nor our use of reason nor in any kind of immediate utility-value.[4] It is a human construction of relationality with the not-known, the other and the uncertain.[5] This is because 'belief' is never something individual that can be privately mastered; it presupposes a particular relation of credibility with someone or something else, making it something *a priori* intersubjective and subject to external alteration.[6]

Discussing several famous theorists of the term—Augustine, Pascal, Antoine Arnauld, C.S. Peirce, William James, Michel de Certeau, and Bruno Latour—Vecchio shows how the conceptualization of the belief-category by these thinkers was a robust practice, transforming and developing, not just in relation to newly gathered knowledge of the world around us, but first and foremost in relation to other conceptualizations of believing itself. This is important, as it relativizes the often teleologically thought relation between knowledge and belief, with the former often considered as becoming more and more dominant at the expense of the latter through societal processes of knowledge-accumulation.[7] Such conceptions would not only result in teleological accounts of the entangled histories of knowledge and belief, but would also have important secondary effects, such as the conviction among historians, anthropologists, philosophers and social scientists, that conceptualizing and articulating belief was exclusively rooted in our accurate knowledge and representation of what beliefs are, rather than *also* being a part of the history of believing in its own right and the different motives for shaping and directing what this category encapsulates.

The overview provided by Vecchio is not in any way linear, however and, as a result, goes against the idea that narrating and conceptualizing belief somehow stands outside the history of believing. It presents the practice of articulating belief and engaging with other, historical languages of believing as a philosophical and socio-cultural question, a problem which needs to be addressed from generation to generation.[8] Questions such as "What is belief, exactly?" are not fully explained by their search for

---

[4] Ibid., 188–189.

[5] A similar argument was recently put forward in a book by Agustín Fuentes, *Why We Believe: Evolution and the Human Way of Being* (New Haven: Yale University Press, 2019).

[6] Vecchio, "Modi e questioni del credere", 188–189; de Certeau, "L'institution du croire", 61–80.

[7] Michel de Certeau, "Les révolutions du « croyable »", in: Michel de Certeau, *La culture au pluriel* (Paris: Seuil, 1993 [1st ed. 1974]), 17–32.

[8] Vecchio, "Modi e questioni del credere", 189–90.

epistemic accuracy and propositional content; they are also performative instruments for engaging with these dense, historical languages. What space do we enter when we are reflecting on belief? This is a historical question, where the goal is not to find what beliefs are substantively, but how they are spoken, written, used and practiced, by actors, networks and institutions.[9]

From such an anthropological perspective on beliefs-as-signifiers, imagining otherness—whether it be in a religious-theological context, a social-institutional context, an economic-commercial context, or a political-ideological one—is something that we necessarily do at all times, since we simply cannot *not* symbolize our social other.[10] In this sense, when thinking and reflecting on the other, we always enter into the semiotic-historical matrix of belief, even when we attempt to overcome the very limitations of the category itself. Speaking and narrating 'belief', in this understanding, is much broader than its typically religious, symbolic or irrational meaning, instead referring to a historical network of meanings which must be navigated and made operational. The semantic history of 'belief' further underscores this historical proliferation, with its several linguistic variants continuously crossing over into domains of commerce, jurisprudence and politics.[11] This has led certain sociologists of religion, like Danièle Hervieu-Léger, to conceptualize the secularizing processes of the twentieth century less as a disappearance of religion, than as a re-composition of societal relations of belief, leading to religious practices to manifest themselves beyond their typical institutional domains such as the Church.[12]

Under the impetus of this growing awareness of 'belief's' synchronic diversity, historians have returned to the past, seeking to reconstruct the different pathways of these modalities of believing, the most prominent recent examples of which being John H. Arnold and Ethan H. Shagan.[13] Especially the latter, and his seminal work *The Birth of Modern Belief*

---

[9] de Certeau, "L'institution du croire", 78–79.

[10] Alain Boureau, "Croire et croyances", in: *Michel de Certeau: Les chemins de l'histoire*, eds. Christian Delacroix, François Dosse, Patrick Garcia & Michel Trebitsch (Paris: Éditions Complexe, 2002), 134.

[11] Royannais, "Michel de Certeau: l'anthropologie du croire", 506n19.

[12] Cf. Danièle Hervieu-Léger, *Le Pèlerin et le Converti* (Paris: Flammarion, 1999); Ibid., "La religion, mode de croire", *Revue du Mauss* 22, no. 2 (2003): 144–158.

[13] John H. Arnold, *Belief and Unbelief in the Middle Ages* (London: Hodder Arnold, 2005); Shagan, *The Birth of Modern Belief*.

(2018), is of interest to me here, as Shagan seeks to understand how, what he terms, regimes of belief developed *in relation to each other* across social, cultural and religious domains.[14] In his historical narration of belief's unfolding as an eventually modern category, Shagan problematizes belief's contemporary status as a simple and obvious category, with supposedly little need for further explanation.[15] Rather, he argues that this had not always been the case: in the Middle Ages and the early modern period, novel ways of imagining and conceptualizing 'believing' were consistently invented and that, as such, different modes of believing were opposed to each other as tools of contestation, for example during the Reformation and Counter-Reformation, during the Scientific Revolution and during the Enlightenment's debates between philosophy and religion.[16]

Like Vecchio, Shagan distinguishes different modalities of believing from each other: doctrinal-rational, mystical-experiential, dogmatic-institutional and cognitive-propositional.[17] Going beyond such a typology, however, Shagan aims especially to uncover why certain modalities were more dominant than others during particular historical contexts, and how they achieved a hegemonic status as a 'regime of belief'. Specifically, he wants to provide an alternative account for the typical representation of Western secularization, arguing that the history of European Christianity, philosophy and science was less marked by its secularization through reason than by the several transformations made upon the category of 'belief'.[18] He divides this history in three successive regimes of credulity, medieval, confessional and modern: whereas the first two regimes were characterized by Christianity's desire for a space of autonomous self-identification, in the face of external (ancient philosophy) and internal (confessional conflict) threats, the third, modern regime saw belief escape from Christianity's clutches, migrating instead into society itself and becoming the preferential space for individual, sovereign judgement.[19] Modernity, in other words, was not so much a regime of credulity where beliefs diminished, but where they instead multiplied, where all sorts of

[14] Cf. Arnold, *Belief and Unbelief*, 7–15.
[15] Shagan, *The Birth of Modern Belief*, 1–4.
[16] Ibid., esp. chapters 2, 5 and 6.
[17] Ibid., *passim*. Shagan does not claim to provide any kind of exhaustive list of kinds of believing, but presents his book as "an essay with an argument rather than an exhaustive survey of its subject" (27).
[18] Ibid., 28–29.
[19] Ibid., 283–84.

propositional claims were now classified under the header of 'beliefs' and able to be articulated in such a language.[20]

In the context of this book, Shagan provides an excellent springboard for an investigation of early sociology's usage of belief as an instrument of social analysis and self-historicization, not in the least because of its chronology, as it stops right at my own starting point, the late eighteenth century marking the beginning of the social sciences. Furthermore, his central claim—that the modern regime of belief is characterized by its proliferation, making 'belief' a very open and malleable category—will play a central role in my anthropological approach of the classical sociologists. Like Shagan, I will aim to trace the different practices of meaning-attribution, performed by the early social scientists, to the notion of 'belief', as a way of further analysing how it functioned in conceptualizing, not only their religious and non-Western counterparts, but the very notion of 'sociology' and 'the social scientist' itself as well.

The only marked difference is that (a) I will not limit the discussion of such practices to the realm of the religious, and (b) that, rather than regimes, I will speak of languages of belief, emphasizing less the aspect of hegemonic contestation and focus more on its function as a tool of navigation, negotiation and self-government. Shagan himself also emphasizes this point in his conclusion—"None of them were absolute – regimes of the mind are porous and contested, or else they would not change over time"—but this aspect played a less important role in his book, because of its narrative focus on the birth of modern belief.[21] Here, my aim is less focused on the big narrative questions such as the origin of sociological modernity or its relation to processes of secularization. I limit myself to the different interventions made by early sociologists within these languages of belief, and to how these languages allowed them to construct their own sociological language of belief. The main benefit of Shagan's work is that it functions as a historical background, complemented by Vecchio's typology of different modalities of believing. In combination, they can provide a more exhaustive framework for approaching the different strategies employed by the sociological moderns in their navigation of historical languages of belief.

---

[20] Ibid., 278–81.
[21] Ibid., 283.

A Historical Anthropology of Belief and Its Languages: Michel de Certeau

So what would an anthropology of this history of believing look like exactly, especially in relation to the historical field of the burgeoning social sciences in nineteenth-century France? While anything resembling a fully fledged methodology, to the best of my knowledge, does not yet exist, some important first steps have already been undertaken now more than forty years ago, by the French Jesuit, anthropologist and historian, Michel de Certeau.[22] In a series of articles completed near the end of his life, de Certeau pinpointed a number of important elements such an anthropology should seek to integrate.[23] These were, in no particular order: (1) the performative character of the belief-act as a practice of differentiation; (2) its phenomenological distinction from knowledge-propositions; (3) the creative agency (which he called the poetic function) inherent within the collective practice of believing; (4) the important part played by the institution in regulating and stabilizing the collective stream of belief-practices, and (5) a fragmentary but fundamental reflection on the mediating role played by narratives, between spontaneous beliefs binding collectives and the institutions appropriating these.[24]

Combined, these scattered reflections bring forth a social-historical reality where several different kinds of actors—social collectives generated

---

[22] On de Certeau's life and work, cf. François Dosse, *Michel de Certeau: le marcheur blessé* (Paris: La Découverte, 2002).

[23] de Certeau, "Une pratique sociale de la différence: croire", 363–383; Ibid., "L'institution du croire", 61–80. An abbreviated version of the 1981 text was translated into English: Michel de Certeau, "What We Do When We Believe", in: *On Signs*, ed. Marshall Blonsky (Baltimore: Johns Hopkins University Press, 1985), 192–202. A collection of essays on the practice of believing, titled *La faiblesse de croire*, was published posthumously in 1987, focusing on de Certeau's relation to Christianity experienced in its modern-day decay: Michel de Certeau, *La faiblesse de croire*, ed. Luce Giard (Paris: Seuil, 1987).

[24] These articles have received some attention by other authors, especially sociologists and anthropologists of religion at the beginning of the twenty-first century, but interest has waned since: Louis Panier, "Pour une anthropologie du croire. Aspects de la problématique chez Michel de Certeau", in: *Michel de Certeau ou la différence chrétienne*, ed. Claude Geffré (Paris: Les Éditions du Cerf, 1991) 37–59; Boureau, "Croire et croyances", 125–140; Dosse, *Michel de Certeau*, ch. 36; Royannais, "Michel de Certeau: l'anthropologie du croire", 499–533; Albert Bastenier, "Le croire et le cru: Les appartenances religieuses au sein du christianisme européen revisitées à partir des travaux de Michel de Certeau", *Social Compass* 54, no. 1 (2007): 13–32; Tomas Orylski, "L'itinéraire du croire dans la démarche de Michel de Certeau", *Revue des sciences religieuses* 82, no. 2 (2008): 245–251.

through spontaneous beliefs; institutions seeking to organize said beliefs into efficient and manageable rationalities; reflective, individual agents searching for a meaningful place *in-between* these forces—are in permanent negotiation with each other. Each of these actors has as their goal to construct a particular type of relation with its heterogeneous respondent ('God', 'Society', 'Truth', etc.) in order to create, so to speak, a desired outcome ('meaning', 'communication', 'social harmony', 'solidarity', 'productivity', 'presence', and so on).[25] For de Certeau, what brings a practice of belief into existence is the preliminary reality of absence: the invisible God, the inexperienced consciousness of my neighbour, the hidden movements of the market, the unarticulated intentions of my helper, the unknown value of future commodities.[26] It is through different kinds of practices—one's self-sublimation into a mob, the utter obedience and surrender delivered to God, a devotion given to the Church, the respect for ritualistic objects shared with others, a self-imposed openness displayed to the unknown—that these absences can be negotiated and mediated, in order to produce a kind of performative relationality, the belief-relation.[27] The anthropologist, then, is mainly concerned with investigating the different techniques through which actors keep this belief-relation alive (often categorized as *living faith*) which is less defined by any sort of truth-substance contained within the belief-propositions than in the fact that believers are able to turn their beliefs into action, communication and an experiential sense of time (what the early twentieth-century French philosopher Henri Bergson would term 'duration').[28]

Belief, as such, is considered more in the sense that the pragmatists like C.S. Peirce and William James understood it, as something that is inherent to social life and which is intimately connected to our actions in everyday life.[29] It is because we believe and put our faith in others that we are able to efficiently organize ourselves, without spending our every waking

---

[25] de Certeau, "Une pratique sociale de la différence: croire", 372–377; Boureau, "Croire et croyances", 134–135; Royannais, "Michel de Certeau: l'anthropologie du croire", 509.

[26] de Certeau, "Une pratique sociale de la différence: croire", 363–67; Royannais, "Michel de Certeau: l'anthropologie du croire", 518.

[27] de Certeau, *La faiblesse de croire*, 282–83.

[28] de Certeau, "L'institution du croire", 62. On the concept of duration (*durée*), cf. Henri Bergson, *Essai sur les données immédiates de la conscience* (Paris: Félix Alcan, 1889).

[29] Cf. for example, Charles Sanders Peirce, "Philosophy and the Conduct of Life (1898)", in: *The Essential Peirce: Selected Philosophical Writings, Volume 2 (1893–1913)*, ed. The Peirce Edition Project (Bloomington and Indianapolis: Indiana University Press, 1998), 27–41.

moment verifying the propositional claims of those around us. Or as Patrick Royannais, theologian and de Certeau-expert, would formulate it: "Man practices difference because he has no other choice than to consign himself to the other, without verifying, without knowing whether the other is telling the truth or not [...] What would the love of a man be who would have his wife followed in order to be certain that she is faithful to him [my translation]?".[30] The typical understanding of belief—as the sign of the symbolic and as the opposite of knowledge—is, for the Certallian anthropologist, relativized in two directions: belief is not something uniquely reserved for those institutions with which they are usually associated (churches, pseudoscience, culture), and there are no such things as spaces devoid of beliefs (laboratories, classrooms, state bureaus, mathematical models, concepts, etc.).[31] Relations of belief are historical compositions, which continuously form and reform themselves, and which need to be traced by the anthropologist.[32]

According to de Certeau, then, 'beliefs' are made up of relations which are historically variegated through perpetual processes of negotiation, involving fluctuating intermediaries, reflective discourses and governmental institutions.[33] Such mediations are concentrated on two distinct levels: the institutional and the narrative.[34] Institutions are particularly influential cogs in the machinations of belief: they are able to direct the instable belief-relation created between respondents by acting as a guarantor, ratifying the beliefs (through dogma, symbolism, liturgy, cult, rules of belief, etc.) while making itself the ultimate horizon of said beliefs.[35] In this way, institutions generate from a complex mess of incoherent beliefs a type of order: they create a class of authorized respondents (elders, priests, theologians, judges, experts, etc.) as well as provide a program for the

---

[30] Royannais, "Michel de Certeau: l'anthropologie du croire", 509: "L'homme pratique la différence parce qu'il ne peut faire autrement que d'en se remettre à l'autre, sans vérifier, sans savoir si l'autre dit vrai ou non. [...] Que serait l'amour d'un homme qui ferait suivre sa femme pour être certain qu'elle lui est fidèle ?".

[31] Ibid., 510; de Certeau, "L'institution du croire", 63–68.

[32] Jean-Claude Monod, "Inversion du pensable et transits de croyance: la trajectoire de sécularisation et ses écarts selon Michel de Certeau", *Revue de Théologie et de Philosophie* 136, no. 4 (2004): 341–43.

[33] de Certeau, "Une pratique sociale de la différence: croire", 363; de Certeau, "L'institution du croire", 77–79.

[34] de Certeau, "L'institution du croire", 79–80.

[35] Ibid., 78–79.

judgement of beliefs, constructing as such a coherent body.³⁶ At the same time, such institutional mediations carry with them a great danger, and this is the danger Latour referred to as that of Double Click: if an institution starts overly rationalizing its processing of beliefs—i.e. as mere carriers of information rather than transformation—while becoming further and further detached from its original mechanisms of 'make-believe', it will become harder and harder to believe in the institution itself.³⁷ De Certeau himself has tried to schematize a similar process occurring to the Catholic Church in his article "The Formalities of Practice From Religious Systems to the Ethics of the Enlightenment (the Seventeenth and Eighteenth Centuries)", showing how the Church became increasingly entangled with rationalist-enlightened and governmental-administrative discourses, creating more and more confusion and unbelief among both clergy and the faithful.³⁸

The creation of institutions and the navigation of its dogma is not the only way belief is mediated, however. Through narration, actors are able to embed themselves within this broader and conflictual history of believing, giving meaning to their own understanding of what believing is. According to de Certeau, narrative interventions are ways we can try to balance belief's spontaneous and poetic quality with its potential rationalization in the institution, constantly searching for the best of both worlds.³⁹ De Certeau further illustrates this process with a reference to a scene in Charlie Chaplin's 1923 film *The Pilgrim*, where an escaped convict is caught between two possible futures at the US-Mexico border, one of incarceration and one of violence and unrest. Unable to choose, he starts walking across the border, keeping one foot in each country, pondering the possible benefits of either problematic fate.⁴⁰ In other words, narrative reflections on 'belief', the articulation of its usefulness and role in social life, is a practice in its own right, an attempt at striking a productive balance between nourishing living faith and directing proper government

---

[36] Ibid., 76–77.
[37] Latour, *Rejoicing*, 21–22; de Certeau, "L'institution du croire", 79.
[38] Michel de Certeau, "The Formality of Practices: From Religious Systems to the Ethics of Enlightenment", in: Ibid., *The Writing of History*, transl. by Tom Conley (New York: Columbia University Press, 1988), 147–205.
[39] de Certeau, "L'institution du croire", 79–80.
[40] Ibid., 79.

through the benefits of institutionalized beliefs.[41] This constitutes a complex balancing act which, as I will show throughout the book, consistently preoccupied the sociological moderns in their engagement with the category of belief.

The Anthropology of Sociological Belief

As I have already mentioned, such an anthropology of belief (as a relational practice of difference) found some success in the sociology of religion, in the work of Danièle Hervieu-Léger, Patrick Michel, Albert Bastenier and Alfredo Teixeira.[42] It allowed these sociologists and anthropologists to rethink what it means to be religious in these modern times, when the old institutions of belief were fading while new spiritual movements were expressing themselves beyond the traditional demarcations of the sacred and secular.[43] This is in line with de Certeau's own existential project as a Jesuit who became increasingly disillusioned with what Christianity had become, his own research being fuelled by a search for new ways of constructing a meaningful relation with the divine.[44] Another fruitful avenue has been the history of early and medieval Christianity, with the Certallian anthropology proving to be an invaluable instrument for unearthing the social-intellectual dynamism of Middle Age Christian belief practices. Especially noteworthy in this regard is the work of French medievalist Alain Boureau, who, starting out from de Certeau's notion of the practice of belief as a relational one in need of permanent renewal, set out to investigate the reasons for Christianity's efficaciousness in erecting a particularly durable system of beliefs, despite its apparent strangeness

---

[41] Philippe Büttgen, "Le contraire des pratiques: Commentaires sur la doctrine de Michel de Certeau", in: *Lire Michel de Certeau. La formalité des pratiques*, eds. Philippe Büttgen & Christian Jouhaud (Frankfurt Am Main: Vittorio Klostermann, 2008), 94–95.
[42] Patrick Michel, "Pour une sociologie des itinéraires des sens: Une lecture politique du rapport entre croire et institution", *Archives de sciences sociales des religions* 38, no. 82 (1993): 223–38; Ibid., "La « religion », objet sociologique pertinent?", *Revue du Mauss* 22, no. 2 (2003): 159–70; Bastenier "Le croire et le cru", 13–32; Alfredo Teixeira, "Pour une anthropologie de l' « habitat institutionnel » catholique dans le sillage de Michel de Certeau", *Revue d'histoire des sciences humaines* 23, no. 2 (2010): 117–139.
[43] Danièle Hervieu-Léger, "Le partage du croire religieux dans des sociétés d'individus", *L'année sociologique* 60, no. 1 (2010): 41–62.
[44] Michel de Certeau & Jean-Marie Domenach, *Le christianisme éclaté* (Paris: Éditions du Seuil, 1974).

and complexity.⁴⁵ By focusing on the narrative interventions organized by the Church, Boureau was able to show how Christianity's broad reflective class—theologians, monks, priests, and the laity—was able to keep the Christian faith alive through its endless practices of commentary and repetition, performatively recreating the Christian event par excellence, the death of Christ on the cross.⁴⁶

Then again, it should not come as a surprise that a reconceptualization of what belief is and does should reinvigorate the study of the classical religions and its institutions. But, of course, this was not the only purpose of such an anthropology. de Certeau's discussion of the mathematician Georg Cantor in his article "L'institution du croire" and how the latter found it difficult *to believe* his empirical findings is, in this sense, indicative, emphasizing the fact that the exact sciences were also confronted with the social and institutional issue of belief-negotiation.⁴⁷ The history of knowledge-production, in other words, has coincided with a history of belief-negotiation as well, according to de Certeau. And although these encounters have mostly been understood and articulated as one of repression (designating non-knowledge-based beliefs as 'superstition', 'magic', 'pseudoscience', 'ideology' and so on), at the same time, this meeting has itself also been an avenue of dialogical inspiration, with cognitive psychologists and analytical philosophers finding new forms of appreciation for the role of metaphorical thought within the scientific imagination.⁴⁸ The ambition of de Certeau's anthropology, then, was to bring these domains of scientific knowledge-gathering and religious meaning-distribution into view together through a shared framework of belief-languages, describing and tracing their interactions without referring to evaluative frameworks of physical or metaphysical truth.⁴⁹

---

⁴⁵ Alain Boureau, *L'Événement sans fin: Récit et christianisme au Moyen Âge* (Paris: Les Belles Lettres, 2004), 9.

⁴⁶ Ibid., 10–11.

⁴⁷ de Certeau, "L'institution du croire", 64–65.

⁴⁸ On this dialogical process, cf. Dan Sperber, *Explaining Culture: A Naturalistic Approach* (Oxford: Blackwell Publishing, 1996); Ibid., "Intuitive and Reflective Beliefs", *Mind & Language* 12, no. 1 (1997): 67–83; Maarten Boudry, Michael Vlerick & Taner Edis, "The end of science? On human cognitive limitations and how to overcome them", *Biology & Philosophy* 35, 18 (2020): 1–16; Ibid., "Demystifying Mysteries. How Metaphors and Analogies Extend the Reach of the Human Mind", in: *Metaphors and Analogies in Sciences and Humanities: Words and Worlds*, eds. Shyam Wuppuluri & A.C. Grayling (Cham: Springer, 2022), 65–83.

⁴⁹ de Certeau, "L'institution du croire", 65.

Such an ambitious goal, however, brought forth its own obstacles. One of these obstacles was the difference in status between rational and non-rational beliefs, which needed to be made symmetrical. Of course, by doing this, de Certeau did not mean to say that forms of knowledge-gathering and forms of institutional belief-formation are somehow the same. The French historian had no intention whatsoever to equate philosophy and science to something like religion, or to claim that modern science was in some way a secularized version of theology. Like Latour, de Certeau wanted to distinguish knowledge from belief on a phenomenological basis:

> The difference that distinguishes it [believing, MVD] from *seeing* or *knowing* is not at first notable for the truth value of which a proposition is susceptible – to which an entire epistemology has been devoted – but by this inscription of *time* in a subject-to-subject relationship. When this relationship can no longer be sustained and structured by temporalization, it will evolve into a relationship of (knowing) subject to (known) object.[50]

For de Certeau, to know something is to close the space-time between the knowing subject and known object; the known object is grafted and territorialized into a scientific discourse which approximates physical reality as closely as possible.[51] To believe something, however, is phenomenologically different: existing between two subjects, belief owes its existence to the shared ability of these subjects to technically preserve the space-time between them.[52] It is a tenuous relation, dependent on our skills in regulating the movement of said space-time between believers (through rhetoric, charm, haggling, pleading, promising, reasoning, bluffing, …), sustaining such a space through a mutual commitment by multiple subjects occupying such a domain and built upon a network of gifts and debts.[53] We cannot force another into a shared belief in the way we can force an object to be known; it requires a certain art.[54]

---

[50] de Certeau, "What We Do When We Believe", 193.

[51] de Certeau, *The Practice of Everyday Life*, 115–130. It is this consideration of knowledge which Latour exactly criticized as founding the 'Grand Partage', cf. Bruno Latour, "Comment redistribuer le Grand Partage?", *Revue de synthèse* 110 (1983): 226–231.

[52] de Certeau, "Une pratique sociale de la différence: croire", 372–377.

[53] McCarthy, "Modalities of Belief", 613.

[54] Neil Levy, *Bad Beliefs: Why they happen to good people* (Oxford: Oxford University Press, 2022), 132–148. This art has also become a central topic for political philosophers, cf. for example, Elizabeth F. Cohen, *The Political Value of Time: Citizenship, Duration, and Democratic Justice* (Cambridge: Cambridge University Press, 2018).

The distinction between believing and knowing, in other words, lies in its nature towards experiential space and time: whereas knowledge is marked by the desire to bridge any gap between two separate points through informational means, a belief-relation requires this gap to remain in order to allow the subject some leeway (for haggling, bargaining, convincing; the ability to *change positions and negotiate*, in other words).[55] This does not mean, however, that there is any kind of fundamental opposition between these two forms of relating to objects, from a Certallian point of view: knowing makes use of beliefs as a material foundation and believing itself is a highly rational form of behaviour rooted in generalized knowledge propositions. They simply indicate the complex yet highly interdependent nature of our socio-cognitive mechanisms.[56] From this regard, it becomes apparent that any kind of science is composed of both these dimensions, meaning that it is both an epistemological as well as a social-cultural undertaking.[57] The same can be said, for that matter, of religions, which sometimes make knowledge-claims on the state of the world besides their primary purpose of evangelization and the securing of salvation.[58]

The social and human sciences can, then, also be interpreted from this historical-anthropological perspective on practices of believing.[59] It constitutes an epistemological undertaking, but it is also, like any other knowledge apparatus, susceptible to socio-cultural and institutional processes. Sociologists do not just describe, analyse and gather data on their particular research object; they also, by doing this, inevitably form their own particular belief-community in which they share specific theoretical convictions, methodological presuppositions, and hegemonic research programs, and in which they suffer institutional effects and mechanisms through their interaction with universities, sociological paradigms and the

---

[55] de Certeau, "Une pratique sociale de la différence: croire", 373–74.

[56] Quine & Ullian, *The Web of Belief*.

[57] This has been studied under the headers of social epistemology and sociology of knowledge, cf. Steve Fuller, *Social Epistemology* (Bloomington and Indianapolis: Indiana University Press, 2002).

[58] On this history of religion and its relation to the knowledge of the world, cf. Peter Harrison, *The Territories of Science and Religion* (Chicago: The University of Chicago Press, 2015).

[59] Boureau, "Croire et croyances", 128–135.

research desires of subsidizing governments and companies.⁶⁰ The category of 'belief', then, manifests itself in the history of social science in a double capacity: one is concerned with the epistemological dimension, and is committed to accumulating a better understanding of how the social dimension effectively works, how societal beliefs evolve and function, positively or negatively, in the constitution of social groups and structures. In this history, sociology can be evaluated for its effectiveness or ineffectiveness in describing such belief-objects and -relations, through its process of first delimiting and defining what 'belief-objects' are and then analysing the demarcated social field according to the stipulated methodological principles.

The other, however, is the one I am mainly concerned with here: it is an understanding of 'belief' as a phenomenological practice and speech act, which has a history of its own, and where sociology is approached as a historical discourse which has sought to participate and intervene within this history. The history of sociology then transforms into one where the discipline can be considered as a collection of techniques for negotiating the different possibilities for social becoming and unfolding through the means of sociological knowledge, as a unique instrument for navigating languages of belief.⁶¹ This is an understanding of sociology, less as an individual and intellectual practice, than as a societal-historical phenomenon.⁶² Formulated in this manner, there is no contradiction between an anthropological approach to the history of beliefs as understood by de Certeau, and the history of the social sciences itself, the latter simply representing another set of techniques rather than a distortion or aberration of the different modes of existence.

The French sociologist Pierre Bourdieu has also already tried to conceptualize such an anthropological, meta-sociological perspective in his

---

⁶⁰ To give just one specific example, investigating the life of the Durkheimian tradition, cf. Philip Smith, *Durkheim and After: The Durkheimian Tradition, 1893–2020* (Cambridge: Polity Press, 2020).

⁶¹ Piotr Sztompka, "Modernization as Social Becoming: Ten Theses on Modernization", in: *The Art and Science of Sociology: Essays in Honor of Edward A. Tiryakian*, eds. Roland Robertson & John Simpson (London: Anthem Press, 2016), 163–171.

⁶² This phenomenological perspective on sociology is mostly associated with the work of Edward A. Tiryakian, cf. Edward A. Tiryakian, *Sociologism and Existentialism: Two Perspectives on the Individual and Society* (Englewood Cliffs, NJ: Prentice Hall, 1962); Ibid., *The Phenomenon of Sociology: A Reader in the Sociology of Knowledge* (New York: Appleton – Century – Crofts, 1971).

short article "Sociologues de la croyance et croyances des sociologues" (1987), which can further complement de Certeau's historical anthropology, with some of the unique challenges presented by the sociological discourse. In the article, Bourdieu attempts to describe the meeting point of sociology and religion by reflecting on the specific status of the sociologist itself and their navigations of 'beliefs' as a way of doing sociology of religion.[63] The sociology of religion is especially representative of these challenges, according to Bourdieu, because of this overt, dual manifestation of beliefs: beliefs in this domain are not just the object of investigation for the sociologists of religion, the latter are in a kind of belief-relation themselves with their religious object. This is not, and Bourdieu makes sure to repeatedly emphasize this point, the question of whether or not the sociologist is a believer in God, miracles, reincarnation or religious dogma.[64] Rather, it is a different kind of belief, a sociological belief: by this Bourdieu means the non-knowledge-based relation cultivated by the sociologist with the religious object, their particular relation to the religious field, the degree of social reality committed by the sociologist to their religious object.[65]

This is what Bourdieu refers to as the *illusio*, the semiotic parameters set out by religious believers, towards which the sociological observer cannot be impartial nor is it possible to falsify these claims in a scientific manner. They must differentiate and evaluate, in some way or another, these parameters while constructing their own particular relation with these parameters, as they are impossible to ignore for any sociologist of religion: "and who can say that they do not at least relate to it, if only in a negative sense, through non-indifference [my translation]?"[66] As Bourdieu attempts to articulate in his own way here, the sociologist-actor must intervene in the historical languages of belief, simply to enter into it. It is this disposition that the sociologist must reconstruct for themselves, even though, as Bourdieu commented at the beginning of his article, this can prove to be an arduous and unpleasant task. It requires a great deal of honesty and self-examination, which can be confronting for those who believe themselves to be free of any non-epistemological relations in their scholarly

---

[63] Bourdieu, "Sociologues de la croyance et croyances de sociologues", 155–161.
[64] Ibid., 157.
[65] Ibid.
[66] Ibid., 159: "et qui peut dire ne pas y appartenir, au moins négativement, à travers la non-indifférence?"

endeavour. Yet it is worth this 'punishment', says the famous French sociologist, as it can help sociology achieve a more scientific account of the religious field.[67]

While Bourdieu considers such a thick description of the sociologist's own field of so-called belief-relations to be primarily beneficial for the scientific credentials of the sociological practice itself, it is easy to see how this fashioning of the sociological self is an important historiographical tool as well, as it serves as another call to reconstruct the relation between sociology and religion, not from an exclusive epistemological viewpoint, but from an intellectual-historical and anthropological perspective as well.[68] The history of the imagination of the sociological self, through its negotiation of belief, makes it possible to paint a nuanced picture of sociology's historical relation with religion, one that is neither one of complete misrepresentation nor of modernist enlightenment. Instead, it is something that is continuously invented and reinvented by the sociological actor, through a series of constructions, both of the religious other and the sociological self.

Such an approach has little to say of the substantive sociological work being done by the sociologists themselves. Here, I am not so much concerned with the historical accuracy of the conceptual tools, say, by Durkheim's distinction between mechanical and organic solidarity. It is, rather, to consider the sociological operation as its own historical object, a network of self-articulated relations with religious objects, which can be traced and investigated, using the semantic field of 'belief' as an entry point to reconstructing the history of the sociological belief/knowledge-compositions. Furthermore, such an investigation can take many different forms, focusing on institutional mechanisms, contextual background or social-historical networks. For the sake of clarity, however, I will focus here on just one single aspect, which is the employment by the sociological moderns of narratives to navigate these belief-languages. How did classical sociologists narrate the category of belief, and how did these narrations impact their own imaginations of the social-scientific and religious domains?

Whereas Bourdieu urged his fellow sociologists to more actively reflect on their own positioning and unspoken commitments, it can also be

---

[67] Ibid., 155.
[68] Ibid., 160.

argued that early sociologists have been implicitly producing such reflections from the very beginning. While the discipline of sociology came into existence to provide a more scientific analysis of society, it proved a difficult if not impossible task to dispose its social-scientific register of any narrative elements, with only quantitative social sciences, such as economics and social demography, eventually coming close to such technical rigidity.[69] The social-scientific analysis of the sociologists, theoretically conceived and made rigid through methodological principles, still needed to introduce itself, embed itself into a longer history of past accounts and analyses, as to make clear to the reader the improvements that were made, how the objective results were obtained, how the problematic nature of the sociologist's subjectivity was removed as much as possible. It is via this narrative residue that these sociological interventions into historical languages of belief can best be reconstructed.[70] By investigating the different narrative strategies employed by some of the more famous classical sociologists, as well as their interactions amongst each other within the sociological community, we can reconstruct this distinctive history, gaining further insight into how and why the sociologists engaged with the religious field in the way they did.

And, finally, through de Certeau's and Bourdieu's anthropological approach, the history of sociological engagements with the belief-category becomes something less comprehensively marked by one overarching narrative, such as modernity or secularization.[71] It is an approach that is actor-based, where we can trace the different ways modalities of believing were negotiated in an empirical fashion, while avoiding historical-philosophical and normative traps.[72] This, after shedding the framework of its own sociological prejudices, frees up the way we can think the imagination of belief among the moderns: no longer solely judged on their supposed role in the secularization of Christian religion or their part in the technocratic nature of the modern age, they are rather considered autonomously, as proposing their own project within the history of believing. They too tried, in their

---

[69] William H. Sewell Jr., *Logics of History: Social Theory and Social Transformation* (Chicago: University of Chicago Press, 2005), 12–13.

[70] On the links between narrative and duration, cf. Paul Ricoeur, *Temps et récit* (Paris: Seuil, 1983–1985), 3 vol.; Ibid., *La Mémoire, l'histoire, l'oubli* (Paris: Seuil, 2003).

[71] Boureau, "Croire et croyances", 132–34.

[72] Dan Sperber, "Apparently Irrational Beliefs", in: *Rationality and Relativism*, eds. Martin Hollis & Steven Lukes (Cambridge, MA: MIT Press, 1982), 179–180.

own unique way, to give meaning to the practice of belief as a way to better understand social life, negotiating the many potential benefits of the category with its associated risks and dangers. It allows us to think of the moderns' interactions with belief in a non-monolithic manner, where there is still room for individual diversity and dynamism, rather than a discursive imposition of a modernist orthodoxy, dictating belief to necessarily be a kind of private mental act. While this turn towards the interior was undoubtedly a macro-historical trend followed by many classical sociologists, an exclusive focus on this hegemonic regime would hide the subtlety of what believing ultimately meant to both sociological thinkers and their complex, extensive textual bodies, and how these historical languages themselves impacted the different ways one could think of oneself as a 'social scientist'.

Conclusion

How can we approach the moderns' different navigations of the belief-category and its wider semiotic matrix, without getting caught up in the standard narratives of either modernist self-proclaimed objectivism or of post-secular critiques of said supposed objectivism as little more than rhetorical varnish hiding their power-based mechanisms at play? In this chapter, I have discussed a number of methodological tools—pluralizing the belief-category; anthropologically dividing the history of sociology into epistemological and existential dimensions—as a means of shedding and going beyond these standard narratives. In this way, we can bring the chaotic historical origins of sociology, its transformation into the scientific discipline of modernity and our contemporary critiques of this modernity into a shared perspective, investigating the role played by the sociological language of belief in this process.

In this manner, we can attain a more historical view of the different ways the belief-category was employed by the sociological moderns, how it was used for negotiating their relation with the religious object, and how it, in return, cultivated their imagination of the sociological project itself as well. From this point of view, the engagement between the histories of sociology and religion is multifaceted: rather than being either a singular history of enlightenment or domination, both sociology and the different lived religions (Christianity, Judaism, Islam) are considered as distinct episodes in the history of believing. We can think of this metaphorically: instead of occupying a single, shared public space, the sociological moderns and religious non-moderns can be seen as populating a vast landscape, with only occasional boundary encounters and conflicts in an otherwise relatively tranquil life. The different languages of belief then represent not so much the contested object itself, the ultimate prize to be won or lost, but rather the mere boats to reach the border destinations. To think 'belief', I argue, is a necessary condition for sacred-secular interaction. What we still need to investigate is how these different journeys shaped the formation of something like 'sociology' itself.

CHAPTER 4

Early Experiments in the Sociological Operation I: Languages of Belief Within the French Eighteenth-Century Knowledge Culture

Introduction

The early period of the sociological discipline in France was marked by its close vicinity to a spiritual language and symbolism.[1] It weren't only the Catholic reactionaries wary for another French Revolution and fascinated by the social mechanisms directing communal life who were responsible for this. Even 'scientist' thinkers like Henri de Saint-Simon and Auguste Comte, who aimed to conceptualize social cohesion in a more scientific manner, were profoundly influenced by visions of a socially harmonious Christian society during the Middle Ages, as well as the social functions taken up by religious rituals and dogma.[2] The main question for these

---

[1] Paul Bénichou, *Le Temps des Prophètes: Doctrines de l'Âge Romantique* (Paris: Gallimard, 1977); Nicole Dhombres & Jean Dhombres, *Naissance d'un pouvoir: sciences et savants en France (1793–1824)* (Paris: Payot, 1986); Jack Hayward, *After the French Revolution: Six Critics of Democracy and Nationalism* (New York: New York University Press, 1991); Andrew Wernick, *Auguste Comte and the Religion of Humanity: The Post-Theistic Program of French Social Theory* (Cambridge: Cambridge University Press, 2001).

[2] Mary Pickering, *Auguste Comte: An Intellectual Biography*, Vol. I (Cambridge: Cambridge University Press, 1993); W. Jay Reedy, "The historical imaginary of social science in post-Revolutionary France: Bonald, Saint-Simon, Comte", *History of the Human Sciences* 7, no. 1 (1994): 1–26; Antoine Picon, "La religion Saint-Simonienne", *Revue des sciences philos-*

© The Author(s), under exclusive license to Springer Nature Switzerland AG 2024
M. Van Dam, *Languages of Belief and Early Sociology in Nineteenth-Century France*,
https://doi.org/10.1007/978-3-031-70023-1_4

social theorists was how such unity could be recuperated in a post-revolutionary Europe, where the dynamism and diversity of individual(ist) thoughts and actions was perceived to be at an all-time high.[3]

How can we explain such proximity, and what does it mean for our understanding of classical sociology? While such early social-scientific interventions made by social philosophers like Auguste Comte into the domain of the spiritual have suffered plenty of ridicule and bewilderment, not in the least by their own peers, recent scholarship has made it clear that any exhaustive engagement with these early nineteenth-century thinkers requires a contextualized discussion of such spiritual imaginations of society.[4] Prominent grand narratives, such as those of secularization, modernity, and the relation between science and religion have since been much more thoroughly historicized, untangling the dichotomous representation of such early sociologists as either religious-conservative or progressive-secularist.[5] As a result, we have a much more nuanced view of both the French nineteenth-century intellectual climate, and the (reasonable) motivations for thinkers of society like Bonald, Saint-Simon, and Comte to persist with faith-based tropes, through both the shared context of religious revival at the time and the individual pathways of these figures all being defined by a rediscovery of faith and its social importance.[6]

---

ophiques et théologiques 87, no. 1 (2003): 23–37; Jacques Rancière, *Proletarian Nights: The Workers' Dream in Nineteenth-Century France*, transl. by John Drury (London: Verso, 2012).

[3] Bruno Karsenti, *Politique de l'esprit: Auguste Comte et la naissance de la science sociale* (Paris: Hermann Éditeurs, 2006), 2–5.

[4] Andrew Wernick, "Introduction", in: *The Anthem Companion to Auguste Comte*, ed. Andrew Wernick (London: Anthem Press, 2017), 1–22; Warren Schmaus, Mary Pickering, & Michel Bourdeau, "Introduction: The Significance of Auguste Comte", in: *Love, Order, & Progress: The Science, Philosophy, & Politics of Auguste Comte*, eds. Michel Bourdeau, Mary Pickering, & Warren Schmaus (Pittsburgh: University of Pittsburgh Press, 2018), 3–24.

[5] Richard Schaefer, "Program for a New Catholic *Wissenschaft*: Devotional Activism and Catholic Modernity in the Nineteenth Century", *Modern Intellectual History* 4 (2007): 433–462; Julian Strube, "Socialist religion and the emergence of occultism: a genealogical approach to socialism and secularization in 19th-century France", *Religion* 46, no. 3 (2016): 359–388.

[6] Mary Pickering, "Auguste Comte and the Saint-Simonians", *French Historical Studies* 18, no. 1 (1993): 211–236; Stewart J. Brown, "Movements of Christian awakening in revolutionary Europe, 1790–1815", in: *The Cambridge History of Christianity, Vol. VII: Enlightenment, Reawakening and Revolution 1660–1815*, eds. Stewart J. Brown & Timothy Tackett (Cambridge: Cambridge University Press, 2008), 575–595; Pierre Musso, "Religion and political economy in Saint-Simon", *The European Journal of the History of Economic Thought* 24, no. 4 (2017): 809–827.

In the previous chapter, I have tried to further outline a historical-anthropological method for investigating the meetings between historical sociology and the belief-category. In this chapter, I will set out to further historicize these meetings, and this in two ways. First, I will contextualize, what I have called in the introduction, the sociological operation, as originating in the post-revolutionary crisis of the late eighteenth and early nineteenth centuries and the many public-intellectual debates it set off between social-Catholic reactionaries and their modernist-reformist opponents. I will argue that these debates were largely centred on dealing with the historical legacy of the Enlightenment, and its many successes and failures, focusing on its impact on understanding (and misunderstanding) what it meant 'to believe'. And secondly, I aim to show how these debates resulted in the construction of multiple narrative strategies of sociological self-historicization, through which several early sociological actors tried to differentiate their own understanding of social life while simultaneously presenting their own unique response to the societal crisis of the age.

As such, I aim to show how one of the key mechanisms of sociological self-historicization—the engagement with historical languages of belief as an instrument of sociological imagination—was historically constituted and made possible within the French knowledge culture at the end of the early modern period.

The Formality of Belief: From an Ethics of Enlightenment to the Social Facts of Societal Structures

In his famous chapter in *The Writing of History*, "The Formality of Practices: From Religious Systems to the Ethics of Enlightenment (the Seventeenth and Eighteenth Centuries)", Michel de Certeau relates the story of an early modern divorce, the separation between religion and morality, and the many different effects this divorce had on the way certain things could be thought: religious belief in the seventeenth and eighteenth centuries turned into an object, ethical motivations became an individual matter, the government of the moral domain transformed into a field of contestation between the Church and the State.[7] This was, in other words, a formal transformation, one where the content of religious practices

---

[7] de Certeau, *The Writing of History*, 147–205.

largely remained consistent—the Church remained a very powerful actor in society at the end of the early modern period, church attendance was generally consistent and the reality of a divine realm was still almost universally presupposed—but where important transitions were taking place on what can be called the 'theoretical' level, both inside the religious system (reformists, liberals and enlightened theologians) as well as outside (philosophical sceptics, atheists, political theorists, historians of religion).[8] For de Certeau, the end of the early modern period then came to represent a seismic shift in the particular status occupied by religion in the public domain, a shift the tremors of which could still be easily felt in de Certeau's own time of writing, the tumultuous decades of Parisian intellectual life of the 1960s and '70s.[9]

It would be wrong, however, to assume that the story essentially ends there, at the end of the eighteenth century, as if the socio-philosophical groups became permanently divided (enlightened *philosophes* versus theologians) and the societal conflicts set in stone (the politics of Church-State relations, the ethical discussion on the (non-)existence of the soul, etc.). The divorce itself, after all, was the achievement of a contingently formed historical alliance of philosophers *and* theologians, who had the shared intention of incorporating the persistent flow of new historical and scientific data into a more coherent, objective and universal worldview. This is, in many ways, what the project of Enlightenment ultimately embodied, confronting increasingly fossilized institutional bodies of knowledge, like the Church and the feudal State, with non-institutionalized claims of truth: the chaotic and unpredictable nature of Christian love, the duties and rights of individual citizens, the historical nature of religious systems, and the complexity and pervasiveness of principles of matter.[10] As recent research on the Enlightenment has made clear, this was by no means a purely secular undertaking, with several Christian movements—Reform Catholics, Augustinian Jansenists, Arminian Protestants, enlightened ultramontanists, Jesuit theologians, and many more—playing a crucial role in this formal transition, through their own theological-philosophical work on the limits of doctrinal knowledge.[11]

---

[8] Ibid., 148.

[9] Cf. Michel de Certeau, *La prise de parole, et autres écrits politiques* (Paris: Seuil, 1994).

[10] Dan Edelstein, *The Enlightenment: A Genealogy* (Chicago: University of Chicago Press, 2010).

[11] Monique Cottret, *Jansénismes et lumières: pour une autre XVIIIe siècle* (Paris: Albin Michel, 1998); J.G.A. Pocock, "Historiography and Enlightenment: A View of Their

But while this accidental alliance of multiple Enlightenments was rooted in a collectively experienced 'truth' during the seventeenth and eighteenth centuries—that moral action cannot be universalized by such a deeply historicized institution like Christianity *alone*—this same contextual nature of formal change lay at the root of the increased tension characterizing the Enlightenment project at the end of the eighteenth century and at the beginning of the nineteenth century.[12] The new, enlightened theories of morality, built on the principles of appeasement, neutrality and tolerance, were shown to be nearly powerless in the face of the century's revolutionary violence, undermining the system's supposed social and political efficaciousness.[13]

Consequently, questions were inevitably raised with two of the Enlightenment's intellectual pillars, its moral individualism and its conceptual universalism, two frameworks which turned out to be rather unsuitable for what were a number of social crises at the beginning of the nineteenth century: the ideologically explosive aftermath of the French Revolution, the declining social conditions induced by increased industrialization, and a widespread sense of collective fear, distrust and confusion after the attack on traditional institutions such as the monarchy and the Church.[14] The Enlightenment system of ethics was, in other words, by no means a complete success nor an established hegemony dominating the moral discussions within the public domain from early modernity onwards. The novel composition of enlightened morality, which had been so central in the separation of religion and morals, was itself permanently fragmenting and re-composing, not signalling a permanent historical divorce, but rather introducing a transition which was being performed again and again, in fluctuating forms.[15]

History", *Modern Intellectual History* 5, no. 1 (2008): 83–96; Dale K. Van Kley, *Reform Catholicism and the International Suppression of the Jesuits in Enlightenment Europe* (New Haven & London: Yale University Press, 2018).

[12] Michel de Certeau, Dominique Julia & Jacques Revel, *Une politique de la langue* (Paris: Gallimard, 2002 [first published 1975]).

[13] Several historians even argue that the enlightened moral theories were conducive towards the revolutionary violence, cf. Dan Edelstein, *The Terror of Natural Right: Republicanism, the Cult of Nature, and the French Revolution* (Chicago: The University of Chicago Press, 2009); Timothy Tackett, *The Coming of the Terror in the French Revolution* (Cambridge, MA: The Belknap Press of Harvard University Press, 2015).

[14] Frédéric Brahami, *La Raison du Peuple: Un héritage de la Révolution française (1789–1848)* (Paris: Les Belles Lettres, 2016), 31–39.

[15] Boureau, "Croire et croyances", 128–135.

Turning to the eighteenth-century philosophers' own historical imagination it becomes clear, however, that these valid critiques of the enlightened system of ethics represented less of a fundamental break with the Enlightenment itself, than its continuation and development, only intensifying the earlier interventions made by their enlightened predecessors by seeking to define what "being enlightened" actually was.[16] This contestation of a universalist program of enlightened morality, then, should be understood as an internal development, the Enlightenment system of ethics as being true to its word, a genuine *system* where multiple voices and angles were being practised in order to continually further the shared historical project. In the words of Dan Edelstein, the Enlightenment, as soon as it began historicizing itself, formed a kind of "matrix in which ideas, actions, and events acquired new meaning".[17] By this, he means that the importance of the Enlightenment as a historical phenomenon lay in its performative function as a narrative framework, where *naming* your intellectual practices as 'enlightened', and so effectively partaking in a social and collective undertaking, was the very foundation of the movement.[18] "The Enlightenment", says Edelstein, referencing Paul Hazard's great work *La crise de la conscience européenne* (1935), "constituted a *prise*, not a *crise de conscience*".[19] It was a social-intellectual movement on thinking thought anew, rather than any sort of substantial transformation of thought itself.[20]

The different names given to these movements critiquing the Enlightenment project—the Counter-Enlightenment, Romanticism, historicism, etc.—then represent less of an attempt at effectively characterizing a genuine, burgeoning tradition than signalling a growing preoccupation with the act of historical naming itself, the practice of epochal categorization being the goal in itself.[21] This process of self-

---

[16] Didier Masseau, *Les ennemis des philosophes. L'antiphilosophie au temps des Lumières* (Paris: Albin Michel, 2000).

[17] Edelstein, *The Enlightenment*, 13.

[18] Ibid., 13–18.

[19] Ibid., 13. Cf. Paul Hazard, *La crise de la conscience européenne (1680–1715)* (Paris: Boivin, 1935).

[20] Ibid.

[21] The historiographical validity of these names and categorizations remains highly contested, cf. J.G.A. Pocock, "Enlightenment and Counter-Enlightenment, Revolution and Counter-Revolution: A Eurosceptical Inquiry", *History of Political Thought* 20, no. 1 (1999): 125–139; Jeremy L. Caradonna, *The Enlightenment in Practice: Academic Prize Contests and Intellectual Culture in France, 1670–1794* (Ithaca: Cornell University Press, 2012); James

identification and –historicization—as being enlightened, enlightened alternatively, or not enlightened at all—became the very core of the late eighteenth- and early nineteenth-century intellectual culture, which was highly factionalized among different groups who attempted to claim the 'true meaning' of certain categories.[22] This context of intellectual contestation was not limited to the question of "what is Enlightenment?". The domain of religion and morality, which had stood at the centre of much philosophical deliberation during the seventeenth and eighteenth centuries, was also submitted to a similar treatment. This meant that the discussion was now no longer exclusively concerned with the actual object of religion, its internal make-up and meaning, but also with its particular place in history, its external movement as a historical tradition in relation to other traditions.[23]

Ian Hunter has aptly demonstrated this development through his discussion of the concept 'secularization', which, according to him, was an early nineteenth-century invention as a novel way of *giving meaning* to religion from the perspective of a (philosophically self-identified) rationalizing society.[24] The concept itself had been formed during the early modern period, but signified something very different at the time. It did not refer to any sort of loss of religious beliefs, which is one of the typical manners in which it was understood for a large part of the twentieth century.[25] Rather, 'secularization' was the term used to signify "the transfer of ecclesiastical properties and territories to civil ownership or control".[26] It was a term employed exclusively in the context of public law and diplomacy, originating during the time of the religious wars in the Holy Roman Empire when the peace treaties of Münster and Westphalia (1648) were built around the distribution of ecclesiastical property in order to reach agreeable settlements as well as prevent future discord.[27] Its usage,

Schmidt, "The Counter-Enlightenment: Notes on a Concept Historians Should Avoid", *Eighteenth-Century Studies* 49, no. 1 (2015): 83–86.

[22] James Schmidt, "Misunderstanding the Question: 'What is Enlightenment?': Venturi, Habermas and Foucault", *History of European Ideas* 37, no. 1 (2011): 43–52.

[23] Pocock, "Historiography and Enlightenment", 83–86. Cf. also de Certeau, *The Writing of History*, 147–205.

[24] Ian Hunter, "Secularization: The Birth of a Modern Combat Concept", *Modern Intellectual History* 12, no. 1 (2015): 1–32.

[25] Peter Harrison, "Introduction: Narratives of secularization", *Intellectual History Review* 27, no. 1 (2017): 1.

[26] Hunter, "Secularization", 5.

[27] Ibid.

however, completely changed in the early nineteenth century: not because the historical conditions of religious belief had changed in any dramatic fashion—the Reformation and Counter-Reformation had rather led to an intensification of religious devotion and practice[28]—but because of the aforementioned changes in intellectual culture, where philosophies of history came to dominate as means of philosophical (self-)exploration.[29]

Secularization attained its modern-day meaning, referring to a downward shift in the potentiality of religious belief through the increase of reason and science, in the broader context of an intellectual culture of struggle and contestation. This intellectual culture was mainly concerned with the topic of self-government, and the ability of philosophical reason to autonomously provide an existential diet for such government.[30] Concepts and ideas, in such a culture, represent techniques, instruments through which a mode of existence can be built in the most robust fashion possible.[31] The conceptual success of 'secularization', then, was derived less from its historical accuracy per se, than from its ability to function as a performative intellectual and ideological tool.[32] To speak of secularization as a historical and social process was not just to describe something, but also very much to bring something into existence, a horizon through which communities could imagine themselves.[33] For this reason, historians of religion and science such as Ian Hunter and Peter Harrison have chosen to speak of "narratives of secularization", in order to lay bare how the

---

[28] Hunter (2015, 8n15) points to the work of Heinz Schilling as providing a useful overview of this religious intensification, cf. Heinz Schilling, "Confessional Europe", in: *Handbook of European History 1400–1600: Latin Middle Ages, Renaissance and Reformation, vol. 2, Visions, Programs and Outcomes*, eds. T. A. J. Brady, H. A. Oberman, and J. D. Tracy (Leiden: Brill, 1995), 641–82.

[29] Hunter, "Secularization", 29–31.

[30] Michel Foucault, "Qu'est-ce que les Lumières?", in: *Michel Foucault, Dits et Écrits, vol. II: 1976–1988*, eds. Daniel Defert & François Ewald (Paris: Gallimard, 2001), 1381–1397.

[31] Cf. Quentin Skinner, *Visions of Politics, Vol. I: Regarding Method* (Cambridge: Cambridge University Press, 2002); J.G.A. Pocock, "The historian as political actor: polity, society, and academy (1996)", "The politics of history: the subaltern and the subversive (1998)", and "The politics of historiography (2005)", which are all gathered in his anthology, *Political Thought and History: Essays on Theory and Method* (Cambridge: Cambridge University Press, 2009), 217–271.

[32] Hunter, "Secularization", 24.

[33] On historical imagination as a technique of subjectivation, cf. Reinhart Koselleck, *Futures Past. On the Semantics of Historical Time*, transl. by Keith Tribe (New York: Columbia University Press, 2004), esp. chap. 14, "'Space of Experience' and 'Horizon of Expectation': Two Historical Categories", 255–275.

concept is a "conflation of descriptive, explanatory, and normative elements" as well as how "the normative commitments entailed in the various narratives [...] shape both the marshalling of facts and the explanation of those facts".[34] To write and think 'secularization' was to articulate what Eric Schliesser has termed a "philosophical prophecy", rooted in reason and historical patterns, and was meant to act as a guide for further thought and behaviour.[35]

The history of 'belief' as a concept and category is, in this regard, not dissimilar to the one with which it is so closely associated, 'secularization'. Like the latter, 'belief' was a notion during the nineteenth and twentieth centuries through which historical, religious and social change came to be thought (through its opposition to science and reason), with multiple meanings being ascribed to it in order to ground a certain narrative and philosophy of history.[36] This is not to say that the Enlightenment model of representational belief became actively problematized, something that only became an explicitly articulated tradition in the second half of the twentieth century in several disciplines under the header "critical theory".[37] Rather, by this I mean that the contexts in which 'belief' attained a prominent place intensified and proliferated. Not just the concrete object of philosophical inquiry-say, as it was in John Locke's *An Essay Concerning Human Understanding* (1689) or in David Hume's *A Treatise of Human Nature* (1739–1740)—'belief' also became the instrument of comparative and ethnographic investigation, the area of governmental policy and political intervention, and a popular tool for public discussion.[38] In other words, 'belief' was becoming, besides its varied philosophical and theological meanings, a common sensical category with seemingly little need of elaborate explanation, which instead could explain all kinds of social phenomena through its mere existence as 'beliefs' and 'opinions'.[39] And

---

[34] Harrison, "Introduction", 1–2.
[35] On this term, cf. Eric Schliesser, "Philosophical Prophecy", in: *Philosophy and its History: Aims and Methods in the Study of Early Modern Philosophy*, eds. Mogens Lærke, Justin E. H. Smith, Eric Schliesser (Oxford: Oxford University Press, 2013), 209–235.
[36] Bruno Karsenti, "Destin du culte des morts", *Incidence* 2 (2009): 136–154; Arnold, "Believing in Belief", 236–242.
[37] B.J. Good, "Belief, Anthropology Of", in: *International Encyclopedia of the Social & Behavioral Sciences*, eds. Neil J. Smelser & Paul B. Baltes (Amsterdam: Elsevier, 2001), 1141. Also, cf. supra chap. 1.
[38] Cf. Shagan, *The Birth of Modern Belief*.
[39] Ibid., 268–276.

yet, paradoxically, behind this common sensical and unproblematized understanding provided by an enlightened intellectual culture, lay a rich history of differentiated interpretations and tactical employments by groups and traditions of thinkers.[40]

I will argue that the usage of the belief-category became something which was employed in a more circumstantial, creative and governmental fashion, a conceptual anchor point which allowed the philosophical-historical author their own unique ordering of the constellation populated by such stars as 'society', 'history', and 'religion', with the primary intent being a narrative performance of the social order.[41] This essentially became possible through the proliferation of its meanings—propositional, cognitive, social, representational, cultural, individual as well as collective—as it became a typical signifier for comparative-historical research without much rigorous definition. 'Belief' was (and is still today) a vague and ambiguous category, underdetermined by the histories of Christianity and enlightened philosophy, which, in turn, made it into an excellent crutch to enter a new and original dialogue with these histories.

Belief and the Birth of the Social Sciences in the Early Nineteenth Century

It was in this particular context, where the Enlightenment model of representational belief transformed into a conceptual space of contestation through which 'society' could be thought and discussed on a historicized self-reflective level, that the idea of a science of the social was able to fully originate.[42] In this sense, the uniqueness of the early nineteenth century was not so much its employment of the society-category as a matrix of understanding—social explanations for societal behaviour are as old as the existence of society itself—than the conceptualization of its own viewpoint as historically unique, in the way philosophers like Louis de Bonald, Henri de Saint-Simon and Auguste Comte presented their teleological perspectives.[43]

---

[40] Cf. for example: Revel, "Forms of Expertise", 255–273.

[41] de Certeau, "L'institution du croire", 61–80.

[42] Frédéric Brahami, "Sortir du cercle Auguste Comte, la critique et les rétrogrades", *Archives de Philosophie* 70, no. 1 (2007): 42.

[43] Robert Wokler, "The Enlightenment and the French Revolutionary Birth Pangs of Modernity", in: *The Rise of the Social Sciences and the Formation of Modernity: Conceptual*

In other words, the notion of a new social science was mainly built on its self-differentiation with the Enlightenment regime of reason and belief, which was characterized by the early sociologists as too rationalistic and unable to comprehend the internal complexity and functionalism of society.[44] The enlightened ambition, to come closer to an End of History by means of analytical clarity and uniformity, was considered by its nineteenth-century inheritors as a failure as well as a genuine social danger because it ironically provided a tool for social-historical transformation, as well as, ultimately, laying the foundations for revolutionary violence.[45]

In her recent article, "Aux sources de la sociologie" (2017), Laurence Kaufmann framed this historical context as being characterized by the broad incorporation, prevalent especially among the philosophical-revolutionary class, of a *nominalist* attitude, the understanding of things such as 'society', 'the church' and 'the state' as being composed of both real-materialist elements and social-constructionist facets.[46] While this disposition played a crucial role in making possible the imagination of a societal revolution—the authority of the Church and the monarch being symbolic rather than rooted in anything fundamental—it simultaneously played a central role in making something as a "science of society" possible as well, as the configurated nature of society (real/artificial; materialist/symbolic; individual/collectivist, etc.) created an epistemological vacuum, in which the kinds and the relational aspects of this configuration needed to be interpreted and explained.[47]

Within this vacuum, such as it unfolded in post-revolutionary Europe and especially France, several groups and factions quickly founded themselves, through, amongst other strategies, claims of having found the right division of a scientific-empirical perspective and its non-scientific other, social belief, superstition, and opinion.[48] The integralist nature of the new

Change in Context, 1750–1850, eds. Johan Heilbron, Lars Magnusson, & Björn Wittrock (Dordrecht: Springer Dordrecht, 1998), 35–37.

[44] Robert Wokler, "From the Moral and Political Sciences to the Sciences of Society by Way of the French Revolution", *Jahrbuch fur Recht und Ethik* 33 (2000): 33–46.

[45] For another example of this process, cf. de Certeau, Julia & Revel, *Une politique de la langue*.

[46] Laurence Kaufmann, "Aux sources de la sociologie. Science et politique de la « société » au 18ᵉ siècle", *L'Année Sociologique* 67, no. 2 (2017): 338.

[47] Ibid., 348–349.

[48] Josephson-Storm, "The Superstition, Secularism, and Religion Trinary", 4–5.

social science, as being able to incorporate multiple facets of social life which were seemingly contradictory, was an immediate response to its enlightened predecessor, a knowledge culture which was seen as overly one-dimensional in its emphasis on systematic knowledge and manufacturability. Reason and faith needed to be properly balanced, it was argued, instead of the unbalanced emphasis on rationality put forward by enlightened *philosophes*, which had ultimately led to the social confusion, individualism and a loss of community experienced in the early nineteenth century.[49]

This conception of Enlightenment culture was, as Robert Wokler has already shown, in many ways a myth. Yet the foundational narrative allowed the creation of a clear-cut discursive space, where the social relation in society stood at its centre. So the early nineteenth-century commentators go on to argue that, in order to restore this sense of community, a form of belief, trust and faith in the community needed to be salvaged. Whether this form be traditionally religious, philosophically secular, or modernistically spiritual, this was to be argued for by different claimants and factions.[50] The modernist secularization-narrative—that the progression of science and reason would eventually make all kinds of faith-based interaction avoidable and largely useless—seems to have appeared only later on, with English philosopher and social theorist John Stuart Mill being an early propagator of such a narrative.[51] The social-intellectual struggle in early nineteenth-century France did not presuppose such a disappearance. The engagement with belief was rather considered as a necessary step for understanding both what happened in early modern society as well as what an ideal society should look like.

This eventually led to a kind of combative public knowledge culture where highly distinct groups—Catholic reactionaries, revolutionary socialists and spiritual positivists—intensely debated such questions as the ideal structure of society, its most optimal forms of social government and the role that was still to be played by religion. As a result, these groups and

---

[49] Frédéric Brahami, "Individu, pouvoir, société dans la pensée contre-révolutionnaire", in: *Le libéralisme au miroir du droit. L'État, la personne, la propriété*, ed. Blaise Bachofen (Lyon: ENS Éditions, 2008), 145–163.

[50] Hunter, "Secularization", 4.

[51] Gilbert Faccarello, "Saeculum", *European Journal for the History of Economic Thought* 24, no. 4 (2017): 625–28.

their charismatic leadership figures would come to be associated with an early form of the social sciences, as they took society and its structures to be a holistic phenomenon which needed to be coherently analysed and explained.[52] 'Society', then, transformed into an analytical lens through which all human life, relations and power could be explained, moving away from previously hegemonic explanatory frameworks such as the state, the monarch and/or the juridical sphere.[53]

While these explanations were first and foremost instrumental in nature for these ideological formations, i.e. as providing a practical solution to concrete problems experienced in the wake of the French and Industrial Revolutions, they still very much laid the foundation of later sociological programs, despite their intense political and ideological colouring.[54] During such a chaotic period in French and European history, it was seemingly impossible to separate the broader context from its burgeoning social-scientific programs, as the two were inextricably bound to each other.[55] As such, it was during this period in time, in a society increasingly experienced as incohesive, that the eighteenth-century discourse on sociability, society and social cohesion reached another level, intensified by the experiences of fear and crisis prominent during the revolution.[56] The revolutionary violence of the Terror had shown the necessity of a *science sociale*, one which could better understand the socio-psychological make-up of Man and, through this knowledge, conserve society from Man's all too violent tendencies.[57]

---

[52] Brahami, *La Raison du Peuple*, 177–182.

[53] Karsenti, *D'une philosophie à l'autre*, 155–174; Michel Foucault, *Il faut défendre la société: Cours au Collège de France (1976)*, ed. François Ewald and Alessandro Fontana (Paris: Gallimard/Seuil, 1997), 117; Frederick Neuhouser, "Conceptions of Society in Nineteenth-Century Social Thought", in: *The Cambridge History of Philosophy in the Nineteenth Century (1790–1870)*, eds. Allen W. Wood & Songsuk Susan Hahn (Cambridge: Cambridge University Press, 2012), 651–675.

[54] Karsenti, *Politique de l'esprit*, 5–8.

[55] Philippe Steiner, "French political economy, industrialism, and social change (1815–1830)", in: *Economic Development and Social Change. Historical Roots and Modern Perspectives*, eds. Yiorgos Stathakis & Gianni Vaggi (London: Routledge, 2006), 232–256.

[56] Sophie Wahnich, "Désordre social et émotions publiques pendant la période révolutionnaire", in: *L'invention de la société. Nominalisme politique et science sociale au XVIIIe siècle*, eds. Laurence Kaufmann & Jacques Guilhaumou (Paris: Éditions de l'École des Hautes Études en Sciences Sociales, 2003), 227–259.

[57] Wokler, "The Enlightenment", 45.

It was in this context that the category of belief represented such a potentially productive concept, with its rich and multifaceted history standing in direct opposition to what was then perceived to be the Enlightenment's ambition with the category, which was to make it as rigid and singular as possible in order to fully sharpen its edges as an analytical instrument of interpretation.[58] This stood in direct contrast to the newly developing sociological disposition, which was rather to explore such incongruous histories of meaning in their fullness, as a means of capturing the complex movements which make society the dynamic organism that it is. It was in this manner that the history of belief was able to enter such a fruitful partnership with the historical project of sociology, as the two were able to consistently use one another, so to speak, as a means of reinvention and reimagination.

Conclusion

The knowledge culture in late eighteenth-century France was marked by a couple of trends which were decisive in creating a productive space for a discipline like sociology to unfold itself, as well as enable the category of belief to function as a crucial, dialogical instrument for sociologists as a way of thinking society, its religious manifestations and themselves. These trends were, on the one hand, a growing prevalence of thinking the identity of the community through philosophies of history.[59] On the other, French philosophers were swayed by a return of nominalism and the notion of 'society' as something that was both partly real and partly constructed.

While this created space was populated by a number of actors, not in the least the revolutionaries who wanted to *make* a new kind of society through political imaginations, it was this space which was also taken up by those actors who became moved to investigate a "science of society", as a kind of thought which could make sense of the often paradoxical nature of social life. Furthermore, as I have argued in these past chapters, the category of belief transformed into a uniquely suitable prism for

---

[58] Shagan, *The Birth of Modern Belief*, 248–249.

[59] Judith Revel, "'What Are We at the Present Time?' Foucault and the Question of the Present", in: *Foucault and the History of Our Present*, eds. Sophie Fuggle, Yari Lanci, & Martina Tazzioli (New York: Palgrave Macmillan, 2015), 13–25.

imagining such a science. The notion of 'belief' was able to function as the symbolic core of the sociological operation because it exerted a particular gravitational force on the components within this operation: first of all, it was able to integrate the different and often contradictory intentions of the sociological moderns—as an instrument of politicization *and* depoliticization; as a tool for sacralization *and* secularization—into a single language. And secondly, the conditions enacting the birth of sociology, the opening up of a discursive space for contesting the meaning of 'society', was embodied and reflected within the category of belief and its own increasing contestability as a tool to think the religious and social-scientific domains.

CHAPTER 5

Early Experiments in the Sociological Operation II. The Christian Sociologism of Louis de Bonald

Introduction

The holistic-historical perspective, typical of a structuralist sociology, has often been associated with a group of Catholic anti-revolutionary reactionaries of the early nineteenth century. Figures such as Louis de Bonald, Joseph de Maistre, and Félicité de La Mennais are regularly mentioned as forefathers to the sociological canon for this very reason.[1] The role of these Catholic reactionaries in the eventual foundation of sociology—especially Bonald's through his influence on Auguste Comte and Émile Durkheim[2]—has already been elaborately noted and discussed, by prominent historians and philosophers of social science such as Robert Nisbet, Robert Spaemann, Pierre Macherey, Sandro Chignola, Jean-Yves Pranchère, Giorgio Barberis and Flavien Bertran de Balanda.[3]

---

[1] Wokler, "The Enlightenment", 45–46.

[2] Flavien Bertran de Balanda, *Louis de Bonald. Philosophe et homme politique. Une tradition dans la modernité, une modernité dans la tradition 1754–1840* (Paris: CNRS Éditions, 2021), 18.

[3] Robert A. Nisbet, "The French Revolution and the Rise of Sociology in France", *The American Journal of Sociology* 49, no. 2 (1943): 156–164; Ibid., "De Bonald and the Concept of the Social Group", *Journal of the History of Ideas* 5 (1944): 315–331; Ibid., "Conservatism and Sociology", *American Journal of Sociology* 58, no. 2 (1952): 167–175; Robert Spaemann, *Der Ursprung der Soziologie aus dem Geist der Restauration: Studien über*

The early sociological emphasis on structural interpretations, the social group as the locus of intervention, and the idea of society as an interconnected and organic whole, can mostly be traced back to these thinkers.[4] And after being largely ignored for a long time, or simply being labelled as little more than reactionary conservatives, their work has received more scholarly attention in recent decades, both substantially as well as contextually.[5] What this renewed literature on the social Catholics and their early sociological theories has shown is that these were in fact serious thinkers, who thoroughly engaged with both the Enlightenment tradition and the French Revolution.[6] The latter, in contrast to conventional opinion, was not so much seen by Bonald and Maistre as an apocalyptical disaster which rang in societal degeneration, than as the entire historical spectrum laid bare in all its extremes, the "unprecedented collection of weakness and of strength, of disgrace and of greatness, of delirium and of reason, of crimes and even of virtues, its head in heaven and its feet in hell".[7]

The counter-revolutionaries were, then, like those enlightened *philosophes* before them, the living embodiment of voices seeking historical elevation, fascinated by the chaos left behind by men, trying to make such bloody spectacles meaningful through thought, reason and language.[8] But while secondary literature has increasingly focused on this important nuance, it has yet to fully lay bare how these Catholic reactionaries shaped themselves as well as their readership through particular narrative strate-

---

L.G.A. de Bonald (München: Kösel, 1959); Pierre Macherey, "Aux sources des rapports sociaux. Bonald, Saint-Simon, Guizot", *Genèses* 9 (1992): 25–43; Sandro Chignola, *Società e costituzione. Teologia e politica nel sistema di Bonald* (Milan: Franco Angeli, 1993); Jean-Yves Pranchère, "Totalité sociale et hiérarchie: La sociologie théologique de Louis de Bonald", *Revue européenne des sciences sociale* 49, no. 2 (2011): 145–167; Ibid., "The Social Bond in Maistre and Bonald", in: *Joseph De Maistre's Life, Thought, and Influence: Selected Studies*, ed. Richard Lebrun (Montreal: McGill-Queens University Press, 2001), 190–219; Giorgio Barberis, *Louis de Bonald. Ordre et pouvoir entre subversion et providence* (Paris: Desclée de Brouwer, 2016).

[4] Nisbet, *The Sociological Tradition*, 12–13.

[5] Cf. for example: Matthijs Lok, Friedemann Pestel & Juliette Reboul (eds.), *Cosmopolitan Conservatisms: Countering Revolution in Transnational Networks, Ideas and Movements (c. 1700–1930)* (Leiden: Brill, 2021).

[6] Flavien Bertran de Balanda, "Evil Raised To Its Highest Power. The Philosophy of the Counter-Enlightenment, a Project of Intellectual Management of the Revolutionary Violence", *The Philosophical Journal of Conflict and Violence* IV, no. 1 (2020): 52–72.

[7] Louis de Bonald, *Législation primitive*, 64–65, cited and translated by Flavien Bertran de Balanda, "Evil Raised To Its Highest Power", 70.

[8] Masseau, *Les ennemis des philosophes*, 419–423.

gies, preparing the stage for what can be called a sociological operation. For the social Catholics were not simply satisfied with furthering the Enlightenment project, they aimed to supersede it, bringing philosophy and religion into harmony, in order to ameliorate societal cohesion to its fullest potential.[9] The science of the social was to be a language capable of transcending the fiery conflict which had been raging during the revolutionary period between the secular and the spiritual domain, rejecting the Enlightenment register of tolerance and interaction and searching instead for richer, more deepfelt ways for experiencing religious life and liberty.[10] One of these ways was to be found in the notion of society itself, conceived by these early Catholic sociologists as an organic entity composed of interdependent parts.

This meant, then, that the Catholic sociologists saw it as their task, not to convert philosophical non-believers to Catholicism, but rather to generate new forms of shared believing, among both *philosophes* as well as Christians. It was society, approached as a universal historical category, through which all human and non-human relations could be framed and understood. The most prominent Catholic sociologist, Louis de Bonald, explicitly articulated this goal in his 1796 book *Théorie du pouvoir politique et religieux*, in which he declared that "the great trial of Religion and Philosophy has already gone on for too long".[11] It was time for a new *societal* perspective, which could show that faith and reason were by no means opposed, but perfectly complementary. And Bonald aimed to show this, not just by redefining how faith and reason related to each other, but by also elaborating a historical language which could bring rationalists and believers into a more socially potent synthesis, the vision of a naturally constituted society the way it was meant to be.[12]

The next sections, then, will be devoted to the work of Louis de Bonald, and this in two ways: first, by looking at how the French vicomte concretely constructed a sociological belief-language which attempted to bind the philosophical and religious opponents of the eighteenth century together; and second, by looking at how Bonald used techniques of

---

[9] Zachhuber, "Individual and Community", 18.

[10] Thomas Kselman, *Conscience and Conversion: Religious Liberty in Post-Revolutionary France* (New Haven: Yale University Press, 2018), 13–48.

[11] Louis de Bonald, *Théorie du pouvoir politique et religieux, dans la société civile, démontrée par le raisonnement & par l'histoire* (S.l.: s.n., 1796), vol. II, 3: "[l]e grand procès de la Religion & de la Philosophie n'a que trop duré".

[12] Ibid., 1–7.

self-historicization in order to create a sociological space in which his ideal social-Christian society could unfold itself. The choice of focusing on Bonald, instead of a de Maistre or de la Mennais, is mainly practical and contextual: practical, because the French nobleman built up the most coherent and elaborate oeuvre among his peers, even if it was poorly written, as Alexandre Koyré remarked; contextual, because he is most often considered by later historians of social science as an influential forefather of sociology.[13]

Situating Louis de Bonald: Catholic Reactionary, Philosopher, Thinker of Society

The life and background of Bonald was fairly stereotypical for a Catholic reactionary: born into a landed aristocratic family originating in the old French province of Rouergue, Bonald was educated both at home as well as in Paris and Juilly during his teenage years, coming into contact with philosophy, the classics and history at the hands of the Oratorians.[14] He would serve in the military, being stationed at the court in Versailles and would later return to his hometown in Millau, where he would become involved in its political life, eventually being appointed as mayor of the town in 1785.[15] His life had all the hallmarks of what one would expect of a country nobleman and would most likely have continued to be so, were it not for the revolutionary events of the year 1789. Still in his office as mayor, Bonald at first positively embraced the many changes being rung around the country, putting them into place as the responsible dignitary. Popular with the local populace, Bonald was now elected as mayor—instead of being royally appointed—and oversaw the increased political involvement of the Millau citizenry.[16] It was only with the introduction of the Civil Constitution of the Clergy in July 1790 that Bonald actively began to turn against the Revolution, leading to his eventual exile and

---

[13] Alexandre Koyré, Leonora Cohen-Rosenfield (transl.), "Louis de Bonald", *Journal of the History of Ideas* 7, no. 1 (1946): 56–73; Erwan Moreau, "À propos de Louis de Bonald et de sa sociologie", *Sociétés* 150, no. 4 (2020): 140.
[14] Bertran de Balanda, *Louis de Bonald*, 28–30.
[15] Ibid., 30–36.
[16] Ibid., 37–39.

resistance against the French government.[17] The first important work he wrote, the aforementioned *Théorie du politique et religieux*, was written in Switzerland and outlined his own vision on what he considered to be the proper relation between political and religious power.[18] He would eventually return to France in 1797 and become an important intellectual voice in French political culture, gaining notoriety especially for his role in reinstating the laws against divorce in 1816 and the Anti-Sacrilege Act of 1825, which made the act of blasphemy (theoretically) punishable by death.[19]

It should come as no surprise, then, that Bonald has long suffered from a bad reputation, his philosophical contribution considered as little more than a rhetorically articulate representation of the counter-revolutionary ideological program.[20] But that is not how I aim to approach the work of the conservative French vicomte. While it is true that the language of intellectual culture should be understood as the product of collective programs and factions, it is not the case that this materialist process can then sufficiently explain the authorial voice of someone like Bonald.[21] Rather, the latter should be understood as also undertaking a unique attempt at acting upon this material language, using tools of reflection and abstraction in order to shape the robust mass of the former into an autonomous and individual performance.[22] In other words, Bonald was not *just* a counter-revolutionary proto-sociologist, participating in a political-ideological struggle for the meaning-allocation of religion, social science and society. From an intellectual-historical perspective, he also employed the discourse of counter-revolutionary proto-sociology as a means of carving out an existence for himself in the face of history and the nineteenth-century registers of 'society', 'religion' and 'belief'.[23] Unlike Ian Hunter,

---

[17] Ibid., 44–47.

[18] Flavien Bertran de Balanda, "La Théorie du pouvoir de Louis de Bonald (1796) ou l'édification d'une métaphysique sociale de la royauté", *Annales historiques de la Révolution française* 403, no. 1 (2021): 45–62.

[19] Flavien Bertran de Balanda, "Louis de Bonald et la question du divorce, de la rédaction du Code Civil à la loi du 8 mai 1816", *Histoire, économie & société* 36, no. 3 (2017): 72–86.

[20] Bertran de Balanda, *Louis de Bonald*, 18.

[21] On the materialist basis of culture, cf. Sperber, *Explaining Culture*.

[22] de Certeau, "L'institution du croire", 74.

[23] On pragmatic sociology, especially one that is compatible with a critical meta-perspective on the history of sociology itself, cf. the work of Laurence Kaufmann and Philippe Gonzalez: Gonzalez & Kaufmann, "The Social Scientist, the Public and the Pragmatist Gaze", 1–30.

who considers such spiritual meditations and practices of the self as "spiritual weapons", I think these reflective practices cannot be explained away by their place of origin in a highly politicized and ideological context.[24] While their broader effects contained undoubtedly political elements—Bonald providing the counter-revolutionaries with plenty of ammunition from his own personal ideological arsenal[25]—his own entry into the sociological operation through a government of self and others belongs to its own philosophical and intellectual history.[26]

At the same time, we need not stray too far into the opposite direction, making the whole history of social science into a chronological sequence of singular voices. This, all things considered, small-scale undertaking of the French reactionary philosopher did not determine the historical path of social science, like some seem to suppose who have been worried about sociology's conservative origins and who have sought to distance the sociological canon from thinkers like Bonald, such as Pierre Macherey and Anthony Giddens.[27] Bonald was never able to steer the pathway of sociology into a kind of conservative or reactionary determinism, as he was himself thoroughly embedded within and limited by his own historical environment. Instead, I believe his texts should be approached as the narrative tools of an individual actor, who used techniques of self-historicization as a way of navigating these complex contexts surrounding him. The French vicomte could employ such techniques to set up a potential language for thinking society's historical becoming and its future horizons. For Bonald, the ultimate purpose of such a language would be that it could be shared and performed with others, potentially assisting in the foundation of a new Christian-sociological community. Bonald's attempts at constructing such a Christian-sociological community—through narration, negotiation, and contestation of historical languages of belief—is what I will focus on here.

---

[24] Hunter, "Secularization", 29.

[25] Keith Michael Baker, *Inventing the French Revolution* (Cambridge: Cambridge University Press, 1990), esp. chapters 2 and 3, 31–85.

[26] Bruno Karsenti, "Autorité, société, pouvoir: le science sociale selon Bonald", in: *L'invention de la société: nominalisme politique et science sociale au XVIIIe siècle*, ed. Laurence Kaufmann & Jacques Guilhaumou (Paris: Éditions de l'École des Hautes Études en Sciences Sociales, 2003), 261–286.

[27] Zachhuber, "Individual and Community", 25.

Making Solidarity Between the Philosophical and Religious Classes: Belief in the Work of Louis de Bonald

Central to this undertaking of writing a new kind of community was his creative and tactical engagement with the notion of 'belief'. From the very beginning of his remarkably consistent oeuvre, Bonald sought to take a middle ground, between the philosophical-rationalistic culture of the Enlightenment and the devout and submissive flock of his fellow Christian believers. This middle ground was not analytical but pragmatic: if the two opposing forces were to be joined together once again, concessions would have to be made. That this compromising attitude would be met with suspicion was already expected by Bonald in advance. In the 'Avertissement' of his second volume of the *Théorie du pouvoir politique et religieux*, which focuses on the constitution of religious society, the author seeks to assure his Christian readers that his submission of Christian truths to principles of reason is no reason to be scandalized. His use of reason is only to show "the necessity of Man's beliefs", that "your cult is reasonable" and that he is only following in the footsteps of "the most orthodox writers who have tried to make the most impenetrable dogmas of religion understandable to reason".[28] Furthermore, he made sure to add that there could be no doubt about the sincerity of his disposition towards the notion that religion demands the believer to submit his individual reason to the general reason of religious society and that "there will always remain", beyond the pieces of evidence provided by reason, "in the *how* of its inaccessible mysteries, more than enough obscurity to put into practice the faith of the Christian, to humble man's reason and to appal the pride of the false sage".[29]

Bonald sought, in other words, to paint a picture of human life which was able to take into account its entire complexity: the necessity of reason paired with the ineradicable nature of divine mysteries; the brightness of history coupled with the blindness of the faithful; the endless proliferation of individualities and the transcendental stillness of the singular whole.[30] The struggle between faith and reason, which had dominated the early

---

[28] Bonald, *Théorie du pouvoir politique et religieux*, vol. II, ii.
[29] Ibid.
[30] Bertran de Balanda, *Louis de Bonald*, 53. Cf. also Gérard Gengembre, « Les concepts et l'Histoire » (PhD diss., Université de Paris IV, 1983), 205.

modern period through religious wars, inquisitions, witch trials and anti-superstitious atheism, served as the ultimate metaphor for this paradoxical reality. For too long, both philosophers and religious believers had been unable to see the singular nature of these two intertwined processes, leading to a fruitless civil war, with only death as a result.[31] Instead of struggle, claimed Bonald, the two belong to a single natural law: "FAITH PRECEDES REASON IN ORDER TO SHAPE IT, WHILE REASON FOLLOWS FAITH IN ORDER TO AFFIRM IT [my translation]."[32]

Faith and reason form two distinct yet complementary aspects of Bonald's epistemology, which he approached not just in a physical-materialist manner, but also as an essentially social undertaking, especially when it came to societal and moral matters.[33] When it comes to matters of *community*—living and working together, cooperating and dividing our labour, trusting the work and insights of others—we cannot abandon our belief and trust in others, no matter their actual grasp on the factual reality of things:

> It is assuredly through our faith in others that we are exclusively able to use certain substances to nourish and clothe ourselves, or where we are able to entrust our life to the arts which serve to house us or transport us from one place to the other, although the use of these things is of a totally different order for us than the movement of the earth or the moon's attraction. We even often put the reason of others in place of our own for things that are less necessary and less usual; and the surveyor who enters, the hundredth, in a boat, does not consult beforehand whether the load will not be too strong relative to the volume of water it displaces, but he trusts in the interest and experience of a boatman who has no other knowledge than his own daily practice [my translation].[34]

---

[31] Louis de Bonald, *Législation primitive, considérée dans les derniers temps par les seuls lumières de la raison*, vol. II (1802), in: *Œuvres complètes de M. de Bonald*, vol. II (Brussels: La Société Nationale, 1845), 45: "Il serait temps cependant de faire cesser cette guerre civile, et même domestique, entre la foi et la raison, où tout périt, raison et foi, et ce combat opiniâtre entre les esprits, qui ne laisse sur le champ de bataille que des morts."

[32] Ibid.: "LA FOI PRÉCÈDE LA RAISON POUR LA FORMER, ET QUE LA RAISON SUIT LA FOI POUR L'AFFERMIR."

[33] Moreau, "A propos de Louis de Bonald", 143.

[34] Louis de Bonald, *Recherches philosophiques sur les premiers objets des connaissances morales* (1818), cited in: Moreau, "A propos de Louis de Bonald", 144: "C'est assurément sur la foi d'autrui que nous usons exclusivement de certaines substances pour nous nourrir et nous vêtir, ou que nous confions notre vie aux arts qui servent à nous loger ou à nous transporter d'un lieu à un autre, quoique cependant l'usage de ces choses soit pour nous d'une tout autre

It is by our faith in others—their interest and practical experience, which go beyond epistemic boundaries—that we are able to do our own work, further displaying our essential social interdependence within society. The very social foundation of our knowledge-construction is only further proof for Bonald that matters of trust, belief and faith are not made dispensable through our modernist process of intensified rationalization; indeed, they are structural elements of our way of living and knowing together.[35] Mechanisms of morality are not mere figments of our imagination, they are socially constituted realities gradually built up by historical time and are, as such, beyond our mere intellectual grasp, in the same way "that the movements of heavenly bodies are beyond our physical capacities".[36] We can only submit to them, through shared forms of believing, and commit to their eternal truth and wisdom.[37] From this, it is possible for Bonald to make another induction: that forms of religious government are structural as well, and, as such, indispensable. This was the starting point of much of his sociological work which sought to uncover the natural forms of society, much like it was for later sociologists such as Auguste Comte and Émile Durkheim.[38]

Bonald's dialectical approach to faith and reason was also the main principle of his historical narrative of societal formation, through their form and interaction. The two, argues the French vicomte, are interlocked

---

conséquence que le mouvement de la terre ou l'attraction de la lune. Nous mettons même souvent la raison des autres à la place de la nôtre pour des choses moins nécessaires et moins usuelles; et le géomètre qui entre, lui centième, dans un bateau, ne consulte pas auparavant si la charge ne sera pas trop forte relativement au volume d'eau qu'elle déplace, mais il se fie à l'intérêt et à l'expérience d'un batelier qui n'a d'autre connaissance que sa pratique journalière."

[35] Louis de Bonald, *Démonstration philosophique du principe constitutif de la société* (Brussels: La société nationale, 1845 [1st ed. 1830]), 255: "On savait alors, parce que l'on croyait."

[36] Ibid., 264: "Ainsi toute doctrine qui tendrait à en contredire les dispositions, à en ébranler la croyance, à en dénaturer le sens, même par voie de conséquence, ne saurait être la matière de nos discussions publiques; et ce code du monde moral est, je le répète, hors de notre compétence intellectuelle, comme le mouvement des sphères célestes est hors de notre action physique."

[37] Ibid., 246: "Ce qu'on croyait vrai en physique sous Aristote et Tichobrahé, peut ne l'être plus aujourd'hui; ce qu'on croyait vrai en morale aux premiers jours de la société, en religion aux premiers jours du christianisme, eu politique aux premiers jours de la monarchie, est vrai encore et le sera toujours."

[38] Pranchère, "Totalité sociale", 153.

in a *historical* sequence: reason is sculpted out of the material of commonly held beliefs, after which reason itself becomes an instrument for reaffirming beliefs. In this, Bonald follows the Aristotelian scheme of the *Topics*, and the sequential progression of insight through the interaction between *endoxa* ('reputable beliefs') and their logical assessment through philosophical means.[39] This historical process is dictated by the progress of truth itself and is, as such, not impacted by so-called 'false beliefs'. Even those belong to the same exhaustive structure which Bonald recognizes as the entirety of human existence, and ultimately lead to the same end: "because nothing is lost in the progress of truth, and in the science of moral relations as well in those of numerical relations, we arrive at true results, even from *false starting positions*".[40]

In other words, Bonald's particular modality of belief was not understood as a blind obedience to either an invisible God or an internally experienced divine encounter, the so-called leap of faith more commonly associated with the early modern mystics and hermits.[41] Rather, he considered belief to be something that is inspired by our ability to discern the presence of the sacred at work within the observable historical pattern forming past and present, and taking the shape of *social custom*.[42] Such a process of socialized and shared belief is the very foundation of society itself, according to Bonald, as our communicating of ideas, knowledge and physical bodies makes us into a collective body:

> This is the condition of sociability, and the general law on which society rests, that men receive from each other their physical existence through descent, their moral existence through speech and their forms of knowledge, even in its religious form, comes to them by communication, according to the word of the apostle, *fides ex auditu*.[43]

---

[39] Cf. for example Joseph Karbowski, "Complexity and Progression in Aristotle's Treatment of *Endoxa* in the *Topics*", *Ancient Philosophy* 35, no. 1 (2015): 75–96.

[40] Bonald, *Législation primitive*, vol. II, 46.

[41] Shagan, *The Birth of Modern Belief*, 154–59.

[42] Bonald, *Démonstration philosophique*, 56–57n1.

[43] Bonald, *Législation primitive*, vol. II, 226: "Telle est la condition de la sociabilité, et la loi générale sur laquelle repose la société, que les hommes reçoivent les uns des autres l'existence physique par la génération, l'existence morale par la parole, et que les connaissances même religieuses leur viennent par communication, selon cette parole de l'apôtre, *fides ex auditu*."

We can hear each other and listen to one another, and therefore the very notion of loyalty and togetherness becomes possible.[44] To further elaborate on his point of the existence of these sources of belief-inspiration, Bonald turned to both the history of the Christian religion and the social mechanisms of his own present time, giving the example of Christian self-sacrifice and how it is crucial in preserving the constitution of religious and political society. The historical existence of 'spiritual orders' such as the Benedictines and the Franciscans were instrumental in transforming "useless men" into collective bodies fully devoted to the service of religious and political societies, with the rules of monastic life as useful tools for the societal provision of spirit, heart, and meaning through the vows of obedience, poverty and chastity:

> Religious society drew from natural society those men who were useless to it, and formed them into bodies whose members devoted themselves entirely to the service of civil society, devoting, in order to be useful, their *spirit* through a vow of obedience, their *heart* through a vow of poverty and their *senses* through a vow of chastity [my translation].[45]

These monastic orders were able to inspire acts of social trust and belief to the broader populace, by acting as small theatres of idealized behaviour— "C'étoient des petites sociétés"—through their sacrifice of life and property, and serving as Christ-like exemplars which manifested the natural social state of man.[46]

The historical institution of monastic orders was, according to Bonald, a way for society to limit man's desire for domination, while embedding its protection of the weak. As such, all types of orders were created— religious-military orders aimed at protection, nursing orders aimed at care, mendicant orders focused on preaching, orders dedicated to the preservation of knowledge, and contemplative orders, which are described

---

[44] Bonald, *Législation primitive*, vol. I, 40: "*La croyance vient de l'*ouïe. *Comment entendront-ils, si on ne leur* parle ? *comment leur parlera-t-on, si l'on n'est* envoyé ?"

[45] Bonald, *Théorie du pouvoir politique et religieux*, vol. II, 271: "La société religieuse arrachoit à la société naturelle des hommes qui lui étoient inutiles, & elle en formoit des corps dont les membres se dévouoient tout entiers au service de la société civile, en consacrant à son utilité leur *esprit* par le voeu d'obéissance, leur *coeur* par le voeu de pauvreté, leurs *sens* par le voeu de chasteté."

[46] Ibid., 271: "C'étoient de petites sociétés, qui, pour l'utilité de la société générale, faisoient à Dieu le sacrifice de *l'homme & celui de la propriété.*"

by Bonald as asylums for those ardent souls with excessive sensibility—which would manifest man's weakness and poverty at the very heart of society, acting as the very engine that makes compassion, charity, and hospitality possible for those people "qui s'élève difficilement aux idées spirituelles".[47] These orders embodied "a living and *visible* proof [my italics]" of the transformative capacity of religious belief, with those too attached to their own temporal self-interest becoming *other* through the self-imposed *habit* of charity.[48]

This led Bonald to the paradoxical ascertainment that poverty itself, at least as a mendicant existence, was necessary for the perfect constitution of both religious and political society. In societies where there is no one to assist, "all hearts are closed off to compassion, all hands to charity, all homes to hospitality".[49] The *practice* and the *example* of charity are elements which cannot be absolved if civil and religious societies are to be preserved, essentially admitting that "we will always have the poor among us".[50] By claiming poverty as a permanent societal condition, Bonald was then simultaneously critiquing the developing governmental policy of abolishing mendicancy at the end of the eighteenth century, which he claimed only led to poverty becoming a more universal (and less controlled) phenomenon:

> It is well worth noting that, from the moment onwards, when the governments worked most ardently on banning poverty, or rather begging, from their states, has been the time of the most general dispossession and, as a result, most universal destitution [my translation]![51]

---

[47] Ibid., 272–273.

[48] Ibid.: "Enfans de la providence, ils étoient pour le peuple, qui s'élève difficilement aux idées spirituelles, une preuve vivante & visible que la religion prend soin de ceux qui se dévouent au service de la société. Ils entretenoient dans l'habitude précieuse de la bienfaisance, des hommes trop attachés à leurs intérêts temporels."

[49] Ibid., 273: "Dans des sociétés où il n'y aura personne à assister, *tous les cœurs seront fermés à la compassion, toutes les mains à la bienfaisance, toutes les demeures à l'hospitalité.*"

[50] Ibid., 273: "Aussi le pouvoir conservateur de la société religieuse, & par conséquent de la société civile, qui sait de quel prix sont pour la conservation de la société la pratique & l'exemple de la charité, nous dit lui-même *que nous aurons toujours des pauvres au milieu de nous.*"

[51] Ibid., 273: "[F]ait bien digne de remarque, que le moment où les gouvernemens, travailloient avec le plus d'ardeur à bannir de leurs états la pauvreté, ou plutôt la mendicité, ait été l'époque de l'expropriation la plus générale, & par conséquent de l'indigence la plus universelle !"

What they were banning, according to Bonald, was nothing less than the capacity to observe faith *in action*. The retention of such religious 'rules-of-life' at the very heart of society was crucial in the eyes of Bonald, as such corporate bodies provided an exemplary ideal of self-sacrifice and solidarity through their selfless service to God and society.[52]

In this sense, Bonald took an analytical form typical of the Enlightenment tradition—the evaluation of social, human beliefs according to their societal utility—to turn what were enlightened policies of governance—the eradication of human poverty—on their head. This was a rather standard tactic employed by Christian apologists during the eighteenth century, such as Nicolas-Sylvestre Bergier (1718–1790) and François-Xavier de Feller (1735–1802), who aimed to selectively appropriate the identity and language of the Enlightenment, while steering its messages towards an end result which was more commensurable with religious worldviews.[53] Bonald himself also explicitly inscribed himself into this tradition, taking up the belief-language of the Enlightenment but simultaneously aiming to alter it in a fundamental way. One way he did this was by separating the historical phenomenon of the Enlightenment from those figures typically considered to be its standard philosophical representatives, such as Rousseau, Voltaire, Helvétius, baron d'Holbach. By claiming that Christians were just as able as anybody to *see* and *know* "which roads lead to lights ('lumières', *Enlightenment*) and which is the place where the shadows live", Bonald aimed to broaden the project of the Enlightenment to include Christian practices of faith and devotion as historical manifestations of enlightened reason *in practice*.[54] The project of Enlightenment, with its love of reasonableness, clarity and analytical rigour, was a virtuous one, according to Bonald, but could not be claimed by a single intellectual class, such as the philosophers.

---

[52] Ibid., 279–283.

[53] cf. Jeffrey D. Burson, "Nicolas-Sylvestre Bergier (1718–1790): An Enlightened Anti-Philosophe", in: *Enlightenment and Catholicism in Europe: A Transnational History*, eds. Jeffrey D. Burson & Ulrich L. Lehner (Notre Dame, IN: University of Notre Dame Press, 2014), 63–88; Didier Masseau, "L'idée et la pratique de la retraite dans le combat antiphilosophique", *Dix-huitième siècle* 48, no. 1 (2016): 41–56; Matthijs Lok, "François-Xavier de Feller ((1735–1802) et l'élaboration des Contre-Lumières européennes", in: *Rhétorique et politisation: De la fin des Lumières au printemps des peuples*, eds. S.-A. Leterrier & O. Tort (Arras: Artois Presses Université, 2021), 119–128.

[54] Bonald, *Législation primitive*, vol. II, 47: "Et les chrétiens aussi ont étudié l'homme et son esprit, la société et son contrat, la nature et son système, et ils savent sur quelles voies se trouve la lumière, et quel est le lieu où habitent les ténèbres."

Instead, a new synthesis needed to be made which could transcend the deficiencies of both religious and political society. Bonald's tactical usage of enlightened language was one such way in which the French philosopher sought to achieve a more natural harmony between the two societies. Another example of this was his acceptance of the rationalistic framework for thinking about religion, applying the enlightened division of religious beliefs and political action onto his own work.[55] Throughout the *Théorie du pouvoir religieux et politique*, Bonald defined religious society as being essentially concerned with the government of intellectual and spiritual life, i.e. the internal constitution of man, the rules of morality and the control of man's desire against its turn towards potential depravity.[56] This came down to the conservation of a single belief, which was the faith in the unity of God and the immortality of the soul.[57] Political society, on the other hand, had as its purpose the conservation of social man through the active government of his external actions and practices. The political domain was, in other words, the domain of the physical-practical.[58]

Once again, Bonald emphasizes that the two domains are inextricably entangled, and yet, his correlation of the religious with the internal, spiritual and dogmatic strongly echoes the enlightened tendency of compounding religion's increased spiritualization, privatization and individualization, as something that essentially manifests itself in the mind of the individual believer.[59] At other times, such as in the *Démonstration philosophique*, Bonald further added to such an enlightened approach to beliefs, by discussing the different religious denominations of the Reformation in an ethnographic-comparative manner, differentiating them through their unique sets of dogmatic convictions.[60] Religion, Bonald seems to argue, belongs to the world of ideas and representations, rather than the world of physical objects: it is simply faith in God and His true doctrine.[61]

This, however, should not immediately lead to the conclusion that Bonald fell into any kind of trap of modernity, seemingly unaware of the

---

[55] On this division, cf. de Certeau, *The Writing of History*, 166–68.
[56] Bonald, *Théorie du pouvoir politique et religieux*, vol. I, 54.
[57] Ibid., 50.
[58] Ibid., 54.
[59] Shagan, *The Birth of Modern Belief*, 209–210.
[60] Cf. for example, Bonald, *Démonstration philosophique*, 124–140.
[61] Ibid., 379.

ultimately secularizing effects of such a division between internal-individualist beliefs and social-external action.[62] Rather, I would argue that such an appropriation of an enlightened language of analytical division belonged to a broader rhetorical strategy, one which sought to integrate as much moderate elements as possible—both religious as well as philosophical—in order to create the most robust community of believers in his religious and political society as he could, while discarding only the most dangerous opponents to the wayside. These opponents—materialists, atheists and propagators of the revolutionary 'general will'—were excommunicated from the natural-historical spectrum flanked by reason and faith, as they were labelled by Bonald as those who were *truly* blinded, not by divine grace, but by their own limited and very human pride.[63]

Such a perspective becomes further confirmed when we consider that Bonald was not particularly coherent or logically exhaustive in his usage of the belief-category. For while he selectively applied an enlightened-rationalistic division of beliefs and practices (e.g. when he made the distinction between *those who believe it and those who practice it*, "qui la croyent et qui la pratiquent"), at other times, the French vicomte severely muddled this analytical distinction, emphasizing instead that a belief only constituted a genuine belief when it was practised and led to concrete social action.[64] Simply holding the belief in one's mind, or even speaking it among the belief-community, was not sufficient, according to Bonald, as such an approach to dogma would inevitably result in a societal slide towards materialism and atheism.[65]

In order to incorporate both enlightened and Christian understandings of belief, Bonald made the distinction between "foi de sentiment" and "foi d'opinion": while the latter can be understood as a propositional attitude based in judgement and evaluation, the former is much more rooted in feeling and affection, an intuitive desire towards the divine and the

---

[62] This has been a common trope among Catholic apologists in their critiques of modernity, cf. Shagan, *The Birth of Modern Belief*, 8–10.

[63] Bonald, *Théorie du pouvoir politique et religieux*, vol. I, x: "C'est donc sur une fatalité aveugle, sur une division sans terme, ou un équilibre incertain de pouvoirs que l'homme élève, malgré la nature, à l'aide de l'orgueil & de l'ambition, l'édifice de la société."

[64] Bonald, *Théorie du pouvoir politique et religieux*, vol. II, 5.

[65] Ibid., 37: "Une société se disant religieuse qui se contente de *parler* de l'existence de Dieu & de l'immortalité de l'ame ne peut conserver ni l'une ni l'autre de ces vérités. Elle tombe donc nécessairement dans l'athéisme & le matérialisme."

sublime which has no need for an internal understanding through rationality.⁶⁶ It is because of this instinctively felt spontaneity, according to Bonald, that a 'sentimental faith' is much more natural and innate for most people, as we are much more easily convinced, not by those who want to *understand* God, but by those who *need* God for a source of hope and consolation in the face of life's calamities:

> It undoubtedly won't be disputed that a sentimental faith is in most men, and perhaps in all men, much stronger and much more profound than a faith-by-opinion. Who believes most, who believes best in the fundamental truths of God's existence and the immortality of the soul, those who have listened, often without understanding it, to a scientific discourse on this matter given by a most eloquent speaker, or the widow, the child overwhelmed with grief, who offer their tears to the Supreme Being for the husband or father that death has taken from them, who implore Him to receive him into His bosom and who mix this religious act with an indefinable hope that they are not separated forever from their objects of affections and regrets [my translation]?⁶⁷

Beliefs, in other words, are indeed propositional attitudes and mental representations, intellectually rational and socio-culturally differentiated. But they are *also* manifestations of a need for God, heartfelt pleas for His assistance and guidance in times of distress and sorrow. The appearance of beliefs in society encompasses all facets of man's experience, both their desire for reason and understanding as well as their existential fear of loss and loneliness. Beliefs, for Bonald, are multiple things at the same time, taking up different functions in relation to specific contexts. Again, we see how the proliferation of belief-meanings enables a sociological reading of society's multifaceted composition.

---

⁶⁶ Ibid., 33–35.
⁶⁷ Ibid., 36–37: "On ne contestera pas sans doute que la foi de sentiment ne soit dans la plupart des hommes, & peut-être dans tous les hommes, bien plus ferme & bien plus profonde que la foi d'opinion. Qui est-ce qui croit le plus, qui est-ce qui croit le mieux aux vérités fondamentales de l'existence de Dieu & de l'immortalité de l'ame, de celui qui a écouté, souvent sans le comprendre, un discours scientifique sur cette matière, par l'orateur le plus disert, ou de la veuve, de l'enfant accablés de douleur, qui offrent leurs larmes à l'Être-Suprême pour l'époux ou le père que la mort leur a ravi, qui le conjurent de le recevoir dans son sein & qui mêlent à cet acte religieux cet espoir indéfinissable qu'ils ne sont pas séparés pour toujours des objets de leurs affections & de leurs regrets ?"

But if a society is to survive, argues Bonald, if it is to remain a collective community founded on shared beliefs and love for one another, this enlightened-propositional sort of understanding of belief, where to believe means to have an opinion and make a judgement on a certain condition of the world, this kind of belief can then only be limited to a very small group of people: theologians, clergy, philosophers. In contrast, sentimental beliefs, what Bonald considers to be instinctive feelings of neighbourly love and a spontaneous faith in a merciful God made necessary by the painful reality of social life, these kinds of belief need to be expressed by every single member of the community.[68] The twin human motivations behind these two kinds of belief, faith and reason, are able to coexist and flourish together, but they are not symmetrical registers nor are they equal partners. They are deeply historicized functions, who each have both their ideal and historical state, with the social philosopher (or later, the social scientist) having the task of bringing these ideal and historical states into a proper form of communication. It is through history, and its accurate interpretation and subsequent narration, that this form of communication can be installed, bringing the natural-historical constitution of religious and political society back into existence. It is through an analysis of society's socio-natural condition and the story of its historical unfolding that the false conflict between philosophy and religion could be resolved, in the eyes of Bonald, lifting both up from their individual status as rationalists and cultists into a shared status as *societal believers*.[69]

NARRATING BELIEF AND NATURAL SOCIETY INTO EXISTENCE: BONALDIAN TECHNIQUES OF SELF-HISTORICIZATION

One of the important shifts occurring in Bonald's work, which makes him an immediate precursor to the later sociologists and which differentiates him from his own enlightened predecessors, was his conjunction of a philosophy of history with a normative account of what a well-functioning

---

[68] Ibid., 37: "La religion ou la foi pratique de l'existence de Dieu & de l'immortalité de l'ame est amour & intelligence; mais si elle doit être amour pour tous, elle ne peut être intelligence que pour une petite nombre."
[69] Ibid., 5: "… *Dans son sein rejetons cette guerre, Que sa fureur envoye aux deux bouts de la terre.* D'autres ont défendu la religion de l'homme; je défends la religion de la société: ils ont prouvé la religion par la religion même; je veux la prouver par l'histoire."

and sustainable society should be.⁷⁰ This was something that Bonald himself alluded to in his introduction to the first volume of the *Théorie du pouvoir politique et religieux*, when he alerted the reader to this transition. He signalled this shift by actively distinguishing his own work from that of the most famous thinker of society in the eighteenth century, Montesquieu (1689–1755). In contrast to the latter, which he first praises for his book *L'Esprit des lois* (1748), Bonald argued that his own book did not just limit itself to "the search for the motive or *spirit* of the things that are", but looked beyond this identification of the spirit of things for "the principles of how things should be".⁷¹ Rather than look at such things as climate as a means of explaining the particular developments of societies, one needed to grasp "the first principles of a society" in order to understand its subsequent development, according to Bonald.⁷² For the French vicomte, it was through the knowledge of these first principles that one could evaluate whether a society was properly governed and if the current states of these societies were actually in the condition they were meant to be.

By this, Bonald did not just aim to give a normative-idealist account of any sort of society, a political-philosophical imagination of what a just and righteous community would look like in theory. Rather, his account of society was rooted in concrete histories and sought to uncover the rational laws and principles guiding and directing human community-formation.⁷³ These could be found, according to Bonald, in history, reason and an accurate ethnographic analysis of social practices and institutions.⁷⁴ Social practices and institutions were then, first and foremost, historical indicators of any given society's degree of proper constitution. Comparing different regimes of belief throughout society's past, Bonald wanted to show "the *necessity* of what man *should* believe".⁷⁵ His work, in other words, had an explicitly prescriptive purpose: if we allow society's subjects and objects

---

⁷⁰ Moreau, "A propos de Louis de Bonald", 144–145.

⁷¹ Bonald, *Théorie du pouvoir politique et religieux*, vol. I, xv.

⁷² Ibid.

⁷³ Ibid., 130: "Je ne dis pas, voilà mon système; car je ne fais pas de système; mais j'ose dire: voilà le système de la nature dans l'organisation des sociétés politiques, tel qu'il résulte de l'histoire de ces sociétés. En effet, c'est l'histoire de l'homme & des sociétés qu'il faut interroger sur la perfection ou l'imperfection des institutions politiques qui ont pour objet le bonheur de l'un & la durée des autres."

⁷⁴ Flavien Bertran de Balanda, "Deux sciences de l'homme. Idéologie et Contre-Révolution dans le débat anthropologique du premier XIXe siècle", *Cahiers de philosophie de l'Université de Caen*, « Lecture de Cabanis au XIXe siècle », 57 (2020): 71–84.

⁷⁵ Bonald, *Théorie du pouvoir politique et religieux*, vol. II, ii.

to *naturally* unfold themselves, through a form of government based on social knowledge, this is what society would necessarily look like.[76] Through his purported discovery of social laws and a natural and unnatural constitution of religious and political societies, Bonald also claimed a sense of performativity for his own writing: what he described was necessarily true, and therefore, occupied a certain space of existence, be it in reality or in dormant potentiality.[77]

This was also the case when Bonald wrote what was, in his eyes at least, the history of believing and its trajectory of fluctuating societal robustness and perfection. The point of such a history was less the virtue of historical understanding for its own sake, than the attempt at reviving societal belief itself to its most perfect state, to bring the ideal composition of a 'believing and practicing society' back into existence through the correct narration of both its historical unfolding and its causes for potential disruption.[78] In other words, the early sociological work of Bonald was mainly an exercise in the theory and application of proper *gouvernement*.[79] By properly understanding what 'belief' is and does within a historical society, one takes a first step, in the eyes of Bonald, to what he considered to be a well-governed society.

To show this, he turned towards his own context and the dominant approach to the category, the Enlightenment understanding of 'belief'. For Bonald, the main value of the enlightened approach to belief was not its analytical nature nor its conceptual clarity. It was not its ability to uncover any sort of truth about social or religious life. Rather, it was its indirect ability to function as a tool for analysing the social disruption and disharmony which had befallen society's relationship with belief.[80] The analytical categorization of the Enlightenment model of belief—i.e. as a propositional form of mental judgement—was then considered by Bonald to be less a kind of universal, ahistorical framework than as a symbol for indicating the contemporary historical state of society.[81] It signalled the existence of a historical event, one where the perfect complementarity of political-rational administration and religious self-government through

---

[76] Ibid., vol. I, 32–47.
[77] Bertran de Balanda, *Louis de Bonald*, 56–57.
[78] Bonald, *Démonstration philosophique*, 389–390n1.
[79] Karsenti, *D'une philosophie à l'autre*, 65.
[80] Bonald, *Théorie du pouvoir politique et religieux*, vol. I, 307–309.
[81] Ibid., 320.

belief had become disturbed, leading to separated existences for the domains of religious belief and political action.[82]

But had this perfectly complementary society ever existed and, if so, how had it gone wrong? According to Bonald, a perfectly constituted society is one where the collective beliefs and the desired action form a sort of indissoluble overlap, where the borders between the two have almost disappeared. It is only when there is an asymmetry between the two that such a disruption becomes apparent, however, as it inevitably produces "unnatural actions": "Indeed, beliefs opposed to reason inevitably produce in a people actions which are opposed to nature [my translation]."[83] The task of the thinker of societies is then to historically locate such a perfect and natural constitution of beliefs and action, which Bonald set himself out to discover.

For Bonald, the history of society and its relation to belief was, like it was for everything else, a matter of perpetual mediation.[84] This history was marked by governments who were always in search of reaching a kind of harmonic equilibrium, the natural conjunction of a rational organization of a society's constituent parts and its precarious source of spiritual energy, the faith that keeps everything running smoothly.[85] As a way of reading this history and determining to what degree a society was actually suffused with belief, Bonald turned to an alternative parameter, namely the willingness of man in a well-constituted, religious society to sacrifice themselves.[86] The French vicomte argued that, because man is a rational animal, there are a number of consistent interests and desires whenever he gives himself to others (i.e. enters into a community), which need to be met in every type of society and which are fuelled by two central urges: love and fear.[87]

---

[82] Ibid., 321.

[83] Bonald, *Démonstration philosophique*, 386: "En effet, des croyances opposées à la raison produisent inévitablement dans un peuple des actions opposées à la nature."

[84] Karsenti, "Autorité, société, pouvoir", 270–278.

[85] Bonald, *Théorie du pouvoir politique et religieux*, vol. II, 323: "Si chaque religion ou secte différente de religion correspond à une forme particulière de gouvernement, il est évident que, dans chaque société, le gouvernement doit faire un secret effort pour établir la religion qui a le plus d'analogie avec ses principes, ou la religion tendre à établir le gouvernement qui lui correspond; parce que la société civile, étant la réunion de la société religieuse & de la société politique, ne peut, ce semble, être tranquille que lorsqu'il règne un parfait équilibre entre les deux parties qui la composent."

[86] Ibid., 213.

[87] Ibid., 216: "L'homme se donnera donc lui-même par amour & crainte; il se donnera lui-même dans toutes les sociétés, soit religieuses, soit politiques, car *ces sociétés sont sem-*

The human mind is directed, according to Bonald, by a love of preservation and a fear of destruction, with the particular balance of these two impulses governing how man will relate to himself as well as to others. For Bonald, there is an intimate connection between faith and sacrifice, as sacrifice demands both a strong faith present in the believer and a willingness to combat rationalist fears of going against one's self-interest.[88]

The proper constitution of a society is then evaluated by Bonald according to the willingness of man to sacrifice himself for others, as well as abdicate his personal belongings to his fellow members of society.[89] This willingness can be measured in both religious and political societies, each according to their own parameters. In a properly constituted religious society, Bonald argues that this gift is aimed at God Himself and is made up by the most precious gift man can give in love and fear, and that is the gift of his own life.[90] In an ideally constituted political society, on the other hand, it is defined by a willingness of man to offer his own property to society, for the love of others.[91] It is only when man is able to reach a satisfactory degree of sacrificial spirit in both religious and political society, with each being governed by the proper religious dogma and the proper form of political administration, that one can speak of a perfectly constituted society.

Such a ready desire for sacrifice of the self and property was, according to Bonald, dependent on the level of 'constitution' achieved by religious and political societies, with the most perfect religious society leading to the most perfect possible 'sacrifice':

> Therefore, the less a religious society will be perfect or constituted, the less perfect the feeling or love will be, the less the action through which the sentiment manifests itself will be perfect, the less the sacrifice will be perfect, so to say, the less the gift of man and that of property will be perfect.
>
> *Therefore, within a religious society most perfectly made or most constituted, the sacrifice will be the most perfect it is possible, that is to say, the society will*

---

blables, & elles ont une constitution semblables."
[88] Ibid., 214.
[89] Ibid.
[90] Ibid.
[91] Ibid., 215.

> *make to the Divinity, in the most perfect manner, the most perfect gift of man and of the purest and most perfect property* [my translation].[92]

A perfectly constituted society, in other words, consists of a whole body which is perfectly interdependent, with each function complementing the other, where beliefs and practices exist in a synchronic manner, without being able to distinguish which one precedes the other. So, in other words, while there exists a philosophical-categorical distinction between beliefs and practices, in a well-constituted society this distinction is practically meaningless. The mistake of the enlightened *philosophes*, in the eyes of Bonald, is to confuse such a categorical instrument for a real-life reality, making them unable to properly understand and interpret the spiritual malaise of the late eighteenth- and early nineteenth-century society.

Bonald gives the example of Joan of Arc, and asks whether it matters if everyone at the court of Charles VII *truly* believed whether the peasant girl was genuinely divinely inspired. This is a question which fascinated eighteenth-century thinkers, stemming from their increased inclination towards a correspondence theory of true beliefs, which sought to evaluate propositional claims according to their rootedness in factual truth.[93] But this, so says Bonald, is besides the question. What truly mattered was not the veracity of Joan of Arc's claims, but the historical synchronicity between her claims and the spiritual state of the community: it was the collective belief which France, *at that specific time*, truly required in order to save itself and come together across both religious and political societies.[94] This was what some like Voltaire, in his critique of the medieval

---

[92] Ibid., 220–221: "Donc, moins la société religieuse sera parfaite ou constituée, moins le sentiment ou l'amour sera parfait, moins l'action par laquelle le sentiment se manifeste, sera parfaite, moins le sacrifice sera parfait, c'est-à-dire, moins le don de l'homme & celui de la propriété seront parfaits. *Donc, dans la société religieuse la plus parfaite faite ou la plus constituée, le sacrifice sera le plus parfait qu'il est possible, c'est-à-dire que la société fera à la Divinité, de la manière la plus parfaite, le don de l'homme le plus parfait & de la propriété la plus pure & la plus parfaite.*"

[93] On this reception, cf. Nora M. Heimann, *Joan of Arc in French Art and Culture (1700–1855): From Satire to Sanctity* (Aldershot: Ashgate, 2005).

[94] Bonald, *Théorie du pouvoir politique et religieux*, vol. I, 554: "Il ne s'agit pas de savoir si toute la cour de Charles VII croyoit que Jeanne d'Arc fût inspirée: l'armée, le peuple, les Anglois eux-mêmes le croyoient, & tous agissent d'après cette persuasion. C'en est assez pour que j'aie pu dire avec vérité, que la religion a sauvé la France. Au reste que la pucelle d'Orléans fût inspirée ou non, elle n'en est pas moins l'héroïne de la nation."

superstition, failed to understand, which is the reality of its influence.[95] Beliefs, in this particular instance, are less a collection of cognitive and ideological convictions on the reality of something, than a call to action, a slight nudge to help us act, in the words of Bossuet, which aid us in overcoming our inhibitions where the fullest extent of our reasonable capabilities does not suffice:

> and when reason concedes the necessity of the God-man's real presence within society, as well as the necessity of mutual sacrifice or the gift of oneself, of man to God and of God to man, it calls faith to its aid against these senses which persist in disregarding the presence of God veiled beneath the elements and appearances, and against the passions which persist in dismissing a restraint that impedes them: the heart says, I believe, and desperate reason recalls those consoling words of M. Bossuet: "saying: I believe, represents more the effort within us towards producing such a grand act, rather than the absolute certainty of having produced it (*Histoire des Variations*) [my translation].[96]

Beliefs, for Bonald, are less a single definable thing, than a spectrum of historical modalities, something which he handily makes use of to juggle his historical narrative of different political and religious constitutions and their unique mediations. In the socio-theological scheme of Bonald, 'to believe' can be both a synonym for a social action (*this same sacrifice, this same belief...*, "ce même sacrifice, cette même croyance..."[97]) as well as something mental and individual, and detached from the chosen form of conduct (*divided perhaps by belief but uniting themselves [...] in order to defend the fundamental truths of the social order*, "divisés peut-être de croyance mais se réunissant [...] à défendre les vérités fondamentales de

---

[95] Ibid., 555.
[96] Bonald, *Théorie du pouvoir politique et religieux*, vol. II, 242: "& lorsque la raison avoue la nécessité de la présence réelle de l'homme-Dieu au milieu de la société, & la nécessité du sacrifice mutuel ou du don du soi-même, de l'homme à Dieu & de Dieu à l'homme, elle appelle la foi à son aide contre les sens qui s'obstinent à méconnoître un Dieu voilé sous des espèces ou des apparences, & contre les passions qui s'obstinent à rejeter un frein qui les importune: le cœur dit, je crois, & la raison éperdue se rappelle ces paroles consolantes de M. Bossuet; « dire: je crois, est plutôt en nous un effort pour produire un si grand acte, qu'une certitude absolue de l'avoir produit (*Histoire des Variations*) »."
[97] Ibid., 240.

l'ordre social").⁹⁸ The only reason this is not some massive contradiction within his work, is because Bonald approached belief not as a singular substance but as a historicized signifier, something which displays and manifests the degree of a society's constituted nature.

Such an instrumental approach to beliefs enabled Bonald to articulate his own vision on the role of religion and politics within society, as if it was dictated by history itself. This vision was embodied by a single principle, manifested in one true belief unable to be touched by the contingencies of time: this is the idea that God is a unity and that the soul is immortal.⁹⁹ All of these social enterprises, these attempted formations of community, could be abstracted, in the eyes of Bonald, into a particular search for a relationship with the ultimate societal respondent, the transcendental God, the One who is a "fair giver of goods and evils, of rewards and punishments", the very power which brings society into existence.¹⁰⁰ To think a social philosophy, was to think beyond individual man, and to look towards the figures which could represent all, the man-King in society, the man-God of Christ in the universe, as communicators with this transcendental power.¹⁰¹ It was through these intermediary figures—who find themselves *in-between* the temporary realm of society and the ahistorical realm of God¹⁰²—that the ministers of society could negotiate the social cohesion of their community, through a self-administered willingness to sacrifice themselves and their property for the sake of others.¹⁰³

Bonald's intermediary approach to community-formation was centred on a number of corporate bodies who supposedly had a 'natural'

---

⁹⁸ Bonald, *Législation primitive*, vol. II, 43.

⁹⁹ Bonald, *Théorie du pouvoir politique et religieux*, vol. I, 50.

¹⁰⁰ Bonald, *Démonstration philosophique*, 110.

¹⁰¹ Ibid., 32–33: "Les écoles de philosophie moderne, matérialiste ou éclectique, ont fait la philosophie de l'homme individuel, du moi, qui joue un si grand rôle dans leurs écrits; j'ai voulu faire la philosophie de l'homme social, la philosophie du nous, si je peux ainsi parler, et ces deux pronoms, moi et nous, distinguent parfaitement les deux manières différentes de philosopher."

¹⁰² Bonald, *Législation primitive*, vol. II, 42: "le ministre, semblable au rayon qui joint le centre à chaque point de la circonférence, placé entre le pouvoir et le sujet, pour lier la volonté de l'un à l'obéissance de l'autre. Telles sont les lois générales de toute société, et les harmonies du monde moral."

¹⁰³ Bonald, *Démonstration philosophique*, 108: "Le sacrifice est le don de soi que le ministre fait au pouvoir, au nom et dans l'intérêt des sujets, et par lequel il offre la société tout entière, en offrant l'homme et la propriété, qui composent toute la société."

disposition towards a selfless lifestyle, such as the nobility and the regular clergy, who had received this disposition both through structural and historical factors. When such groups were allowed to flourish within society, it had the effect of creating suitable conditions for social trust and belief to flourish throughout the religious and political societies as well.[104] At the same time, this meant that Bonald approached belief as something that could be won and lost to society.

This was exemplified by the contemporary crisis experienced in the early nineteenth century through rampant individualism and 'functionless' poverty.[105] In the face of such a crisis, the synchronicity between belief and social action could only be recuperated through the simple means of speaking and interacting within the community in order for these propositions to once again turn into articles of faith (something which was seen and believed) and which could incite collective action. This is effectively what social laws *were*, according to Bonald, with societies eventually becoming aware, historically, of certain rationalistic principles and which were subsequently internalized as customs, principles, laws and beliefs:

> Everything is *true* in the principles, everything is *real* in the people. Laws aren't *written in the depths of men's hearts*, as claimed by the sophists, because man could ignore or deny them; they are not uniquely bound to tradition, because man could forget them: but once revealed to man through the word, this unique instrument so necessary to all forms of moral knowledge, they are fixated by the writings of nations, and they become as such a universal, public, invariable, external rule; a *law* which, at no point in time nor in any place, can be ignored, forgotten, suppressed, altered, ... [my translation].[106]

---

[104] Ibid., 108–110.

[105] For Bonald's analysis of this degeneration, cf. his article "Sur la mendicité" in: Bonald, *Démonstration philosophique*, 335–349.

[106] Bonald, *Législation primitive*, vol. II, 42–43: "Tout y est *vrai* dans les principes, tout y est *réel* dans les personnes. Les lois n'y sont pas *écrites au fond du coeur des hommes*, comme le veulent les sophistes, car l'homme pourrait les méconnaître ou les nier; elles ne sont pas uniquement confiées à la tradition, car l'homme pourrait les oublier: mais une fois révélées à l'homme par la parole, moyen unique et nécessaire de toutes ses connaissances morales, elles sont fixées par l'écriture pour les nations, et elles deviennent ainsi une règle universelle, publique, invariable, extérieure; une *loi* qu'en aucun temps et en aucun lieu personne ne peut ignorer, oublier, dissimuler, altérer...".

Bonald then saw it as his task to narrate what a perfectly constituted society looked like and how it unfolded, with the purpose of once again revealing and speaking these truths of the social and thus inspiring his fellow members of civil society into more desirable behaviour, as a reborn moral collective.

Unsurprisingly perhaps, this ideal composition was historically to be found, according to Bonald, in Catholic dogma and a monarchical-aristocratic government. Catholic dogma's history is portrayed by Bonald as one of increasing perfectibility, the end result of a complex diachronic process where human society was seeking to find its natural constitution. Whereas Judaism was able to found a monotheistic religion and Egyptian culture was able to construct a perfect form of administrative government, both were still lacking, with the Jewish people not having a sound system of politics and the Egyptians not finding a suitable system of religious devotion.[107] It was only with the birth of Christianity, said the French social theorist, that both of these—a monarchical system of government and a cult of monotheism—were able to be combined in a natural and harmonious order.[108]

This was a perfection not simply imposed from above, argued Bonald, but one which grew and developed historically, in accordance with the social and geographical conditions, into a marriage of human nature, philosophical reason and the social laws of society, each one complementing the other in a trinitarian embrace of self-perfection.[109] The societal principle of conservation was able to be entrenched at the Council of Nicaea in 325 CE, making Christian dogma as "that which man must believe and act upon".[110] The historical victory of Christianity as a religious and political system, both as an internally rational constitution as well as an ideology which was carried and defended by its martyrs against a hostile Roman government, was won through its codification. In this way, its originally transient status as a body of peoples and beliefs was transformed into a physical and structural entity, symbolized by its Nicaean dogma and the object of the Holy Cross: "she will sport her sacred standard upon the

---

[107] Bonald, *Théorie du pouvoir politique et religieux*, vol. II, 59–60.
[108] Ibid., 63.
[109] Ibid., 64.
[110] Bonald, *Législation primitive*, vol. II, 104.

ruins of paganism, this sign *that she had to conquer*, and before which all the kings of the world must one day bow down to."[111]

The earthly victory of Christianity was, then, simultaneously contingent and necessary, according to Bonald, as both the temporal and the sacred timelines coincided in this particular worldly event, echoing the typical narrative structure in Christianity of the Incarnation.[112] With the codification of the Nicaean dogma, Christian belief turned into a universal law, and yet, this in itself did not make it historically binding as the current predicament of a non-constituted modernity made apparent to Bonald. So how did it, temporarily, go wrong? Throughout his work, Bonald provides a long list of contributing factors: the destabilization of the family unit, the rampant growth of capitalism, the appearance of migratory social groups, both religious (mendicants) and militarily (mercenary armies), the increasing division of labour, unbalanced migration to urban areas, infidelity and divorce becoming more common and so on.[113]

What all of these things had in common, however, was their de-territorialized nature, individuals and groups which were no longer bound to anything, had no relation to property and, as such, were unable to become part of collective bodies rooted in law, nature and history.[114] While some of these factors were simply caused by social and demographic transitions, others were the result of philosophical misgivings, such as those of the so-called early modern libertines, the sceptics and atheists who advocated for a complete freedom of thought and action.[115] Such a split between the domains of thought and one's particular place within the social body also created the aforementioned rupture between belief and action which had become rampant within the Enlightenment knowledge culture, meaning that both the former and the latter lost their rootedness

---

[111] Ibid.: "elle arborera sur les ruines du paganisme son étendard sacré, ce signe dans *lequel elle devait vaincre*, et devant qui tous les rois de la terre devaient un jour se prosterner."

[112] Boureau, *L'événement sans fin*, 20.

[113] Bonald, *Législation primitive*, vol. II, *passim*.

[114] Ibid., 151.

[115] On the *libertins érudit*, cf. Jean-Pierre Cavaillé, "Libertinage, irréligion, incroyance, athéisme dans l'Europe de la première modernité (xvie-xviie siècles). Une approche critique des tendances actuelles de la recherche (1998–2002)", *Les Dossiers du Grihl* [En ligne], 1–2 | 2007, last consulted on the 27th of October 2022. URL: http://journals.openedition.org/dossiersgrihl/279.

and their very purpose, ultimately leading to a "corruption of mores, [and] a weakening of the laws".[116]

It is at this point that the task of the social scientist comes to the fore once again, which Bonald saw in the recognition and condemnation of such disruptive splits as those made by the libertines, which broke up the Christian singularity of dogmatic belief and well-regulated social action.[117] As the societal qualms would necessarily sort themselves out on a cosmological-theological scale, according to Bonald—the victory of Christianity being historically and ontologically necessary—the social scientist could, however, also aid in this reparation of the religious and political constitution, by acting as a mediating vessel helping towards the goal of proper societal self-government through communication and education.

Elsewhere, Bonald gives another concrete example of the corrosive effects of de-territorialization when he discusses the historical evolution of the role of the priest in society, as an example of a ministerial figure who had gradually become less and less efficient in the government of the religious body. But why had this happened? By analysing the social and historical conditions of priestly life, Bonald argued that he was able to pinpoint the reason for this: as urban settlements began to proliferate, they began to build their own churches and rectories.[118] Priests then started moving to these new settlements, joining the secular living communities instead of remaining within the original structure of priestly life, where they lived in a closed community with fellow priests supervised by a superior.[119] As a result, the strength of their religious government began to wane, forms of moral corruption, among both priests and populace, increased, and social isolation became a fundamental problem.

It was as a result of different types of historical contingencies—the invasions of the Vikings, the Crusades, the wars of kings against their vassals, the weakness of administrations, the proliferation of donations—that

---

[116] Bonald, *Législation primitive*, vol. II, 221: "La licence de penser et d'agir, parée de tous les attraits du bel esprit, et quelquefois des dehors de la vertu, d'intelligence avec les passions, pénétrait au sein de la société domestique, y corrompait les moeurs, en affaiblissait les lois, et l'attaque à force ouverte que cette audacieuse philosophie méditait contre la société publique, n'était retardée que par gouvernements la force d'inertie de partout imprévoyants, et qui s'endormaient au bord des abîmes."

[117] Ibid., 224–227.

[118] Ibid., 113.

[119] Ibid., 113–114.

"confusions" had been able to arise: the clergy suddenly having responsibilities and property relations which went against the very spirit of their duties, which was to sacrifice and fully dedicate themselves to God and their flock in a collective fashion.[120] Instead, they found themselves increasingly drawn away from their communities. To Bonald, it was not so much that individualism was an evil in itself: other social actors, like the nobleman, thrived in their more remote form of existence, as it allowed them a calm life which helped them in the performance of their governmental duties.[121] The problems arose when different modes of existence became confused and mixed, when the priest and nobleman were made to live in conditions which went against the spirit of their original constitution.[122]

The solution, according to Bonald, was straightforward: the natural order of the living conditions needed to be restored and the first principles which constituted these social functions needed to be respected and preserved. The class of priests were to be brought together, once again, in shared living quarters through the aggrandizement of parishes, and the people would journey to them for sermons, transforming every church visit into a pilgrimage, and thus making it the more heartfelt experience it originally was in earlier times.[123] As such, the menace of social isolation—of both the priests as well as the believers—would be combatted, and proper religious constitution would be restored, as the ritual of devotion would once again be made up by the joined performance of religious belief and social community at the place of worship, *as it was meant to be*.[124] While such reforms (i.e. a return to the ancient form of religious discipline) would not be beneficial for the individual quality of life, it would lead to societal benefits, according to Bonald, thus making it a sacrifice worth making for the greater good of the community.[125]

It was through the natural-historical composition of faith, property and social laws that men, families, and professions could be *made into* collective bodies, with such a corporatist spirit essential in the fabrication of a

[120] Ibid., 115.
[121] Ibid., 112.
[122] Ibid., 116–117.
[123] Ibid., 162.
[124] Ibid., 163.
[125] Ibid., 164.

sense of solidarity akin to the organic economy organizing the Holy Trinity itself.[126] Faith, if it were to have any social meaning for Bonald, was not something that could be dependent on just an individual 'who believes', however authentic such a belief could be. Faith required an institution, something which could harness all these individual 'beliefs', with the function of the social scientist being to police them into uniformity and to protect them from internal confusion.[127] What was needed, according to Bonald, was a return to the institutions of the Church, the nobility, and the family, a return to religion itself as the basis of social life, since only the relation between God and man could exercise the authority to bring about both social and spiritual harmony.[128]

His narrative techniques of self-historicization played a crucial role in trying to bring about this vision of what religious and political societies needed to look like. It provided his own interventions, as a social mediator, with a sense of legitimacy, as he had the task of stepping outside of both history and the several societies, and detecting the 'unnatural' elements which had brought about the corruption of belief and moral behaviour. Furthermore, by creatively engaging with the multiple historical meanings of belief (individual/collective; enlightened/religious; social/intellectual), Bonald constructed a dynamic historical scheme where societies reached different levels of synchronicity between belief and social action. His was not just another Christian narrative of divine Incarnation. Rather, he tried to bring this tradition together with the Enlightenment tradition of ethnographic analyses of belief, to find a new synthesis, one which could accommodate the different meanings of belief as well as the current crisis of faith and social cohesion experienced by French civil society in the early nineteenth century into a single story.

---

[126] Bonald, *Théorie du pouvoir politique et religieux*, vol. III. On the importance of the triadic structure of the Holy Trinity for Bonald's vision of society, cf. Jacques Alibert, *Les triangles d'or d'une société catholique. Louis de Bonald théoricien de la Contre-Révolution* (Paris: Téqui, 2002). For a more critical note on Bonald's appropriation of a social corporatism and his omission of its more historical, bottom-up solidarity-mechanisms, cf. W. Jay Reedy, "The Traditionalist Critique of Individualism in Post-Revolutionary France: The Case of Louis de Bonald", *History of Political Thought* 16, no. 1 (1995): 65–66.

[127] Bonald, *Démonstration philosophique*, 135.

[128] Bonald, *Démonstration philosophique*, 422.

Conclusion

The social-theoretical work of the French reactionary vicomte, Louis de Bonald, left its marks on the development of sociology throughout the nineteenth century, despite its polemic, religious and, at times, vehemently anti-modernist tone. In the work of Comte and Durkheim, it resurfaces via such notions as the "Religion of Humanity" and "organic solidarity", echoing Bonald's understanding of the social body as a totality which is structurally defined by the interdependence of its different parts. But this considerable influence on the development of social science was not limited to mere conceptual tools. It also signalled the beginning of a sociological engagement with historical languages of belief which was able to lend itself to the formation of a new kind of philosophy and mode of existence.[129] Bonald, as both a philosopher and devout Catholic, found himself occupying a middle ground between these two different cultures and embarked on a project attempting to mediate a renewed bond, not merely bringing the two cultures of reason and Christianity together as individual traditions but seeking to have them undergo a shared transformation into a unified body of societal believers.

Bonald's sociological project was then both an analytical-epistemological undertaking as well as a historical-existential one, a discursive intervention in both the history of knowledge and the history of self-government. A crucial instrument in this process of attempted fusion was the category of belief, which had been employed by both traditions in their distinct manners. Finding himself in the chaotic remnants of an Enlightenment intellectual culture, where belief became both an individual propositional attitude and an ethnographic descriptor for differentiating cultures, Bonald played a complex game with the category. Instead of prioritizing either its enlightened-philosophical or Catholic meaning, the French philosopher employed it as an empty signifier, selectively using it in its different meanings—enlightened, ritualistic, Catholic, social—in his attempt to build a performative narrative. This was a historicized, socio-theological narrative of corporatist bodies—such as the nobility, the priesthood, the monks, the ministers—which gradually perfected themselves as society developed through their combination of natural beliefs and social action into a perfect and singular union. It was an attempt at transforming both

---

[129] Karsenti, *D'une philosophie à l'autre*, 57–90.

an Enlightenment culture of individualism and excessive reason as well as a fragmenting Christianity into a novel and vibrant synthesis.

It was the category of belief and its variety of historical meanings which allowed Bonald to mediate the histories of philosophy and religion, attempting to bring both into narrative communication. To believe meant many different things, historically differentiated and complex; but to love, to sacrifice, to come together, meant just one thing, according to Bonald, to commit oneself to divine revelation. This single truth was something Bonald aimed to convey by piercing through the many different registers which were beginning to accumulate in both enlightened-philosophical and religious-theological systems. As an ailment to this condition of increasing differentiation, what needed to be reached was the social fact, that which truly moved society and its actors into a harmonious, cohesive whole. By writing, exploring and articulating a Christian-philosophical science of the social, the natural constitution of societies could once again be reached and installed through proper regimes of self-government.

While it is understandable that the later sociological tradition has clearly indicated its distance from a thinker like Bonald—not in the least because of his anti-liberal attitudes towards women and others who did not strictly adhere to the ideal of the Catholic family structure—this should not blind us from the importance of Bonald's contribution to the formation of the sociological operation. What Bonald was able to do in his narrative articulations on society was the operationalization of the gap between distinct discourses of enlightened reason and those of religious collective self-sacrifice, using the complexity of the category of belief—its individual as well as social nature, its dialectical oppositions with practice and rationality, its multiple meanings across religious, cultural and intellectual domains—as a means of constructing his own unique intervention and positioning.

Bonald—using belief to conceptualize corporatist bodies and institutions as hybrid combinations of beliefs and action—displayed one technique of operationalizing this gap; others would do so in their own manner as well. The multiple historical languages of belief provided a means of imagining a discourse on society beyond enlightened philosophy and institutional religion. Furthermore, it allowed Bonald to carve out a place and a responsibility for what he considered to be the social scientist: it was the latter's responsibility to analyse the different social conditions of believing, and his moral and societal duty to preserve these perfect conditions as well as their respective domains from confusion and contamination by illicit historical migrations and transfers. The social scientist, in the eyes of Bonald, was first and foremost a guardian, a gatekeeper who would seek to preserve the different constitutions of each society (religious, political, …) in their most perfect and harmonious state. The conservation of belief as a singular doctrine—faith in the unity of God and the immortality of the soul—was perceived as a central task for safeguarding communal life and stimulating energies of social cohesion and solidarity.

But this productive relation with historical languages of belief also bound that which would later become sociology, in a sense, to its religious other, with all its benefits as well as its considerable limits. The contextual particularity which created this discursive opportunity—the experience of limitations to both rational individualism and religious collectivism—gradually disappeared in the sociological tradition. But as I will show in later chapters, the mechanisms of this formal structure employed by Bonald as a means to navigate the two domains kept on persisting.

CHAPTER 6

Early Experiments in the Sociological Operation III. The Socialist Sociologisms of Saint-Simon and the Saint-Simonists

Introduction

The seventeenth and eighteenth centuries saw the birth of what Ethan Shagan has termed 'modern belief', the newly found hegemony of a regime of belief which understands this notion as the field of sovereign judgement.[1] At the same time, the proliferation of the category's meanings transformed it into a creative conceptual field as well, one where the different understandings of the term could assist theorists and philosophers in constructing novel imaginations of such fields as religion, politics and science.[2] The birth of modern belief, in other words, transformed the concept into a space of contestation, one which would be profoundly exploited in the social, religious and intellectual crisis which unfolded after the French Revolution.[3]

This was, essentially, what the French counter-revolutionary and philosopher Louis de Bonald had envisioned as an explicit goal of his own writings on society: he employed the plurality of belief-meanings to make

---

[1] Shagan, *The Birth of Modern Belief*, 207–249.
[2] Ibid., 268–276.
[3] Guillaume Cuchet, *Une histoire du sentiment religieux au XIXe siècle. Religion, culture et société en France, 1830–1880* (Paris: Les Éditions du Cerf, 2020).

the distinction between happy and unhappy conditions of belief, erecting a historical narrative of belief's perfectibility in Christian-monarchical society and its subsequent disruption. It shouldn't come as any particular surprise, however, that a convinced Catholic like Louis de Bonald would be invested in something like the preservation of our social capacity to believe. His desire to redirect some of its historical meanings towards a broader collective project which could integrate both religious and secular self-interests was a goal which enticed many of his fellow Catholic reactionaries as well. But it would be misguided to presume that such engagement with historical languages of belief as an instrument for the imagination of the social domain would be limited to the Catholic context. Many other, non-Catholic programs existed as well, where historical languages of belief were engaged with as a way of thinking both the place of the social scientist and their relation to the religious domain.

In this chapter, I will turn to such a non-religious context, namely the group of the Saint-Simonists and their engagement with the notion of belief as a lever to imagine sociological interventions. As I will argue throughout this chapter, this engagement represented less of a clear-cut program of preserving society's ability to believe, as it was for Bonald, than as an instrument to discover what it meant to think socially and cultivate a truly sociological mode of existence. The category of belief represented, for the Saint-Simonists, a narrative instrument of conversion and transformation towards becoming a person who could fully embrace the paradoxical and multifaceted nature of social life. Again, the semiotic flexibility and historicity of 'belief' played a crucial role in this regard. For the Saint-Simonists, while their approach of the category first started out as a typical enlightened understanding of 'beliefs'—as a kind of raw mental material, distinct from knowledge, through which cultures and populations could be known and subsequently governed—they eventually added other meanings to this category, as they came to experience the intellectual complexity of social groups and their different cultural layers. It was the elasticity of belief as a concept, so I argue, which allowed the Saint-Simonists to inhabit this space between a highly theoretical philosophy of historical progress and a lived experience of eclectic proletarian practices of meaning and spirituality.

Saint-Simon: Between Sociology, Socialism and Religion

Before we can look at how this transformational process unfolded among the Saint-Simonists, we must start with the figure whose name came to represent an entire movement, Claude-Henri de Saint-Simon. Born into a noble but poor family during the second half of the eighteenth century, Saint-Simon lived a tumultuous life, its eventful character strongly mirroring the state of French civil society around the birth of the modern period. A gifted and headstrong young man, Saint-Simon tried his hand at several ventures typically associated with the noble gentleman, first partaking in the American Revolutionary War as a French military officer while later turning his attention to the business opportunities made possible by the French Revolution, selling national property in association with a Prussian diplomat.[4] He would eventually settle for a life of scholarship and patronage, using his modest means to both educate himself in the technical and medical sciences, and, where possible, financially support promising young minds in furthering their scientific endeavours.[5] The limited nature of his own funds, however, meant that this generous spending ultimately led to his later life being marked by consistent poverty, with the former nobleman himself becoming dependent on charity in order for him to be able to write his own socio-scientific pamphlets and books.[6] In the final years of his life, he would be supported by a small band of loyal disciples until his death in 1825, after which these disciples would dedicate themselves to making the work of Saint-Simon known across the world.[7]

The socio-philosophical work of Saint-Simon itself takes up an ambiguous place in the history of sociology: on the one hand heralded for his early and original vision of a rationalistic social science and put forward by Émile Durkheim as a more formative influence to the discipline than his one-time assistant, Auguste Comte, he also carries with him, on the other hand, a more controversial legacy, as the founder of a socialist cult which explicitly represented itself as theocratic and dogmatic, and which was

---

[4] Pickering, *Auguste Comte*, 60–61.
[5] Emile Durkheim, *Socialism and Saint Simon*, ed. Alvin W. Gouldner, transl. by Charlotte Sattler (London: Routledge & Kegan Paul Ltd, 2009), 54.
[6] Ibid.
[7] Pamela M. Pilbeam, *Saint-Simonians in Nineteenth-Century France: From Free Love to Algeria* (Basingstoke: Palgrave Macmillan, 2014).

later disbanded and outlawed by the French government in 1832.[8] This complex heritage has meant that the life and work of Saint-Simon has been perceived to have not one, but multiple points of impact on the history of social sciences: not only its general, epistemological development as a science, but also its status as a discourse for conceptualizing religion, the discipline's early contextual engagement with religious history, and its role as an intellectual source for socialist ideology.[9]

In this, he closely resembles his contemporaries, Louis de Bonald and Auguste Comte, with whom he is often grouped as a class of early sociologists who were simultaneously concerned with the development of a social *science* and with the historical transition from a Christian-religious civil body towards a more modern, scientific-industrial society.[10] While this grouping is categorically legitimate—as I am discussing them all in these chapters as well—I argue that it would be a mistake to classify their interventions as all being of the same kind. For while they shared a similar entry point for thinking society—the problem of shared belief and its historical moment of crisis—their answer to this problem differed not only substantially, but formally as well. By this, I mean that the particular historical value of these different social theorists in the construction of the sociological operation was formally distinct: while someone like Bonald employed the languages of belief as a tool for thinking Christianity and enlightened philosophy in a single, comparative framework, Saint-Simon, and his followers the Saint-Simonists in particular, engaged with this category as a means of interpreting social action and as an instrument for concretely navigating social life.[11] Bonald and the Saint-Simonists did not just have

---

[8] On the totalitarian roots of the Saint-Simonist dogma, cf. Georg G. Iggers, *The Cult of Authority: The Political Philosophy of the Saint-Simonians* (The Hague: Martinus Nijhoff, 1970 [1st. ed., 1958]).

[9] Florence Hulak, "Sociologie et théorie socialiste de l'histoire. La trame saint-simonienne chez Durkheim et Marx", *Incidence. Revue de philosophie, littérature, sciences humaines et sociales 11* (2015): 83–106; Strube, "Socialist religion and the emergence of occultism", 364–66; Philippe Regnier, "Entre politique et mystique, sécularisation et resacralisation. Pour une nouvelle approche de la religion saint-simonienne", *Archives de sciences sociales des religions* 190, no. 3 (2020): 87–108.

[10] Keith Michael Baker, "Closing the French Revolution: Saint-Simon and Comte", in: *The Transformation of Political Culture 1789–1848*, edited by François Furet and Mona Ozouf. (Oxford: Pergamon, 1989), 323–39; Macherey, "Aux sources des rapports sociaux", 25–43 Reedy, "The historical imaginary of social science", 1–26.

[11] Cf. infra.

different *ideas* about society and its particular constitution. They also differed in how their imagination of the sociologist and social science related to their concrete duties and actions in the social domain itself. And my argument here is that it is this formal differentiation which has up to this point been insufficiently emphasized and reflected upon.

This nuanced but important difference goes some way in explaining the persistent issues scholars are having in recognizing the unique composition of the Saint-Simonist narratives of belief and its designs of a social-scientific program, the uniqueness of which resides, so I argue, rather in their attempted collapse of sociological theory and practice into a singular mode more so than in their particular usage of a Christian-inspired terminology, a trait it shared with most of the social thinkers of the time.[12] The lack of a sensibility towards the formal dimension can be seen as a direct result of how the sociological canon is conventionally given shape. The typical understanding of sociology's canonization—as a group of social theorists who had different ideas and theories on the historical-structural workings of social reality and the methods required for studying such a reality—has made it more difficult to ascertain formal distinctions, as early sociologists were differentiated according to the originality and accuracy of their particular models of society. This was clearly the case for someone like Durkheim, whose reading of Saint-Simon centres around his philosophical-theoretical 'invention' of positivist philosophy and positivist social science. And it is this primordiality, this having of a philosophical thought *before* Comte, which guarantees his historical worth, which is his fundamental contribution to the development of sociology:

> *Saint-Simon was the first* who resolutely freed himself from these prejudices. Although he may have had precursors, never had it been so clearly asserted that man and society could not be directed in their conduct unless one began by making them objects of science, and further that this science could not rest on any other principles than do the sciences of nature. And this new science – he not only laid out its design but attempted to realize it in part. We can see here all that August Comte, and consequently all that the thinkers of the nineteenth century, owe him. In him we encounter the seeds already developed *of all the ideas which have fed the thinking of our time*. We

---

[12] Iogna-Prat & Rauwel, "Introduction", 17. On this Christian-inspired terminology, cf. Julien Pasteur, *Les héritiers contrariés. Essai sur le spirituel républicain au XIXe siècle* (Paris: Les Belles Lettres, 2018).

have just found in it positivist philosophy, positivist sociology. We will see that we will also find socialism in it [my italics].[13]

In other words, Saint-Simon's entry into the sociological canon was a result of his ability to extract himself from his peers through intellectual means, an original thinker who advanced the progress of the discipline through the powers of his exceptional mind.

While such an authorial vision of intellectual history is by no means uncommon, there is an obvious source of tension there for a thinker like Saint-Simon, who not only continuously emphasized the network-like structures of social-intellectual formation, but who also inspired a very dynamic and vibrant sociological language, which was picked up by a whole host of original Saint-Simonist thinkers, like Prosper Enfantin, Saint-Amand Bazard, Olinde and Eugene Rodrigues, Jean Reynaud, Émile Barrault and Michel Chevalier.[14] For this reason, scholars like Stefania Ferrando have increasingly begun to blur the lines between Saint-Simon, the author and Saint-Simon, the symbol of a particular sociological language, and have started to instead focus more on the different techniques, practices and compositions which were being made inside of a collective Saint-Simonist framework, in order to better articulate its true originality.[15]

From this perspective, it also becomes more apparent that the move away from the singular author towards the discursive enterprise does not equate to a transition from a social-scientific to a political-ideological perspective.[16] Not only were these Saint-Simonists serious thinkers and proper scientists in their own right, their organization into a school, language, and applied method of the Saint-Simonist doctrine were important steps in the historical development of sociology as well, as the Saint-Simonists' practices within the social domain added a more descriptive, empirical and

---

[13] Durkheim, *Socialism and Saint Simon*, 67.

[14] Pierre Musso, *La religion industrielle. Monastère, manufacture, usine. Une généalogie de l'entreprise* (Paris: Fayard, 2017).

[15] Stefania Ferrando, "Le 'détournement' de la révolution. Continuité historique et conflit social chez Saint-Simon", *Archives de Philosophie* 80, no. 1 (2017): 33–54.

[16] For a counter-argument to this, which does make the opposition between a more positivist-scientific project of Saint-Simon and its ideological and religious politicization by his school, cf. Picon, "La religion Saint-Simonienne", 23–37.

socially active dimension to the discipline's imaginary.[17] And as I will try to argue here, it is in this transition, and its formal differentiation from Bonaldian and Comtean modes of sociological self-conceptualization, that we can gain further insight into the particular importance of Saint-Simonism within the history of the social sciences and its different engagements with historical languages of belief.

A Case of *mentir-vrai*? Historiographical Interpretations of the Saint-Simonists and Belief

Whenever the topic of 'belief' arises in the discussion of Saint-Simon and Saint-Simonism by sociologists and historians, this generally takes the form of a single question: "Did the Saint-Simonists genuinely *believe* in that peculiar religious movement that they had created, with all of its symbolism, rituals and miracles?"[18] And it isn't hard to understand why this question would fascinate later commentators on the movement, as their socialist explorations of spirituality, especially in the final era of the Saint-Simonist collective (1830–32), stood in stark contrast to their foundational values of possessing a rigidly scientific worldview, of cultivating a rational-utilitarian model of social life and of being highly critical towards irrational and superstitious practices, values which had been especially prominent in the work of Saint-Simon himself.[19]

The question of Saint-Simonist belief in their own religious message of social evangelization wasn't, for historians like Philippe Regnier and Antoine Picon, so much a yes-or-no question, as it was a call for a thorough contextualization, one which could further explain this eclectic status of Saint-Simonism as a rationalist *and* mystical movement.[20] As a result, historians like Regnier and Picon have pointed out several facets of Saint-Simonism as areas of further research in order to properly approach

---

[17] Philippe Regnier, "Du Saint-Simonisme comme science et des Saint-Simoniens comme scientifiques: généralités, panorama et repères", *Bulletin de la Sabix* 44 (2009), last consulted on the 13th of December 2022, http://journals.openedition.org/sabix/626.

[18] Picon, "La religion Saint-Simonienne", 24.

[19] Musso, "Religion and Political Economy", 811; Michel Bellet, "On the Utilitarian Roots of Saint-Simonism: From Bentham to Saint-Simon", *History of Economic Ideas* 17, no. 2 (2009): 41–63.

[20] Philippe Regnier, "Entre politique et mystique, sécularisation et resacralisation. Pour une nouvelle approche de la religion saint-simonienne", *Archives de sciences sociales des religions* 190, no. 3 (2020): 87–88.

the movement's role within the history of nineteenth-century religion: its evolution across time, going from the early work of Saint-Simon to his later focus on religion to its eventual reception among his followers; how this Saint-Simonist doctrine was effectively practised, both by those within the leadership group as well as those more loosely associated with the movement, such as the many bourgeois sympathizers who provided the group with final support; and how these Saint-Simonist gospels were received among those proselytized to, the labourers and the city folk who were searching for ways of improving their dire causes, either monetarily or spiritually.[21]

From such a contextualist point of view, the question of belief transforms into a matter of motive and background. Why did Prosper Enfantin, the de facto leader of the Saint-Simonist group during their late, religious phase, place such an emphasis on the poetic, the spiritual, the mystic in his reflections on social life and the purpose of the Saint-Simonist cult? For someone like Regnier, this can mostly be explained by Enfantin's character and desire, which was the character of an industrial engineer who sought the most efficient ways to communicate with the proletarian masses and to lead them towards their shared goals of a society-wide social emancipation. The language of miracles, hope and love were, in this instance, the most effective tools for aligning the workers with the Saint-Simonists.[22] This did not make the Saint-Simonist faith something false or illusionary, according to Regnier, who employed the term *mentir-vrai* as a way of capturing the movement's nuanced attitude towards its faith. It simply indicated a realist disposition among the leaders of the Saint-Simonist group, who wanted, above all else, to implement concrete social reform.[23]

Such a contextualist approach to the question of belief among the Saint-Simonists opens up the possibility of further integrating such socialist-utopian groups more thoroughly within the history of nineteenth-century religious and spiritual movements, which is something that historians like Guillaume Cuchet, Dominique Iogna-Prat, and Alain Rauwel have recently begun to do.[24] But one thing which still proves to be a hard

---

[21] Ibid., 87–108; Picon, "La religion Saint-Simonienne", 34–37.
[22] Ibid., 103–104.
[23] Ibid., 104.
[24] Cf. the theme issue directed by Dominique Iogna-Prat and Alain Rauwel for the journal *Archives de sciences sociales des religions* (vol. 190, no. 3) in 2020, titled 'Autour de Comte et Saint-Simon: Reconfigurations socio-religieuses post-révolutionnaires', or Cuchet's *Une histoire du sentiment religieux au XIXe siècle. Religion, culture et société en France, 1830–1880*.

task for most is to reflect on how this religious project of the Saint-Simonists was actually tied to their vision and imagination of a social science, the two often remaining fully separated as distinct projects of the early nineteenth-century social reformists. And yet, it is with regard to this relation that the question of belief among the Saint-Simonists reaches another level of importance, I would argue, as this matter of belief as a historical practice among this movement brings these two domains into communication. This was apparent to Saint-Simon and the Saint-Simonists themselves as well: throughout their writings, they engage with, reflect on and conceptualize what believing actually meant, both for themselves and for others, those who were in need of direction by the Saint-Simonist doctrine.

In this chapter then, I will turn to a discussion of how 'belief'—as a category, as a signifier of distinct historical languages—manifested itself within Saint-Simonist thought and action, how it was broached by these reformists and also how it, as a result, reversely impacted the Saint-Simonists as well, the historicity of the category itself partly dictating the ways it could be employed and manipulated. I will argue that these Saint-Simonist language games in interaction with the belief-category generated an innovative and original spirit within the movement, laying bare a number of facets which would come to be indicative of later social science and its reflections on the relationships between theory and practice.

A Saint-Simonist Philosophy of the Present: Modernity and the Arrival of the Cartesian Regime of Belief

The Saint-Simonist engagement with belief as a means of imagining both social life and its ideal form of (scientific) analysis was intellectually far-reaching. As I will argue in the next three sections, it allowed them to articulate an original philosophy of modernity, a program of class politics and a new, experiential kind of knowledge of society. Moreover, these were innovative readings of what believing meant and could mean, and provided novel arguments for what a social science could look like.

As such, the Saint-Simonists constructed a direct challenge to the early sociological program developed by the Catholic-reactionary school in the wake of the French Revolution, so forcefully put into words by the French vicomte Louis de Bonald. This intellectual contest between the two social theorists was not just one that was retroactively imagined by those twentieth-century sociologists like Robert Nisbet seeking to construct a disciplinary canon. Saint-Simon himself positioned his own interpretation of the history of religion—and its relation to the birth of a new social science—directly against that of the reactionary school, represented in his eyes by both Bonald and Chateaubriand, the latter complementing the former's rationalist interventions through, what Saint-Simon termed, his considerable literary talent.[25] Saint-Simon performs this positioning in a short entry in the second volume of the *Introduction aux travaux scientifiques du dix-neuvième siècle* (1808), "Sur la religion", in which he summarizes his own philosophical analysis of the current situation in France in a clear and succinct fashion.[26] While Saint-Simon effusively praised the work of the French vicomte—his writings described as being "full of life" and as "fit to rejuvenate science and literature"—he was accused of being guilty of a capital error: Bonald had been mistaken on the unitary principle which fundamentally guides social forces.[27]

A central component to this critique was Bonald's historical evaluation of Christian belief and its role in present-day nineteenth-century France. According to Saint-Simon, it was historically unconvincing to convey the unitary spirit of society to deism, Bonald's argument that it was Christian dogmatism, i.e. the belief in an immortal God, which could guarantee a society that was unified, active and altruistic.[28] Rather, Saint-Simon put forward an alternative series of arguments: the current predicament befalling society could not be explained by its abandonment of Christian dogma, but should be explained by society's present inability to develop a new religion which properly coincided with the concrete beliefs prevalent within French civil society around the start of the 1800s.[29] The Catholic religion, in its form at the beginning of the nineteenth century, was nothing more than a mere material shell: whatever force it still possessed, this

---

[25] Claude-Henri de Saint-Simon, "Introduction aux travaux scientifiques du dix-neuvième siècle, vol. II (1808)", in: *Œuvres choisies de C.-H. de Saint-Simon, précédées d'un essai sur sa doctrine*, vol. I (Brussels: Fr. Van Meenen et Cie, 1859), 202.

[26] Ibid., 202–215.

[27] Ibid., 211: "Ses ouvrages, malgré cette imperfection capitale, me paraissent les plus estimables productions qui aient été mises au jour depuis plusieurs années. Il est un point de vue duquel ils sont admirables; ils sont pleins de vie; ils sont faits pour inspirer de l'enthousiasme aux savants et aux littérateurs; ils sont propres à rajeunir la science et la littérature."

[28] Ibid., 212.

[29] Ibid., 211.

was to be explained more by the considerable institutional power it once had and this power's aftershocks, rather than any sort of present spiritual authority typical of living faiths.[30] The Christian system of beliefs, in other words, the Catholic dogma which had been the centre of Bonald's narrative of a properly constituted religious and political society, had completely lost its force, according to Saint-Simon. Narrating this dogma back into existence, as Bonald wished to do, would make little to no difference, in the eyes of the social reformer.

What Saint-Simon termed as "the march of the human spirit" confirmed this: while the appearance of the Christian religion, and its doctrinal-institutional implementation by St. Paul, had massively furthered the social government of human society for a number of centuries—creating a European confederation, steering both scientific and literary production to new heights and providing a Christian ethic of labour for the stimulation of the social and political economy—this institution had gradually begun to diminish in power from the fifteenth century onwards.[31] This diminishment was not the result of external, political and economic factors, as Bonald had tried to argue, which, in the latter's narrative, had subsequently led to "confusions" in the composition of faith and social action.[32] Rather, according to Saint-Simon, this had been the simple result of intellectual progress: the appearance of great scientific minds such as Copernicus, Kepler and Galilei created a new and better understanding of the physical workings of the world, an understanding which could not have been provided via the doctrinal institutions populated by the clergy.[33]

Most importantly, perhaps, this shift in the positioning of the core of society's self-understanding, from the Church and theologians to a class of scientists and philosophers massed in academies and universities, brought forth an important transition in what it meant to believe in society. Saint-Simon was adamant to make clear, first of all, that such a transition did in no way equate to an abolition of a need for spiritual authority itself, as later emphasized by two of his most prominent followers, Enfantin and Bazard

---

[30] Claude-Henri de Saint-Simon, "Le Nouveau Christianisme (1825)", in: *Œuvres choisies de C.-H. de Saint-Simon, précédées d'un essai sur sa doctrine*, vol. III (Brussels: Fr. Van Meenen et Cie, 1859), 330.
[31] Saint-Simon, "Introduction aux travaux scientifiques, vol. II", 205–208.
[32] Cf. supra, ch. 4.
[33] Saint-Simon, "Introduction aux travaux scientifiques, vol. II", 208.

in the *Doctrine Saint-Simonienne* (1829).[34] "Man is a religious being", argued Enfantin and Bazard, "who develops", meaning that while systems of belief can rise and fall according to societal needs and demands, the ultimate need for such a system of belief always remains.[35] While it is crucial that institutions embodying such systems of belief, like the Christian Church, do not become able to impose a regime of non-performative beliefs, i.e. beliefs disconnected from the needs of society, at the same time, it is imperative that ultimately such a system is effectively implemented, one that is able to convincingly guide human behaviour and which is rooted in the current desires and needs of society.[36]

This had been the great error of the century before. While the enlightened revolutionaries had been justified in throwing off the yoke of the Christian system of beliefs, which had already long been surpassed by the events and practices of progressing human history, these revolutionaries had been mistaken in their presupposition that now all forms of spiritual authority had become obsolete. They had failed to realize that

> society will not be able to advance but on the condition of a communal faith, which would further impassion all sympathies by bringing all wills together, which would satisfy those of the highest intelligence by only presenting theories justified by observation, which would submit those of inferior capacities to those of superior capacities, bringing all together through the love of a new destination [my translation].[37]

The liberal attitude of the enlightened moderns—"where the sovereignty of each individual consciousness was proclaimed"—had functioned well as an instrument of reform and deconstruction against the institution of the Church, but could not, on its own, function as a governmental system in its own right.[38] For Saint-Simon and the Saint-Simonists, a new regime of

---

[34] Saint-Amand Bazard & Barthélemy Prosper Enfantin, *Doctrine Saint-Simonienne: Exposition* (Paris: Librairie Nouvelle, 1854 [1st ed. 1829–30]), 404–415.

[35] Ibid., 405.

[36] *De la religion Saint-Simonienne. Aux élèves de l'École polytechnique* (Brussels: Laurent Frères, 1831), 41.

[37] Ibid.: "la société ne pourrait avancer qu'à la condition d'une foi commune, qui exalterait encore toutes les sympathies en reliant toutes les volontés, qui satisferait les plus hautes intelligences en ne présentant que des théories justifiées par l'observation, qui soumettrait enfin les capacités inférieures aux capacités supérieures, en les unissant toutes dans l'amour d'une destination nouvelle."

[38] Ibid.

belief needed to be cultivated, which could "unite all in the love of a new destination", as such a communal faith would allow societies to collectively advance. The new system of belief suited to modern society would need to be one that was able to incorporate all moral, scientific and technological progress, and was to be extracted from the new scientific and philosophical insights which had been achieved from the fifteenth century onwards.

This turn to the spiritual authority of science was best encapsulated by the works of Francis Bacon and René Descartes and the novel anti-theological truth they proclaimed: "MAN MUSTN'T BELIEVE BUT THOSE THINGS ACKNOWLEDGED BY REASON, AND CONFIRMED BY EXPERIENCE."[39] This transition led to an important loss in (spiritual) authority for the class of Christian theologians and priests, who were no longer able to dominate the means of intellectual and social government, but which had to now actively compete against alternative systems of belief, as put forward by the class of physicists.[40] It was a struggle they were never going to win, with even radical programs such as those advanced by the French seventeenth-century bishop Bossuet—arguing for the complete egality of all men—only briefly gaining a temporary advantage, while having severe and unforeseen side-effects as well.[41] The final blow in this contest between competing systems of belief was delivered by Isaac Newton, according to Saint-Simon, who was able to find a unitary principle which could integrate both a system of belief as well as the new scientific method: this was the principle and fact of universal gravitation.[42]

Whereas the deistic principle of an immortal and eternal God was unable to account for the intellectual advancement of humanity, the physicist principle did have this advantage. It made possible, as soon as it was sufficiently disseminated throughout Europe, "a general assault on Christian religion" via the publication of the *Encyclopédie*, advocating for

---

[39] Saint-Simon, "Introduction aux travaux scientifiques, vol. II", 209: "L'HOMME NE DOIT CROIRE QUE LES CHOSES AVOUÉES PAR LA RAISON, ET CONFIRMÉES PAR L'EXPERIENCE."

[40] Ibid., 209–210: "Les Théologiens n'eurent pas longtemps l'avantage: les Physiciens reprirent promptement le dessus."

[41] Saint-Simon puts responsibility for the events of the French Revolution in the hands of Bossuet, as his egalitarian proclamation lit a fire which could not be controlled, cf. Saint-Simon, "Introduction aux travaux scientifiques, vol. II", 210n(1).

[42] Ibid., 211.

the "idea of universal gravitation to serve as the foundation for the new scientific system and *as a result for the new religious system as well*".⁴³ Saint-Simon, while less critical of religion than the materialist branch of the Enlightenment *philosophes*, was convinced that the deistic system had run its course as a framework for capturing the collective stream of beliefs prominent in modern society, especially those prevalent among the class of the intellectual elite. Unlike Bonald then, who used his analysis of the different modalities of belief to conclude that Catholic dogma was the framework which best captured the composition of belief and social action, Saint-Simon argued that deistic dogma was an institution like any other and didn't transcend the particularities of its historical age:

> Each age has its character, each institution its time span.
> RELIGION AGES IN THE SAME MANNER AS OTHER INSTITUTIONS. SIMILAR TO OTHER INSTITUTIONS, IT NEEDS TO BE RENEWED AFTER A CERTAIN WHILE. EACH RELIGION IS A BENEFICIAL INSTITUTION AT ITS POINT OF ORIGIN. PRIESTS ABUSE IT WHEN THEY ARE NO LONGER RESTRAINED BY THE BRAKE OF OPPOSITION, WHEN THEY NO LONGER HAVE ANY MORE DISCOVERIES TO MAKE IN THE SCIENTIFIC DIRECTION THAT THEY RECEIVED FROM THEIR FOUNDER: IT THEN BECOMES OPPRESSIVE. WHEN RELIGION HAS BECOME OPPRESSIVE, IT FALLS INTO CONTEMPT, AND ITS MINISTERS LOSE THE CONSIDERATION AND FORTUNE THAT THEY HAD ACQUIRED [my translation].⁴⁴

---

[43] Ibid., 211: "Quand la découverte de Newton fut suffisamment répandue en Europe, les lettres laïcs français se coalisèrent pour donner un assaut général à la religion chrétienne. Ils firent une Encyclopédie, ouvrage dans lequel ils démontrèrent, relativement à toutes les parties de la connaissance humaine, que les travaux faits d'après l'impulsion donnée par Descartes, étaient infiniment supérieurs à ceux qui étaient sortis du système de croyance inventé par Jésus; ils ont fait sentir que l'idée de gravitation universelle était celle qui devait servir de base au nouveau système scientifique et *par suite au nouveau système religieux*."

[44] Ibid., 213: "Chaque âge a son caractère, chaque institution sa durée. LA RELIGION VIEILLIT DE MÊME QUE LES AUTRES INSTITUTIONS. DE MEME QUE LES AUTRES INSTITUTIONS, ELLE A BESOIN D'ÊTRE RENOUVELÉE AU BOUT D'UN CERTAIN TEMPS. TOUTE RELIGION EST UNE INSTITUTION BIENFAISANTE A SON ORIGINE. LES PRÊTRES EN ABUSENT QUAND ILS NE SONT PLUS CONTENUS PAR LE FREIN DE L'OPPOSITION, QUAND ILS N'ONT PLUS DE DÉCOUVERTES A FAIRE DANS LA DIRECTION SCIENTIFIQUE QU'ILS ONT RECUE DE LEUR FONDATEUR: ELLE DEVIENT ALORS OPPRESSIVE. QUAND LA RELIGION A ÉTÉ OPPRESSIVE, ELLE TOMBE DANS

For Saint-Simon, the Christian religion does not stand outside of historical time, unlike it did for Bonald, making it susceptible to the typical mechanisms characterizing the development and degradation of any institution: as an institution becomes successful through its virtuous constitution, it gradually fails to evolve as quickly as the world around it, eventually falling prey to forces of corruption in its attempts at staying relevant through means different from its original constitution. The world had simply moved beyond the theology and practice of Christian belief.

So while Bonald and Saint-Simon both employed the historiographical prism of multiple forms of believing as a way of reading the historical developments within society—the loss of belief's social efficaciousness with Bonald through faulty constitutions, the Cartesian revolution of positivist beliefs for Saint-Simon—they arrived at vastly different conclusions on the state of the present spiritual crisis and how to get out of it. For Saint-Simon, the Cartesian moment ensured that a complete return to a deistic system was impossible: the intellectual class of elites had moved on from such Christian belief practices and could only believe those things that could be proven with reason and confirmed by experience. For them, community-forming beliefs could only be found in the principle of universal gravitation. This, in the early nineteenth century present, was the principle which best encapsulated the nature of modern believing, according to Saint-Simon, and which ought to serve, in his eyes, as the educational and ideological premise for the spiritual formation of both children and the ignorant, even though this principle needed to be "dressed up as something sacred" for the latter to be able to properly commit to it.[45]

This categorical distinction between an elite governmental class and an ignorant population which needed to be governed through symbolic manipulation is something which also returns in Saint-Simon's broader

LE MÉPRIS, ET SES MINISTRES PERDENT LA CONSIDÉRATION ET LA FORTUNE QU'ILS AVAIENT ACQUISES."

[45] Saint-Simon elaborated on this in his entry "Sur l'unité de cause" in the *Introduction*, cf. Saint-Simon, "Introduction aux travaux scientifiques, vol. II", 216–19, esp. 219: "les opinions scientifiques arrêtées par l'École devront ensuite être revêtues des formes qui les rendent sacrées, pour être enseignées aux enfants de toutes les classes et aux ignorants de tous les âges." It was an idea which was present throughout his work, appearing already, in a slightly different form, in the *Lettres d'un habitant de Genève* (1802), before being "further developed in his 1813 *Mémoire sur la science de l'homme* and his *Travail sur la gravitation universelle* (1813)", cf. Michael Drolet, "A nineteenth-century Mediterranean union: Michel Chevalier's *Système de la Méditerranée*", *Mediterranean Historical Review* 30, no. 2 (2015): 161n1.

understanding of the sciences and their historical trajectories. In his own unique take on the history of the sciences, the French social theorist argues that this history can be divided into two separate scientific dimensions, composed of those sciences which focus on the particular on the one hand and of those sciences which focus on general principles on the other. According to Saint-Simon, this history is marked by a principle which dictates that the intellectual classes could only be focused on one of these dimensions at a time, with the two chronologically alternating.[46] Individual scientific cultures in different historical periods, in other words, focused on either a science of the particular—such as physics, biology, chemistry, botany, etc.—or on a science of the general, such as theology and moral philosophy, but never both at the same time. This had also already been the case for what Saint-Simon considered to be 'the Saint-Simonist school': they had mostly been focusing on the science of the particular and had not yet committed enough resources to a 'general science'.[47] Yet it was through general science, and its applications, argued the social reformer, that religious systems were ultimately constructed, as he defined the latter as "the collection of applications from general science as a means through which the enlightened could govern the ignorant".[48]

Through these distinctions—regimes of belief, systems of scientific investigation—Saint-Simon was able to construct his own historical narrative of societal change: according to the ambitious social reformer, society had found itself in a moment of transition, no longer able to undergo a full obedience to the deistic system, but also not yet able to construct a physicist religion.[49] It reminded him of another pivotal point in history, more specifically the time when Late Antique society shifted from polytheism to deism, an extended period where different classes believed different things: "the intellectuals were deists, the ignorant believed in multiple Gods [my translation]."[50] A similar scenario was unfolding now in the early nineteenth century as a result of scientific progress: "Physicism for the

[46] Saint-Simon, "Introduction aux travaux scientifiques, vol. II", 213.
[47] Saint-Simon discussed these disciplines in the first volume of the *Introduction*, where he tried to give a state of the art of the sciences.
[48] Ibid.: "LA RELIGION EST LA COLLECTION DES APPLICATIONS DE LA SCIENCE GÉNÉRALE AU MOYEN DESQUELLES LES HOMMES ÉCLAIRÉS GOUVERNENT LES HOMMES IGNORANTS."
[49] Ibid, 214.
[50] Ibid.: "les savants étaient deists, les ignorants croyaient à plusieurs Dieux."

educated, and Deism for the ignorant class [my translation]."[51] In this sense, the framework of multiple historical regimes of belief not only allowed Saint-Simon to ground his own historical narrative on the "march and progress of the human spirit", but also to construct a complex analysis of social-intellectual classes and their different modes of government.

From Philosophy to Prescriptive Ethic: Believing Alternatively as a Saint-Simonist Moral Practice

While Saint-Simon's philosophy of the present laid bare the current conditions governing society—not just of belief, but of reason, industry and work as well—it did not present an immediate and obvious answer to society's ills. Rather, it showed the need of a clearly articulated governmental ethics, one which could actively intervene and give shape to a new society in the best and fairest way possible. After all, Saint-Simon's project was not merely an intellectual one; it was complemented, especially in the later part of his life, by a normative moral program which took as its guiding principle the improvement of the life of the poorest and most numerous classes.[52] He would turn this principle into the central argument of his final and unfinished work, *Le Nouveau Christianisme* (1825), in which he tried to unearth how a religion in modern industrial society should look like, i.e. one that would be capable of fully incorporating the new (scientific and rationalist) conditions of believing prevalent in such a society.[53] In this work, he advocated for a new and transformed iteration of Christianity, one where all of its institutions would start out from the idea of universal fraternity and the goal of the improved well-being of the poorest class:

> The new christian organisation will orchestrate the temporal institutions, as well as the spiritual institutions, from the principle that *all men must behave themselves towards one another as brothers*. It will direct all institutions, of whichever nature it will be, towards increasing the well-being of the poorest classes [my translation].[54]

---

[51] Ibid.: "le Physicisme pour les gens instruits, et le Déisme pour la classe ignorante."
[52] Durkheim, *Socialism and Saint Simon*, 121.
[53] Musso, "Religion and Political Economy", 823–24.
[54] Saint-Simon, "Le Nouveau Christianisme (1825)", 325: "La nouvelle organisation chrétienne déduira les institutions temporelles, ainsi que les institutions spirituelles, du principe que *tous les hommes doivent se conduire à l'égard des uns des autres comme des frères*. Elle dirig-

As the number of students and proselytes gradually increased around Saint-Simon and his early socialist legacy, a network began to form which set out to impose the social reformer's vision onto the French social and industrial life of the early 1800s, their undertaking intensifying after the death of Saint-Simon especially thanks to the efforts of one of his most dedicated followers, the mathematician Olinde Rodrigues.[55] Rodrigues and the other Saint-Simonists saw it as their task to transform their advanced knowledge of the workings of social life into an active disposition, which could subsequently function as the foundation of an ever-expanding community.[56] A good example of this mindset can be found in the Saint-Simonists' series of presentations given to the students of the *École Polytechnique* in Paris in 1830, in which they set out their doctrine in an attempt at drawing further support and commitment to their cause.[57] Here, their analysis of the conditions of believing and knowing of past and present was not merely theoretical, it was the basis of a moral appeal for a new kind of politics.[58] Their understanding of the historical spirit had transformed the Saint-Simonists into judges who had to decide who and what belonged to an unreachable past and those who carried within themselves the seed of the future:

> We, true judges of the camp, we who know the march of humanity, its point of departure and its spirit of progress, we are capable of discerning from within the midst of these confused elements of a society in disorder, both those characteristic facts of a past which must disappear, as well as those, carrying the germ of the future, which must increase and develop in an infinite manner, as well as those, finally, which draw their importance from the particular nature of the present era, which are destined to vanish with it [my translation].[59]

era toutes les institutions, de quelque nature qu'elles soient, vers l'accroissement du bien-être de la classe la plus pauvre."

[55] Durkheim, *Socialism and Saint Simon*, 130–131.
[56] Picon, "La religion Saint-Simonienne", 28.
[57] Olivier Pétré-Grenouilleau, *Saint-Simon. L'utopie ou la raison en actes* (Paris: Biographie Payot, 2001), 394–95.
[58] *De la religion Saint-Simonienne*, esp. the fifth discourse, termed 'Appel', 55–64.
[59] Ibid., 43: "[N]ous, véritables juges du camp, nous qui connaissons la marche de l'humanité, son point de départ et le sens de son progrès, nous sommes en état de discerner au milieu des élémens confus de cette société en désordre, et les faits caractéristiques d'un passé qui doit disparaître, et ceux qui, portant le germe de l'avenir, doivent s'accroître et se

These presentations proved to be quite fruitful, as the students of the *École* formed the core of the eventual Saint-Simonist apostolate, that group of followers who set out to apply Saint-Simonist doctrine in real life.[60] Saint-Simonism, then, gradually transitioned from a philosophical exercise centred around a single theorist into an activist network, with followers and disciples going around to ateliers and workshops in Paris, before eventually moving on to other industrial centres, like Dijon and Lyon.[61] Saint-Simonists like Jean Reynaud would give speeches (or 'sermons', as the reformist movement would call them) to gatherings of up to 3000 people, others would go into workshops and ateliers, speaking to local workers in attempts at converting them to their cause or convincing them to form worker associations.[62]

While this interaction between ambitious, ideological elites and the proletarian classes is highly fascinating in its own right, what interests me here is how this particular transition, from theoretical reflections by Saint-Simon to concrete activism by a complex network, impacted the Saint-Simonist engagement with the notion of believing as a practice. And an impact it did have, as the confrontation with both the complexity of the workers' problems and the sheer diversity of the needs and desires of the proletarian individuals showed the limits of mere social theorizing. When confronted with the social reality, it occurred to Prosper Enfantin, one of the leaders of the movement after the passing of Saint-Simon, that the very structures of the new, positivist regime of belief, could be oppressive in its own right, as it obscured what were the genuine desires of a substantial part of the proletarian classes:

> up to this point we haven't been anything for them but philanthropic doctors, we have not yet made them live our Saint-Simonist life. Yes, the work we accomplish today is a material work, a work of industry; it is the flesh that we rehabilitate, that we sanctify; but recall what Eugène [Rodrigues, Saint-Simonist writer and ideologue; MVD] has said: *the sacred fire of enthusiasm is not kindled in the weakly fireplace of philanthropy*. Certainly, we have done

---

développer indéfiniment, et ceux enfin qui, tirant toute leur importance de la nature particulière de l'époque présente, sont destinés à s'évanouir avec elle."

[60] Jean-Pierre Callot, "Les polytechniciens et l'aventure saint-simonienne", *Bulletin de la Sabix* 42 (2008), last consulted on the 21st of December 2022, https://journals.openedition.org/sabix/131; Cuchet, *Une histoire du sentiment religieux au XIXe siècle*, 29–30.

[61] Pilbeam, *Saint-Simonians in Nineteenth-Century France*, 38.

[62] Ibid., 38–39.

well to enter the worker's chambers, to take him out, to make him associate with his brothers, we have done well furthermore to found workshops, to ensure the improvement of the moral, intellectual and physical fate of those children who have come to us; but we would renounce the mission Saint-Simon has given us, and we would almost deserve the accusations thrown at us, if we reduce the new temple to the measly proportions of a barracks or rather a poorhouse. It is not merely help that the poorest and most numerous classes expect from the sons of SAINT-SIMON; THEY WANT AN ENTIRELY NEW LIFE, a life of religion and poetry; they need greatness, glory; they need artists who impassion and guide them; the worker wants feasts; the idler still pays, but no longer inspires; it is not only industry that we do, it is *worship*; usefulness is no longer enough for us, we want beauty; we have entered among the workers asking them to share their sufferings and tears; but don't forget that in order for them to see in us anything other than chaplains of Christ, we must bring them a glorious and joyful enthusiasm, and spread it with them and through them throughout the world [my translation].[63]

One of the central principles of Saint-Simonist dogma conveyed that the positivist era of human history, in which they considered themselves to have now arrived, constituted an overlap between human self-interest and

---

[63] Barthélemy Prosper Enfantin, "Deuxième enseignement (20 novembre 1831): l'histoire", in: *Œuvres de Saint-Simon et d'Enfantin*, vol. XIV (Paris: E. Dentu, 1868), 73–74: "jusqu'ici nous n'avons été pour eux que des docteurs philanthropes, nous ne les avons pas fait vivre de notre vie Saint-Simonienne. Oui, l'œuvre que nous accomplissons aujourd'hui est une œuvre de matière, une œuvre d'industrie; c'est la chair que nous réhabilitons, que nous sanctifions; mais rappelez-vous ce qu'a dit Eugène: *le feu sacré de l'enthousiasme ne s'allume point au chétif foyer de la philanthropie*. Certes, nous avons bien fait d'entrer dans la chambre de l'ouvrier, de l'en tirer, de l'associer avec ses frères, nous faisons bien encore de fonder des ateliers, de veiller à l'amélioration du sort moral, intellectuel et physique de ces enfants qui viennent à nous; mais nous abdiquerions la mission que Saint-Simon nous a donnée, et nous mériterions presque les accusations qui seront lancées contre nous, si nous réduisions le temple nouveau aux mesquines proportions d'une caserne ou plutôt d'un hospice. Ce ne sont point des *secours* que la classe la plus pauvre et la plus nombreuse attend des fils de SAINT-SIMON; ELLE VEUT UNE VIE NOUVELLE TOUT ENTIÈRE, une vie de religion et de poésie; il lui faut du grand, de la gloire; il lui faut des artistes qui l'exaltent et qui l'entrainent; l'ouvrier veut des fêtes; l'oisif en paie encore, mais n'en inspire plus; ce n'est pas seulement de l'*industrie* que nous faisons, c'est du *culte*; l'utile ne nous suffit plus, nous voulons du beau; nous sommes entrés chez les travailleurs en leur demandant le partage de leurs souffrances et de leurs larmes; mais n'oublions pas que pour qu'ils voient en nous autre chose que des aumôniers du Christ, nous devons leur rapporter un glorieux, un joyeux enthousiasme, et le répandre avec eux et par eux sur toute la terre."

collective duties.⁶⁴ The worker, in the Saint-Simonist economy, would enjoy their labour through the love they felt for their brethren and their lot through the *teachings* of their Saint-Simonist priests, thus furthering the progress of human spirit, science and industry in harmonious and automatic fashion.⁶⁵ The confrontation with the workers' reality severely complicated this vision, as Enfantin articulated in his own words, as the workers wanted more out of life than labour alone. They had, as the French philosopher Jacques Rancière has so elegantly shown in his book *Proletarian Nights* (*La Nuit des prolétaires: Archives du rêve ouvrier*, 1981), dreams of their own, dreams which were not sufficiently articulated by their class position alone.⁶⁶ Their struggle with intellectual reductionism was something the Saint-Simonists themselves were, at least partly, responsible for, their theory of societal progress being fundamentally rooted in a class theory of industrial labour, where the work served as the very condition of collective emancipation.⁶⁷

This, as Enfantin discusses in the passage above, has limited the efficacy of the Saint-Simonist priests, who had as their spiritual function the government of the workers' beliefs towards desirable social action, their conversions through intellectual means—founded on the premise of positivist demonstrations—not sufficient to actually *move* the workers into action. Such an overly intellectual disposition had caused a series of miscommunications between the Saint-Simonists and the worker class, with the latter coming to view the former as a cheap source of charity. As a result, the Saint-Simonists needed to adjust their self-presentation by integrating the complex ambiguity of the workers' reality into their own ethic, for a true communion between the elite and proletarian classes to unfold. Saint-Simon's original conception of proletarian belief—as something that was only of interest because of its potential function as a site of Saint-Simonist government—no longer sufficed, according to Enfantin, as the proletarian beliefs were much more eclectic than what Saint-Simon had imagined.⁶⁸

---

⁶⁴ *De la religion Saint-Simonienne*, 22: "Par nous, en effet, et pour la première fois, l'*intérêt* et le *devoir* se trouvent complètement conciliés, harmonisés."
⁶⁵ Saint-Simon, "Le Nouveau Christianisme (1825)", 330–31: "Le véritable christianisme commande à tous les hommes de se conduire en frères à l'égard les uns des autres […] ainsi le clergé doit s'occuper principalement d'enseigner aux fidèles la conduite qu'ils doivent tenir pour accélérer le bien-être de la majorité de la population."
⁶⁶ Rancière, *Proletarian Nights*.
⁶⁷ Musso, "Religion and Political Economy", 822.
⁶⁸ Cf. supra.

This has been well analysed by Rancière, who saw in this historical meeting of tensions and contradictions the central value of the Saint-Simonist ideology and practice as a reformist movement.[69] The Saint-Simonists' use of a religious language acted, according to Rancière, like a veil, with no particular content in itself other than politics, its spiritual symbolism mainly functioning as a crutch through which it could communicate with the still-deistic proletariat. Yet, when needed, this rather vacuous religious language was surprisingly effective, as it could impose a non-materialist logic onto a series of events in order to make possible a selfless politics of association. In the densely philosophical language of Rancière:

> To resolve the dilemma is really to remain in the contradiction. The "religion" has no content other than politics. But this politics can break off compromises with the forces of egotism only by means of the transcendence of a religion that typifies a world order in the image of its ends or offers the model of an action freed from the chain of necessity. At the undefined boundaries of "simple reason," the republican cult of virtue and the mysticism of the living universe meet in this transcendent religion of fraternity that alone can ground a politics of association among human beings.[70]

For Rancière, what defined the Saint-Simonist movement, more than anything else, was its composite form as a coalescence of different early nineteenth-century discourses, those of civic republicanism, new-age mysticism and socio-economic solidarity. The status of the Saint-Simonists' religious language as a kind of superficial veneer was not to its detriment, in the eyes of Rancière, an ideological white lie meant for the proletarian classes. Rather, it was its greatest strength, allowing it to act as a kind of guest house, welcoming and harbouring all kinds of different voices, wills and desires, a trait which was especially useful in the politically turbulent times of the late 1820s and early 1830s, which saw the threat of European war as a result of fighting in Poland as well as the chaotic events leading to the 1830 July Revolution in France.[71]

It was in this eclectic space that the functionality of the Saint-Simonist form of religious speech truly came to the fore. For Saint-Simonists like Abel Transon, another *Polytechnicien* who felt himself called to the cause

[69] Rancière, *Proletarian Nights*, 179.
[70] Ibid., 179–180.
[71] Ibid., 181.

and who started spreading the utopian message of Saint-Simon across France, this religious language provided a crucial additive to the movement's more rationalist social philosophy, as the latter simply proved itself unable to fully move people's spirits and souls, *to lift up the world around them*:

> for it isn't to the intellectuals that he gave the power to touch men. Intellectuals don't have the words that stir the soul, that give life, that enlighten. Oh! since Archimedes they have not found a base from which their levers could lift up the world [my translation].[72]

Founding such an understanding of successful communication between social classes, of what it takes to effectively construct a social bond, was another interpretation by the Saint-Simonists of what it meant to believe. While Saint-Simon's rationalistic approach to the category was productive in its own right—for analysing the current state of the world and for articulating a new kind of politics—it proved to be unable to consistently sustain an actual Saint-Simonist ethics, with ethics meaning here a concrete form of existence within the social domain.

And yet, this did not mean that the categorical framework of 'belief' itself was abandoned for being too rationalistic. Rather, its historical and categorical pliability allowed it to function as the site of Saint-Simonist self-reflection and -transformation. Rancière already mentions this alternative approach to 'believing' by referring in the quote cited above to the Saint-Simonist idea of "the mysticism of the living universe". As I will try to show in the following passages, this was an idea which was an immediate result of their proselytizing practices in workshops and ateliers. In these transformative encounter with the workers, the Saint-Simonists uncovered and gradually put into words a new imagination of belief, one which wasn't knowledge-based, but was more akin to a leap of faith: to have faith, according to the Saint-Simonists, was to believe that the stranger represented their fraternal equal, who could just as equally transform you as be transformed by the gospel brought to their

---

[72] Abel Transon, "Morale du monde", in: *Religion Saint-Simonienne. Recueil de prédications*, Vol. I (Paris: Au bureau du Globe, 1832), 421–422: "car ce n'est pas aux savans qu'il a donné de toucher les hommes. Les savans n'ont pas la parole qui remue l'ame, qui donne la vie, qui fait la lumière. Oh! depuis Archimède, ils n'ont pas trouvé d'appui à leurs leviers pour soulever le monde." These pamphlets—*Religion Saint-Simonienne*—were part of a series, and will hereafter be abbreviated as *RSS*.

doorstep.[73] It was then, unlike Bonald's Catholic-rationalist commitment to a transcendental proposition or Saint-Simon's earlier socio-cultural understanding of belief as a type of opinion, a new kind of *blind* belief in the "mysticism of the living universe", which was mobilized by the Saint-Simonists. This was a transformative understanding of the practice of belief, which required the believer to surrender himself to humanity beyond the economic logic dictated by the chain of necessity. Such a conceptualization of belief was based on the experiences of the Saint-Simonist apostles in encountering the workers as a life-changing event, which was something that could not be encapsulated within the scientific speech of observation and knowledge.[74]

At first, this should not come as a surprise. Both Saint-Simon and his later followers proactively conceptualized social beliefs and its proper forms of government as being class-based, meaning that positivist demonstrations would be directed towards the intellectual elite, while the popular and ignorant classes would need to be, at first, enticed with a non-rational language of cult and faith.[75] In this sense, non-positivist systems of beliefs—the deism of the popular masses, as mentioned earlier—were integrated into the broader scheme of Saint-Simonist government, but they were done so at first purely from a utilitarian perspective, in their attempt at recreating some of the most effective techniques of the Catholic cult. In Catholicism, the arts had been a crucial instrument for the cultivation of Catholic belief: poets could provide memorable recitations, musicians could use their craft to further amplify these recitations into the hearts and souls of the believers, painters and sculptors could attract the attention of the believing flock onto desirable scenes, and architects could design temples for housing these rituals.[76]

The Saint-Simonists' turn to such techniques was designed, in their eyes, as a way of making those wary Catholic believers, sceptical of non-deistic reformism, more at ease with the Saint-Simonist message, showing how Saint-Simonism and Catholicism were not so different after all. Through ritualistic language and spiritual symbolism, the Saint-Simonist

[73] Rancière, *Proletarian Nights*, 103–104.

[74] Transon, "Morale du monde", 422.

[75] Saint-Simon, "Le Nouveau Christianisme (1825)", 334. At other times, this distinction was flattened, with Saint-Simonists stating that nobody, both intellectuals and the ignorant, believed in anything anymore, *except* positivist demonstrations, cf. *De la religion Saint-Simonienne*, 27.

[76] Ibid., 359–360.

movement could guide those remaining Christians towards a viable future, as they were seen by the social reformists as wandering into the future blindly, their minds and bodies telling them to believe in a Christian God which was no longer there. "Poor credulous soul", lamented the Saint-Simonist preacher, Emile Barrault, "what are you doing? You are still looking up at the sky, but the sky is deserted [my translation]!"[77] Their Christian God having abandoned them, Barrault invited the lost Christian souls into the temple of Saint-Simon, where, even though the Saint-Simonist elites themselves did not believe in such mystical reveries, they would be welcomed, cared for and loved, and would be safe from any mockery.[78]

The Saint-Simonists, in other words, aimed to combine their rationalistic knowledge of the social world with a rationally manufactured tolerance of all its irrationalities, pointless symbolisms and superstitions, embracing these through a self-prescribed ethic of unconditional love.[79] Their philosophical example in this was seventeenth-century thinker Baruch Spinoza, whose unitary conception of reality sought to go beyond the typical distinction of materialism and spiritualism.[80] Like him, the Saint-Simonists "had recognized [...] that thought and the extent are attributes of a singular and infinite substance". But they sought to go even beyond the great early modern philosopher, by not just understanding this principle of substance monism but by actively committing to this principle as an object of love and devotion, as something that is felt by those positivist believers to be alive and animated.[81] It was only by constructing a new religion on the basis of this principle, that this accommodationist approach

---

[77] Emile Barrault, "Dégout du présent, besoin d'avenir", *RSS. Recueil de prédications*, Vol. I (Paris: Au bureau du Globe, 1832), 487: "Pauvre ame credule [...] que fais-tu? Tu regardes encore au ciel, mais le ciel est désert !".

[78] Ibid., 487–88.

[79] *De la religion Saint-Simonienne*, 21: "il y a des raisonnemens qui précèdent l'action; il y a des actions inspirées qui précèdent le raisonnement; mais il n'y a ni action ni raisonnement qui ne soient engendrés par l'amour, en comprenant sous ce mot *amour* tout ce qui tient au désir, au sentiment, à la volonté. Ainsi la vie, c'est l'amour."

[80] Bazard & Enfantin, *Doctrine Saint-Simonienne*, 418–420.

[81] *De la religion Saint-Simonienne*, 22: "Enfin nous ne sommes point *unitaires* de la même façon que Spinosa; car après avoir reconnu, comme lui, que la pensée et l'étendue sont les attributs de la substance une et infinie, nous sentons cette substance animée, vivante, et nous l'AIMONS. Notre conception n'est donc pas, comme la sienne, purement *philosophique*; elle est éminemment RELIGIEUSE."

to social reality could be translated into an effective form of spiritual government, one which would be able to combat the social crisis of the age.[82]

In this chaotic assemblage of different beliefs and their associated classes—scientists, artists, industrialists, deists, the ignorant, the superstitious—it is up to the Saint-Simonist priest to bring these all together, and direct them towards a shared, common goal, the goal of intellectual and moral progress.[83] The goal of the priest, in other words, was to shape solidarity and communion, and to use the means required to ensure obedience. The task of the priest was to *make*-believe: "To govern, that means to excite, to harmonize, to direct efforts towards the goal loved by all; to obey, that means to follow a path which is easier, gentler, and quicker. Authority and obedience are nothing but the political transformation of the love which brings all men together in God [my translation]."[84] "Everywhere, the PRIEST *associates*": using their knowledge of the social, their understanding of their particular domain, and their ethic of unconditional love, the Saint-Simonist priest has the responsibility of forming communities into being.[85]

For someone like Philippe Regnier, as mentioned above, the employment of multiple understandings of the belief-category by the Saint-Simonists—not just the promotion of their own Cartesian regime of positivist belief they themselves were committed to, but also integrating non-positivist languages of hope, mystical love, blind faith and the unknowable—represented a case of '*mentir-vrai*', an intellectual tool for manipulating the ignorant masses to direct them towards desirable outcomes.[86] This is not an unfair interpretation: Enfantin himself often thought of these kinds of interventions in this manner, defined by Regnier as "a science and technique for conducting humanity, [...] for example

---

[82] Ibid., 14–19.

[83] Emile Barrault, "La Hiérarchie", *RSS. Recueil de prédications*, Vol. I (Paris: Au bureau du Globe, 1832), 191.

[84] Ibid., 196: "Gouverner, c'est exciter, harmoniser, diriger les efforts vers le but aimé de tous; obéir, c'est suivre une route plus facile, plus douce et plus prompte. L'autorité et l'obéissance ne sont que la transformation politique de l'amour qui unit tous les hommes en Dieu."

[85] Emile Barrault, "Le Sacerdoce", *RSS. Recueil de prédications*, Vol. I (Paris: Au bureau du Globe, 1832), 220: "Partout, le PRÊTRE associe".

[86] Philippe Regnier, "L'institution et son en-dehors: la théorie littéraire des saint-simoniens", in: *Philologiques I. Contribution à l'histoire des disciplines littéraires en France et en Allemagne au xixe siècle*, eds. M. Espagne & M. Werner (Paris: Éditions de la Maison des Sciences de l'Homme, 1990), 211–237.

with the aid of 'miracles', in order to make them [i.e. the ignorant masses] hear truths in the present to which they will only have access to in the future".[87] Someone like Antoine Picon also questions the authenticity of the religious fervour of some Saint-Simonists, although he is quick to add "that it is perhaps not very useful to probe in detail the minds and hearts [of the Saint-Simonists]".[88]

But rather than asking the question whether the Saint-Simonists genuinely believed in their messages of mystical love and hope or whether they were merely manipulating an impressionable crowd through their employment of an artificial deistic language, I would argue that we should look at what this use of a deistic language meant for their ability to think and historicize themselves, as Saint-Simonists. How did this usage of a blind faith in the mystic universe affect the ways they conceptualized their own roles and functions within social life? When it comes to evaluating the Saint-Simonist engagement with non-positivist forms of belief, in other words, we need to make the distinction between a governmental discourse of others (the remaining deistic believers) and one of themselves. Whereas the Saint-Simonist understanding of governing others through a language of non-positivist belief was essentially utilitarian, its social-existential employment of governing themselves was focused on the transformation the Saint-Simonists have undergone in their encounter with the workers' reality: "we were then above all *doctors* and not yet APOSTLES. With us, religion was on the theoretical level, political, hateful and warlike, a form of morality, a pure critique. Today, religion makes our hearts jump and our tears flow [my translation]".[89]

The Saint-Simonists, in their speeches to workers, often emphasized their own moments of conversion and transformation, from being disconnected intellectuals who mainly thought of religion as a social tool to

---

[87] Regnier, "Entre politique et mystique", 103: "une science et une technique de conduite de l'humanité, assez lucide sur le processus de fabrication des croyances pour intégrer la conviction que, parfois, l'« homme supérieur », le « grand poète », doit tromper les foules, à l'aide par exemple de « miracles », pour leur faire entendre au présent des vérités auxquelles elles n'accéderont que dans l'avenir."

[88] Picon, "La religion Saint-Simonienne", 35–36.

[89] Émile Barrault, "Au Père Enfantin", in: *RSS. Recueil de prédications*, Vol. I (Paris: Au bureau du Globe, 1832), i-ii: "alors nous étions surtout *docteurs* et non pas encore APÔTRES. Chez nous, la religion était à l'état de théorie, la politique, haineuse et guerrière, la morale, une pure critique. Aujourd'hui la religion fait tressaillir nos cœurs et couler nos larmes."

being genuine *apostles*, where the speaking of Saint-Simonist love and fraternity has changed into something which deeply stirs their own souls, not just those they were eager to convert. The point of these kind of utterances, I would argue, was not so much their degree of authenticity, whether they were truly moved by Saint-Simonist doctrine or not. But rather, its importance lay in such utterances' ability to signal a moral-epistemic transformation of the Saint-Simonists themselves, as they came to truly inhabit the social domain, cultivating an experiential understanding of their fellow man and the religious bonds they shared. This was a form of 'knowledge' which was beyond the disembodied theories of the likes of "Grotius, Volney and Bentham" and which was instead fully rooted in the naked event of the social encounter, where the Saint-Simonist, argued Transon, had needed to learn to shed his rationalist prejudices of human selfishness and let themselves be formed by the reality of the future friend they came upon.[90]

By speaking to the worker, listening to them, touching them and being touched, the Saint-Simonists could witness what belief actually meant as it unfolded itself in action, where the mere act of believing and its shared experience was able to sustain itself, without having any need of abstraction or theorization:

> But I believe in my hope, our efforts will not be in vain. The bond, *however weak, however vague it may still be*, which has been imperceptibly formed between you and us and which becomes more and more precious to us, must give our words more and more strength. If our zeal somewhat surprises you, you already have faith, like us, in the coming emancipation of the most numerous class. *This faith is the most robust foundation of the new temple.* [my italics and translation].[91]

The weakness and vagueness of the belief-bond between the apostles and the workers is, at the same time, its most robust source of strength.[92] The

---

[90] Transon, "Morale du monde", 422.

[91] Barrault, "Dégout du présent, besoin d'avenir", 471: "Mais j'en crois mon espoir, nos efforts ne seront pas perdus. Le lien, quelque faible, quelque vague qu'il soit encore, qui de vous à nous s'est insensiblement formé et nous devient de plus en plus cher, doit rendre notre parole de plus en plus confiante. Si notre ferveur quelquefois vous étonne, déjà pourtant vous avez foi comme nous à l'affranchissement prochain de la classe la plus nombreuse. Cette foi c'est le plus solide fondement du temple nouveau."

[92] On this paradoxical weakness of believing, cf. de Certeau, *La faiblesse de croire*, esp. 299–305.

simple fact that one can believe through mere hope and that this tenuous act already generates a kind of social bond in itself—'we choose to believe together'—is a novel realization of how social life works which the Saint-Simonists attributed to the everyday encounters they had within society.[93] This was a reflexive problematization of what belief actually constitutes which was very different from the other conventional imaginations of it in Saint-Simonist thought, both its argumentation for a Cartesian belief system as the new hegemonic regime in modernity as well as its utilitarian use of popular beliefs as an instrument of government for the ignorant masses. To have a blind faith in the mystical workings of the universe was not something that was, in other words, merely limited to those deists who were still living in the past and who needed to be brought into the future by a better-informed Saint-Simonist elite. The Saint-Simonists themselves conveyed that they also needed such faith: it is what bound the different classes together in the new temple of Saint-Simon. Can we still speak of something like *mentir-vrai* when the Saint-Simonists used the concept of belief to turn the looking glass back at themselves as well? As I will argue in the next section, it is this reflexivity which would represent another important contribution of Saint-Simonism to the history of the social sciences and its employment of belief-languages.

TOWARDS A HIDDEN KNOWLEDGE OF THE SOCIAL: BELIEF AND EXPERIENCE IN SAINT-SIMONIST THOUGHT

As a result of their short but intense period of success as missionaries in the different urban centres, the Saint-Simonist followers briefly became a cause célèbre throughout France and its neighbouring countries.[94] Both the spiritual-symbolic language of the movement and its effective employment of public opinion was an early manifestation of a social-cultural phenomenon which would come to saturate French civil society in the next decades, with famous figures like Allan Kardec (pseudonym of Hippolyte-Leon-Denis Rivail) and novelist Victor Hugo popularizing discussions on the existence of spirits, souls and the possibility of reincarnation.[95]

---

[93] Barrault, "Dégout du présent, besoin d'avenir", 472–473.
[94] Pilbeam, *Saint-Simonians in Nineteenth-Century France*, 44–68.
[95] Lynn L. Sharp, *Secular Spirituality: Reincarnation and Spiritism in Nineteenth-Century France* (Lanham/Boulder: Lexington Books, 2006); Guillaume Cuchet, *Les voix d'outre-tombe. Tables tournantes, spiritisme et société au XIXe siècle* (Paris: Éditions du Seuil, 2013).

Saint-Simonism, even after its disbandment in 1832, would still play an important role in these discussions, both through the activity of former members like Jean Reynaud as well as being a source of inspiration for other socio-religious revivals, with Frédéric Ozanam, one of the founders of the Saint-Vincentians, being particularly impressed by the Saint-Simonist practices of entering the social field itself, rather than merely describe it from the outside.[96] As an unintended result, however, the Saint-Simonist techniques of religious speech have mainly come to be understood in this context of spiritual revival and social evangelization, instead of also being seen as a part of the modern histories of knowledge-production and belief-negotiation. The increased emphasis on religiosity by the later Saint-Simonists only seems to further confirm this to later historians of social science, as they often contrast it to the more theoretical-scientific approach put forward by Saint-Simon himself. Later sociologists, such as Durkheim in his account of Saint-Simonism's place within the sociological canon, often also echoed this division. The concrete practices of the Saint-Simonist movement often remain underexplored in the context of the history of the social sciences, the critiques made by Saint-Simonists like Abel Transon and Émile Barrault against a theoretical knowledge of social life seemingly taken at face value by later commentators.

Yet this division between a sociological phase marked by Saint-Simon's social philosophy and a religious-political phase characterized by the development of a collective socio-reformist movement unnecessarily obscures the interesting epistemic developments produced by this facet of Saint-Simonism. Take for example this passage, by the painter Machereau during the events brought forth by the July Revolution (1830) and described in his own 'Profession of Faith' (1831):

> On that day, and only on that day in my past life, did I glimpse, in the midst of the people revolting as a single human being, the future that I find today. I felt myself alive with the life of those around me when my hand, covered with the muck of the heroic street, shook the honorably callused hand of the worker, the smooth white hand of the student, and even the hand of the bourgeois idler; it was always a human being moved by my fears and my hopes. A secret flame, a divine voice, revealed a UNIVERSAL

---

[96] Cuchet, *Une histoire du sentiment religieux au XIXe siècle*, 55–60.

ASSOCIATION to me. O my fathers, of all the news I yearned for, what good news it brought me! That instantaneous movement that brought me closer to a human being and worked its effect in the two of us as in every being, that feeling which invited me to gently reveal secrets to a human being whose name and life I had no need to know in order to confide in him, said to me: No, human beings are not born to hate, they are born to love; yes, association and love are their needs. Ah, I no longer miss that paradise promised to the mere spirituality of my being alone. Henceforth I will touch and hear and see loving beings who are alive with my life.[97]

The lyrical language of Machereau's profession makes it fit easily into the abovementioned frameworks of a revived religious romanticism, one where the revolutionary politics of July 1830 becomes intimately entangled with a religious-spiritual utopianism of "universal association".[98] But another facet is here at play, which is that Machereau uncovers a new way for understanding and relating to others in public life through his everyday experience of wandering the street during the July Revolution, an experience which gives him an insight into both the true state of humanity ("human beings [...] are born to love; yes, association and love are their needs") and into his own rationally and historically infused prejudices ("No, human beings are not born to hate [...] Ah, I no longer miss that paradise promised to the mere spirituality of my being alone").

The confrontation with the other in the street then provided the Saint-Simonist with another kind of knowledge, the kind which could only be attained through touch and embodiment, a kind of standpoint epistemology *avant la lettre*.[99] Again, the act of believing, of having faith in another ("that feeling which invited me to gently reveal secrets to a human being whose name and life I had no need to know in order to confide in him") functioned as a crucial narrative prism through which a Saint-Simonist like Machereau could reflect on his own life, reason and intervention. In this way, such reflections on the practice of believing constituted both a continuation of Saint-Simon's project of analysing the social history of belief as well as its inversion. But how was this the case?

---

[97] Machereau, "Profession of Faith", *L'Organisateur*, March 5th, 1831, cited in: Rancière, *Proletarian Nights*, 181–182.
[98] Rancière, *Proletarian Nights*, 182.
[99] On standpoint epistemology, cf. Briana Toole, "Recent Work in Standpoint Epistemology", *Analysis* 81, no. 2 (2021): 338–350.

First, it represented its continuation as Saint-Simon had also approached the category of 'belief' as a tool for thinking the sociologist in history, as a way of further outlining the purpose of the social scientist. Why had something like a social science suddenly become necessary around the eighteenth and nineteenth centuries, according to Saint-Simon? One of the reasons would be that it would be able to investigate such things as beliefs and their role in society in an objective and scientific manner, alongside other formative elements of social life such as institutions, forms of government and the structures of societal organization.[100] Social beliefs were considered by Saint-Simon as semi-propositional claims (to use current-day terminology), which could be differentiated according to their degree of falsification, with society steadily progressing from ancient polytheistic to Christian-theological to eventually Cartesian-positivist beliefs.[101] Within this scheme, the social scientist had a purely theoretical relation with beliefs, in the eyes of Saint-Simon, standing outside their domain of government as an observer. In the Cartesian regime of belief which Saint-Simon thought they had entered, only those beliefs were adhered to which could be demonstrated as being true.[102] Saint-Simon considered the social scientist to be someone who would contribute to science and society by conceptualizing a new sort of social religion ('the new Christianity') purified from all of its superstitions and useless beliefs.[103] A belief without a corresponding demonstration of its truth in reality had become an anachronism for Saint-Simon, something which no longer had any place in the modern system of positivist belief.

What the missionary encounter with the workers made clear, however, was that such a belief/knowledge-composition had its own fundamental limits: another kind of knowledge of the social could be found exclusively in the touch of the "callused hands", in the actual experience ("I will touch and hear and see loving beings who are alive *with my life*") of the

---

[100] Wokler, "From the Moral and Political Sciences to the Sciences of Society", 36–40.

[101] Saint-Simon, "Introduction aux travaux scientifiques, vol. II", 205–209.

[102] *De la religion Saint-Simonienne*, 27: "Et pour croire à lui, pour se vouer à l'accomplissement d'une œuvre si belle, accoutumé qu'on est à ne reconnaître de pouvoir légitime que celui de l'intelligence, on veut de la science, des démonstrations, du positif: personne aujourd'hui, grands et petits, *ignorans* et *savans*, ne croit à rien plus qu'à tout cela! Eh bien, Messieurs, St-Simon peut en donner. Voici ce que son école vous dit par ma bouche."

[103] Saint-Simon, "Le Nouveau Christianisme (1825)", 301.

social conditions as they were enacted in real-time. The original, more theoretical belief/knowledge-composition articulated by Saint-Simon—organizing and differentiating the different propositional regimes of belief through (socio-historical) knowledge—had to be augmented by the experiences of the Saint-Simonist missionaries: social beliefs, even those without any immediate correspondence to social reality, do persist in the Cartesian age, as they retain an important social function.

This function, according to the Saint-Simonists, is that we do gain something through such a thing as blind faith which is an existential understanding of what it means to be human: through a naked surrender to our fellow man, their dreams, their eclectic aspirations beyond the restrictions of their class become accessible to us.[104] Of course, this fundamental tension which was produced through the modernist intensification of the theory/practice-divide is something that haunts the entire history of social science, made up of the seemingly eternal struggle between the idealist representation of the material conditions of reality, and its concrete experience by the oppressed classes themselves, which are, by necessity, more complex and diverse than can be captured by rationalized representations of this reality.[105] And this realization becomes articulated at intermittent points in this history, for example in the 1960s and '70s, when historians like Rancière and E.P. Thompson reacted against an intellectual Marxism which was becoming too disconnected from the everyday reality experienced by the working classes themselves.[106]

Another example can be traced back to the 1930s, when someone like Simone Weil, the French philosopher and political activist, also became captivated and fascinated by this tension between the theoretical reflections on industrializing life and its actual, practical experience, as she left her teaching job at a girls' *lycée* to go and work in a factory, in order to actually *live* what it is like and to phenomenologically describe how one is formed and shaped into a 'worker'.[107] These writings would eventually be bundled in the book *La condition ouvrière* (1951), in which she

---

[104] Barrault, "La Hiérarchie", 201.
[105] Donald Reid, "Introduction", in: Rancière, *Proletarian Nights*, xiii-xxxv.
[106] E.P. Thompson, *The Making of the English Working Class* (London: Victor Gollancz Ltd., 1963).
[107] Robert Sparling, "Theory and Praxis: Simone Weil and Marx on the Dignity of Labor", *The Review of Politics* 74, no. 1 (2012): 87–107.

chronicled her experiences as a factory worker in the late 1930s, further displaying, through her very existence and practices as a worker, the blind spots inherent in the works of the Marxist-intellectual class, through their lack of lived experience with what it means to *be a worker*.[108]

Furthermore, this sociological tension is intimately connected to the fact that Weil herself was someone who is difficult to place exclusively within a secular tradition; she was as much a socialist intellectual as she was a devoted Christian later in life, this individual complexity undoubtedly related to her wariness of a theory uprooted from reality.[109] But, as Scott B. Ritner argues, this is less a confirmation of her separation of a Marxist tradition than an example of a tradition in action, where intellectual and existential lacunae are addressed and reflected upon.[110] Similar figures have popped up in the history of the sociological tradition, often at the fringes of the discipline, as an almost automatic mechanism for balancing a previous trajectory of excessive theorization. It were often women, like Jane Addams (1860–1935), the American social worker and sociologist, who would take up such a role, as she would combine her daily practices of community organization with reflections on the relation between these practices and social theory. Eventually, the sociological discipline has tried to articulate such self-reflexivity into the core of the operation itself, as, in the second half of the twentieth century, action research increasingly became a tradition onto itself. Via this method, the researcher not merely describes, but actively participates in the social context or organization studied, incorporating these experiences into the research results themselves.[111] Another iconic work in this regard, again originating in the fringes in more ways than one, was written by Jeanne Favret-Saada, who laid bare how a seemingly irrational practice, like an "unwitching ritual", could only be properly understood when the researcher actively

---

[108] Simone Weil, *La condition ouvrière* (Paris: Gallimard, 1951).

[109] For Weil's reflections on 'uprootedness': Simone Weil, *L'Enracinement, prélude à une déclaration des devoirs envers l'être humain* (Paris: Gallimard, 1949).

[110] Scott B. Ritner, "Simone Weil's Heterodox Marxism: Revolutionary Pessimism and the Politics of Resistance", in: *Simone Weil, Beyond Ideology?*, eds. Sophie Bourgault & Julie Daigle (Cham: Palgrave Macmillan, 2020), 185–205.

[111] Mary Jo Deegan, "Jane Addams, the Hull-House School of Sociology, and Social Justice, 1892 to 1935", *Humanity & Society* 37, no. 3 (2013): 199–278; on action research, cf. Jacques M. Chevalier & Daniel J. Buckles, *Participatory Action Research: Theory and Methods for Engaged Inquiry* (London: Routledge, 2013).

participated in the lifeworld of witchcraft, a world closed to scholars who exclusively employ instruments of reason and abstraction.[112]

It is in this vein that the Saint-Simonist movement should also be viewed within the broad history of the social sciences, I argue, in its self-reflexive problematization of positivist social theory through the Saint-Simonists' experiences of encountering the workers in their concrete everyday *life*. In this sense, their contribution to the construction of the sociological operation expands, beyond the sociological theory and ideas of Saint-Simon, towards a complex body of techniques accumulated by a network of sociological actors for dealing with social and religious practices. Their application of the Saint-Simonist doctrine onto their own life was not so much an abandonment of the socio-scientific spirit for a venture into the domain of utopian politics, as much as it represented this spirit coming into action, their quest for fully understanding the workings of society still fuelling their missionary behaviour and decision-making. As such, I would argue that any investigation of the Saint-Simonist influence into the development of late nineteenth-century social science should involve the writings and activities of these later Saint-Simonists, in order to further understand how their own forms of standpoint epistemology and action research relates to the later, more institutionalized forms of these methods within the discipline.

Conclusion

"A Modern is someone who believes that others believe", said Latour in his *On the Modern Cult of the Factish Gods*, and it is not difficult to see how someone like Claude-Henri de Saint-Simon would fall under this category.[113] Presenting himself as someone who could uncover the different stages of belief-systems throughout history, Saint-Simon even went so far as putting forward his own vision for a new religion, a "new Christianity", the main benefit of which would not be any sort of salvation of the soul but rather its ability to improve the worldly life of the poorest classes.[114] All of this, while also proclaiming to *only* believe that which is reasonable and demonstrable, and Saint-Simon can be considered as perhaps one of

---

[112] Cf. Jeanne Favret-Saada, *Les Mots, la Mort, les Sorts: la sorcellerie dans le bocage* (Paris: Gallimard, 1977); Ibid., *Désorceler* (Paris: L'Olivier, 2009).

[113] Latour, *On the Modern Cult*, 2.

[114] Saint-Simon, "Le Nouveau Christianisme (1825)", 322–323.

the Founding Moderns, whose understanding of religion exclusively went through the informational category of belief and, as such, could not imagine any sort of purpose to religion beyond the socially effective.[115]

And this evaluation isn't exactly unjustified either: throughout his own work, the French social reformist mainly approached the category of 'belief' in the way his enlightened predecessors like Condorcet and the Ideologues did as well, as individual mental states originating in cultural environments and institutions, through which the social scientist could observe the historical spirit in societies. For Saint-Simon, the state of collective belief needed to conform to the historically conditioned structures of society. In nineteenth-century France, this meant a system of belief which was sympathetic to the scientific mind, one which valued curiosity and creativity, and one which consistently sought to verify these beliefs, through critical examination, demonstration and communication.

The previously hegemonic system of beliefs, that originating in the Christian belief of the Incarnation of Jesus Christ, was considered to have become unsuitable, in the eyes of Saint-Simon, as it no longer conformed to the changed structures of society. At the same time, this did not mean that Saint-Simon completely abandoned the idea of religion. Unlike his enlightened predecessors, the social reformist was convinced that something like a spiritual authority needed to be sustained within society for it to function properly, and thus sought to conceive of a new kind of religion, a "new Christianity", which would be conform to a modern society, one which was, moreover, struggling with ways of dealing with socio-economic inequality and changing conditions of living and working. It was only by providing all different social classes with a shared purpose and goal, argued Saint-Simon, that a well-governed and functioning society could arise again.

The category of 'belief' was a central component within this socio-philosophical scheme of the social reformist, as it allowed Saint-Simon to approach both the history of religion as well as its future as something intimately connected to the organization of society and as something that could be ideologically and intellectually tinkered with, an instrument more than anything through which the mind and subsequently the behaviour of the different classes could be governed. Again, this seems to largely confirm the typical critiques of later commentators of such sociological moderns as

---

[115] Latour, "Beyond belief", 28–29.

Saint-Simon, which is that they understood little of the complex make-up of the religious phenomenon and, furthermore, that 'belief' was a crucial instrument in this misunderstanding, transforming religion into something social and informative, and with little other purpose than its worldly impact as an instrument of communal formation.

In this chapter, however, I have aimed to counter such a critical evaluation of Saint-Simon's use of the belief-category, and this in two ways. First of all, instead of only focusing on the writings of Saint-Simon himself, I have considerably broadened the view of what can be called the Saint-Simonist engagement with historical languages of belief, by also looking at the Saint-Simonist movement as well as their concrete practices as missionaries of Saint-Simonist dogma. And secondly, I have tried to approach this Saint-Simonist engagement with this category in a more historical manner, by not only looking at how Saint-Simon conceptualized the category, but by also integrating how this conceptualization subsequently impacted the Saint-Simonist ideology as well.

As a result, I would argue that quite a different picture of the Saint-Simonist employment of the belief-category appears, one which goes far beyond the merely informative and instrumental as is sometimes posited. As I have tried to show throughout this chapter, 'to believe' meant many things within the Saint-Simonist tradition. While its first iteration, as a theoretical concept in the work of Saint-Simon, was rather restrictive in its positivist meaning, this restrictive nature, at the same time, ultimately also allowed the Saint-Simonists to self-reflexively problematize this notion, when confronted with situations in social life which did not conform to Saint-Simon's original iteration of 'belief'.

And this is where the multifaceted history of the concept shows itself to be valuable: because 'believing' actually did mean many different things throughout the ages, when Saint-Simon's original iteration of positivist belief fell flat in the face of social reality, this did not lead the Saint-Simonist program to an intellectual collapse under the pressure of its own weight. The multiple meanings could coexist alongside each other thanks to the pluralist nature of the category's history, making additional iterations also 'true', with the added remark that they were true dependent on the particular context and status of the sociological observer in question. The elasticity of belief's semiotic matrix allowed these multiple iterations of belief, not only to coexist, but to transform into a productive interaction between sociological theory and practice.

In the case of the Saint-Simonists, this meant that the theoretical class distinction between a positivist elite and a superstitious worker class made by Saint-Simon gradually evolved from an epistemological trickle-down scheme where the intellectuals unilaterally defined what 'believing' meant into an interactive system of mutual exchange, where the concrete reality of the working classes and their acts of believing provided their own unique form of social knowledge which had the power to alter the theoretical models of the Saint-Simonists. 'Belief', in other words, in all its historical ambiguity of meaning enabled the construction of a narrative space in which the Saint-Simonists could develop and test their different instruments of social analysis, where believing could signal different things at different times and providing a sense of how religious practices, speech acts and rituals were rich and complex phenomena in their own right.

CHAPTER 7

Sociology as Institution and as Spiritual Authority: Languages of Belief in the Work of Auguste Comte

Introduction: The Advent of Positivism

In the second half of the eighteenth and the first half of the nineteenth century, the formation of the social sciences in France had been intimately connected to the social and political turmoil characteristic of the era: the French Revolution, the Terror, the Napoleonic Wars, the Bourbon Restoration and the July Revolution, all of these events were both influenced by vehement intellectual debates on the state of society and influential in shaping different epistemic responses to these events and their impact on society.[1] This period eventually culminated in the European revolutions of 1848, a final explosion of social unrest which was, once again, strongly affected by a political-intellectual culture populated by different reformist movements, many of which called upon their own analyses of society and its structures as arguments for reform and/or revolution.[2] And then, something seemingly changed: as intensely as the revolutionary era had erupted, so quietly did it eventually taper out, the liberal reforms granted throughout different European countries apparently sufficient for soothing the revolutionary spirits of the mid-nineteenth century. At least,

[1] Brahami, *La Raison du Peuple*, 9–26.
[2] Craig Calhoun, "Classical Social Theory and the French Revolution of 1848", *Sociological Theory* 7, no. 2 (1989): 210–225.

this is how later historians have come to approach this era, with most forms of historiographical periodization ending the revolutionary political culture at this stage, its format of public revolutionary struggle being substituted for a new politics of parties, parliaments, imperialist expansion and colonization.[3]

Interestingly enough, the history of the social sciences has consistently adopted this scheme of periodization as well, mainly using it as a way to distinguish between a pre-scientific and early scientific period of sociology.[4] Typically, early nineteenth-century figures like Louis de Bonald and Henri de Saint-Simon were then approached as political philosophers and reformers who had begun to theorize an undertaking such as social science, without actually being sociologists themselves.[5] Of course, this is a serious topic of debate in its own right, with many scholars making the case that eighteenth- and early nineteenth-century thinkers of society, like Bonald and Saint-Simon, need to be engaged as properly belonging to the history of social science.[6] That being said, it seems self-evident that a difference exists between the state of social science in the early nineteenth century and the form that it gradually began to take in the second half of the nineteenth century, when some of the so-called founders of the discipline, Émile Durkheim and Max Weber, started to articulate and outline a scientific ethos, focus and methodology which is still formative of the discipline to this very day.[7]

---

[3] Louis Bergeron, François Furet & Reinhart Koselleck (eds.), *Das Zeitalter der europäischen Revolution 1780–1848* (Frankfurt am Main: Fischer Bücherei, 1969); William H. Sewell Jr., *Work and Revolution in France: the Language of Labor from the Old Regime to 1848* (Cambridge: Cambridge University Press, 1980); François Furet & Mona Ozouf (eds.), *The French Revolution and the Creation of Modern Political Culture, vol. 3: The Transformation of Political Culture 1789–1848* (New York: Pergamon Press, 1987).

[4] Johan Heilbron, Lars Magnusson & Björn Wittrock (eds.), *The Rise of the Social Sciences and the Formation of Modernity: Conceptual Change in Context, 1750–1850* (Dordrecht: Kluwer Academic Publishers, 1998); Frédéric Brahami, *La Raison du Peuple: Un héritage de la Révolution française (1789–1848)* (Paris: Les Belles Lettres, 2016).

[5] Heilbron, *French Sociology*, 42–44, in which Saint-Simon is referred to as a "political reformer" who "lacked the scientific competence and the rigor this would require and mistakenly gave priority to social and economic reform". Someone like Bonald is not mentioned throughout the book.

[6] Moreau, "A propos de Louis de Bonald", 140.

[7] On the potential role of the sociological canon today, cf. Steven Lukes, "Sociology's inescapable past", *Journal of Classical Sociology* 21, no. 3–4 (2021): 283–288.

Much like it was in the broader Western European political culture, the burgeoning sociological culture around the middle of the nineteenth century witnessed a decline in emphasis on immediate social reform, as the political and social anguish of post-revolutionary France settled down and was replaced by a desire for a more depoliticized science of society and social life.[8] As Johan Heilbron has shown, the new generation of scholars born in the 1820s, like Ernest Renan and Hippolyte Taine, became highly critical of the spiritualist language which was rife within the early social sciences and instead turned towards the socio-scientific cultures prevalent in Germany and Great Britain, where much more emphasis was being placed on scientific rigour and method.[9] The metaphysical components and the intricate entanglement with Christianity's fate in modernity, aspects which were so constitutive of the early nineteenth-century ventures into social science, were gradually being cut loose from the discipline itself, with the new movement of positivist sociologists seeking to ally the young discipline with the natural sciences and other young and promising disciplines, such as psychology.[10] Whereas early philosophers of society, such as Bonald and Saint-Simon, had still sought to either modernize the Christian religion or to evolve beyond it towards more socially emancipatory forms of religiosity, the positivists, undoubtedly affected by half a century of spiritualist dominance and a lack of scientific progress, aimed to thoroughly shift the emphasis of the young socio-scientific discipline away from religious concerns and more towards the true, materialist foundations of social life.[11] This did not mean that religion was no longer of any concern—it was still a central theme and research object of positivist sociology—but it did signify an important shift in the status of the religious domain for the positivist sociologist, as simply another facet of social life to be studied and investigated rather than as the privileged entry point for thinking about society.[12]

---

[8] Bruno Karsenti, "Le problème des sciences humaines. Comte, Durkheim, Lévi-Strauss", *Archives de Philosophie* 63, no. 3 (2000): 445–465.

[9] Heilbron, *French Sociology*, 22.

[10] Ibid., 59–70.

[11] Ibid., 24–26.

[12] On the context of 'religion' in the sociological culture of the late nineteenth and early twentieth century, cf. Mitsutoshi Horii, "Historicizing the category of 'religion' in sociological theories: Max Weber and Emile Durkheim", *Critical Research on Religion* 7, no. 1 (2019): 24–37.

Where the status of 'religion' changed, so too did the status of 'beliefs' for the positivist sociologist. Again, as it was for the domain of 'religion', this shift was not absolute: as I have shown in the chapters before, the employment of the belief-category was already multifaceted in the first half of the nineteenth century in the societal reflections of Bonald, Saint-Simon and the Saint-Simonists, and it continued to be so in the second half of this century. And yet, it can be argued that the category began to take on a more uniquely sociological meaning at this time, and this for several reasons. First, the increasing turn towards scientific rigour and method forced positivist sociologists to be more clear about the epistemological tools which they were employing, stimulating further exercises in defining their concepts.[13] And second, the category of 'belief' represented an especially suitable avenue for discussions of disciplinary demarcation: it was a concept through which sociologists engaged with their philosophical, and especially, Kantian heritage, and it provided a source of contestation with that other, quickly developing science in the second half of the nineteenth century, psychology.[14]

This gave, understandably, the notion of 'belief' a primarily epistemological dimension, as something which concerned, first and foremost, such questions as the cognitive make-up of the human mind, the state of interconnection between thought and action, and the relationship between the individual consciousness and their social environment. Perhaps, then, it is here, with the advent of positivist sociology and the discipline's gradual institutionalization within the university, that we can locate those sociological moderns lamented by Bruno Latour, who imposed an informative mode of the belief-category as the privileged instrument for understanding and approaching the phenomenon of religion, clearing the path for its continuous misunderstanding throughout the next century.[15] Recent

---

[13] Cf. for example: Marcel Mauss, "Métier d'ethnographe, méthode sociologique", Extrait de la "Leçon d'ouverture à l'enseignement de l'histoire des religions des peuples non civilisés". *Revue de l'histoire des religions* 45 (1902): 42–54. Digital edition (pages 3–9), last consulted on the 20th of September 2023, http://classiques.uqac.ca/classiques/mauss_marcel/oeuvres_3/oeuvres_3_09/metier_ethnographe.html: "Sachant que les rites et les croyances sont des faits sociaux, difficiles à saisir, nous devrons toujours rechercher, messieurs, quel est leur véritable forme, leur mode d'existence, de transmission, de fonctionnement (7)."

[14] On the development of psychology and its impact on the sociological discipline, cf. Joly, *La révolution sociologique*, 27–132.

[15] On Latour's critique of the belief-category, cf. supra ch. 2.

scholarship in the critical religion-tradition—which is interested in investigating the socially constructed religious-secular distinction as a research object[16]—often points in a similar direction, looking at how classical sociologists like Durkheim and Weber were formed by their roles as prominent intellectual voices within the colonialist-imperialist states of nineteenth-century Imperial Germany and the Third Republic, using such categories as 'religion' to naturalize "the value orientation of the state with which each of them was associated".[17]

In the following three chapters, I will investigate how these shifts within the sociological discipline concretely materialized in the work of two of the most famous positivist sociologists, Auguste Comte and Émile Durkheim. As I have done in the previous chapters, I do this by looking at how they conceptualized, practised and negotiated the category of 'belief' throughout their texts, in order to reconstruct how these sociologists navigated the complex and deeply historical semantic network of 'belief'. The guiding question throughout these chapters will be whether and how the positivist negotiation of the belief-category genuinely constituted a process of secularization, both for themselves in their identification as secular sociologists and for those others whose belief-practices they described and interpreted.

The Peculiar Case of Auguste Comte

In this first of these three chapters on positivism and its engagement with the category of belief, I will focus on the work of Auguste Comte. In this aforementioned shift from a more religiously inspired and -influenced social science towards a more methodologically robust and academically institutionalized sociology, the life and work of Comte symbolizes a kind of transitional phase in which the specifics of this shift were conceptualized and partially implemented. Considered by many to be the founder of both positivism and sociology, the French philosopher has an ambiguous and often contradictory legacy, with the unifying principle of his work mostly being dependent on the part of it which was particularly emphasized by his later interpreters. This could range from Comte being essentially

---

[16] Timothy Fitzgerald (ed.), *Religion and the Secular: Historical and Colonial Formations* (London: Equinox, 2007); William Arnal & Russell T. McCutcheon, *The Sacred is the Profane: The Political Nature of "Religion"* (Oxford: Oxford University Press, 2013).

[17] Horii, "Historicizing the category of 'religion'", 35.

viewed as an anti-metaphysical philosopher of science to someone who ultimately aimed to reinvent religion and who considered himself to be the Grand Priest of a newly formed positivist religion.[18]

Like those early nineteenth-century social scientists before him, Comte had been strongly influenced by the events and aftermath of the French Revolution.[19] Born in 1798 to a conservative Catholic family in Montpellier, Comte was instead drawn to the republican ideals of the Revolution, quickly distancing himself from the counter-revolutionary sympathies which were common both to his parents and to most people living in the south of France.[20] He would move to Paris to study at the École Polytechnique, learning about the beneficial role science could play in the organization of society, before being expelled in 1816 for insubordinate behaviour.[21] In the years following, he would enter into the social circles of the famous reformist Henri de Saint-Simon, acting as his assistant and contributing several texts to Saint-Simonist journals, both under his own name as well as under the name of Saint-Simon himself.[22] The two would eventually break ties in 1824 after a dispute on the authorship of the *Plan des travaux scientifiques nécessaires pour réorganiser la société* (1824), with Comte, after the split, becoming the leading thinker on the role of science within society while the Saint-Simonists would turn more towards religiosity and spirituality under the new leadership of Prosper Enfantin.[23]

In the years following his association with the Saint-Simonists, Comte became a central figure in the set-up of a positivist tradition and this through the writing and publication of the *Cours de philosophie positive* (1830–42), a six-volume work on the history and philosophy of the sciences.[24] Comte was one of the first philosophers to theorize what were

---

[18] These two approaches can even appear in the same anthology, cf. for example: Johan Heilbron, "Auguste Comte and the Second Scientific Revolution", in: *The Anthem Companion to Auguste Comte*, ed. Andrew Wernick (London: Anthem Press, 2017), 23–41, and Thomas Kemple, "Comte's Civic Comedy: Secular Religion and Modern Morality in the Age of Classical Sociology", in: *The Anthem Companion to Auguste Comte*, ed. Andrew Wernick (London: Anthem Press, 2017), 159–174.

[19] Pickering, *Auguste Comte*, 3.

[20] Ibid.

[21] Schmaus, Pickering, & Bourdeau, "Introduction: The Significance of Auguste Comte", 11.

[22] Ibid., 11–12; Pickering, *Auguste Comte*, 102–103.

[23] Ibid., 12; Pickering, "Auguste Comte and the Saint-Simonians", 218.

[24] Auguste Comte, *Cours de philosophie positive* (Paris: Rouen Frères & Bachelier, 1830–42), 6 vol.

effectively revolutionary changes occurring in the make-up of science itself, as the second half of the eighteenth century saw an increasing division of labour within what was earlier simply known as 'natural philosophy', with different disciplines (mathematics, biology, chemistry) applying themselves to different facets of life.[25] What Comte added to this historical event was the insight that knowledge and science turned out to be things which were historically and socially developed as well, with different stages in human development having different cultures of knowledge-production.[26] This was his theory of the three stages—the theological, metaphysical and positive stages—which sought to explain both the historical shape of knowledge as well as its contemporary form as a multi-disciplinary undertaking.[27] Furthermore, it was this insight—the need for a historical and systematic synthesis of the sciences—which provided the discipline of sociology with its own rightful place in the hierarchy of the sciences, as that form of knowledge which could reflect on the historical development of knowledge itself within a societal context.[28] According to someone like Johan Heilbron, it was this differential theory of science which represented Comte's major contribution to the history of social science, as it "laid the foundation for sociology as a relatively autonomous science".[29]

At the same time, such an emphasis on the epistemological facet of Comte's work has been highly contested in its own right—as the polemic between Heilbron and fellow Dutch sociologist Dick Pels has shown, concerning Heilbron's supposedly selective reading of the French philosopher—as such an exclusive focus pushes the later, more speculative work of Comte firmly to the background.[30] This contestation has only been amplified since the turn of the twenty-first century, with Comte's writings

---

[25] Heilbron, *French Sociology*, 41–43.
[26] Ibid., 43.
[27] Ibid.
[28] Ibid., 44–45.
[29] Heilbron, *The Rise of Social Theory*, 271.
[30] On this polemic, cf. Dick Pels, "Historisch positivisme", *Amsterdams Sociologisch Tijdschrift* 18, no. 1 (1991): 118–139; Johan Heilbron, "Intellectuele geschiedenis als sociologisch probleem", *Amsterdams Sociologisch Tijdschrift* 18, no. 1 (1991): 140–160; Dick Pels, "Dupliek. Nogmaals: Heilbron's Comte", *Amsterdams Sociologisch Tijdschrift* 18, no. 1 (1991): 161–164; Dick Pels, "Reviews: Johan Heilbron, The Rise of Social Theory. Cambridge: Polity Press, 1995", *History of the Human Sciences* 9, no. 1 (1996): 113–131; Johan Heilbron, "Auguste Comte and historical epistemology: a reply to Dick Pels", *History of the Human Sciences* 9, no. 2 (1996): 153–159.

on altruism, love and the Religion of Humanity garnering more and more scholarly interest since that time.[31] In the eyes of other Comte-specialists, like Michel Bourdeau, Frédéric Brahami and Mary Pickering, the French philosopher cannot be reduced to his status as a philosopher of science and pioneering positivist, as he was, in their eyes, also someone who was sceptical of intemperate scientism and who was less than convinced to consider 'science' as a solution to every kind of problem.[32] According to these scholars then, Comte's extensive forays into the domains of religion and spirituality did not so much represent an aberration of Comte's thought but its fullest extension, marking his most remarkable achievement in the history of social science as someone who was able to explore and reflect on sociology's epistemological *and* existential dimensions.[33]

The fact that he was able to produce such an eclectic body of work is a further indication of how Comte was constantly drawn to both the past era of a spiritualist politics and the coming era of positivism, with his sociological interventions being marked by the desire to strike a harmonious balance between the two in which they would fully complement each other.[34] As argued by Warren Schmaus, Mary Pickering and Michel Bourdeau, this eclecticism does not imply that there were different phases in Comte's work, one positivist-scientific and the other religious-moralistic, as it has often been interpreted by both his peers (such as John Stuart Mill) and by later historians and sociologists.[35] The seeds of his Religion of Humanity can be found in the later volumes of the *Cours* and the same commitment to positivism pervades the volumes of his *Système politique*.[36] Rather than signal any kind of fundamental shift within his work, it indicates that Comte realized the value of both a reasonably organized society and a philosophy which could make sense of the human desire for (irrational) meaning and emotionality, and sought to find ways of articulating a way of thought which could find room for both.

---

[31] Cf. "Auguste Comte et la religion positiviste", *Revue des sciences philosophiques et théologiques* 87, no. 1 (2003); "Autour de Comte et Saint-Simon. Reconfigurations socio-religieuses post-révolutionnaires", *Archives de sciences sociales des religions* 190, no. 3 (2020).

[32] Pickering, *Auguste Comte*, 577.

[33] Michel Bourdeau, "Auguste Comte et la religion positiviste: présentation", *Revue des sciences philosophiques et théologiques* 87, no. 1 (2003): 19–20.

[34] Pickering, *Auguste Comte*, 4.

[35] Schmaus, Pickering, & Bourdeau, "Introduction: The Significance of Auguste Comte", 20.

[36] Ibid., 19–21.

When we turn to the question of 'belief' and the role it played within the work of Auguste Comte, however, it becomes apparent that this perceived distinction between the epistemological and religious phases within Comte's life thoroughly impacts later studies of this category in the work of the French philosopher. Not a great deal has been written on Comte's understanding of the belief-category up to this point—although the revived interest in positivist religion has somewhat invigorated such investigations[37]—and most of what has been written tends to emphasize either its philosophical facets and connections (Bourdeau) or its political function in Comtean thought as a tool for proper government (Brahami).[38] Such specialized readings should not come as a surprise either, since, even though Comte's employment of the category was consistent throughout his oeuvre, it did not constitute one of his central concepts, in the way, for example, 'altruism' or 'the law of three stages' did.[39] But this leaves us with the question of how Comte concretely used the category within his intellectual toolset as an instrument to move across these different domains. What is still missing, in other words, is a look at how Comte employed these different meanings of the belief-category within his own work, both as a coherent philosophical project and as a means of thinking both his own sociological program and his historical status as a sociologist. In the next sections of this chapter, I will seek to answer this question. As I have argued in previous chapters, it is by looking at these different narrative strategies of articulating 'belief' that we can gain a better understanding of how someone like Comte envisioned the complex relationship between an unfolding social science and the persistent desire of human societies for religious meaning and spiritual authority.

---

[37] Bourdeau, "Auguste Comte et la religion positiviste", 10–11.

[38] Bourdeau, "Pouvoir spirituel", 1095–1104; Frédéric Brahami, "De la nécessité du pouvoir spirituel chez les modernes: Comte, critique de l'âge critique", *Archives de sciences sociales de la religion* 190 (2020): 127–141.

[39] The centrality of 'belief' was strongly related to his conviction that "dogmatism [...] was the natural mental state of humanity", which made matters of belief crucial in any form of government, cf. Schmaus, Pickering, & Bourdeau, "Introduction: The Significance of Auguste Comte", 18.

The Comtean Passage: Moving Sociology Beyond the Reactionary Debates of the Early Nineteenth Century

The previous chapters have given an indication of how the category of belief—its ambiguous grammar, its flux of historically distinct meanings, its ability to take on multiple modalities—played a central role in the early formation of the sociological discipline through its ability to function as a communicative surface in relation to this other crucial discourse of early modern social government, Christian religion. The difficulty of fully capturing the notion of 'belief', experienced by both Louis de Bonald and Saint-Simon in their early sociological philosophies, was clearly noticed by one of Saint-Simon's former assistants, Auguste Comte.[40] While Comte obviously valued both thinkers as important voices in the debate on the need for a moral regeneration of society, he had a troubled relationship with them, especially with Saint-Simon, as the two experienced a personal fall-out at the end of the latter's life as I have mentioned above.[41]

With the counter-revolutionary reactionaries like Bonald, de Maistre Chateaubriand and Felicité de Lamennais, Comte maintained a relationship which was much more straightforwardly intellectual, as the two parties shared an interest in the organic constitution of society as well as in the (beneficial) role religiosity played in the organization of civil society during the Middle Ages.[42] These thinkers of the so-called "retrograde school" emphasized the importance of spiritual power without envisioning its eventual appropriation of temporal power, like Saint-Simon and the Saint-Simonists did.[43] Comte, like many of his contemporaries, noticed the gap in spiritual authority and commonly shared moral principles throughout the Europe of the nineteenth century, which made any hope for a

---

[40] For a recent overview on the life and works of Auguste Comte, cf. Wernick, "Introduction", 1–22.

[41] Pickering, *Auguste Comte*, 157.

[42] Andrew Wernick, "The Religion of Humanity and Positive Morality", in: *Love, Order, & Progress: The Science, Philosophy, & Politics of Auguste Comte*, eds. Michel Bourdeau, Mary Pickering, & Warren Schmaus (Pittsburgh: University of Pittsburgh Press, 2018), 237.

[43] Carolina Armenteros, "The Counterrevolutionary Comte: Theorist of the Two Powers and Enthusiastic Medievalist", in: *The Anthem Companion to Auguste Comte*, ed. Andrew Wernick (London: Anthem Press, 2017), 94.

community with solid foundations fruitless in his eyes.⁴⁴ He was particularly swayed by the example of the Holy Alliance, the coalition binding the monarchies of Austria, Prussia and Russia together after the Napoleonic Wars, which had been used and discussed by the abbé Lamennais as a typical case of how such a collective could never properly work if it lacked a legitimate spiritual power and exclusively leant on temporal and heterogeneous elements.⁴⁵

Modern Europe, in other words, could not simply move beyond Catholicism without finding a suitable replacement for its spiritual authority. Furthermore, Comte had learned from the retrograde school that societies, in fact, could die, meaning that the real danger of disorder needed to be contained through a renewed spiritual doctrine, which could replace the negative, critical metaphysics which had dominated the current age.⁴⁶ And yet, according to Comte, the Catholic reactionaries were in many ways themselves partly responsible for this current condition, through their refusal to recognize the 'pastness' of Catholic-feudal society, as they desired to anachronistically restore the body politic to its medieval-feudal condition.⁴⁷ Instead, what was needed was the imposition of spiritual power in a positive system of belief corresponding to the industrial conditions of the modern age, with this conviction forming the basis of Comte's later project of a Religion of Humanity.⁴⁸

Historical discussions on Comte and his eclectic group of predecessors have focused mostly on the different kinds of interactions between these figures: their degree of intellectual inspiration, the politics of their ideologies and affiliation, and the overlaps of their socio-cultural milieus.⁴⁹ And while these are essential sources of research in their own right, here I am not so much concerned with the figure of Comte as a sociological author

---

⁴⁴ Comte, "Considérations sur le pouvoir spirituel (Mars 1826)", 214: "[I]l reste incontestable que ce système ne saurait avoir aucune solidité, si les diverses nations étaient abandonnées, d'une manière fixe, aux seules impulsions temporelles, sans les subordonner à aucune doctrine morale commune, établie et maintenue par un pouvoir spirituel quelconque."

⁴⁵ Ibid., 214n(1).

⁴⁶ Andrew Wernick, "The 'Great Crisis': Comte, Nietzsche, and the Religion Question", in: *The Anthem Companion to Auguste Comte*, ed. Andrew Wernick (London: Anthem Press, 2017), 124–125. On the terminology of "the retrograde school", cf. Comte, "Considérations sur le pouvoir spirituel", 197n(2).

⁴⁷ Ibid., 124.

⁴⁸ Karsenti, *Politique de l'esprit*, 50–51.

⁴⁹ Reedy, "The historical imaginary of social science in post-Revolutionary France", 1–26; Armenteros, "The Counterrevolutionary Comte", 91–115.

than as a historical actor seeking to navigate his own textual interventions within the broader history of belief, its different languages and its meanings. The work of Louis de Bonald and Henri de Saint-Simon then still plays an important role within this alternative historiographical framework but in a slightly different guise: these authors are less approached as providing a holistic body of sociological theory in their own right—which could be represented correctly or wrongly by Comte—but as historical embodiments of a burgeoning sociological culture, a culture which Comte wanted to fundamentally give shape.

For someone like Comte, having the opportunity to reflexively position himself qua 'sociologist' coincided with his own self-conceptualization as a social philosopher who occupied a unique meta-historical position. Both the inventor of a new religion and its Grand Priest, Comte imagined his own philosophical work in a similar vein, acting as a communicative bridge between multiple realms. His task as Grand Priest was to bring the spheres of objective and subjective life into communication. This categorical distinction between subjective and objective existences was already a staple within philosophy since the time of Aristotle (with Comte remarking that it was Immanuel Kant who was responsible for most neatly articulating it), but it attained a particular prominence in Comte's philosophy as the foundational principle of positivism, the latter being considered responsible for its systematization.[50] While objective life was characterized by its physical-materialist laws which governed the living in an automatic fashion, subjective life, on the other hand, was marked by its genuinely social and moral nature, as such an existence was able to extract itself from the rigid laws imposed on objective life.[51] Peculiarly perhaps, Comte associated such a subjective existence with the population of the dead, those who had literally become freed from the constraining laws of time and materiality and which could subsequently aid Humanity in its government through their exemplary status as those previously living men and women who were *morally worth* remembering.[52]

Past, present and future; the borders of objective and subjective life; the split between physical and spiritual existence: all of these dimensional

---

[50] Auguste Comte, *Catéchisme positiviste, ou Sommaire exposition de la religion universelle, en onze entretiens systématiques entre une Femme et un Prêtre de l'Humanité* (Paris: Chez Carilian-Goeury et V^{or} Dalmont, 1852), 41–42.

[51] Ibid., 163.

[52] Ibid., 167–168.

ruptures were experienced as subjectively constitutive by both the living and the dead, yet, remarkably, they were able to be transcended by the French philosopher as a result of his intimate understanding of both physical and social reality.[53] The positivist priest, according to Comte, was able to live two lives simultaneously, the priest being a representative of the two worlds in each dimension, allowing for the moral and spiritual coordination of the population within the objective realm.[54] Everything flowed through these singular points of dimensional cross-contamination, with the positivist priests considered by Comte to be the exclusive class capable of overseeing the complex social and material mechanisms driving all populations, both living and dead.[55]

For Comte then, the appearance and development of positivism represented a watershed moment in history, as new tools had been uncovered which could generate a new spiritual harmony. This also furthered his conviction that the culture of public discussion from around the turn of the nineteenth century, with its endless debates on the status of religion and spiritual power in society, had been misleading and illusory. Comte viewed it as his task to effectively close this public space of contestation and return to a society characterized by a harmony of beliefs and opinions. One of the ways the French philosopher attempted to realize this closure was by conceptualizing the historical appearance of the retrograde and progressive schools as a sign of modernity's composition itself.[56] From this viewpoint, the status of Bonaldian and Saint-Simonist sociology for Comte was then not so much of an alternative theory on the state of modern society than of a rich layer of socio-historical material, its main function being to provide the sociological observer with further insight into society's contemporary condition.[57]

At this point in time, certain readers might remark that to take such a view seriously is to simply take over Comte's own positivist language uncritically, a language furthermore which was often controversial for its perceived authoritarian tendencies as well as its political-ideological

---

[53] Karsenti, *Politique de l'esprit*, 159–160.
[54] Ibid.
[55] Jean-François Braunstein, "La religion des morts-vivants. Le culte des morts chez Auguste Comte", *Revue des sciences philosophiques et théologiques* 87, no. 1 (2003): 61–62.
[56] Brahami, "Sortir du cercle", 43; Brahami, "De la nécessite du pouvoir spirituel", 127–129.
[57] Brahami, "Sortir du cercle", 46–47.

ambiguity.[58] The Comtean philosophy of science has been considered by certain scholars as being autocratic in its structure, with its intentional purpose of hierarchizing the sciences and articulating a universal system of positivist philosophy and politics as an expression of this structure.[59] Reducing the work of Bonald and Saint-Simon to symbolic expressions of modern history rather than as proper social-philosophical voices in their own right could then be seen as confirming this autocratic scheme, in which Comte stands at the centre of modernity, passing his unique judgement along the way. I would argue, however, that entering the Comtean concept-space does not equate to its uncritical affirmation. My goal here is not simply to reconstruct this space, but rather to see how it operates, using the category of 'belief' as a means of making its textual mechanisms visible.

Turning to the work of Comte itself now, where and how did the French sociologist discuss the notion of belief? For Comte, the question of belief and its role in modernity was a constant throughout his life. While many scholars distinguish between the first and second part of his intellectual life—the first characterized by his conceptualization of a philosophy of science, the second by his work on positivist politics and the Religion of Humanity[60]—such a distinction cannot be made with regard to the belief-category, as this topic took on a central importance in both parts of Comte's life. Both his philosophy of science as well as his Religion of Humanity were fundamentally concerned with the question of belief (in regard to reason and demonstration in the former, and its government and institutionalization in the latter). The central text on this topic is undoubtedly his 1826 text "Considérations sur le pouvoir spirituel" in which Comte explicitly reflects on the category and its role within modern society in relation to the division of labour, the development of science and the decay of institutionalized religion.[61] But while this text is one of the few which reflexively problematizes the category—alongside his

---

[58] Mary Pickering, "Conclusion: The Legacy of Auguste Comte", in: *Love, Order, & Progress: The Science, Philosophy, & Politics of Auguste Comte*, eds. Michel Bourdeau, Mary Pickering, & Warren Schmaus (Pittsburgh: University of Pittsburgh Press, 2018), 250–253.

[59] Friedrich Hayek, *The Counter-Revolution of Science: Studies on the Abuse of Reason* (Glencoe: The Free Press, 1952). Cf. also Michel Bourdeau's response: Michel Bourdeau, "Fallait-il oublier Comte? Retour sur The Counter-Revolution of Science", *Revue européenne des sciences sociales* 54, no. 2 (2016): 89–111.

[60] Andrew Wernick, "Introduction", 7.

[61] Comte, "Considérations sur le pouvoir spirituel ", 177–216

"Considérations philosophiques sur la science et les savants" (1825) and the *Catéchisme positiviste* (1852)—again, the category and its extended language manifests itself throughout the Comtean oeuvre.

Furthermore, three distinct meanings can be extrapolated from Comte's engagement with the term: (1) it presented a means of reading the condition of modernity and the role of the sociologist; (2) it constituted a concrete problem of spiritual government and the loss of institutions; and (3) finally, it functioned as a crucial heuristic for understanding the complex historicized and socialized nature of Man.[62] As I will argue throughout this chapter, this accumulation of belief's meanings was no coincidence: for Comte, the proliferation of ways of believing and its lack of communication, calibration and spiritual government constituted a central problem for the so-called sociologist-priest, a problem which necessitated the use of multiple tactics for tackling it. In the next three sections, I will discuss each of these meanings and Comte's tactical approaches of them.

Narrating the Sociological Government of Beliefs: Aristotle, St. Paul, Gall

Like many of his contemporaries in the first half of the nineteenth century, Comte arrived at the question of belief through a preoccupation with spiritual power, or, to be more precise, its lack thereof in a modernizing, post-revolutionary society in France.[63] As a result, the French sociologist would dedicate his investigations of the social domain, the sciences and religion towards answering the question of spiritual power's role and form in modernity, starting out from the normative premise that no society could persist without a kind of spiritual authority, an institution which could direct the populace in their thought and action.[64]

Following this premise, it should come as no surprise that Comte put the emphasis on the virtual-theoretical domain and its effect on social life: the origin, organization and distribution of ideas, opinions, and beliefs, and the interaction between competing theoretical registers, such as science and theology. In the positivist philosophy of Comte, the theoretical operation always preceded the pragmatic direction of politics, meaning it

---

[62] Karsenti, *Politique de l'esprit*, 201; Bourdeau, "Pouvoir spirituel", 1095–1104; Kemple, "Comte's Civic Comedy", 164.

[63] Bourdeau, "Pouvoir spirituel", 1095–1096.

[64] Brahami, "De la nécessité du pouvoir spirituel", 128–129.

was absolutely crucial to identify the "principle according to which social relations must be coordinated".[65] The 'spirit of the system', not only unearthed by the theoretical procedure but also articulated by it, serves as the direct condition of possibility through which temporal powers can determine "the mode of repartition of power and the ensemble of administrative institutions", so as to conform to spiritual authority.[66] The main object of such a politics by Comte was, in essence, the rule of "opinion".[67] When Comte speaks of opinion, however, he does not refer to its meaning common today as the (instable) individual judgement of something which contrasts with (stable) objective facts. Rather, for Comte, opinion can achieve a similar form of stability through the fixation of beliefs, which can subsequently reconstruct spiritual authority.[68] This fixation is the very goal of the Comtean 'sociologist': not to intervene on the action of subjects (*faire agir*), but on the plane of thought and opinion (*faire penser*, *faire croire*) in order to correspond the beliefs of the subjects to the spiritual theory of social action.[69]

To put it in more familiar terms, Comte aimed to establish new 'articles of faith', transforming a body of opinion (*endoxa*) into spiritual authority on the back of a philosophical discourse, performing his own institutional operation in the process (positivist science). In order to further legitimize this operation, Comte sought to embed himself into a long history of beliefs and their reflexive organization. In his epistemic organization of

---

[65] Vincent Guillin, "Comte and Social Science", in: *Love, Order, & Progress: The Science, Philosophy, & Politics of Auguste Comte*, eds. Michel Bourdeau, Mary Pickering, & Warren Schmaus (Pittsburgh: University of Pittsburgh Press, 2018), 132.

[66] Auguste Comte, *Plan des travaux scientifiques nécessaires pour réorganiser la société* (Paris: Les Éditions Aubier-Montaigne, 1970 [1st ed., 1822]), 68–69: "La formation d'un plan quelconque d'organisation sociale se compose nécessairement de deux séries de travaux, totalement distinctes par leur objet, ainsi que par le genre de capacité qu'elles exigent. L'une, théorique ou spirituelle, a pour but le développement de l'idée-mère du plan, c'est-à-dire du nouveau principe suivant lequel les relations sociales doivent être coordonnées, et la formation du système d'idées générales destiné à servir de guide à la société. L'autre, pratique ou temporelle, détermine le mode de répartition du pouvoir et l'ensemble d'institutions administratives les plus conformes à l'esprit du système, tel qu'il a été arrêté par les travaux théoriques. La seconde série étant fondée sur la première, dont elle n'est que la conséquence et la réalisation, c'est par celle-ci que, de toute nécessité, le travail général doit commencer. Elle en est l'âme, la partie la plus importante et la plus difficile, quoique seulement préliminaire."

[67] Bourdeau, "Pouvoir spirituel ", 1096.

[68] Ibid., 1096.

[69] Karsenti, *Politique de l'esprit*, 56.

social beliefs, Comte traced his own genealogy of social science back to Aristotle, as he, in the words of Vincent Guillin, "not only aimed at discovering the laws of the historical development of social phenomena but also tried to define the historical conditions of possibility of the knowledge of these laws".[70] In other words, the basis of his science was not just his analytical processing of empirical observation, but also its integration of preceding propositions (a *history*), as he identified the authorities who could legitimately articulate the social dimension.[71]

As with Aristotle, Comte recognizes the social dimension of belief: when we believe, we believe, first and foremost, someone 'other' by our faith in them.[72] A good example of this can be found in the division of labour, which, according to Comte is not solely a materialist matter:

> it is first and foremost also intellectual and moral, that is to say it also demands, besides a practical submission, a certain degree of real confidence, be it in the capacity or in the integrity, of the special organs who are now exclusively entrusted with a function which was hitherto universal [...] Every day, as a necessary consequence of the thorough subdivision typical of contemporary human work, each of us is, in many ways, dependent on the capability and morality of a whole host of actors nearly completely unknown for the very maintenance of our own lives, the ineptitude and perversity of which having grave consequences for often a great number of people [my translation].[73]

The proper functioning of society rests on our collective ability to trust and believe in the words and actions of our fellow man as well as the institutions tasked with organizing particular branches of social life.[74] Any

---

[70] Guillin, "Comte and Social Science", 138.

[71] Cf. Certeau, "Une pratique sociale de la différence", 377–380.

[72] Bourdeau, "Pouvoir spirituel", 1098.

[73] Auguste Comte, *Cours de la philosophie positive*, 50th lesson, 279, cited in: Bourdeau, "Pouvoir spirituel", 1098: "elle est aussi et surtout intellectuelle et morale, c'est-à-dire qu'elle exige, outre la soumission pratique, un certain degré correspondant de confiance réelle, soit dans la capacité, soit dans la probité, des organes spéciaux auxquels est ainsi exclusivement confié désormais une fonction jusqu'alors universelle. [...] Chaque jour, par une suite nécessaire de la grande subdivision actuelle du travail humain, chacun de nous fait spontanément reposer, à beaucoup d'égards, le maintien même de sa propre vie sur l'aptitude et la moralité d'une foule d'agents presque inconnus, dont l'ineptie ou la perversité pourraient gravement affecter des masses souvent fort étendues."

[74] In this, he echoes Bonald's own recuperation of the Aristotelian belief/knowledge-composition, cf. supra ch. 5.

disturbance in this kind of everyday belief could have grave consequences for a society's well-being.

The ambition, for Comtean positivist politics, was to direct this stable, everyday body of beliefs to a particular logic of social rationality, that of an altruistic love for the other. The premise underlying this ambition was the idea that dogma—the state of a fixed set of beliefs induced by an acceptance of authority—was the natural condition of man.[75] Scepticism, according to Comte, was nothing more than a mental manifestation of humanity in crisis during periods of transition when one dogma becomes substituted for the other (i.e. Christianity which was to be replaced by positive philosophy).[76] Furthermore, within the Comtean ontological framework, man was not meant for a life of sterile reasoning, constantly talking about the life they are supposed to lead.[77] Man, so says Comte, is meant for a life of action, which is only possible if people have a collective faith in both the actions of others as in the integrity of the spiritual class—those few who are meant to live a life of contemplation—who are supposed to govern their beliefs.[78] Within religious positivism, individual thought is something that can be given up. The only thing that is unconditional is the duty to love.[79]

Because of the omnipresence of these instances of social faith in the actions of the other, such levels of trust cannot sustain constant demonstration. In other words, what is necessary for the creation of any genuine moral and intellectual communion, according to Comte, is the innate disposition to believe spontaneously in total obedience of a spiritual authority, echoing the experience already captured in a systematized fashion by Catholic philosophy. This is, ultimately, what *faith* was for Comte.[80]

---

[75] Comte, "Considérations sur le pouvoir spiritual", 204: "Le dogmatisme est l'état normal de l'intelligence humaine, celui vers lequel elle tend, par sa nature, continuellement et dans tous les genres, même quand elle semble s'en écarter le plus."

[76] Ibid., 204.

[77] Ibid., 204: "Ni l'homme, ni l'espèce humaine ne sont destinés à consumer leur vie dans une activité stérilement raisonneuse, en dissertant continuellement sur la conduite qu'ils doivent tenir."

[78] Ibid., 204.

[79] Bourdeau, "Pouvoir spirituel", 1097.

[80] Comte, "Considérations sur le pouvoir spiritual", 207: "se trouve expliquée cette vieille expérience du genre Humain dont la philosophie catholique, d'après cette connaissance profonde, quoi que essentiellement empirique, de notre nature qui la caractérise si éminemment, a systématisé le résultat général, en présentant directement comme une vertu fondamentale, base immuable et nécessaire du bonheur privé ou public, la *foi*, c'est-à-dire la disposition à

However, this did not mean that Comte professed, like the Saint-Simonists, a blind faith, one that was based on the transformative encounters with the unknown other. Rather, Comtean faith is completely based on scientific principles, meaning that, even if it is inefficient to constantly demand demonstration, technically this could be achieved as each proposition was supposed to be verifiable.[81]

What was required, according to Comte, in further ingraining these dispositions of social faith was an institutionalization of the Comtean dogma of altruistic faith, a project which he considered to be executed for Christianity by St. Paul and which the French sociologist would seek to perform for the new Religion of Humanity.[82] In the eyes of Comte, it was St. Paul, more than anyone else, who should be considered as the founder of Christianity, through his development of a Christian doctrine rooted in both nature and grace.[83] Reacting against the selfishness of early Christianity, which was marked by an obsession with salvation and led to a gradual abandonment of social life by Christian believers, St. Paul reoriented the focus of the Church towards a harmonization of the believer's disposition towards the two cities.[84] His vision of a permanent struggle between nature and grace provided a schematic through which the complexity of Man—their selfish and altruistic penchants manifesting within the same person—could be addressed through cult and devotion.[85]

Comte, however, would seek to move beyond the monumental work of the Apostle, as he attempted to combine Aristotelian philosophy of science with a new program of a universal religion built on altruism and love of

croire spontanément, sans démonstration préalable, aux dogmes proclamés par une autorité compétente: ce qui est, en effet, la condition générale indispensable pour permettre l'établissement et le maintien d'une véritable communion intellectuelle et morale."

[81] Bourdeau, "Pouvoir spirituel", 1099.
[82] Wernick, "The Religion of Humanity", 217.
[83] Karsenti, *Politique de l'esprit*, 192.
[84] Auguste Comte, *Système de politique positive, ou Traité de sociologie, Instituant la Religion de l'Humanité*, Vol. III (Paris: Chez Carilian-Goeury et V^{or} Dalmont, 1853), 410–416.
[85] Comte, *Catéchisme positiviste*, 126–127: "Le grand saint Paul, en construisant sa doctrine générale de la lutte permanente entre la nature et la grâce, ébaucha réellement, à sa manière, l'ensemble du problème moral, non seulement pratique, mais aussi théorique. Car cette précieuse fiction compensait provisoirement l'incompatibilité radicale du monothéisme avec l'existence naturelle des penchants bienveillants, qui poussent toutes les créatures à s'unir mutuellement, au lieu de se vouer isolément à leur créateur."

the other.[86] The crucial event which had made this new composition possible was the research done by German physiologist Franz Joseph Gall (1758–1828), whose scientific work on the make-up of the human brain laid the foundations of both scientific and pseudo-scientific disciplines like psychology and phrenology.[87] Via Gall's so-called cerebral revolution, the Pauline conception of a struggle between nature and grace could be seen for what it was, a useful fiction which mistook human benevolence as a divine gift when, in reality, both our selfish and altruistic tendencies were located within the same social brain.[88]

The positivist discipline of sociology, then, was rooted in a genuine knowledge and reality of human behaviour and beliefs—human action as being oriented by both the frontal part of the brain ("sympathetic impulsions", "intellectual faculties") and the posterior side ("personal instincts")[89]—which allowed the possibility, according to Comte, of harmonizing religious and scientific worldviews through a spiritually coordinated government of contextualized beliefs, the spiritual class of sociologist-priests guiding the community in the type of faith required for the occasion.[90] This novel form of classification and its realization, in its reading of the history of beliefs, made Comte into a new kind of subject, someone who was able to live through objective (i.e. materially and socially conditioned) and subjective (i.e. as aware of the reality of these forms of conditioning) lives simultaneously, granting him the unique position of Grand Priest within the Religion of Humanity.[91]

The Institutionalization of Beliefs: Cult and Education

The second facet of Comte's engagement with the historical languages of belief concerned the role of the sociologist in concretely enacting such a disposition towards desirable beliefs within the community. The question remained for Comte: how could such a fixed set of beliefs exactly be

---

[86] Ibid., xxiii: "Sans elle, je n'aurais jamais pu faire activement succéder la carrière de saint Paul à celle d'Aristote, en fondant la religion universelle sur la saine philosophie, après avoir tiré celle-ci de la science réelle."
[87] Pickering, *Auguste Comte*, Vol. I, 303–305.
[88] Comte, *Catéchisme positiviste*, 128–129.
[89] Ibid., 129.
[90] Comte, *Système de politique positive*, Vol. III, 617.
[91] Karsenti, *Politique de l'esprit*, 196.

established among the populace? Comte expanded on this question in his *Catéchisme positiviste*, a summary of his positivist system of ideas in the form of a catechistic dialogue between a Comtean priest and a female interlocutor.[92] Two key aspects stand out in the creation of a universally harmonious community rooted in altruism and solidarity: cult and education. First of all, the veneration of the Grand-Being (*le Grand-Être*) was intended to cultivate through sentiment that which each study of positivist dogma concludes: that true unity can only be established by living for the other.[93] The symbolic manifestations of the public positivist cult—the establishment of Paris as a positivist Mecca, the creation of a new liturgical year celebrating the entirety of Humanity itself, or the adoration of the Mother and Child in codified paintings and sculptures—had as function solely to create collective habits, with the Priest emphasizing how the organization of this public cult was intended to mimic cerebral functions.[94] The practical domain of the Religion of Humanity aimed at perfecting human order, first physically, then intellectually, and finally, and most importantly, morally.[95]

In the eyes of Comte, the natural morality of man needed to be cultivated, while reducing as much as possible, those impulses which were contradictory to the general good, such as selfishness:

> Hence the need for developing, through a special action, that natural morality which is present in man, in order to reduce, as much as possible, the impulses of each person to the degree necessary for general harmony, in order to habituate the voluntary submission of the particular to the common interest from childhood onwards, and in order to constantly reproduce in active life, with all of its necessary influence, a consideration of the social point of view [my translation].[96]

---

[92] Comte's use of the catechism as a narrative form further confirms the point made by Carolina Armenteros that the positivist philosopher was really "a man of the eighteenth century", cf. Armenteros, "The Counterrevolutionary Comte", 113.

[93] Comte, *Catéchisme positiviste*, 228: "Toute l'étude du dogme positif conduit à conclure que notre véritable unité consiste surtout à vivre pour autrui. Le culte est ensuite destiné principalement à développer les sentiments qu'exige une telle disposition."

[94] Ibid., 208.

[95] Ibid., 231.

[96] Comte, "Considérations sur le pouvoir spirituel", 206: "De là donc la nécessité de développer par une action spéciale ce qu'il y a dans l'homme de moralité naturelle, pour réduire, autant que possible, les impulsions de chacun à la mesure voulue par l'harmonie générale, en habituant dès l'enfance à la subordination volontaire de l'intérêt particulier envers l'intérêt

From childhood onwards, an obedience to the common good needed to be instilled, as personal interest was, as much as possible, suppressed. The imposition of cult was one such "special action". The most crucial task, however, was reserved for the education of the people. Education, in the philosophy of Comte, should be understood in the broadest sense possible. It was a task taken up by a separate class of priests, who, alongside the mothers of the pupils, were to oversee nearly every facet of the pupil's life in order to fully implement an altruistic mindset internalized by the student.[97] Apart from a highly specific program aimed at children and young adults, the priests were responsible for the continuous intellectual and moral formation of all classes, something which had served the Catholic Church well during its own period of spiritual authority.[98] Through the positivist clergy, the people then could receive a constant stream of universal education, which would allow most people to focus on their daily activities, as any potential conflicts could be settled via the spiritual class.[99]

Through universal education and the veneration of cult, the love for the other could become totally ingrained within the individual subject, making it so strong that it could even overcome the strongest of impulses, such as sexual instinct: "Our young followers will be accustomed, from childhood, of viewing the triumph of sociability over personality as the principle purpose of man. They will prepare themselves to one day overcome the sexual instinct by combatting, early on, the nutritional instinct, which are naturally linked through the proximity of the respective organs [my translation]."[100] It is hard to see something other than complete indoctrination as the goal of positivist politics, and it should come as no surprise that many after Comte saw in him nothing but the progenitor of totalitarianism, Eric Voegelin even going so far as to proclaim that "the satanic Apocalypse of Man began with Comte and has become the

---

commun, et en reproduisant sans cesse dans la vie active, avec tout l'ascendant nécessaire, la considération du point de vue social."

[97] Comte, *Catéchisme positiviste*, 240.
[98] Pickering, *Auguste Comte*, Vol. I, 645.
[99] Comte, *Catéchisme positiviste*, 239–240.
[100] Ibid., 248: "Nos jeunes adeptes seront habitués, dès l'enfance, à regarder le triomphe de la sociabilité sur la personnalité comme la principale destination de l'homme. Ils se prépareront à surmonter un jour l'instinct sexuel en luttant, de bonne heure, contre l'instinct nutritif, qui d'ailleurs s'y lie naturellement d'après la contiguïté des organs respectifs."

signature of the Western crisis".[101] Such critiques were already prevalent during his own time, with many labelling his system as "theocratic" after the appearance of his *Considerations sur le pouvoir spirituel* in 1826, something which could completely undermine his philosophy as Comte himself was well aware of.[102] And yet, the fundamental question occupying his philosophy—how to make beliefs stable?—was one taken up by many others, like Charles Sanders Peirce (1839–1914) and the pragmatists, even though their recourse to intellectual and spiritual authority for the establishment of such stability incurred much less controversy.[103]

Furthermore, from our own Certallian perspective employed here, it becomes clear how Comte was, first of all, (perhaps too) well aware of the eventual necessity of an institutional operation for the procurement of fixed beliefs, as his own narrated self-historicization shows, drawing a genealogical line from Aristotle through St. Paul to himself.[104] His sociological program of societal self-improvement was completely rooted in his own positivist reading of the history of believing, as he sought to emulate previously successful mechanisms of collective make-believe in a new, modern form. His Religion of Humanity had as purpose to close off the ungoverned stream of new beliefs (responding to the Aristotelian analysis of the structural development of knowledge and belief), by having his own positivist philosophy take up all mental space. His intellectual class of positivist priests-sociologists appropriated the authority to shape opinion and beliefs through their own exclusively contemplative existence (echoing the Christian monopolization of contemplation via its monastic orders), making every other type of reasoning, e.g. a self-interested mindset who would chase material fortune above selfless altruism, illegitimate.[105] The

---

[101] Cited in: Mike Gane, "Comte and his Liberal Critics: From Spencer to Hayek", in: *The Anthem Companion to Auguste Comte*, ed. Andrew Wernick (London: Anthem Press, 2017), 206.

[102] Pickering, *Auguste Comte*, Vol. I, 356. The fact that some philosophers, like John Stuart Mill, were able to see past such characterizations to find the nuance of his political philosophy, profoundly touched Comte, cf. ibid., 528.

[103] Bourdeau, "Pouvoir spirituel", 1099–1104.

[104] Cf. supra.

[105] Comte, *Catéchisme positiviste*, 254: "Sans excéder sa juste autorité, le pouvoir spirituel peut aller, en effet, jusqu'à prononcer, au nom du Grand-Être, l'indignité radicale d'un faux serviteur, devenu dès lors incapable de participer aux devoirs et aux bienfaits de l'association humaine. [...] Alors le coupable, quelque riche ou puissant qu'il soit, se verra quelquefois, sans éprouver aucune perte matérielle, graduellement abandonné de ses subordonnés, de ses domestiques, et même de ses plus proches parents. Malgré sa fortune, il pourrait, dans les cas

community of believers would *de facto* excommunicate the non-believer, as any kind of non-altruistic behaviour would lead to social marginalization and collective shunning.

In this sense, Comte formulated his own attempt at providing society with the tools for controlling the collective stream of beliefs, a source he considered to be typical of societal disruption through its unpredictability and dynamic nature. By constructing a closed-off narrative, with an exhaustive history of Humanity being assisted by a positivist philosophy of history and a detailed calendar, Comte sought to complete History and effectively end it. In his positivist calendar, each day would be connected with a specific object of devotion (Monday—Marriage; Tuesday—Paternity; Wednesday—Filiation; Thursday—Fraternity; Friday—Domesticity; Saturday—The Woman, or Love; Sunday—Humanity), in order to still provide society with a complete human experience, without however feeding its self-destructive tendencies.[106]

This was very similar to the temporal politics of the French revolutionaries at the end of the eighteenth century, who wanted to break with the past and impose their own control on the social experience of time by creating a new calendar and dating system.[107] And finally, Comte stipulated the full appropriation of the semiotic space of aesthetic representations, as it became exclusively filled with positivist images, like the Goddess through the image of the Mother and Child, delineated according to minute detail, with each detail intended to correspond to the 'completeness' of human biology.[108] This was an extreme conclusion to the institutional operation performed by Comte, a logical endpoint to the idea of a philosophical system proposed by Aristotle, which, in the epistemic chaos of the modern age, meant a complete appropriation of all intellectual authority in order to prevent any intrusion of potential otherness into the lifeworld of the believer.

While Comte was able to construct a sociology where the proper government of beliefs was its primary function, at the same time, his scientific system is a good, if somewhat extreme example, of how such an

---

extrêmes, être réduit à se procurer directement sa propre subsistance, parce que personne ne voudrait le servir."

[106] Ibid., 215.

[107] Sanja Perovic, *The Calendar in Revolutionary France: Perceptions of Time in Literature, Culture, Politics* (Cambridge: Cambridge University Press, 2012).

[108] Comte, *Catéchisme positiviste*, 207.

institutional operation closes off the ability, not only to reason independently, but also to imagine differently. The very notion of belief becomes, for Comte, a singular modality: it is the cognitive capacity to submit to spiritual authority, its success marked by the spiritual governor's ability to anticipate any obstacles to this capacity. It is the lens through which he views, not just his own positivist dogma, but his Catholic precedents as well. He begins his catechism with the final proclamation of his *Cours philosophique sur l'histoire générale de l'Humanité*, which shows how this positivist modality made thinking belief in a diverse manner impossible:

> In the name of the past and the future, the theoretical servants and the practical servants of HUMANITY will take over the general direction of earthly affairs in a dignified manner, in order to finally construct a True moral, intellectual and material providence; as such, irrevocably excluding from political supremacy all the various slaves of all the Gods, catholic, protestant, or deistic, as being both backward and disruptive [my translation].[109]

Comte is performing two exclusions simultaneously: first, he historicizes other forms of belief—Catholic, Protestant, deistic—as being both historically behind and disruptive. But secondly, he places all these types of faith, linked through their dogmatic nature, on a singular trajectory. Other modalities of believing, like the Saint-Simonist conception of the transformative encounter, don't have a place at all within the Comtean framework. They have become 'unthinkable'.

Keeping Beliefs Alive Within a Positivist Knowledge Culture: Comte on Prayer

In the previous section it became apparent how Comte imagined himself as occupying a uniquely privileged position: the Grand Priest not only oversaw directing the stream of beliefs within society, he also didn't allow for any kind of divergence. Alternative beliefs, those that didn't correspond to positivist criteria of demonstration and verification, were

---

[109] Ibid., v: "Au nom du passé et de l'avenir, les serviteurs théoriques et les serviteurs pratiques de l'HUMANITÉ viennent prendre dignement la direction générale des affaires terrestres, pour construire enfin la Vraie providence, morale, intellectuelle, et matérielle; en excluant irrévocablement de la suprématie politique tous les divers esclaves de tous les Dieu, catholiques, protestants, ou déistes, comme étant à la fois arriérés et perturbateurs."

necessarily rooted in fiction and thus harmful to the general good of society.[110] Here, Comte seems to comply to the image later commentators painted of him, as an autocratic thinker who wanted to generalize his own system of classification for such categories as 'religion', 'society' and 'belief', while creating the conditions for making alternative meanings for such signifiers conceptually impossible. And while this vision of Comte as an enlightened sociologist-despot is by no means misplaced, in this section I would like to briefly make the case that his engagement with the category of belief wasn't as one-sided as it might appear, even though later readers of the French sociologist and his work have found this nuance hard to take seriously.

In the work of Comte, this nuance can be articulated through the robustness of the belief-category and the challenges that it posed to the Comtean system of positive government: the stream of collective belief-practices provided not just the material base of the sociological solution for modernity through its ideal government, it also represented a considerable theoretical problem for Comte. On the one hand, Comte realized, as we have seen, that to let this stream go ungoverned would lead, as the post-revolutionary period had shown, to societal chaos. To do its opposite, however, to govern this stream of collective beliefs too restrictively, as the Comtean system was at risk of doing, would result in a static society with no source of dynamism left whatsoever, with the death of society as an inevitable result.[111] Comte was aware of this risk of restrictive government and, in order to prevent such catastrophic scenarios, he realized that the sociological class would need to be able to generate their own stream of new beliefs. The positivist spiritual exercises were his answer to this problem. Here, I will focus on one such an exercise, prayer.[112]

By closing off the ability of the community to spawn new beliefs which weren't rooted in positivist philosophy, the positivist system ran the risk of becoming sterile and of losing that typical quality of religions to reinvent, reshape and reimagine themselves. For someone like Comte, this meant that it was not sufficient for sociology to be a merely informative

---

[110] Auguste Comte, "Sommaire appréciation de l'ensemble du passé moderne (avril 1820)", in: Auguste Comte, *Système de politique positive, ou Traité de sociologie, Instituant la Religion de l'Humanité*, Vol. IV: Appendice général du système de politique positive (Paris: Chez Carilian-Goeury et V^{or} Dalmont, 1854), 41–42.

[111] Brahami, "De la nécessité du pouvoir spirituel", 136.

[112] Comte, *Catéchisme positiviste*, 170–174.

discipline. It had to *produce* opinion as well.¹¹³ The task of 'sociologie'—given shape as a new 'Religion of Humanity' in his *Système de politique positive* (1851–1854)—had been to incorporate the transformative capacities of religious speech into an institution founded on rational and technocratic principles.¹¹⁴ But technocratic rationalism, realized Comte, was unable to fully bring communities together, which necessitated the integration of a third facet between those of mental thought and social action.¹¹⁵ This facet was the facet of affection, love as the motor of community-formation, which, furthermore, was the natural, most base state of the human condition, according to Comte: "we get tired of thinking, and even of acting; never do we get tired of loving. This is the natural solution that the positive theory of the soul presents towards the famous question so vainly contested among the metaphysicians, concerning the irregularity or the continuance of the highest vital functions [my translation]."¹¹⁶ The metaphysical question Comte is referring to is essentially the question of transformation, those practices of non-informative speech spontaneously organizing social association.¹¹⁷

How could these two seemingly opposed forms of relationality—the immediate subject-object relation of a rationalist positivism versus the transformative economy of communal affection—be brought together? Comte saw the solution in the ritualistic practice of prayer, which could weld these opposed modes together, while resulting in the stimulation of the most noble forms of action:

> Besides the habit of good deeds, nothing tends to develop the sympathetic instincts better than the familiar practice of heartfelt expressions of sentiment. Finally purged of all selfish characteristics, prayer now consists of a full and direct effusion of our best feelings. Acquiring in such a manner a greater

---

¹¹³ Karsenti, *Politique de l'esprit*, 56.

¹¹⁴ Ibid., 188–189.

¹¹⁵ Auguste Comte, *Système de politique positive, ou Traité de sociologie, instituant la Religion de l'Humanité*, Vol. I (Osnabrück: Otto Zeller, 1967 [1st ed., 1851]), 682.

¹¹⁶ Ibid., Vol. I, 690: "on se lasse de penser, et même d'agir; jamais on ne se lasse d'aimer. Telle est la solution naturelle que la théorie positive de l'âme fournit envers la célèbre question si vainement agitée entre les métaphysiciens, sur l'intermittence ou la continuité des plus hautes fonctions vitales."

¹¹⁷ For Comte, this was a question already engaged by the philosopher-economists of the Scottish Enlightenment, like David Hume, Adam Smith and Adam Ferguson, as he considered them to be his precursors in developing a middle position between natural self-interest and selfless altruism, cf. Wernick, *Auguste Comte*, 123n20.

moral efficacity, it also becomes more common, as it is addressed to beings which are more well-known and more sympathetic. To pray is to love and to think at the same time, if the prayer remains purely mental; sometimes loving by thinking, sometimes thinking by loving, according to the dominant disposition. But, if the prayer also becomes something spoken, according to its true nature, then prayer constitutes loving, thinking and even acting at the same time. In this way, purified prayer offers the best summary of life; and, reciprocally, life, in its most noble facet, consists of a long prayer [my translation].[118]

In this passage, Comte explores the "universal connectedness" of intelligent thought, activity, and morality within a religious system, and how a spontaneous moral life can be compatible, and even ameliorated, with a rational understanding of it. The act of praying, approached by Comte as a habitual activity, combines intelligent reflection and affective sentiment, so much so that they flow into each other.[119] Going even further, when spoken aloud in its "natural form", prayer brings about—i.e. as a performative practice—an idealized type of behaviour through this conjunction of heart and spirit, necessitating a constant and spontaneous type of moral activity.[120] Life and prayer become seemingly indistinct from each other, with prayer functioning as a sort of theatre, a miniature summation of the noble life, while life itself becomes understood as a long prayer, a permanent spiritual exercise.[121]

The role of positivist science, in other words, was not of replacing the practice of affective speech—with its many ritualistic, metaphorical and

---

[118] Comte, *Système de politique positive*, Vol. II, 76: "Après l'habitude des bonnes actions, rien ne tend à mieux développer les instincts sympathiques que la pratique familière des dignes effusions. Purgée enfin de tout caractère égoïste, la prière comporte désormais une pleine expansion directe de nos meilleurs sentiments. En acquérant ainsi plus d'efficacité morale, elle devient aussi mieux usuelle, puisqu'elle s'adresse à des êtres mieux connus et plus sympathiques. Prier, c'est tout ensemble aimer et penser, si la prière reste purement mentale; tantôt aimer en pensant, et tantôt penser en aimant, suivant la disposition dominante. Mais, si la prière devient aussi orale, selon sa vraie nature, alors prier constitue à la fois aimer, penser, et même agir. Ainsi, la prière purifiée offre le meilleure résumé de la vie; et, réciproquement, la vie, sous son plus noble aspecte, consiste en une longue prière."

[119] Karsenti, *Politique de l'esprit*, 202.

[120] Ibid., 202.

[121] This is similar to the Ignatian understanding of prayer as a type of spiritual meditation leading to a specific type of social action, cf. Philip Sheldrake, *Explorations in Spirituality: History, Theology and Social Practice* (New York: Paulist Press, 2010), esp. ch. 5: "Prayer and Social Engagement: Interiority and Action", 93–105.

poetic elements—with any sort of clear and straightforward rationalist discourse. Rather, the added value of positivism lay in its ability to show how the need for collective rituals and performances was biologically detectable as a neurological function.[122] The *knowledge of* transformative speech, as a biologized natural sentiment of Man, does not obscure the socially effective qualities of religious speech, but only brightens them, brings them closer to an optimal state.[123] In other words, religious and knowledge-based forms of speech were not opposed to one another, but were attempted to be brought into conjunction by Comte through such positivist spiritual exercises such as prayer.[124] It was through the conceptualization of such spiritual exercises that Comte made his own classification of something like belief less rigid, as it opened up the possibility of thinking belief beyond its relation to spiritual authority and positivist government.

Conclusion

Auguste Comte's engagement with historical languages of belief formed an important framework for his ability to articulate both his own sociological program and identity, as well as his normative philosophy of social-political government. Throughout his work, the French sociologist transformed the practice of 'believing' into a cognitive, psychological action which was rooted in the complex composition of the social brain and which needed to be directed into desirable behaviours for societal well-being. In this sense, Comte was a precursor to contemporary scholars in the fields of cognitive anthropology, philosophy of mind and neuroethics, which are all concerned with understanding how the brain generates certain beliefs in interaction with its environment, as well as how these cognitive processes are related to others, such as our ability to reason

---

[122] As Karsenti remarked, the Comtean revolution is firstly a cerebral revolution, cf. Karsenti, *Politique de l'esprit*, 196.

[123] Comte, *Catéchisme positiviste*, 162: "L'objet du culte subjectif se réduit donc à une sorte d'évocation intérieure, résultée graduellement d'un exercice cérébral dirigé suivant les lois correspondantes. L'image reste toujours moins nette et moins vive que l'objet, d'après la loi fondamentale de notre intelligence. Mais, puisque l'inverse a souvent lieu dans les maladies cérébrales, une heureuse culture peut rapprocher l'état normal de cette limite nécessaire, fort au delà de ce que l'on a dû croire jusqu'ici, tant que ce beau domaine resta vague et ténébreux."

[124] Karsenti, *Politique de l'esprit*, 58–59n59.

properly.[125] At the same time, Comte's radicalism in this cognitive-sociological program, his dependence on certain pseudosciences, such as phrenology, and his intention to turn these findings into a stringent political project, has led others to conclude that his work on beliefs and religion was yet another instantiation of the Enlightenment's preoccupation with manufacturability, founded on the illusion that the philosopher was able to occupy the infamous 'view-from-nowhere' and, as such, dictate both what belief is and how they should be governed.

In this chapter, I have tried to approach this evaluation in a historical-empirical fashion, closely reading Comte's engagement with the notion of belief in his construction of his own sociological operation. I was able to extract three distinct functions of historical belief-languages in the Comtean project of sociological self-fashioning: first of all, through his reflections on the history of beliefs and their philosophical articulation, Comte was able to signal the unique importance of sociology within modernity, as the science which could combine a scientific analysis of the social with the coordination of its religious form and implementation. The positivist revolution had marked an important point of no return for the societal status of beliefs, with the advancement in the sciences making the compositions and workings of the act of believing ultimately knowable in the eyes of Comte. It was the task of the sociologist to then conceptualize what purposes were left for such practices as 'having faith'.

Secondly, through his collapse of the Pauline nature-grace struggle and his socialization of Gall's cerebral thesis, Comte formulated a project of ideal beliefs' institutionalization, which imagined the role of the sociologist as a member of a spiritual class who would coordinate the direction of societal thought and action. Through his reading of Aristotelian and Pauline systems of make-believe, Comte sought to emulate the historical successes of previous belief systems, such as Christianity, by adapting these systems to the conditions of a modern, positivist society. The knowability of belief systems then necessitated their rigid government, leading to a complete supervision and articulation of the community's mental and representational space.

And finally, while this objectivist understanding and sociological subjectivation has led to the consideration of Comte as a kind of enlightened

---

[125] Cf. for example: Sperber, *On Anthropological Knowledge*; Neil Levy, *Bad Beliefs: Why they happen to good people* (Oxford: Oxford University Press, 2022); Richard Pettigrew, *Epistemic Risk and the Demands of Rationality* (Oxford: Oxford University Press, 2022).

despot, where beliefs are considered as mere instruments for social government and where non-positivist beliefs are to be strictly avoided, in the final section of this chapter I aimed to show how Comte himself was also seemingly aware of the pitfalls of such an approach and constructed his own strategies for avoiding these traps of a belief system devoid of any novel sources of imagination. These strategies were rooted in a Comtean risk analysis of his restrictive program for government of the collective stream of belief-practices, which dictated the need for a series of spiritual exercises.

One of these exercises, prayer, highlighted Comte's continuous attempts at thinking modernity's precarious state, in which an ever-increasing knowledge of our human nature needed to be combined with a continued openness towards the future and those states yet unknown. The act of prayer constituted for Comte a cultivation of such a complex disposition, in which the three crucial facets of human life—loving, thinking and acting—came together in their most natural fashion, creating a moral life which was equally able to deal with forces of dogma and unpredictability.

CHAPTER 8

Narrating Solidarity Through the Division of Belief: Durkheim and the History of Belief Systems

Introduction

In the following two chapters I will make the argument that, what I have called the sociological language of belief reached a first culmination point with the figure of Émile Durkheim. While the famous French sociologist is typically considered as a founding father of sociology as a scientific discipline, I will argue here that, at least as substantial as his conceptualization of an objectivist sociological method, was his contribution of a sociological technique of self-historicization: the understanding of and reflections on what preceded him as a means of giving shape to a sociological mode of existence. But what was it that Durkheim exactly tried to give form to? My argument throughout these two chapters will be that Durkheim attempted to historically sociologize sociology as both a historical institution and as an event in the history of reason. In other words, to be a sociologist, according to Durkheim, was to practise a certain way of historical being. Once again, I will argue that languages of belief proved to be vital instruments in this undertaking, both as a system of negotiation with other modes of existence, as well as functioning as a conceptual-historical signifier for differentiating the sociological operation from previous systems of communal self-exegesis.

In this chapter, I will focus on Durkheim's navigation of languages of belief through his narration of 'solidarity' and his imagination of the sociological function within organic society, focusing on his 1893 work, *The Division of Labour*. I will first, however, commence with a prologue, in which I briefly reconstruct the context of Durkheim's contemporary knowledge culture. This was a knowledge culture, so I will argue, in which the question of whether 'beliefs' could be employed as an instrument of interpreting both the past and the present was highly contested. I use these debates—conducted with both historians (Seignobos) and sociologists (Tarde)—to make clear some of the complexities inherent in Durkheim's operationalization of the category, concluding the prologue by arguing that a proper understanding of the Durkheimian contribution to a sociological belief-language requires us to move beyond the self-presentations of the belief-category provided by both Durkheim and his opponents.

This results, in other words, in a twofold reading against the grain: against the neo-Kantian approach of belief forwarded by the Durkheimian school and against the anti-positivist critiques of neo-Kantian belief presented by thinkers such as Seignobos and Tarde. Instead, what is required is an investigation of how historical languages of belief acted upon and within the Durkheimian text, to gain further insight into what readings of society the Durkheimian sociological apparatus actually made possible.

Through this double counter-reading, we can access a new understanding of some of Durkheim's more famous conceptual schemes, such as his distinction between mechanical and organic solidarity. While this opposition between mechanical and organic solidarity is often presented as representing the chronological demise of belief systems in society, I will instead argue that this constituted a conceptual distinction which functioned on multiple historical and meta-historical levels, through which Durkheim was able to imagine the transformation of belief in organic social life. Furthermore, I will make the case that this distinction was used by Durkheim as a narrative instrument, with which he aimed to lay bare the conditions through which systems of belief attained their social and historical (non-)agency.

PROLOGUE. ON BELIEF AS A CATEGORY OF HISTORICAL
AND SOCIOLOGICAL ANALYSIS: DURKHEIM AND SEIGNOBOS

On the 28th of May 1908, a group of scholars gathered at the Sorbonne in Paris for the annual meeting of the *Société française de philosophie*. Among them was Émile Durkheim, founder of the sociological school in France and burgeoning academic celebrity at the time. The gathering itself would become notorious in its own right, with an intense polemic crystallizing between the sociological school and a group of historians spearheaded by Charles Seignobos, the latter being highly critical of the sociologists' understanding of history.[1] The meeting represents a watershed moment for French historiography in the early twentieth century, as the debate unearthed the many disagreements among historians and social scientists on such matters as causality, the role of psychology in historiography and history's scientific status.[2]

Little, however, has been said on the impact of the event on the Durkheimian School. This shouldn't come as a surprise. With Seignobos using his opportunity as the sole presenter of a short paper to launch his assault on positivist methodology, Durkheim and his consorts were put on the defensive from the beginning. In response, they regurgitated the standard account of the Durkheimian program of socio-scientific investigation: that there exist autonomous social laws which govern social interaction, and that these laws are categorically distinct from their manifestations on the individual level; and, secondly, that these laws are essentially unconscious, and that the only way to penetrate their existence is through a systematic and external analysis of their functions.[3] Nothing that Seignobos said made Durkheim or any of his positivist consorts, like historian Paul Lacombe or philosopher Célestin Bouglé, budge from what they considered to be indomitable truths.[4] Furthermore, the debate was

[1] Robert Leroux, *History and Sociology in France: From Scientific History to the Durkheimian School* (New York & London: Routledge, 2018), 109.
[2] Laurent Mucchielli, "Aux origines de la Nouvelle Histoire en France: l'évolution intellectuelle et la formation du champ des sciences sociales (1880–1930)", *Revue de synthèse* 116 (1995): 55–98; Francisco Sevillano, "La controversia finisecular sobre el método histórico en Alemania y Francia (1883–1908)", *Hispania* 78 (2018): 193–217.
[3] Émile Durkheim, *The Rules of Sociological Method, And Selected Texts on Sociology and its Method*, ed. Steven Lukes, transl. by W.D. Halls (Basingstoke, Hampshire: Palgrave Macmillan, 2013), 160–63.
[4] Paul W. Vogt, "Un durkheimien ambivalent: Célestin Bouglé, 1870–1940)", *Revue française de sociologie* 20, no. 1 (1979): 123–139; Massimo Borlandi, "Lacombe, Durkheim et le

aimed at settling fundamentally historiographical questions: the knowability of the (conscious and unconscious) motivations of past actors, the reality of historical laws and the character of their structural recurrence across time. What was at stake was (social) history's place at the table of science, turning the debate into an almost existential experience for historians.[5] While Durkheim, as he alluded to early in the discussion, considered history to be a crucial instrument in the sociologist's toolset, it did remain just that, an instrument.[6] History for history's sake seemed to be of little interest to him, making much of the debate methodologically irrelevant from a social scientific-point of view.

And yet, the discussion was able to lay bare an important grey area in the Durkheimian sociological apparatus, and that was the status of belief for the sociologist and sociological knowledge. This matter was not called upon during the discussion itself. Durkheim did reference matters of belief several times during the debate, but each time in a conventional manner for his own system of explanation. Beliefs, considered to be the representations of the individual agents concerning their view of the world, only became interesting, for Durkheim, in their falsehood, as effects of an external social agent, such as public opinion or propaganda. When they overlapped with social reality, their truthfulness stemmed not from any individual self-reflection, but from their (accidental) coincidence with the social fact: "In short, we do not accept as such the causes that are pointed out to us by the agents themselves. If they are true, they can be discovered directly by studying the facts themselves; if they are false, *this inexact interpretation is itself a fact to be explained* [my emphasis]."[7] Beliefs, in other words, were considered here by Durkheim to be merely symbolic, their function being either their representation of the social world or their distortion, with the latter case providing the sociologist with an entry point into a (potentially interesting) context of societal self-deception.[8] Within

---

groupe de L'Année sociologique", in: *Histoire et anthropologie de la parenté. Autour de Paul Lacombe (1834–1919)*, ed. A. Fine & N. Adell (Paris: Éditions du CTHS, 2012), 257–268.

[5] Laurent Mucchielli, "Une lecture de Langlois et de Seignobos", *Espaces Temps* 59–61 (1995): 130–136.

[6] Robert N. Bellah, "Durkheim and History", *American Sociological Review* 24, no. 4 (1959): 447–461.

[7] Durkheim, *The Rules of Sociological Method*, 173.

[8] Durkheim discussed the forms and causes of self-deception most explicitly in a brief dialogue with the work of Marx, the latter being correct about the facts of individual and collective self-deception, but deemed mistaken by Durkheim on the Marxist primacy of

such a conceptual scheme, beliefs are merely mechanic: devoid of any ontological weight of their own, they are neutral carriers of information between worlds, going from the social to the historical to the sociological, and back again. Perceived like this, the sociologist *has no beliefs of their own* during the process of socio-scientific analysis, they are in an instrumental relation with these beliefs through which the domain of the social is made visible as a result of objective and systematic interpretation.[9]

So how did this discussion problematize this sociological grey area, in which Durkheim and his consorts were able to convince themselves that they were conceptually and methodologically separated from the world of beliefs? The problematization of the sociological imagination of belief stemmed from elsewhere, namely Seignobos' Pyrrhonist attitude, his scepticism towards the knowability of past actors' motivations at all.[10] His failure to accept the existence of socio-historical laws did not just cause a collapse in communication during the meeting, it resulted in, what can be called, a *crisis of belief* among his positivist interlocutors. It is through this crisis that the Durkheimian sociological operation, and its own forms of self-deception, becomes more visible, allowing us to grasp some of its strategies of self-historicization and -narration, and, as such, reconstruct its outlines.

The crisis of positivist belief becomes more directly visible if we move our focus away from the propositional substance of the discussion and turn to the modal level of the participants' assertions. There, two strategies become clearly demarcated which were employed by the Durkheimians: first of all, there were attempts at finding the most base level of shared ground, in order to taper over the seriousness of the disagreement.

---

economic structures above socio-cultural phenomena, cf. Émile Durkheim, "Marxism and Sociology: The Materialist Conception of History (1897)", in: Durkheim, *The Rules of Sociological Method*, 123–129.

[9] Durkheim, *The Rules of Sociological Method*, 40: "Feelings relating to social things enjoy no pride of place over other sentiments, for they have no different origin. They too have been shaped through history. They are a product of human experience, albeit one confused and unorganized. They are not due to some transcendental precognition of reality, but are the result of all kinds of disordered impressions and emotions accumulated through chance circumstance, lacking systematic interpretation. Far from bringing enlightenment of a higher order than the rational, they are composed exclusively of states of mind which, it is true, are strong but also confused. [...] Feeling is an object for scientific study, not the criterion of scientific truth."

[10] On the tradition of historical pyrrhonism cf. Anton M. Matytsin, *The Specter of Skepticism in the Age of Enlightenment* (Baltimore: Johns Hopkins University Press, 2016).

Common ground was projected onto the historical nature of science, the explanatory importance of societal institutions, and the social embeddedness of individuals.[11] Yet such broad statements were, in the end, little more than superficial illusions, covering what was a profound, almost existential conflict. Seignobos and Durkheim admitted as much in the final exchanges of the discussion, their shallow agreements functioning rather as thinly veiled insults:

> DURKHEIM: Let us rest on that illusion, and let us say that Seignobos, like myself, admits that a society changes individuals.
> SEIGNOBOS: Agreed, but only on condition that the society is conceived of solely as the totality of individuals.
> DURKHEIM: If you prefer it, let us say that the composing of the assembled whole changes each one of the elements to be assembled together.
> SEIGNOBOS: I admit that tautology.[12]

And yet, this attempt, failed as it was, was not unimportant. It shows how sociological principles of method, as sources for truth-finding, were still highly dependent on being believed *together*, despite their self-articulated distancing of the realm of beliefs as a condition of possibility for an objectivist method. As soon as this methodological bond collapsed as a result of Seignobos' incessant scepticism, any sort of productive interaction became almost completely impossible.

As soon as their attempts at 'converting' Seignobos failed, the rest of the discussion then turned towards strengthening the belief-bonds between the positivists themselves, in their shared disavowal of Seignobos' historical scepticism. This manifested itself in the second strategy, where Seignobos' arguments were individualized, as *beliefs* (in a psychological-cognitive sense), in an attempt at disconnecting his words from anything resembling scientific propositions. Instead, his claims were put aside as the statements of a nihilist, a mystic and a threat to the very idea of collective scholarship itself.[13] After Seignobos put in doubt the possibility to extract

---

[11] Durkheim, *The Rules of Sociological Method*, 162, 173.

[12] Ibid., 173.

[13] The debate on mystical scientism was started by Seignobos himself, who (indirectly) admonished the positivists for their tendency to claim certain non-rational claims—such as the existence of a social Spirit—as instead rationally founded. The most explicit accusation of mysticism against Seignobos, on the other hand, is performed by the moral philosopher

psychological data from history through an objective method, Durkheim responded both resolutely and drastically: "If we have no other means of knowing, we must give up history. If we look upon history as you do, those who do not engage in it can comfort themselves and even rejoice that they do not do so. [...] Your method leads to the ultimate degree of nihilism. So why then give such a large place to the teaching of history? It would mean a lot of time wasted to achieve such singularly poor results."[14] Durkheim goes even further afterwards, denying even the possibility of history itself—not just a historical *science*—if the sceptical principles of Seignobos were followed through: "Then we must give up trying to study history. If the historical data are in any way accessible, they are comparable, and the objective method must be applied. Otherwise, *history no longer exists* [my emphasis]."[15] And it weren't just the sociologists who expressed such clear boundaries against Seignobos' historical pyrrhonism. A historian of Greek and Roman Antiquity and father to one of the later founders of the Annales School, Gustave Bloch said: "I am really frightened at the scepticism of Seignobos. What would remain of history if one listened to him? Almost nothing."[16] Someone like Lacombe could only express disbelief with regard to Seignobos' anti-objectivist disposition: "What in the world then impels you to write history?", he asked his colleague.[17]

So when Durkheim is searching for shared ground with Seignobos, or when Bouglé and Lacombe are positing confirmatory assertions of Durkheimian method, or when Seignobos is presented as a disciplinary outsider, we are seeing at work socio-epistemic mechanisms of belief-relations being solidified and disbanded, aspects of the sociological method which were explicitly articulated by Durkheim during the debate.[18] While this is in contrast to the self-presentation of the Durkheimian sociologist

---

Frédéric Rauh (1861–1909) —"Je le répète, le mythologue, ici, c'est vous"—yet these passages are, for some reason, omitted from the translated version of the debate in *The Rules of Sociological Method*. For the full version, in French and including the presentation by Seignobos, cf. Charles Seignobos, "L'inconnu et l'inconscient en histoire", *Bulletin de la Société Française de Philosophie* 8 no. 6 (1908): 217–247. The short discussion between Seignobos and Rauh can be found on pages 246 and 247.

[14] Durkheim, *The Rules of Sociological Method*, 162.
[15] Ibid., 164.
[16] Ibid., 169.
[17] Ibid., 171.
[18] de Certeau, "L'institution du croire", 64–68.

and their rules of a proper sociological method, at the same time, this contradictory state of things does not lie beyond the realm of Durkheimian sociology itself. As Durkheim himself mentions in his debate with Seignobos, historical actors are themselves often unable to accurately capture the forces and true motivations which govern their actions.[19] So when Durkheim attempts to articulate the full extent to which languages of belief functioned within his own operation of sociology in his *Rules for Sociological Method*, he simply proved his own point by being unable to exhaustively do this, as he was limited by his own present condition and the many restrictions imposed upon the present-day actor. To reconstruct the different ways 'belief' functioned within Durkheimian sociology, we cannot rely on Durkheimian self-reflective motivations alone; rather, we must contextualize and reconstruct the different conditions directing Durkheim and his fellow positivists to utter their particular sociological worldviews.

What this debate then shows, is that modalities of belief functioned in multiple ways within Durkheimian sociology, some in a controlled and self-articulated fashion, others less so. This is the dichotomy that the debate ultimately unearthed: whereas Durkheim and the other members of his school were constantly trying to disconnect beliefs from social facts via objective methods (i.e. the conscious motives of individual actors are not and cannot be privileged avenues for penetrating social reality), at the same time, practices of belief seemingly kept imposing themselves on the sociologists which were beyond the means they were, at first glance, willing to give such practices. Or, to put it slightly differently: a key historical motive of Durkheim was to distance the new science of sociology from the governmental history of societal ways of believing, with the scientific method and its rational-theoretical principles seen as crucial instrument for this process.[20] The discussion with Seignobos shows us, however, that to simply take over Durkheim's conceptual articulation of belief in order to understand the historical place of sociology, as a scientific method devoid of such belief-practices, would be to potentially miss out on a crucial dynamic within the constructed sociological system of Durkheimian positivism.

---

[19] Cf. supra.
[20] Cf. Steven Lukes, "Introduction to this Edition", in: Durkheim, *The Rules of Sociological Method*, xi–xxxv.

CRITIQUES OF DURKHEIMIAN APPROACHES TO BELIEF

Seignobos' take on the debate at the Sorbonne, amid this collective state of positivist umbrage, was seemingly one of personal enlightenment. Their crisis of belief served as evidence of his own claims. History, he said, and by extension sociology as well, was still unable to *force* association—on both an intellectual and social level—through reason alone. The inability of the Durkheimian school to impose their form of sociological reason onto the debate acted, as such, as a historical sign: "This discussion shows, better than I would have been able to do, the entire difficulty we have in agreeing in history, even about the most common and apparently the most clear ideas."[21] It acted as further confirmation, in his mind, of the obfuscating effects inherent within Durkheimian sociology through its remaining dependence on "supra-individual realities".[22] While Seignobos specifically referred to the work of German historian Karl Lamprecht and the concepts of *Volksgeist* and *Völkerpsychologie* when he talked about "supra-individual realities" during the debate, it is clear that he included Durkheim's notion of society in this group of concepts as well.[23] The sociological answer to the question of belief was, according to Seignobos, a complete failure. It took what still needed to be explained—the collective consciousness, society, social facts—as the root of its explanatory framework, through its presupposition of the rationalist nature of social life. This wasn't much of an explanation at all for an empiricist like Seignobos, who preferred to have the experiences of individuals speak for themselves.[24] But was Seignobos justified in his critique of Durkheimian approaches to belief, a critique furthermore which was prevalent among the many opponents of sociological positivism? To evaluate this claim, we need to ascertain the particular conditions and motivations of each party's intervention, and whether Seignobos had a correct understanding of how belief manifested itself in Durkheimian sociology.

Their opposition came to a head on the matter of the social mechanisms propelling ancient societies and the knowability of these mechanisms to the present-day researcher:

[21] Durkheim, *The Rules of Sociological Method*, 168.
[22] Ibid., 172.
[23] Seignobos, "L'inconnu et l'inconscient en histoire", 223–28.
[24] Ibid., 228.

SEIGNOBOS: But that can only bring obscurity into them. What can we understand about the social mechanism of ancient collectivities? Very little, and then solely by means of analogies with our society today.

DURKHEIM: It seems to me on the other hand that we understand Australian (aboriginal) societies much better than our own.

SEIGNOBOS: We don't mean the same thing by the word 'understand'. For my part, it seems that we understand much better present-day societies than Australian ones. *It is probably a question of imagination* [my emphasis].[25]

For Charles Seignobos, it is manifestly clear that it is ourselves that we know best. He does not think that we are able to particularly *know* and *understand* the social mechanisms governing the first Aboriginal Australians, because such things require both primary source material and a robust form of external and internal criticism, which can allow the historian to cultivate a hermeneutic relationship with their historical counterpart.[26] This is simply not possible with ancient aboriginal societies as they lack the bare minimum in discursive commonality—i.e. source material and (cultural) language—to set up such a relationship.[27] As such, their experiences are so foreign to us, in the eyes of Seignobos, that the danger of an imposition of our own societal values—"solely by means of analogies with our society today"—is deemed too high. Rather, when faced with such insufficiency of written testimonials of our historical counterparts, we should recognize their estrangement from us, as we simply do not possess the tools with which we can bridge the ultimate divide created by history.[28] Their beliefs, understood as the motivations committing them to their own lifeworld, are unreachable to us, or at least, in the way presumed by Seignobos.

---

[25] Durkheim, *The Rules of Sociological Method*, 171.

[26] Charles V. Langlois & Charles Seignobos, *Introduction to the Study of History*, transl. by G.G. Berry. (New York: Henry Holt and Company, 1904), 142–43.

[27] Ibid., 146–48.

[28] Charles Seignobos, *History of Ancient Civilization* (London: T. Fisher Unwin, 1907), ch. 2.

Seignobos' final remark, however, is not unimportant: "It is probably a question of imagination." How should we understand Durkheim's imagination of Aboriginal beliefs? If we were to remain within a hermeneutic framework like Seignobos, it is not difficult to think we are encountering a kind of imperialistic positivism, one which has little issues with imposing its own universal and rational language onto the beliefs of Aboriginal society. Two questions should be asked first before we could confirm such a perspective, however: first, why does Durkheim think he can breach the social mechanisms of Aboriginal society, and, second, why is it more difficult to understand our own? What is the challenge of knowability inherent in our present-day society and our own beliefs?

Unlike Seignobos, Durkheim does not consider the intricate workings of Aboriginal society beyond the scope of a positivist science. Whereas Seignobos is dependent on the necessary existence of material intermediaries—"books, monuments, inscriptions, and languages"[29]—in order to bridge the historical divide between the present and the past, Durkheim, through his presupposition of the universally human, cognitive capacity of rational belief, is able to make this temporal leap conceptually and rationally, rather than empirically. Again, it is Kant and his notion of 'pure concepts of understanding'—"time, space, number, cause, substance, personality"[30]—that provided Durkheim with access to these societies, with Kantian philosophy coming closest to breaching the elementary forms of rational classification which allows humanity to associate with each other. For a positivist sociologist like Durkheim then, there is a unique kind of conceptual-historical *solidarity* between rational philosophy and ancient civilizations like the Aboriginal Australians, as both are the closest approximations of the social classification of things, even if they both reached this destination in radically different ways—i.e. philosophical reflection and religious totemism.[31] As such, to refer again to his point in the debate with Seignobos, it is a very clear and 'pure' kind of conceptual access to past civilizations, as the rational beliefs of ancient collectivities as well as their concepts of understanding are at their closest point of

---

[29] Ibid.

[30] Durkheim, *The Elementary Forms of Religious Life* (1995), 8–9.

[31] Émile Durkheim & Marcel Mauss, *Primitive Classification*, ed. and transl. by Rodney Needham (London: Cohen & West, 1963), 19–26.

interaction with the social forces that have formed them, not yet having "been refined and revamped by sophisticated thought".[32]

As I have mentioned above, questions over the validity of Durkheim's argument for a conceptual solidarity between past and present through reason were not unique to Seignobos. The central debate in sociological circles at the time concerned this very topic, with Durkheim's main intellectual opponent, Gabriel Tarde, questioning the existence of such supra-individual realities as well, and even accusing Durkheim, much like the latter did of Seignobos, of a mystic undertone haunting his staunch positivism:

> Notice the enormous assumption implied by the current notions that Mr. Durkheim explicitly relies on to justify his chimerical conception; this assumption is that the mere relation between several beings can become itself a new being, often superior to the others. It is strange [it is strange!] to see minds that pride themselves on being above all positive, methodical, minds that hound and harry even the shadow of mysticism, being attached to such a fantastical notion.[33]

Tarde's befuddlement is a reference to positivist sociology's seeming lack of self-awareness, or, at least, their refusal to think their conceptual frameworks fully through. The positivists claimed to investigate the social through what they considered to be 'beliefs': ideas, concepts, and propositions which were, above all, cognitive representations dictated not by individual rational insight but by the broader culture individuals shared.[34] To study belief from a philosophical and psychological perspective had been common since the seventeenth and eighteenth centuries, with the category of belief acting as a kind of container-concept for subjective propositions on the perceived state of the world.[35] Furthermore, the philosophical debate on belief resurfaced as a prominent point of discussion during the 1870s and '80s in France and Germany, as a result of neo-Kantian reflec-

---

[32] Durkheim, *The Elementary Forms of Religious Life* (1995), 6.
[33] Gabriel Tarde, "Les Deux éléments de la sociologie", 75–76, cited in: Émile Durkheim & Gabriel Tarde, "The debate", in: *The Social after Gabriel Tarde: Debates and assessments*, ed. Matei Candea (London & New York: Routledge, 2010), 37.
[34] Steven Lukes, *Émile Durkheim: His Life and Work. A Historical and Critical Study* (New York: Harper & Row, Publishers, 1972), 11.
[35] Shagan, *The Birth of Modern Belief*, 253.

tions on the precise relation between belief and knowledge, with someone like Durkheim being particularly influenced by neo-Kantians like Charles Renouvier and Émile Boutroux.[36] The essentially social nature of beliefs made it particularly attractive as a site of intervention for developing social and human sciences throughout the nineteenth century, as it represented a kind of unique raw material which could give access to a previously untapped source of social knowledge.[37] While psychology occupied itself with the individual manifestations and compositions of belief, sociology and anthropology, so theorists like Durkheim argued, could take care of the collective manifestations.

While this all sounds perfectly reasonable, the very nature of beliefs made its encounter with the social and human sciences problematically ambiguous. After all, the positivist scheme of sociological explanation was dependent on an implicit hierarchy, where beliefs were, by definition, less rational positions to take than views of the world steered by scientific knowledge.[38] This was accompanied by a kind of moral-philosophical ethos taken up by the positivists, where it was deemed valuable and inherently good to absolve oneself, as much as possible, of such beliefs, and to be governed by reason and reason alone.[39] But it was at this point that things were starting to fall apart for someone like Tarde as well as many other anti-positivists. The rationalism put forward by social theorists like Durkheim, as well as their dislike for belief-dependent worldviews, was at direct odds with itself, as sociological positivism was considered to be unable to conceptually account for its own presuppositions still rooted in such beliefs. Such contradictory and almost 'illogical' elements are, according to Tarde, the very substance of social logic and action, a substance which Durkheimian sociology is completely unable to trace, its inability to understand itself decisively displayed.[40] From this point of view, moreover, it became difficult to see its instrumentalization of beliefs as anything else than a system of potential domination, with which forms of non-Western

---

[36] Giovanni Paoletti, "Representation and belief: Durkheim's rationalism and the Kantian tradition", in: *Durkheim and Representations*, ed. W.S.F. Pickering (London: Routledge, 2000), 125.

[37] Leroux, *History and Sociology in France*, 38–39.

[38] Josephson-Storm, *The Myth of Disenchantment*, 15.

[39] Émile Durkheim, *Moral Education: A Study in the Theory and Application of the Sociology of Education*, ed. Everett K. Wilson, transl. by Everett K. Wilson & Herman Schnurer (New York: The Free Press, 1961), 5–6.

[40] Leroux, *History and Sociology in France*, 122–24.

and non-modern knowledge could be set aside as unhistorical, irrational and unenlightened.[41] To use Andrew Pickering's words, sociological rationalism was essentially a way for not taking different worlds seriously.[42]

Tarde's accusation of a positivist paradox, of a rigorous objectivist methodology being founded by the sociologist's *belief* in Society and Science (with capital S) functioning as autonomous coercive forces, has since become a tradition. The main proponent and thinker of Tardean social science, Bruno Latour, has further developed this critique, for example, through his own critical reading of *The Elementary Forms of Religious Life*.[43] In his commentary, *The Elementary Forms* appears not so much as an exploration of religion's social origins, as it acts as a theological meta-language reflecting on the origins of sociology itself, the discovery of society as the true repository of the sacred, as the 'real' embodiment of the One God.[44] The great illusion performed by the moderns, according to Latour, was to convince themselves as well as others that they were able to penetrate the truths of social reality without having to have recourse to beliefs (in God, in transcendence, in metaphysics, etc.), all the while creating new fabricated gods, such as science, society and social fact in which they did believe, and deeply so.[45]

Latour's ambition, continuing Tarde's project, was aimed at returning to the individual, further understanding what truly makes an agent act, socially, without depending on some external *deus ex machina*.[46] Tarde refers literally to a kind of *deus ex machina* being used by the Durkheimian sociologists of his time, which is the notion of the *milieu*, or context to put it more broadly:

> There is a fetish, a *deus ex machina*, that the new sociologists make use of, like an *Open Sesame*, every time they are embarrassed, and it is time to point out this abuse which is becoming truly worrying. This explanatory talisman is the *milieu*. [Ah!] Reach for that word – what more needs to be said? The

---

[41] Cf. for example the discussion of Durkheim and Mauss's primitive classification in: Peter Pels, "Classification revisited: On time, methodology and position in decolonizing anthropology", *Anthropological Theory* 22, no. 1 (2022): 78–101, esp. 81–84.

[42] Andrew Pickering, "The Ontological Turn: Taking Different Worlds Seriously", *Social Analysis* 61, no. 2 (2017): 134–35.

[43] Latour, "Formes élémentaires de la sociologie".

[44] Ibid., 262.

[45] Ibid., 273.

[46] Latour, "Gabriel Tarde and the End of the Social", 128.

milieu is the multi-purpose formula whose illusory profundity serves to disguise the emptiness of the idea. Thus, they have not hesitated to tell us, for example, that the origin of all social evolution should be sought exclusively in the properties "of the internal social *milieu*". [...] As for this phantom-*milieu*, this ghost we delight in summoning up, to which we lend all sorts of marvellous virtues, so that we are exempt from recognizing the existence of the true and truly beneficial geniuses by whom we live, in whom we move, without whom we would be nothing, let us eliminate it from our science as soon as possible. The *milieu* is a nebula which, upon closer inspection, resolves into different stars, of very unequal sizes.[47]

Tarde and Latour, it must be said, made use of a rhetorical device very similar to a *deus ex machina* themselves, in how they presented the concept of Durkheimian society and its explanatory intentions. The simple fact of something akin to a positivist belief, unearthed, somehow represents for the critics of Durkheim a victorious blow, a veritable unmasking of the pseudo-scientific ruse that is positivist sociology. And yet, it was one of Durkheim's immediate predecessors who openly sought to articulate the rules and conditions of a positivist faith, Auguste Comte with his Religion of Humanity.[48] And while Durkheim was undoubtedly somewhat embarrassed by Comte's extravagances and sought to make the social science more scientific and objectively robust, this does not equate to any sort of denialism towards the key insight of Comte: that the positioning of the sociological observer, towards the multiple and shifting social realities must be conceptualized, articulated and integrated into the very framework of social science itself.[49]

The non-believing, rationalist sociologist, as he appeared in the discussions with Seignobos and Tarde, would undoubtedly be philosophically undressed by Tarde's observations, were he to be the only face of Durkheimian sociology. And yet, the truth of the matter is that the figure of the sociological observer is a highly dynamic entity within Durkheimian sociology, through which the matter of sociological belief is explored in different ways. One is through a philosophical reflection on what it means to be a sociologist within an unfolding history of reason, where languages

---

[47] Gabriel Tarde, "Les Deux éléments de la sociologie" (1895), 78–79, cited in: Émile Durkheim & Gabriel Tarde, "The debate", in: *The Social after Gabriel Tarde: Debates and assessments*, ed. Matei Candea (London & New York: Routledge, 2010), 39.

[48] Cf. supra chapter 7.

[49] Karsenti, *Politique de l'esprit*, 56.

of belief serve as multifaceted instruments for capturing the different facets of social reality. This I will elaborate on further in the next chapter. Another is through an imagination of the sociologist within the history of social cohesion, solidarity and societal becoming. It was in his conceptualization of institutions as a historical motor of social change that Durkheim navigated different historical languages of belief to construct his own sociological narrative of socio-historical performativity. This is my focus for the remaining sections of this chapter.

Orienting Durkheim Within the History of Belief: Thinking Society Through the Division of Belief with Comte and Fustel de Coulanges

It has now become apparent that, in order to understand the different ways historical languages of belief manifested themselves within the Durkheimian sociological system, we cannot rely on either the Durkheimian self-presentation nor on its representation within anti-positivist critiques. Rather, we must reconstruct Durkheim's engagement with belief-languages beyond its second-order reflections by either tradition and, instead, orient the French sociologist within the history of belief by reading his navigation of the category against the grain. In somewhat of a Durkheimian fashion, passages in which beliefs are discussed—both as a material means for social analysis and as an avenue for reflections on the nature of society—serve here as a kind of pathway, through which different strategies of the Durkheimian negotiation of the social domain can be laid bare.

The first case I want to explore using this method of reading Durkheim against the grain is his famous study of types of solidarity in *The Division of Labour in Society* (1893).[50] A choice of the *Division of Labour* for investigating Durkheim's engagement with languages of belief might seem strange at first, since the French sociologist rarely reflects on the term itself throughout the work. Instead, the focus lies firmly on the nature of the concept 'solidarity' (mechanical versus organic), its spectrum of manifestations across different historical societies, and the evolutionary

---

[50] Émile Durkheim, *The Division of Labour in Society*, intro. by Lewis Coser, transl. by W.D. Halls (London: Macmillan, 1984).

development of what Durkheim termed as 'the collective conscience'.[51] As a result, subsequent commentary on the work, when embedding it within discussions on modernity and secularization, have focused on the broader category of 'religion' itself rather than its individual components such as beliefs and rites, facets of Durkheimian sociology which are more easily associated with *The Elementary Forms of Religious Life* (1912).[52]

And yet, when carefully read, it becomes apparent that *The Division of Labour* contains a more complex language game of belief than typically estimated. In the standard narrative of Durkheim exegesis (e.g. in the work of Talcott Parsons), the opposition of mechanical and organic solidarity is marked by an ideal-typical distinction between societies marked by homogeneity and shared beliefs and those which are characterized by functional differentiation and interdependence.[53] Furthermore, implicated within this opposition, so it is often argued by scholars, also resides an evolutionary scheme: whereas the most primitive societies organized themselves on the basis of a shared religion and the effacement of difference, modern societies inevitably drifted towards individualism, specialization and the diminishment of religious life.[54] In other words, Durkheim seemed to argue that society transitions from one being dominated by the dissemination of shared beliefs towards one that has lost its need of

---

[51] Philippe Steiner, *La sociologie de Durkheim* (Paris: La Découverte, 2005, [4th ed.; 1st ed., 1994]), 15–21.

[52] Robert Bellah, "Introduction", in: Émile Durkheim, *On Morality and Society*, ed. Robert Bellah (Chicago: Chicago University Press, 1973); Anthony Giddens, *Capitalism and Modern Social Theory* (Cambridge: Cambridge University Press, 1971); David Lockwood, *Solidarity and Schism: 'The Problem of Disorder' in Durkheimian and Marxist Sociology* (Oxford: Clarendon Press, 1992); Talcott Parsons, *The Structure of Social Action* (Glencoe: Free Press, 1949 [1ˢᵗ ed., 1937]), Ibid., "Durkheim's Contribution to the Theory of Integration of Social Systems", in: *Essays on Sociology and Philosophy*, ed. Kurt H. Wolff (New York: Harper & Row, 1960), 118–153, Ibid., *Societies: Evolutionary and Comparative Perspectives* (Englewood Cliffs: Prentice-Hall, 1966); Tiryakian, *Sociologism and Existentialism*; Ernest Wallwork, *Durkheim: Morality and Milieu* (Cambridge, MA: Harvard University Press, 1972), Ibid., "Religion and Social Structure in *The Division of Labour*", *The American Anthropologist* 86, no. 1 (1984): 43–64; Jonathan S. Fish, "Religion and the Changing Intensity of Emotional Solidarities in Durkheim's *The Division of Labour in Society* (1983)", *Journal of Classical Sociology* 2, no. 2 (2002): 203–223.

[53] Smith, *Durkheim and After*, 139–140.

[54] Phyllis Stock-Morton, *Moral Education for a Secular Society: The Development of Moral Laïque in Nineteenth Century France* (New York: SUNY Press, 1988), 127; Horii, "Historicizing the category of 'religion'", 33.

collective systems of belief, organic society being regulated more in accordance with its growing pluralisms.[55]

At first glance, this is a reading which is articulated by Durkheim himself, for example when he refers to the gradual diminishment of proverbs, sayings and maxims within more advanced societies:

> The decrease in the number of proverbs, adages and sayings as societies develop is still further proof that the collective representations are also becoming less determinate. Among primitive peoples, in fact, maxims of this kind are very numerous. [...] More advanced societies are only slightly fertile in this way during the preliminary phases of their existence. Later not only are no new proverbs coined, but the old ones gradually fade away, lose their proper meaning, and end up by not being understood at all. This clearly shows that it is above all in lower societies that they are most favoured, and that today they only succeed in maintaining their currency among the lower classes.[56]

With the increasing division of labour and the subsequent divergences this division has produced within society, such sayings are no longer able to fulfil their original function as a kind of crystallization of a collective sentiment and, as such, gradually disappear.[57] The example of proverbs echoes, according to Durkheim, a larger-scale process, which is the diminishment of the "sphere of religion" within society, a process which has been occurring, in the eyes of the French sociologist, "from the very origins of social evolution".[58]

The understanding of the Durkheimian sociological system as one that indicates a disappearance of belief, or at the very least, approaches historical belief as a form of social connection which has increasingly lost its meaning in modernity should not come as a surprise. Its schematic allocation as a central tenet of mechanical solidarity—"Consequently the ties binding us to society, which spring from a *commonality of beliefs and sentiments*, are much fewer than those that result from the *division of labour* [my emphasis]"[59]—invites the reader to surmise that the transition of one system of solidarity to another is mimicked by societal systems of belief in

---

[55] Smith, *Durkheim and After*, 140.
[56] Durkheim, *The Division of Labour*, 120.
[57] Ibid., 120–21.
[58] Ibid., 120.
[59] Ibid., 101.

a similar manner. In such a scheme, mechanical *beliefs* would suffer the same fate as its equivalents in proverbial expression, to "gradually fade away". A more thorough reading of the *Division of Labour*, however, would suggest that such a representation needs to be further investigated. The question is then: what exactly happens to systems of belief in organic societies? Does the practice of believing follow a transition like the one characteristic of solidarity, from more mechanical processes to organic ones?

While Durkheim does not explicitly answer these questions, as they are not the topic of his investigation, there are several indirect explorations of the theme throughout the book. A key indicator for such a reading is Durkheim's own narrative orientation within the unfolding history of the social sciences, in particular his engagement with both the work of Auguste Comte and Numa Denis Fustel de Coulanges. These two predecessors and important influences to Durkheim appear throughout the work as representative flagbearers for two distinctive approaches to historical systems of belief, both their composition and their transition towards modernity. My argument here is that Durkheim employs these two figures as rhetorical tropes through which he constructs his own complex technique of sociological self-historicization, understood as a uniquely modern mode of existence through its function as a communicative vessel for society's unfolding.

So how do these two figures appear throughout *The Division of Labour*? Fustel de Coulanges's *La Cité antique* (1864) and the *Histoire des institutions politiques de l'ancienne France* (1875, vol. I) were important sources for Durkheim's discussion of Roman law and the beliefs underpinning the institutions of classical societies, and appear sporadically throughout the text.[60] While Durkheim contested several claims of Fustel de Coulanges's *The Ancient City*, such as the latter's argument that the cult of death formed the foundation of primitive religion, it was Fustel's emphasis on the close relation between social-communal beliefs and the historical formation of institutions which formed a central facet of Durkheim's heuristic for identifying mechanical solidarities and their historical transitions.[61] Something like a "collective conscience" could be extracted through a historical-ethnographic method which was very similar to the one

---

[60] On the influence of Fustel de Coulanges on Durkheim, cf. Lukes, *Émile Durkheim*, 59–65.
[61] On the critiques of *The Ancient City*, cf. François Héran, "De la Cité Antique à la sociologie des institutions", *Revue de synthèse* 4 (1989): 367.

employed by Fustel de Coulanges in *The Ancient City*, where social institutions, legal codes and corporations are considered as crystallized forms of "common ideas, interests, sentiments and occupations", expressions, in other words, of a widely shared desire of a moral logic and code:

> It is impossible for men to live together and be in regular contact with one another without their acquiring some feeling for the group which they constitute through having united together, without their becoming attached to it, concerning themselves with its interests and taking it into account in their behaviour. And this attachment to something that transcends the individual, this subordination of the particular to the general interest, is the very wellspring of all moral activity. Let this sentiment only crystallise and grow more determinate, let it be translated into well-defined formulas by being applied to the most common circumstances of life, and we see gradually being constituted a corpus of moral rules.[62]

Compare this to Fustel's understanding of collective beliefs—"The external and tangible laws which appear among men are nothing but signs and symptoms of the moral facts produced within our souls [my translation]"[63]—and the influence becomes markedly clear. Beliefs as social energy bringing societal associations into existence, this is how the category was typically employed throughout *The Division of Labour*, tracking its different trajectories from primitive to modern societies. In this form, it constituted for Durkheim one of the main sources of potential solidarity-formation, the other of course being the so-called division of labour itself.[64] As such, Durkheim was able to operationalize a mechanical understanding of belief systems—semi-propositional attitudes which were easily disseminated among groups through their simplicity, their homogeneity and their direct connection to a prescribed form of collective action—in order to give meaning to a certain type of societal association.[65] While this heuristic

---

[62] Émile Durkheim, "Preface to the Second Edition", in: Durkheim, *The Division of Labour*, xliii.

[63] Numa Denis Fustel de Coulanges, *La Cité antique* (1864), 470, cited in: François Héran, "Le rite et la croyance", *Revue française de la sociologie* 27, no. 2 (1986): 243: "Les lois extérieures et sensibles qui paraissent parmi les hommes ne sont que les signes et les symptômes des faits moraux qui se produisent dans notre âme."

[64] Durkheim, *The Division of Labour*, 172.

[65] Ibid., 64 "From this chapter it can be seen that a social solidarity exists which arises because a certain number of states of consciousness are common to all members of the same society. It is this solidarity that repressive law materially embodies, at least in its most essential

provided a framework for evaluating the social performativity of beliefs—as it did for Fustel de Coulanges, in such oppositions as proto-history/history and Greek-Roman society/Christianity—Durkheim's engagement with Comte suggests another possible reading, in which the history of solidarity and belief relates to the formation and self-understanding of the sociological discipline itself.[66] The mechanical nature of beliefs did not stimulate an approach of history as radically other, as it did for Fustel de Coulanges, but as one which could integrate past and present societies into a single, sociological totality.[67]

Durkheim's engagement with Comte, and the latter's approach to historical languages of belief, was of a completely different order. Comte's sociological method of understanding and integrating belief served not as a form of source material for Durkheim but as a contemporary intervention by a sociological equal, someone who attempted to use social science as a means of connecting past to present societies in a singular model of social modernization.[68] It was Comte's answer to the French post-revolutionary crisis of solidarity and his argument for a renewed and modern spiritual authority, which acted as an access point for Durkheim's own, and fundamentally contrary, perspective. Like Durkheim, Comte had made a similar assessment of the modern, industrializing society as one that came to be characterized by a division of labour and functional differentiation.[69] Such a turn towards specialization had a potentially disastrous side-effect, in the eyes of Comte, namely the loss of a "true relationship to the public interest", with the worker's focus being instead more acutely directed towards private self-interests.[70] This had long been the function of religion in society, as the communicative vessel of an altruistic logic to the 'common conscience', but, thanks to the increasing complexity of society, traditional religions could no longer fulfil this function

---

elements. The share it has in the general integration of society plainly depends upon the extent, whether great or small, of social life included in the common consciousness and regulated by it." Cf. also Smith, *Durkheim and After*, 16.

[66] François Héran, "L'institution démotivée de Fustel de Coulanges à Durkheim et au-delà", *Revue française de sociologie* 28, no. 1 (1987): 67–97.

[67] On this distinction between Durkheim and Fustel de Coulanges, cf. Héran, "Le rite et la croyance", 243–44.

[68] On the influence of Comte on Durkheim, cf. Lukes, *Émile Durkheim*, 67–69.

[69] Durkheim, *The Division of Labour*, 295.

[70] Ibid.

in a satisfactory manner.⁷¹ Rather, said Comte, it was up to modern society to come up with its own specialized organ which could take up the function, previously fulfilled by institutional religion, "constantly to remind us of the concept of the whole and the sentiment of common solidarity".⁷²

Against such a call for a renewed generalist perspective, Durkheim makes a series of critical arguments, positing instead that an organic society, governed by a logic of a division of labour, has its *sui generis* mechanisms of altruistic behaviour, which no longer rely on *a posteriori* principles dictated by a theological-governmental class, but on principles generated spontaneously through the division of labour itself.⁷³ What interests me here, however, is not the substantive-sociological discussion on the precise constitution of organic society and its mechanisms of solidarity, but rather the formal implications of the textual opposition created by Durkheim between Fustellian mechanical-automated beliefs and Comtean organic-reflexive dispositions towards such beliefs. The discussion of Comte's notion of spiritual authority introduces, in other words, into the *Division of Labour* the issue of the reflexive-sociological function, the meta-historical role to be played by the class responsible for observing, reflecting upon and, potentially, directing a society's mechanical beliefs. As I will show in the next section, this meta-historical distinction further complicates Durkheim's perceived transition from mechanical to organic solidarity.

From an Organic to a Mechanical Government of Beliefs: Sociological Faith in the Function of Solidarity

The question of reflexivity and government—the gradual awareness of our intuitive motivations guiding our social behaviour, their subsequent sophistication in ideas, languages, customs, traditions and institutions, and the normative implications for the external observer of these processes—forms a central facet of *The Elementary Forms of Religious Life*.⁷⁴ The narrative distinction between the dimension of an unfolding social life

---

[71] Cf. supra my discussion of Comte's notion of spiritual authority in ch. 7.
[72] Auguste Comte, *Cours de philosophie positive*, vol. IV, 430–431, cited in: Durkheim, *The Division of Labour*, 296.
[73] Durkheim, *The Division of Labour*, 297–301.
[74] Durkheim, *The Elementary Forms of Religious Life* (1995), 6. Cf. also infra, ch. VIII.

and one that comments on and interprets the former is a crucial dynamic in the book, which allowed Durkheim to reflect on the supposed conflict between science and religion as well as the future role of sociology within this debate. The French sociologist sets the scene early in *The Elementary Forms*, when he sketches out the dualistic unfolding of primitive society: added onto the material mechanisms of society-formation (the raw social facts of individual and collective action making society through rites, beliefs and symbols) were, according to Durkheim, endless streams of self-interpretation and -representation, theologians, priests, rulers, political consultants, philosophers and scientists who give their own shape and meaning to this raw social material, resulting in a muddled mess in which it is difficult to surmise what is actually social, that "what might be common to all".[75] Some of these excursions into virtuality, such as mythology and theology, have the inadvertent effect of obscuring and distorting these 'primitive' social states of affairs:

> As it progresses historically, the causes that called it into existence, though still at work, are seen no more except through a vast system of distorting interpretations. The popular mythologies and the subtle theologies have done their work: They have overlaid the original feelings with very different ones that, although stemming from primitive feelings of which they are the elaborated form, nevertheless allow their true nature to show only in part.[76]

Others, like philosophy and science, have more illuminating effects, such as Immanuel Kant's elucidation of the categories of understanding, which, according to Durkheim, was both born out of religion (through the latter's social constitution) and was fundamentally distinct from it, as it fulfilled a function different from that of religion.[77]

This set of distinctions—between automated, spontaneous beliefs constituted by society and those reflexively constituted by *a posteriori* rationalization or mythologization—was less pronounced in *The Division of Labour*, but still implicitly resonated throughout the book through

---

[75] Ibid., 5: "Here it is priests, there monks, elsewhere the laity; here, mystics and rationalists, theologians and prophets, and so on. [...] But how can one find the common basis of religious life under the luxuriant vegetation that grows over it? How can one find the fundamental states characteristic of the religious mentality in general through the clash of theologies, the variations of ritual, the multiplicity of groupings, and the diversity of individuals?"
[76] Ibid., 7.
[77] Ibid., 432.

Durkheim's reflections on spiritual authority and the sociological attitude towards the normative constitution of solidarity.[78] Taking these distinctions into account, we can construct an alternative historical schematic of societies, one which incorporates the Durkheimian view on the development of belief systems within organic society: instead of a singular plane on which societies transition from mechanical to organic systems of solidarity, we have a dual unfolding of society in history, one on the mechanical-material level of spontaneous beliefs and one on the reflexive-virtual level of the interpretation, analysis and government of these beliefs. What Comte had failed to realize, according to Durkheim, was that it had not just been the material conditions of society which had transformed, but the reflexive organs of government themselves as well: "We have ourselves undoubtedly shown that the organ of government develops *with* the division of labour, not as a counterbalance to it, but by *mechanical necessity* [my emphasis]."[79]

What does Durkheim mean by this? First, he means to claim that all social functions, not just the general societal organs but their reflexive addendums (such as theology and science) as well, were now subservient to the new principle of social organization, the division of labour. He gives the example of how the scientific undertaking itself is in the process of integrating this principle:

> The unity of science will thus be formed *by itself*, not by the abstract unity of a formula, one moreover that is too narrowly conceived for the host of things it must include, but *by the living unity of an organic whole*. For science to be one, there is no need for it to keep its gaze wholly fixed upon one single area of consciousness – which is moreover impossible – but it is enough for all those who study it to feel that they are collaborating in the same task [my emphasis].[80]

Much like other facets of social life in organic society, Durkheim is arguing that philosophy and social science are equally coming to a state of collective unity in a natural, *sui generis* and *automatic* fashion.[81] But this argument simultaneously served as a critical commentary on the form of Comte's sociology, which Durkheim considered to be a secularized

---

[78] Steiner, *La sociologie de Durkheim*, 21–25.
[79] Durkheim, *The Division of Labour*, 296.
[80] Ibid., 306.
[81] Ibid.

version of pastoral government, a continuation of the reflexive disposition as it was within mechanical society.[82] To do this, to continue thinking of philosophy as a gateway to a generalist perspective on the whole, was to ignore the changed conditions of intellectual life in modernity.[83] The division of labour had, in the eyes of Durkheim, not only transformed the reality of the everyday believer/worker, who suddenly found themselves in an alternative form of social organization; the task of the intellectual governor/analyst had been thoroughly transformed as well. The Comtean intervention of a reflexive, prescriptive ethic and an externally imposed social rationality represented then not just an alternative approach but a distortion of the sociological function itself, with the counter-productive effect of making specialization untenable.[84]

So what did the sociological function within the division of labour look like, what was the actual make-up of science and philosophy in modern society? Epistemic labour, much like its social and economic equivalent, had been increasingly susceptible to processes of specialization, differentiation and individual complexity.[85] For the social scientist to provide a general synthesis of all these diverging traditions, methods, and propositions would simply be too great an ask, with no single human mind capable of such synthetic capacities.[86] Furthermore, science was not just the summary of a series of propositions, according to Durkheim. Rather, it was a combination of these propositions together with the "hopes, habits, instincts, needs, and presentiments" of the scientists themselves, with these lived experiences crucial in constituting, what Durkheim termed, "the soul" of a science.[87] This was something not translatable to any sort of generalist principle, and could only be properly understood by someone who practised the science itself. The social reality of scientific life, in other words, made it impossible for a philosophical outsider to capture the spirit of the scientific undertaking beyond the level of caricature.[88]

---

[82] Ibid., 301.
[83] Ibid., 298–99.
[84] Ibid., 307.
[85] Ibid., 298.
[86] Ibid., 298–99.
[87] Ibid., 299.
[88] Ibid., 299–300: "To have a part in it, one must set to work and confront the facts. According to Comte, for the unity of science to be assured, it would be sufficient for these methods to be reduced to a unity. But it is precisely the methods that are the most difficult to unify. For, as they are immanent in the sciences themselves, as it is impossible to disen-

Within organic society then, the sociological observer, Durkheim argued, has as a new main task, one that is particular to itself and which conforms to the epistemic division of labour: the evaluation of the state of the different organs and their respective conditions of regulation, making sure that particular organs do not fall into a state of *anomie*.[89] The sociologist does not so much formulate their own social rules for society (in accordance to a desirable societal goal), but rather articulates them in the way they are formulated by the structure of society itself, in the way "these rules emerge automatically from the division of labour".[90] The sociological function is not to create solidarity through moral rules, the guidance of behaviour and the cultivation of desirable beliefs, but to assist society by making it further conscious of itself and the ways it most naturally drifts and interlocks together:

> Thus it is not the brain that creates the unity of the organism, but it expresses it, setting its seal upon it. Some speak of the necessity for a reaction of the whole upon the parts, but the whole also needs to exist. This means that the parts must be already solidly linked to one another so that the whole may become conscious of itself and react accordingly. We should then see, as labour is divided up, a sort of progressive decomposition occurring, not at any particular points, but over the whole extent of society, instead of the ever-increasing concentration observed in reality.[91]

What Durkheim tries to put into words then, through his discussion of the Comtean governmental notion of spiritual authority, is that the transition from mechanical to organic societies then also implied a transformation of the scientist's disposition towards systems of belief. What effectively took place, according to Durkheim, was a kind of curious inversion: on the one hand, the social object of government—the believer, the labourer, the one performing everyday social actions—experienced a reflexive turn through the division of labour, gaining more autonomy and responsibility in their

tangle them completely from the body of established truths in order to codify them separately, one cannot know them unless one has practised them oneself. Yet even now it is impossible for the same man to practise a great number of sciences. These broad generalisations can therefore only rest upon a fairly cursory view of things."
[89] Ibid., 304.
[90] Ibid., 302.
[91] Ibid., 297.

performance of their work in *building the social*.⁹² The governing class of the intellectual elite, on the other hand, entered into a more mechanical, automated disposition, their main task now consisting in assisting society in naturally unfolding itself, to toil away on the external ideals fuelling the "free deployment of all those forces that are socially useful".⁹³

This is what Durkheim effectively refers to when he speaks of the transformation of the organ of government "by mechanical necessity".⁹⁴ While the material base of society transitioned from a mechanical to an organic logic of self-organization, the reflexive class of intellectuals and philosophical governors followed an inverted process: they went from an organic disposition of self-government towards a more mechanical relation with the socially expressed philosophical ideal, a society which was gaining the ability to independently sustain itself on the basis of the shared principles of justice, reason and fairness.⁹⁵ Understood in this manner, Durkheim seems to allow for an implicit distinction between something like a "collective consciousness" and mechanisms of believing: whereas the former gradually disappears as a result of a change in the structures of society, the latter transform and adapt to the new conditions of the social. I will clarify this distinction in this final paragraph of the section.

By my use of Fustel de Coulanges and Comte as narrative instruments rather than as mere interlocutors, *The Division of Labour* transforms into a textual surface which allows for multiple readings at the same time: it was not just a sociological analysis of systems of solidarity and their transformation, but also a philosophical commentary on the history of reason and the particular role to be played by sociology within this history. Durkheim returns to this secondary reading in the final page of his book. There, he reiterates the point that the current crisis of solidarity is not a crisis of intellectualism, meaning that it cannot be resolved by more and more theorizing:

---

⁹² Ibid., 308: "The division of labour supposes that the worker, far from remaining bent over his task, does not lose sight of those co-operating with him, but acts upon them and is acted upon by them. He is not therefore a machine who repeats movements the sense of which he does not perceive, but he knows that they are tending in a certain direction, towards a goal that he can conceive of more or less distinctly."
⁹³ Ibid., 321.
⁹⁴ Cf. supra.
⁹⁵ Durkheim, *The Division of Labour*, 338–39.

> Our disease is therefore not, *as occasionally we appear to believe*, of an intellectual order, but linked to deeper causes. We are not suffering because we no longer know on what theoretical idea should be sustained the morality we have practised up to now. The cause is that certain elements of this morality have been irretrievably undermined, and the morality we require *is only in the process of taking shape* [my emphasis].[96]

What is interesting, first and foremost, is that Durkheim designates the sociological attitude towards the crisis of solidarity as informed by mechanisms of believing ("as occasionally we appear to believe"). With this he does not mean to say that the moralists (like Comte) have fallen prey to non-rational assumptions while Durkheim himself has been able to avoid this trap. No, with this he refers to the shared contemporary sociological condition, which is one of societal and structural transition, both socially as well as epistemologically. This makes an analysis of the present unfolding of a new social morality impossible to assert directly and rationally, in the eyes of Durkheim, making any investigation of sociology's current condition, at least partly, a non-epistemic navigation (here, we may remember Durkheim's claim in the Seignobos-debate that we can better understand historical societies than ourselves).[97] The social object of contemporary sociology—the functions and mechanisms of modern solidarity—does not fully exist yet, so cannot be exhaustively described, nor reflexively brought into existence.[98] The sociologist, in other words, is mechanically necessitated to place their trust, their faith in the prospect that a new form of solidarity will come to impose itself on society, in accordance with its rational and moral principles: "A mechanistic theory of progress then not only does not deprive us of an ideal, *but allows us to have faith that we shall never be without one. Precisely because the ideal depends upon the social environment, which is essentially dynamic, it is constantly changing* [my emphasis]."[99]

So what *can* the sociologist do, in such a case, if not analyse an existing form of solidarity or prescribe a normative form of societal cohesion? Two things, according to Durkheim: (1) the prescription of a moral horizon

---

[96] Ibid., 340.

[97] Cf. supra.

[98] Ibid., 306: "These new conditions of industrial life naturally require a new organisation. Yet because these transformations have been accomplished with extreme rapidity the conflicting interests have not had time to strike an equilibrium."

[99] Ibid., 282.

and (2) the identification of any obstacles impeding its natural unfolding. This is what Durkheim described, throughout the book, as a negative disposition, something that is not guided by a common end (such as the collective conscience) but allows instead to organize "individual wills in an orderly fashion".[100] While Durkheim refers to this mechanism in the book in order to describe a certain kind of solidarity, in this meta-historical reading, it simultaneously refers to the sociological attitude within organic society as well.[101] This is exactly what *The Division of Labour*, especially in this secondary reading, attempted to provide:

> In short, our first duty at the present time is to fashion a morality for ourselves. Such a task cannot be improvised in the silence of the study. It can arise only *of its own volition, gradually, and under the pressure of internal causes that render it necessary*. What reflection can and must do is to prescribe the goal that must be attained. That is what we have striven to accomplish.[102]

The Division of Labour, in other words, was viewed by Durkheim as a means through which society could become further aware of itself and, as such, assist in the mechanical process of the new social morality taking shape. The task of social science, as such, was to prepare the social field for its natural, socio-historical unfolding and it could do this by intervening on the exterior framework: "We need to put a stop to this anomie, and to *find ways of harmonious co-operation between those organs that still clash discordantly together*. We need to introduce into their relationships a greater justice *by diminishing those external inequalities* that are the source of our ills [my emphasis]."[103] This is how Durkheim perceived his own set of reflections in *The Division of Labour*—"That is what we have striven to accomplish"—, as a self-reflexive sociological intervention on the current conditions of social science as a historical institution and as a manifestation of socio-rational being.

---

[100] Ibid., 73.
[101] Ibid., 331.
[102] Ibid, 340.
[103] Ibid., 340.

Conclusion

I have started this chapter with an argument for reading Durkheim's navigation of historical belief-languages against the grain, and this for two reasons: first of all, Durkheim and his school have themselves shown a lack of conceptualization of this very practice, as evidenced by their self-presentation and the subsequent crisis of belief in their discussion with Charles Seignobos. And secondly, critics, like Seignobos and Gabriel Tarde, cannot be relied on either for providing an entry into describing this navigational practice, as they themselves were only partly successful in capturing this positivist undertaking, failing to demonstrate a sufficient understanding of the existential project lurking within Durkheimian positivism. Reading against the grain, with a focus on the category and semiotic matrix of 'belief', we arrive instead at a more complex reading of Durkheim's interactions with this notion.

The case I have focused on in this chapter is the usage of the belief-category in *The Division of Labour* and the different strategies employed by Durkheim in this book for his approach of both solidarity and sociology as a historical institution. Typically understood as a kind of substitute-form for both mechanical solidarity and collective conscience, I have instead tried to show how the imagination of Durkheimian belief functioned on two different levels throughout the book, one concerning the mechanisms of believing as a condition for solidarity, and one as an indirect commentary on the transitions of the intellectual-reflective class in contemporary society. Using Fustel de Coulanges and Auguste Comte as narrative instruments for constructing a formalistic division of belief systems, Durkheim was able to conceptualize a persistence and transformation of mechanisms of believing into organic society.

Because of the difficulty of knowing the sociological condition—as the societal mechanisms and forms of morality were still in the process of calibrating, stabilizing and crystallizing, according to the French sociologist—Durkheim employed a negative method, i.e. identifying what the sociologists no longer were. Whereas the societal believer and the intellectual governor were once diametrically opposed to one another, the transformation of societal structures had now blurred the lines between these social groups. The labourer, argued Durkheim, takes on more and more reflective accountability within organic society, while the sociologist, on the other hand, enters more and more into this space of 'being governed', trusting the collective of society to form itself mechanically and to assist where they can. In this way, through this negative method, Durkheim was able to use the history of solidarity-formation as a reflective commentary on the state of sociology itself and the current space it occupied. This negative method, however, only provided the ability of outlining this space from the outside: *The Division of Labour*, as Durkheim himself alluded to, was a kind of speculative reflection on where the sociologist found themselves and what tools and functions were available to them throughout the transitional phase society found itself in.

Unlike the claims put forward by the anti-positivists, then, it cannot be said that the continued existence of sociological belief represented a fatal blow to the project of sociological positivism. Throughout *The Division of Labour*, this paradoxical state lurked beneath the surface, as a meta-commentary on the condition of the sociologist within modernity. And yet, at the same time, it represented a discursive conundrum for a sociological positivist like Durkheim, as he was largely unable to explicitly articulate what this practice of sociological faith precisely entailed. What does become more clear from such a reading is that the coming of an organic modernity did not constitute the disappearance of the practice of believing for Durkheim. Rather, it represented a shifting and reorganization of its practice across the intellectual and non-intellectual classes.

In the next chapter, I will look at Durkheim's attempts at further occupying and describing this sociological space from the inside, through his engagement with both neo-Kantianism and pragmatism. Using these philosophical traditions as a means of thinking sociology, Durkheim further ensconced himself within this history, so I argue through his engagement with both neo-Kantian and pragmatist conceptions of belief, as a philosophical reflection on the legitimacy of sociology as both an epistemological institution and a sovereign mode of existence.

CHAPTER 9

The Varieties of Sociological Experience. Durkheimian Belief/Knowledge-Compositions

INTRODUCTION

In the previous chapter, I have aimed to show how Durkheim made a sociological language of beliefs operational, employing dual readings of the category by Fustel de Coulanges and Comte as a historical-narrative anchor through which the multifaceted status of forms of believing in modernity could be traced. In this chapter, I want to expand on another aspect of the Durkheimian engagement with belief-languages, which was the French sociologist's reflexive conceptualization of the term itself. Here, the important source of stimulation was both the rising prominence of neo-Kantianism as well as its critiques via pragmatism and Bergsonian philosophy. Both the neo-Kantian and the pragmatist traditions explicitly conceived a theory of belief, which allowed Durkheim to gradually articulate his own theory of belief in relation to both his understanding of sociological research as well as the role of the sociologist itself.

By discussing Durkheim's more philosophical reflections on belief, in relation to pragmatism and neo-Kantianism, we can gain a better understanding of another aspect of interest to us here, which was his consideration of non-Western cultures and practices. Sociological moderns like Durkheim have been accused, both in his own era and today, of being obtuse to non-rational systems of meaning and devotion, imposing instead their own framework of truth and reasonableness onto such cultures and, as such, producing, at best, interpretative misunderstandings or committing, at worst, forms of epistemic injustice and subjugation.[1] One of his contemporaries for example, the largely 'forgotten' French ethnographer Arnold van Gennep, accused Durkheim of treating his research subjects such as the Australian Aborigines in an overly classificatory manner, robbing them of any historical agency and missing any "sense of life" itself.[2]

The category of belief, with its strong Western-Christian undertones and explicitly rationalist premises, often played a central role in such accusations of reductionism, its epistemological framework considered to be too restrictive for a proper understanding of such complex phenomena. By advocating for both a post-secular and ontological turn, contemporary scholars critical of Durkheimian positivism have argued for substituting such frameworks with more symmetrical equivalents, making it possible for non-Western cultures to regain a sense of agency when their religious practices of devotion are being investigated from the outside. By replacing the positivist theory of truth-correspondence and -realism, the latter being lamented for its normative obfuscation of non-rational propositions, they argue that we can attain not only a better understanding of non-Western cultures but of modernity itself.[3]

In this chapter, I aim to further tackle this accusation, by reconstructing Durkheim's, what I have called throughout these chapters, belief/knowledge-composition. It is my argument that the value of Durkheimian sociology was its self-reflective ideal of social layering: the thick description of the different regimes of truth and belief traced by the sociologist in both their utterance and their experience. While these different layers were not all as true as each other, they were all equally 'real', according to Durkheim. The very goal of the sociological project, as he made clear in his discussion of pragmatist philosophy, was not to exclude forms of non-modern categorization, but rather to bring all these forms of categorization together and understand their simultaneous and intersubjective unfolding. It is not necessary then, so I argue here, to abandon the Durkheimian toolset, even if it would be unwise to read and apply Durkheim's works in an overly literal fashion. Rather, it is still of value

---

[1] Latour, "Formes éléméntaires de la sociologie", 259.

[2] Bjørn Thomassen, "The hidden battle that shaped the history of sociology: Arnold van Gennep contra Emile Durkheim", *Journal of Classical Sociology* 16, no. 2 (2016): 182.

[3] Arpad Szakolczai & Bjørn Thomassen, *From Anthropology to Social Theory: Rethinking the Social Sciences* (Cambridge: Cambridge University Press, 2018), 254.

today if approached carefully, especially for when we try to understand the historical process of sociology's self-formation and -imagination.

The chapter is made up of three sections. In the first section, I will discuss Durkheim's theorization of the belief-category and its roots in the neo-Kantian philosophical tradition. In the second section, I will turn towards Durkheim's lectures on pragmatism and how this philosophical tradition, via its critiques of rationalist understandings of belief, problematized Durkheim's own understanding of the category and invigorated a more self-reflexive and -critical attitude with the French sociologist. In the final section of the chapter, I look at how this self-reflexive engagement with the belief-category's multidimensionality enabled Durkheim to further historicize the societal task of sociology itself, as a language which could articulate the existence of multiple social and cultural realities at the same time. I will conclude by arguing that Durkheimian sociology, and its classificatory character, did not so much lack a "sense of life" as it aimed to *give life* to such modern practices as classification and speculative, contemplative thought.

BELIEFS AS REPRESENTATIONS: DURKHEIM AND THE NEO-KANTIAN THEORY OF BELIEF

Throughout Durkheim's work, his philosophical grasp of the concept of belief was generally consistent. This might seem strange in the light of the often-made distinction between "the early and the late Durkheim", the Durkheim of *The Division of Labour in Society* and *The Elementary Forms of Religious Life*, but the simple explanation might just be that this consistency was the result of an underdeveloped theorization itself. According to Giovanni Paoletti, Durkheim did not have a fully articulated notion of what belief precisely was, neither in the first nor the second part of his career, so it makes sense that the term did not become explicitly problematized when Durkheim moved away from discussions of social solidarity towards reflections on collective representations, the symbolic and the sacred.[4]

Despite this lack of a fully expounded framework focusing on the precise meaning of belief, Durkheim still sporadically reflected on the term

---

[4] Paoletti, "Representation and belief", 127; Giovanni Paoletti, "Solidarity as a social relation: history of Durkheim's project. Some remarks about solidarity and 'lien social' in Durkheim's works", *Europeana* 3 (2014): 115–130.

throughout his work, going beyond its mere practical application as a narrative instrument of self-historicization as seen in the previous chapter. A few key characteristics can be extracted on the basis of these sporadic excursions: first of all, to have beliefs, according to Durkheim, meant to accept and give consent to certain propositions signalling a particular state of the world, i.e. representations.[5] Beliefs, furthermore, stemmed from a social origin: they were essentially considered by Durkheim as representational manifestations of the ontological reality of social forces, which gradually seeped into something resembling an articulated discourse, to be used and engaged with by the social group and its descendants.[6] Beliefs, in other words, were the semi-intellectual markers giving access to the plane of the socially Real, the dimension in which collective entities moved and interacted.[7] This socialized nature of belief-propositions was not considered to function as one-way traffic either. In Durkheimian thought, there is considered to be a perennial dialogue at work between the individual and society, with one of the clear purposes of society being perceived by the French sociologist as assisting its individual members in becoming more and more aware of the collective forces socially governing them.[8]

A final aspect of this Durkheimian framework of beliefs was that these were not just socially useful but also *true*:

> Indeed, it is a fundamental postulate of sociology that a human institution cannot rest upon error and falsehood. If it did, it could not endure. If it had not been grounded in the nature of things, in those very things it would have met resistance that it could not have overcome. Therefore, when I approach the study of primitive religions, it is with the certainty that they are grounded in and *express the real* [my emphasis].[9]

Yet this reality of both the believed object and the practice of believing is not the only condition for beliefs to exist. They also need to be shared by a social group of believers and these are experienced collectively, forming

---

[5] Paoletti, "Representation and belief", 127.
[6] Durkheim & Mauss, *Primitive Classification*, 43.
[7] Sue Stedman Jones, "Representations in Durkheim's Masters: Kant and Renouvier. I. Representation reality and the question of science", in: *Durkheim and Representations*, ed. W.S.F. Pickering (London: Routledge, 2000), 37.
[8] Bruno Karsenti, *La société en personnes. Études durkheimiennes* (Paris: Economica, 2006), 160–61.
[9] Ibid., 2.

part of what Durkheim termed 'the collective consciousness'.[10] In this, they are different from knowledge-based propositions concerning our experience of the world, as the former occupy a phase preceding the processes of individualization, rationalization and potential verification inherent to the latter.[11]

At the same time, however, beliefs should not be reduced to purely imitative mechanisms, coercing individuals into forms of action in the way that Tarde understood belief and desire in his book *The Laws of Imitation*.[12] Rather, Durkheim was adamant, both in *The Elementary Forms of Religious Life* as well as in his other works such as *Suicide*, that to believe and to imitate are two distinct modes.[13] When discussing the mimetic practices of the Aboriginal tribes, such as among the Warramunga whose chief imitates the cry of the White Cockatoo during a night long ceremony, Durkheim continuously spoke of rites, not beliefs.[14] Because it is the rites which are "modes of action", while beliefs are "states of opinion", their distinction, while somewhat artificial, still categorically decisive: "Between these two categories of phenomena lies all that separates thinking from doing."[15] To imitate, in other words, is to do something, whereas to believe something is to think, *in a kind of way*.

To continue with the example of religion, then, beliefs express (together with myths, dogmas and legends), "the nature of sacred things, the virtues and powers attributed to them, their history, and their relationship with one another as well as profane things".[16] They are the form of speculative judgement, which is tasked with drawing the lines between those things which are considered to be sacred and those which are profane. Beliefs, then, are a tool of mediation, and to have and to share them constitutes an intellectual operation, even if the actual thought-work is only of secondary importance to their social status. Durkheimian beliefs are, in this understanding, always rational beliefs. As Giovanni Paoletti has already

---

[10] Ibid., 439; Durkheim, *The Division of Labour*, 39.

[11] Émile Durkheim, *Pragmatism and Sociology*, ed. John B. Allcock, transl. by J.C. Whitehouse (Cambridge: Cambridge University Press, 1983), 91.

[12] Gabriel Tarde, *The Laws of Imitation*, transl. by Elsie Clews Parsons (New York: Henry Holt and Company, 1903).

[13] Émile Durkheim, *Suicide: A Study in Sociology*, ed. George Simpson, transl. by John A. Spaulding & George Simpson (London & New York: Routledge, 2002), 74.–76.

[14] Durkheim, *The Elementary Forms of Religious Life* (1995), 357.

[15] Ibid., 34.

[16] Ibid.

persuasively argued, this puts Durkheim right into the neo-Kantian tradition of the late nineteenth century, following other French theorists on rational belief like Charles Renouvier and Victor Brochard.[17] By understanding Durkheim's theory of belief from a neo-Kantian perspective, the complexity and, at times seemingly paradoxical, status of collective representations within Durkheimian sociology becomes more straightforward and coherent. Using Kant's critical philosophy of rational beliefs as a theoretical starting point, Durkheim was able to better locate a unique link between the individual and society, a mental state which was simultaneously affective as well as reasonable, making it a more nuanced avenue for sociological investigation of social ties than other more rigid conceptual instruments such as self-interest and the contract.[18]

The question remains, however, whether Durkheim's reception of neo-Kantian concepts sufficiently describes the French sociologist's engagement with the question of belief throughout his work. There are a few reasons to pose this question in the first place. First, there is the obvious matter that Durkheim's usage of the belief-category is different simply through the fact that it was not intended to serve as the basis of a philosophical theory but as a condition for a sociological method. Paoletti already noted this important distinction, arguing that Durkheim fruitfully expanded neo-Kantian thought by introducing the social dimension of belief.[19] Another crucial addition was the further integration of a historical dimension, which was constructed in dialogue with Fustel de Coulanges and his work on socio-historical institutions, as discussed in the previous chapter.[20] A second remark on the potential insufficiency of the neo-Kantian framing of Durkheimian reflections on belief is that it can find no real place for the impact pragmatism had on the French sociologist's thinking. Some of the most innovative thoughts on belief in the work of Durkheim can be found in his posthumously published lectures on pragmatism, where the positivist sociologist tried to rebut some of the challenges posed to rationalism by pragmatist philosophers such as William James, Charles Sanders Peirce, John Dewey and F.C.S. Schiller.[21] It was by

---

[17] Paoletti, "Representation and belief", 127.
[18] Ibid., 133.
[19] Ibid., 126.
[20] Ibid., 127; Numa Denis Fustel de Coulanges, *The Ancient City: A Study on the Religion, Laws, and Institutions of Greece and Rome* (Kitchener: Batoche Books, 2001 [1864]).
[21] Bruno Karsenti, "La sociologie à l'épreuve du pragmatisme. Réaction durkheimienne", in: *La croyance et l'enquête. Aux sources du pragmatisme*, eds. Bruno Karsenti & Louis Queré

engaging with their pertinent critiques that Durkheim could mould a new, modern form of rationalism:

> Its value is, as has already been mentioned, that it [pragmatism] shows up the weaknesses of the old rationalism, which needs to be reformed if it is to meet the demands of modern thought and take into account certain new points of view introduced by modern science. The problem is to find a formula which will both preserve what is essential in rationalism and answer the valid criticism that pragmatism makes of it.[22]

A crucial addition to Durkheim's notion of belief occurs in this dialogue with pragmatism, which is the acceptance of the fact that belief was not merely a mental and rational construct but also carried within itself a creative force which constructed reality as well.[23] This is, of course, an important departure of the neo-Kantian notion of belief, where little to no room was left for belief as something other than a rational instrument for accepting or rejecting certain propositions on the state of the world. Through pragmatism, belief transformed, for Durkheim, into something that could *alter* propositions, as something that did perform an action rather than remain exclusively limited to the domain of thought.

This second remark ties into a final consideration, which is that the way belief manifested itself in Durkheimian sociology, whether as a universal, cognitive branch of the *individual* human psyche or as a social-performative act *between* subjects, was highly variable. Let me give a few examples to show what I mean. Belief, understood and applied by Durkheim in a self-reflective manner, comes to the fore in *The Elementary Forms of Religious Life* as a kind of unchanging thing: the tribesmen in Aboriginal society *believe* in a number of things, dictated to them by the totemic structure they adhere to, and these beliefs can be gathered, systematized and, subsequently, rationally explained in a coherent fashion by the sociologist.[24] Yet these beliefs themselves were seemingly not considered by Durkheim to be very dynamic on their own accord, as they merely echoed the constitution of the social environment surrounding the tribe. If we encounter historical change in *The Elementary Forms*, it occurs on the level of the collective where beliefs, rituals and the forces of social reality interact,

---

(Paris: Éditions de l'École des Hautes Études en Sciences Sociales, 2004), 317–349.
[22] Durkheim, *Pragmatism and Sociology*, 2.
[23] Ibid., 23.
[24] Durkheim, *The Elementary Forms of Religious Life* (1995), 6–8.

patiently waiting for the sociologist to eventually uncover them: "But a new way of explaining man becomes possible as soon as we recognize that above the individual there is society, and that society is a system of active forces – *not a nominal being, and not a creation of the mind* [my emphasis]."[25] Whereas society was seen as historically autonomous and generative, beliefs (as collective representations) were considered to be merely "creations of the mind", passive signifiers representing the dynamic movements of the social above the individual.[26]

Such a passage is typically read in opposition to Tardean sociology, the latter explicitly denying the existence of such a societal dimension.[27] Another critical reading, as articulated by van Gennep, would point out the rather reductionist character of such passages, with Durkheim simply glancing over Aboriginal beliefs as being largely irrelevant and lacking in socio-historical agency.[28] Here, we encounter something resembling the hierarchical scheme often attributed to positivist sociology in a critique of its practices of epistemological domination, one where the scientific knowledge of the sociologist is charged with processing the narrative forms of self-identification from a different cultural world.[29] The question is then whether this investigative relation between primitive tribes and positivist sociology represents the kind of unilinear epistemic domination as some critics of rationalist positivism have suggested. Durkheim's own philosophical reflections on the status of beliefs for sociological interpretation can provide a better idea whether such critiques are actually valid.

The French sociologist was himself aware of the limits of a positivist-sociological analysis of so-called primitive cultures, contrary to what these critiques seem to imply. Furthermore, it was a source of reflection which

---

[25] Ibid., 448.

[26] Ibid., 227: "That power exists, and it is society. When the Australian is carried above himself, feeling inside a life overflowing with an intensity that surprises him, he is not the dupe of an illusion. That exaltation is real and really is the product of forces outside of and superior to the individual. Of course, he is mistaken to believe that a power in the form of an animal or plant has brought about this increase in vital energy. But his mistake lies in taking literally the symbol that represents this being in the mind, or the outward appearance in which the imagination has dressed it up, not in the fact of its very existence. *Behind these forms, be they cruder or more refined, there is a concrete and living reality* [my emphasis]."

[27] Cf. Gabriel Tarde & Émile Durkheim, "The debate", in: *The Social after Gabriel Tarde: Debates and assessments*, ed. Matei Candea (London & New York: Routledge, 2010), 27–43.

[28] Latour, "Formes éléméntaires de la sociologie", 259, 268.

[29] Martin Holbraad & Morten Axel Pedersen, *The Ontological Turn: An Anthropological Exposition* (Cambridge: Cambridge University Press, 2017), 193.

appeared throughout his work, for example, when Durkheim showed particular attention to the artificiality of the boundaries separating social science and religion. According to him, containing the forces of religion and the sacred, even within the epistemically robust domains of the secular and the scientific, constituted a difficult practice for the sociologist, as these religious-collective forces were, by their nature, 'contagious'.[30] This is an important reason why Durkheim often made sure to emphasize his *identity* as a rationalist, not just as a symbol of recognition or as a usual trope for the validation of rational clarity, but also as a means of containing this contagion through practices of translation:

> This characteristic, sacredness, can be expressed, I believe—and I feel bound to express it—in secular terms. That is, in fact, the distinctive mark of my attitude. Instead of joining with the utilitarians in misunderstanding and denying the religious element in morality, or hypostatizing with theology a transcendent Being, I feel it necessary to translate it in rational language without thereby destroying any of its peculiar characteristics. You will see that, from this point of view, I escape the objection you have made since, confronted with the sacred, of which I affirm the existence, my secular reason retains all its independence.[31]

Beliefs, then, within the Durkheimian framework are not passive by nature in relation to positivist knowledge, they are *made that way* via a scientific-conceptual operation of *translation*. Extracting the belief-content through its supra-historical quality of rationality, Durkheim can uncover certain social laws governing Man and society. Yet this operation also has its clear limits. If we want to know something for certain, i.e. know something scientifically, we have to cut it out of its immediate context of becoming, making it abstract and 'cold': "To be certain, we must affirm something; and to affirm something we have to extract it from the becoming of sensation and classify it."[32] The social-scientific employment of beliefs—as rational and disconnected entities—only represents a segment of their function within society, the segment that is knowable and able to be made visible.

---

[30] Ibid., 323.
[31] Émile Durkheim, *Sociology and Philosophy*, transl. by D.F. Pocock (Abingdon, Oxon: Routledge, 2010), 35.
[32] Durkheim, *Pragmatism and Sociology*, 100.

Beliefs, in other words, are not *just* representations; they are made this way in the sociological operation as a condition of possibility for socio-scientific understanding. Durkheim thus also concedes that beliefs are more than what the sociologist typically makes of them, their place and role in the societal stream of becoming simply not immediately visible and ontologically available to the sociological gaze. So what is the social scientist to do with this invisible appendage, this blind spot in their desire to grasp the meaning of society in its totality? It was by entering into a dialogue with pragmatism that Durkheim was able to articulate a sociological attitude towards this appendage of non-visible beliefs. As a result of this dialogue, Durkheim was able to construct his own intervention in the stream of historical languages of belief, one that went much further beyond a mere classification of non-rational beliefs as being irrelevant or false, as I will show in the following section.

THINKING SOCIOLOGY AS A POSITIVIST INSTITUTION: DURKHEIM ON PRAGMATISM

So what did this spectrum of visible and non-visible beliefs look like? To understand this, we need to turn to Durkheim's engagement with the philosophy of pragmatism, the important text being his posthumously published lectures on the topic in *Pragmatism and Sociology* (1955). The importance of this engagement can be explained by the shift in perspective which occurred, where an alternative facet of social beliefs was investigated by Durkheim. In most of Durkheim's published work, the research emphasis was put on how both beliefs and the institution could be interpreted from a scientific-conceptual perspective (which I have already discussed in the previous chapter), in which the sociologist enters into a particular kind of relationship with the social facts, as described by Durkheim in his *Rules of Sociological Method*. The institution-as-social-fact was considered in Durkheimian sociology as a *thing-in-itself*, which needs to be studied from the outside detached from the subjects and its mental representations.[33] This was the very goal of the *Elementary Forms* as well: "To discover what that object [cult] consists of, then, we must apply […] an analysis similar to the one that has replaced the senses' representations

---

[33] Durkheim, *The Rules of Sociological Method*, 37.

of the world with a scientific and conceptual one. This is precisely what I have tried to do."[34]

Such a perspective, however, was not immediately possible in his discussion of pragmatist philosophy, and this for a number of reasons. First of all, pragmatism did not concern itself with the objective study of institutions but with those of subjective beliefs, experiences and opinion. In the pragmatist philosophy of William James, for example, it was the individual experiences of religious life which took centre stage, not their shared performance nor their institutional embodiment, as Durkheim intended. In pragmatism, it was belief itself that was performative and creative, which could reveal a reality, so pragmatists would argue, unreachable by rationalist principles alone.[35] The separation of thought and action, so central to Durkheim's analysis of religious life, became muddled in pragmatist philosophy, with thought itself representing a particular kind of action in the world through the intimate connection between belief and action.[36]

And secondly, pragmatism aimed to eliminate the positivist distinction between rational belief and objective truth, arguing that such distinctions were merely artificial. Pragmatists argued that seeing how reality is constantly changing, our notion of what is true must be changeable as well. What is 'true' is something that is made and re-made, according to James, in order to accommodate the fluidity of changing reality itself: "These things *make themselves* as we go. Our rights, wrongs, prohibitions, penalties, words, forms, idioms, beliefs, are so many new creations that add themselves as fast as history proceeds. Far from being antecedent principles that animate the process, law, language, truth are but abstract names for its results."[37] To summarize, then, pragmatism tackled the very presuppositions founding rationalist sociology. As such, Durkheim's discussion of pragmatism needed to be a philosophical and methodological reflection on the principles of positivist sociology itself, and a structured argumentation on why these positivist principles came closer to attaining a

---

[34] Durkheim, *The Elementary Forms of Religious Life* (1995), 420.

[35] William James, *The Varieties of Religious Experience: A Study in Human Nature* (London and Glasgow: Collins, 1960), 87–88.

[36] Peirce, "Philosophy and the Conduct of Life (1898)", 33.

[37] William James, *Writings 1902–1910: The Varieties of Religious Experience. Pragmatism. A Pluralistic Universe. The Meaning of Truth. Some Problems of Philosophy. Essays* (New York: Literary Classics of the United States, Inc., 1987), 592.

satisfactory understanding of truth and reality than those of their pragmatist opponents.[38]

The arguments of pragmatists like William James and C.S. Peirce were not necessarily convincing for someone like Durkheim, who had always displayed a strong conviction in the truthfulness of his scientific ambitions.[39] But the challenge of pragmatism did force Durkheim to turn inwards towards self-reflection and -articulation, in order to fully explain positivist principles and counter the pragmatist claims. It raised a number of crucial questions: What are the limits of sociological knowledge? What does the sociologist *do* with those things he or she cannot know? What does belief mean for the sociologist itself, not as an object of study but as a thing inside the mind of the sociologist, *as a historical subject*? It is not that Durkheim hadn't yet thought of these things, as these kinds of philosophical-existential reflections appear throughout his work. But the dialogue with pragmatism demanded that Durkheim articulate these reflections as clear as possible, as the very project of rationalism was threatened by the popularity of pragmatism and Bergsonism, both in academia as among the broader populace.[40] It is not unreasonable to suggest that most of Durkheim's later work was aimed at explicitly meeting this exact challenge, a period of time experienced by him, as well as other rationalists such as German phenomenologist Edmund Hüsserl, as a crisis of reason.[41]

And yet, this historical interpretation of the nefarious role of pragmatist philosophy did not result in an unfair account of his intellectual opponents.[42] On the contrary, Durkheim, throughout the lectures, took the philosophy of pragmatism very seriously, acknowledging their legitimate criticisms of the classical rationalist project and seeking to find the

---

[38] Durkheim, *Pragmatism and Sociology*, 1.

[39] Lukes, *Émile Durkheim*, 370.

[40] Neil Gross, "Durkheim's Pragmatism Lectures: A Contextual Interpretation", *Sociological Theory* 15, no. 2 (1997): 126–149.

[41] Edward A. Tiryakian, "Durkheim and Hüsserl: A Comparison of the Spirit of Positivism and the Spirit of Phenomenology", in: *Phenomenology and the Social Sciences: A Dialogue*, ed. Joseph Bien (The Hague: Martinus Nijhoff, 1978), 39. Husserl explored this topic through his own phenomenological lens in his book published in 1936, *Die Krisis der europäischen Wissenschaften und die transzendentale Phänomenologie: Eine Einleitung in die phänomenologische Philosophie* (for an English translation, cf. Edmund Hüsserl, *The Crisis of European Sciences and Transcendental Phenomenology: An Introduction to Phenomenological Philosophy*, transl. by David Carr (Evanston: Northwestern University Press, 1989)).

[42] Lukes, *Émile Durkheim*, 488.

appropriate answers to these criticisms.[43] Pragmatism represented, then, not so much a foe to be defeated as a tool to think with.[44] The particular status of these lectures was not limited to the attitude of Durkheim, as it can be argued that his sociological approach shifted as well. Whereas Durkheim's standard sociological approach can be phenomenologically characterized as an operation of bracketing social reality in search of ideal objectivities, his engagement with pragmatism was far more existential, with the position of the sociologist uncharacteristically problematized itself.[45] We can represent this transition schematically, by extracting the four main components of Durkheimian analysis: scientific perspective—society—individual beliefs—institutions. The Durkheimian sociologist traditionally occupies the external position of the scientific perspective, mapping how societal structures engage with historical contingencies and intermediary bodies (i.e. institutions), shaping and being shaped by their individual and intersubjective embodiments.[46]

This scheme is different in the lectures of pragmatism, as the sociologist occupied two positions, at the same time: Durkheim was not only an external observer but a historicized object as well. Both positivist sociology and pragmatism occupy similar positions, functioning as intermediary bodies trying to give meaning to a coherent set of belief-propositions, as well as form a particular truth-relationship with the domain of society. In other words, the topic of sociology was not just approached as a science in these lectures but an institution as well, composed of propositions and constituted by a particular function:

> It is here that we can establish a PARALLEL BETWEEN PRAGMATISM AND SOCIOLOGY. By applying the historical point of view to the order of things human, sociology is led to set itself the same problem. *Man is a product of history and hence of becoming; there is nothing in him that is either given or defined in advance.* History begins nowhere and it ends nowhere. Everything in man has been made by mankind in the course of time.

[43] Durkheim, *Pragmatism and Sociology*, 2.
[44] Stéphane Bachiocchi and Jean-Louis Fabiani, "Durkheim's Lost Argument (1895–1955): Critical Moves on Method and Truth", *Durkheimian Studies* 18 (2012): 34.
[45] Carlos Belvedere, "Durkheim as the Founder of Phenomenological Sociology", *Human Studies* 38, no. 3 (2015): 382–83; Armand Cuvillier, "Preface to the French Edition of 1955", in: Émile Durkheim, *Pragmatism and Sociology*, ed. John B. Allcock, transl. by J.C. Whitehouse (Cambridge: Cambridge University Press, 1983), xvii–xviii.
[46] Paul Fauconnet and Marcel Mauss, "La sociologie: objet et méthode", *Grande Encyclopédie* 30 (1901): 11.

> Consequently, if truth is human, it too is a human product. Sociology applies the same conception to reason. *All that constitutes reason, its principles and categories, has been made in the course of history* [my emphasis].[47]

The sociologist becomes fully entangled, historically and existentially, and is itself a particular product of an ongoing historical flow in which one must navigate and negotiate: "[Pragmatism and sociology] are *children of the same era* [my emphasis]", says Durkheim in the very first utterances of his lecture series.[48] Here, the phenomenological composition of Durkheim's perspective radically shifted: from the conceptual relationship, where the sociologist engages with the distinct social reality inhabited by the 'social fact', the framework transitions towards an existential engagement with the social action of historically performing social science. What are we doing, exactly, when we are doing social science?

Such a question was a logical extension of a discussion of pragmatist principles, with the latter being actively concerned with reflecting on the very act of *doing* philosophy, of *giving* meaning to concepts such as 'truth', 'belief', 'reason', and 'reality', and how all of these practices are intimately related to our constitution—historically, psychologically, sensorily—as persons.[49] By engaging with pragmatism, Durkheim was being externally moved to articulate the historical process of how the sociologist intervenes in social reality by performing his own discourse on belief-propositions, and how this discourse relates specifically to scientific and institutional registers.[50] Unlike their rationalist opponents, so says James, pragmatists do not consider truth to be self-evident in its definition. Instead, the very first task of philosophy should be to approach truth in its historicized fullness, to be able to cover truth-claims which include both "'absolute' truth [...], as well as truth of the most relative and imperfect description".[51] Durkheim, as a sociologist being well aware of complexity of social reality and the conceptual difficulty of capturing this particular nature of it, was not unsympathetic to such an ambition. In his most charitable reading, the pragmatist critique of rationalism could be characterized as putting an emphasis on the practical consequences of conceptual thought, and had as

---

[47] Durkheim, *Pragmatism and Sociology*, 67.
[48] Ibid., 1.
[49] James, *Writings 1902–1910*, 489.
[50] de Certeau, "L'institution du croire", 61–80.
[51] James, *Writings 1902–1910*, 919.

its main goal "to liberate thought", "to make the truth more supple" in order to account for the essentially interconnected state of reality.[52]

Durkheim saw the pragmatist tradition as identifying two main intellectual phenomena which imposed limits onto reality, with dogma and conceptual thought being considered as the central perpetrators of such limitations.[53] The accusation of philosophical dogmatism has been a consistent recurrent in the history of rationalism, with philosophical opponents of rationalism constantly pointing out those axioms which still rested on personal beliefs, rather than any universal, rational measure.[54] Pragmatists represented a continuation of this same tradition. They considered as the dogmatic conception of truth the notion "that the true idea is the idea which conforms to things. It is an image, a *copy* of objects, the mental representation of the thing. An idea is true when this mental representation corresponds accurately to the object represented".[55] Such an account of truth, however, was not satisfactory to pragmatists like James and Schiller, as it created, in their view, an ontological and epistemological "chasm"—between the objective and the subjective, between thought and action—where there was none.[56] From the pragmatist perspective, this gap, created through the illusion of a Platonic Idea World, only produced illogical and negative effects: it made light of the reality of the human experience, while providing no convincing argument explaining the existence of the diversity of minds.[57] The prospect of knowledge for knowledge's sake also meant little to pragmatists: to appraise knowledge in such a way would do little more than make it "a god to which one raises altars".[58]

Something similar was argued towards a critique of conceptual thought. Basing himself on the philosophy of Henri Bergson, James tried to make the point that the concept and the real were two antithetical things: whereas the concept is "something definite and distinct [...c]ut from the stream of our experience", "impressions mutually interpenetrate each

---

[52] Durkheim, *Pragmatism and Sociology*, 64, also 36.
[53] Ibid., 11–32.
[54] Richard H. Popkin, *The History of Scepticism: From Erasmus to Descartes* (Assen: Van Gorcum & Comp. N.V., 1960), 214.
[55] Durkheim, *Pragmatism and Sociology*, 11.
[56] Ibid., 16.
[57] Ibid., 21.
[58] Ibid., 14.

other in the sensory flux of images".[59] As such, conceptual life is ruled by "the principle of identity or non-contradiction": to constitute the concept as a model of reality is to think of reality as "made up of stable elements that are entirely distinct from each other and have no reciprocal communication".[60] But this is not how reality manifests itself. Living things move across all kinds of borders, forming networks and creating types of connectivity which defy rationalist demarcations. To project a static concept onto such a fluid whole, would be to miss out on the soul of living things (here, we can remember the accusation of Arnold van Gennep of Durkheim, as lacking a "sense of life"), that essence which gives it life itself:

> what makes up the reality of things is the network of *influences* they exert on each other. My thought acts on my body; it animates it. A movement of my body exteriorizes this thought, and by means of this intermediary my thought communicates with that of others. James writes that things must be able to combine, to 'compenetrate and telescope'. But, he says, 'Intellectualism denies ... that finite things can act on one another, for all things, once translated into concepts, remain shut up to themselves'. Concepts 'make the whole notion of a causal influence between finite things incomprehensible'. From the point of view of conceptual logic, all distinctions are 'isolators'. Contagion of concepts would be confusion, and confusion is the major logical sin.[61]

The same lack of comprehension could be applied to rational concepts of belief as well: to have a belief, is not to express a clearly demarcated state of the world; it means to look forward to the potential accomplishment of a certain action. It is a way to intervene in reality, according to pragmatists, not copy it.[62] This is what Charles Sanders Peirce had in mind when he argued that the notion of belief is inherently meaningless in a scientific language: "Hence, I hold that what is usually and properly called belief [...] has no place in science at all. We *believe* the proposition we are ready to act upon. *Full belief* is willingness to act upon the proposition in vital crises, *opinion* is willingness to act upon it in relatively insignificant affairs.

---

[59] Ibid., 28.
[60] Ibid., 29.
[61] Ibid., 31.
[62] Ibid., 38.

But pure science has nothing at all to do with *action*."[63] Believing, then, is considered by pragmatists to be less a mental attitude towards propositions (as the neo-Kantians proposed) than a practice in its own right, an instrument for both coordinating as well as creating the reality around us.[64] It does, in other words, constitute an action, rather than a mere form of thought.

At this point, the opposition between pragmatist readings of belief and Durkheim's application of the category in the *Elementary Forms of Religious Life* could not be more stark. The static and passive nature of Aboriginal beliefs, in the way they were described by Durkheim, is in complete contrast to how someone like William James would approach them. According to James, these were not merely representations of a society gradually articulating itself, but diverse and creative signifiers in their own right, pseudo-intellectualized instruments which were tasked with navigating the social milieu surrounding them. Approaching them merely as representations would constitute little else than an effacement, a rationalist appropriation of cultural practices with the sole goal of constructing an idealist discourse detached from social reality itself.

Pragmatism and Sociological Positivism on the Poetic Function of Belief

But is this an accurate representation of Durkheim's own navigation of both ethnographic literature as well as languages of belief? To answer this question most clearly, it is best that we return once more to the historical-anthropological framework of Michel de Certeau, making it act as a lens through which both sociological positivism and pragmatism can be compared in a historical and symmetrical manner. In this way, we can think of Durkheim's engagement with pragmatism as essentially centring on the question of the institution in processing propositions on reality. As we saw before, according to Durkheim himself, what binds pragmatism and positivist sociology together in these lectures is their status as historically paralleled schemes of interpretation which consider truth and reason to be societal products. This includes reflective statements on truth and reason as well of course, meaning that sociology and pragmatism are not just social science and philosophy, they are historical institutions. Durkheim

---

[63] Peirce, "Philosophy and the Conduct of Life (1898)", 33.
[64] Durkheim, *Pragmatism and Sociology*, 38–39.

refers to this when he points out how pragmatists like William James are using instruments of logic and reason to critique the constrictive effects of said logic and reason:

> It is, in fact, very difficult to escape from concepts and logical principles. When James tells us that one cannot make something continuous from something discontinuous, is he not using a logical principle? Is he not affirming with the aid of conceptual thought something that touches on reality itself?[65]

It is important to note here that Durkheim is not just criticizing pragmatism for lacking self-awareness of its own reasonableness. Rather, he is pointing out the unavoidably dual nature of every proposition on propositions: we are simultaneously making ourselves discursively as we are being made by historical factors outside ourselves. Here, he is anticipating his own argument for the necessity of sociology's institutional function in the history of reason.

Pragmatists disagreed on the nature of this institutional function: they ultimately viewed their historical role less as "an undertaking to encourage action" than an attack on *pure speculation* and *theoretical thought*".[66] In other words, pragmatist philosophers conceptualized their own historicity, belonging to the history of reason's unfolding, as a philosophical act of deconstruction, giving prominence back to reality over reason.[67] Reality, says William James, exceeds the limits of logic: "Reality, life, experience, concreteness, immediacy, use what word you will, exceeds our logic, overflows and surrounds it."[68] Pragmatism, then, has been brought into the world, not for using reason to make beliefs conform to static concepts, but with the function to 'make sense' of this excess inevitably created through the existence of beliefs which could not be verified by conceptual thought *immediately*.[69] The purpose of thought, according to pragmatists—and this means all thought, with philosophy being considered as an attitude common to all people, not just philosophers[70]—is to organize the entirety of 'potential truth' into a meaningful structure, through which the

---

[65] Ibid., 32.
[66] Ibid., 64.
[67] Ibid., 32.
[68] James, *Writings 1902–1910*, 726.
[69] Durkheim, *Pragmatism and Sociology*, 51.
[70] James, *Writings 1902–1910*, 487–88.

individual can navigate their mental life, satisfactorily, in correspondence with that of reality.⁷¹

The important insight consistently put forward by the pragmatists then is that something like believing has more than one frame of reference which gives it meaning. A belief is not only true or false, it is also an important social practice which has the capacity to found a community through the temporalized nature of its speech act. This is what someone like Michel de Certeau has termed the poetic function of belief: belief-propositions are processed by a community of speakers, not with the intention to construct a hierarchy of knowledge-distinction, but with the goal of creating a space from which otherness can speak without immediately being domesticated through instruments of reason or logic.⁷² It represents an attempt at creating historical duration within a discursive system, leaving the beliefs partially undefined in order to give them a metaphorical quality.⁷³ As such, de Certeau has termed such a metaphorical procedure as "the Trojan horse of interrelational historicity within the city of rationalist legislation [my translation]".⁷⁴ It is a way of *speaking* belief in its performative form: as a social relation which constructs a network of gifts and debts between separate believers, creating a social web characterized by movement and temporalization.⁷⁵

This relation was considered by the pragmatists to be a crucial part of what they viewed as reality, but which was seemingly unable to be thought satisfactorily by rationalism through its dependency on conceptualism and inability to think interrelational influences.⁷⁶ The truth of social life manifests itself in motion, it is constantly becoming.⁷⁷ It could not be captured by being translated into rationalist principles, by being made static through conceptual classification. The goal of pragmatism was to make thought able to express this nature of truth, by emphasizing the latter's creation through social processes of intersubjective dependency:

> Truth lives, in fact, for the most part on a credit system. Our thoughts and beliefs 'pass,' so long as nothing challenges them, just as bank-notes pass so

---

[71] Durkheim, *Pragmatism and Sociology*, 50.
[72] de Certeau, "L'institution du croire", 73.
[73] Ibid., 74.
[74] Ibid.
[75] de Certeau, "Une pratique sociale de la différence: croire", 364.
[76] Durkheim, *Pragmatism and Sociology*, 66.
[77] Ibid., 52.

long as nobody refuses them. But this all points to direct face-to-face verifications somewhere, without which the fabric of truth collapses like a financial system with no cash-basis whatever. You accept my verification of one thing, I yours of another. We trade on each other's truth. But beliefs verified concretely by *somebody* are the posts of the whole superstructure.[78]

This superstructure means that reality is perennially able to integrate *future states* of belief and truth in a pragmatist conception of belief, without presupposing some logically inconceivable disruption to the perfect dominion of objective ideals.[79]

Durkheim considered this sensitivity towards the fluidity of reality and thought's role in managing a possible future to be pragmatism's greatest achievement.[80] It resolved (partially, at least) what remained neo-Kantianism's main flaw: its inability to fully historicize Man and Man-made products, like 'truth', 'belief', 'reason' and 'logic', as well as provide a legitimate place for error and irrationality within the broader history of reason.[81] These concepts were not timeless entities, but historicized frameworks specific to certain cultures and customs: "We can no longer accept a single, invariable system of categories or intellectual frameworks. The frameworks that had a reason to exist in past civilisations do not have it today."[82] This also meant that the duality of Man, as being composed simultaneously of rational and sensory activity, was not sufficiently explained by the mere act of their classification, as was argued to be the case in Kantian philosophy. This still left open important questions as elaborated by Durkheim in another one of his essays on this topic, "The Dualism of Human Nature and its Social Conditions": "How is it that we can participate *concurrently* in these two existences? How is it that we are made up of two halves that appear to belong to two different beings? Merely to give a name to each being does nothing toward answering the fundamental question [my emphasis]."[83] With pragmatist philosophy, we

---

[78] James, *Writings 1902–1910*, 576–77.
[79] de Certeau, "L'institution du croire", 73.
[80] Durkheim, *Pragmatism and Sociology*, 67.
[81] Ibid., 68.
[82] Ibid., 71.
[83] Émile Durkheim, "The Dualism of Human Nature and its Social Conditions", in: Émile Durkheim, *Essays on Sociology and Philosophy*, ed. Kurt H. Wolff (New York: Harper & Row, Publishers, Inc., 1964), 334.

attained a more complex account of sensory activity's role in constituting practices of truth-making.[84]

While pragmatism correctly identified crucial voids within rationalism, namely the problem of non-rational beliefs and the explanation of epistemological innovation, its privileged answer for this lack, the conceptualization of thought and action as inhabiting a single, continuous plane, created more issues than it resolved. According to Durkheim, this pluralism of pragmatism prevented it, similar to neo-Kantianism, of providing an exhaustive account of humanity's dualist historical condition.[85] Furthermore, its anti-rationalistic stance had led it to abandon any prospect of a thorough engagement with speculative truth, knowledge for knowledge's sake, nor did it thoroughly examine, phenomenologically, what the act of contemplation actually entailed.[86] In other words, while it succeeded in laying bare certain blind-spots of rationalism (the misrepresentation of reality through conceptual classification), it continued and even intensified other obfuscations (conceptual classifications as being reality-producing). The discovery of the historicity and non-determination of thought and beliefs should not, says Durkheim, lead us to leave behind what were real and important findings of the Kantian tradition of philosophy: (1) that reason *progresses* in its historical elaboration; (2) that something such as *an extra-individual and impersonal truth exists* which can impose itself onto us from outside ourselves; and (3) that *conceptual fixity can construct a valuable knowledge-relationship*, rather than just create invalid distortions of reality.[87]

To combine the poetic function of belief articulated by pragmatism with the conceptual analysis of rational belief propagated by neo-Kantianism, this is what Durkheim saw as the historical function of positivist sociology *as a self-reflective, historical institution*. Positivist sociology could take up this position as it was equally concerned with preserving the objective authority of impartial truth, as well as understand the social experience of said truths as a part of historical and creative becoming: "Sociology provides us with broader explanations. For it, truth, reason and morality are the results of a becoming that includes the entire

---

[84] Durkheim, *Pragmatism and Sociology*, 72.
[85] Ibid., 68.
[86] Ibid., 76.
[87] Ibid., 76–77, 80, 98.

unfolding of human history."[88] In his engagement with pragmatism and rationalism, Durkheim consistently tried to define sociology as a discourse which can exclusively integrate both of these components. As such, it is the science which, according to Durkheim, was most ideally suited to explore the duality of Man, through its own historical composition as a kind of hybrid between a scientific-conceptual analysis of rational beliefs, and an institutional discourse, functioning as a broad and temporalized framework through which the diversity of society's historical unfolding attains *meaning*. For Durkheim, the inherent advantage of sociological language was its ability to let belief-propositions *speak* as both objective truth and as non-conceptual otherness.[89]

Through its own unique location as a self-historicized discourse, in-between the impersonal and the personal, sociology could subsequently rethink both rationalism and pragmatism, moving beyond the epistemic limitations inherent to both closed-off thought systems. First of all, Durkheim thought he was able to show how, through a phenomenological analysis of the act of contemplation, speculative truth was also creative and performative in its own right.[90] While the conditions of thought and action are fundamentally distinct—thought being characterized by hyper-consciousness and fixity *in* time, as opposed to action being an externalization of oneself defined by flow and movement—this does not mean that thought does not 'add' to reality. Rather, speculative truth, according to Durkheim, is crucial "to *constitute a being who would not exist without it*".[91] It is through reason that we are able to create a particular kind of shared lifeworld, a lifeworld which Durkheim considers to be civilization itself:

> The fact is that truth, the 'copy' of reality, is not merely redundant or pleonastic. It certainly 'adds' a new world to reality a world which is more complex than any other: That world is the human and social one. Truth is the means by which a new order of things becomes possible, and that new order is nothing less than *civilization*.[92]

---

[88] Ibid., 67.
[89] Ibid., 67–68.
[90] According to Karsenti, Durkheim's dualism is in this sense Spinozist, rather than either Cartesian or pragmatist, cf.: Karsenti, *La société en personnes*, 205.
[91] Durkheim, *Pragmatism and Sociology*, 80–82.
[92] Ibid., 92.

The existence of a reasonable lifeworld also satisfies one of the main problems encountered by pragmatism, namely how "several different minds can know the same world at once".[93] The retention of such an objective yet created domain, through the gradual elucidation of reason imposing itself onto the world of experience, can provide an answer to this conundrum.

The pragmatists, when coming across such a statement, would be eager to proclaim the inability of such a lifeworld dictated by rational principles to imagine the social conditions of real life, which are characterized by diversity and personal interaction in a shared construction of experienced truth. Yet such an accusation would be unfair, in the eyes of Durkheim. Sociology does not, unlike rationalist philosophy, universalize this lifeworld. It is an attempt at historically describing and analysing this gradual imposition. As such, it is a lifeworld (1) among others, which (2) furthermore, is collectively constructed in its own right: "These ideas, however, do not originate with individuals. They are *collective representations*, made up of all the mental states of a people or a social group which thinks together."[94] In other words, the poetic function of processing beliefs persists in Durkheimian sociological discourse, as it stipulates that "there is room for a plurality of mental attitudes all of which in a sense are justified".[95] They are justified, as the complexity of reality makes possible an infinite amount of points of view, making personal negotiation between subjects as valid a way of constructing truth as speculative contemplation.[96] While these forms of negotiation are considered by Durkheim to be 'partial truths', this was the same for the pragmatists, who believed that individual processes of truth-construction were still limited by reality and would ultimately lead to a kind of generally agreed upon status quo.[97]

This socially constructed status, furthermore, was not limited to metaphorical statements, but represents a quality inherent in all beliefpropositions, even scientific ones:

> It could well be that certainty is essentially something collective. We are only certain when we are certain that we are not the *only ones* who are certain. Even when we have worked out a personal belief, we need to communicate

[93] Ibid., 85.
[94] Ibid., 84.
[95] Ibid., 91.
[96] Ibid., 91–92.
[97] Ibid., 75.

it, in order to be certain that we are not mistaken. The authority of tradition and opinion is not, of course, exempt from criticism. When we criticize them, however, it is always in their own name. When, for example, we criticize popular prejudices in the name of science, we are using the authority which opinion accords to science.[98]

The transformation of belief-propositions into scientific propositions through processes of rationalization does not extract these propositions out of the lived world of personal interaction, belief and trust; it simply duplicates them, it gives them a position on multiple planes of existence *at the same time*. Through sociology, however, we can follow and trace the pathways of these propositions, historically, in their dual becoming: as concepts and as non-determined utterances of opinion. This unique location, moreover, legitimizes the Comtean desire for a master science, a positivist discourse which could coordinate the proper relations between these two unfolding domains of social life. Yet, unlike Comte, who suffered from epistemological hubris, Durkheim did not envision a governmental dominance imposed by scientific-conceptual thought. Positivist coordination would limit itself to facilitating a genuine dialogue with society as a historical entity, aiming for an ideal relation of mutual understanding between scientific thought and collective consciousness.[99]

To summarize, then, Durkheim sought to replace the animosity of rationalist domestication and pragmatist deconstruction by a kind of sociological principle of tolerance for reality's functional fullness. This was a tolerance of the scientist, who accepted "that it is very likely that no one of us will see the whole of all its aspects",[100] as well as a tolerance of the collective masses, where everyone "must be able to admit that someone else has perceived an aspect of reality".[101] The question that comes up, at this point, is why Durkheim considered sociology to be qualified to act as such a master science, possessing the authority to coordinate both specialized sciences as well as collective representations in such a way? Durkheim himself put forward sociology's seemingly unique relation to society and its own processes of becoming: sociology, by being able to study the full extent of individual and collective representations, allows society to

---

[98] Ibid., 102.
[99] Ibid., 89–91.
[100] Ibid., 71.
[101] Ibid., 92.

become more aware of itself.[102] At the same time, however, this articulation of collective representations is productive in its own right, as it is through articulating thought collectively that society itself comes into existence: "it is thought which creates reality; and the major role of collective representations is to 'make' that higher reality which is society itself."[103] In other words, positivist sociology and society are not just science and object, they are in an active and productive interaction with each other. Here, we are again reminded of the phenomenological character of Durkheimian positivism and its similarity to the work of Edmund Husserl, who described his own project as *"ratio in the constant movement of self-elucidation"*.[104] Society is self-reflectively producing its own rational *becoming* via sociology. It speaks itself into existence.

To Michel de Certeau, this is precisely what an institution of belief presupposes: it *postulates* an authority—Society, God, the Church, the family—which can graft itself onto the place of otherness, making it productive of a social rationality, without able to be fully known through this rationality itself.[105] Durkheim, throughout his work, often referenced the transcendence of society, for which I will give here only one example, taken from his 1906 presentation, "The Determination of Moral Facts":

> Society is something more than a material power; it is a moral power. It surpasses us physically, materially and morally. Civilization is the result of the co-operation of men in association through successive generations; it is essentially a social product. Society made it, preserves it and transmits it to individuals. […] Because it is at once the source and the guardian of civilization, the channel by which it reaches us, society appears to be an infinitely richer and higher reality than our own. It is a reality from which everything that matters to us flows. Nevertheless it surpasses us in every way, since we can receive from this storehouse of intellectual and moral riches, of which it is the guardian, at most a few fragments only.[106]

Because of our own individual limitations and the endlessly growing complexity of society in modern life, we can only know it, conceptually tie it

---

[102] Ibid., 90.
[103] Ibid., 85.
[104] Tiryakian, "Durkheim and Husserl", 43.
[105] de Certeau, "L'institution du croire", 76–77.
[106] Durkheim, *Sociology and Philosophy*, 27.

down, fragmentarily.¹⁰⁷ A large section, then, remains a matter of faith for the sociologist, a reality also remarked by Albert Cuvillier in his preface to the lectures on pragmatism: "The fact of the matter is […] that fundamental to any 'normative science', any system of morality or logic, any 'theory of knowledge', there are one or more principles which are incapable of proof or demonstration in the proper sense of the word, if not of all rational justification."¹⁰⁸ The sociologist's commitment to society itself seems to be one of those principles.

This type of circular reasoning has often led to the critiques already discussed in the sections above, by someone like Bruno Latour, for example, who criticizes Durkheim for postulating the very thing he is purporting to explain.¹⁰⁹ Steven Lukes as well, while less critical than Latour, still remarks that Durkheim seems to miss a crucial distinction, namely "between the truth of a belief and the acceptance of a belief as true".¹¹⁰ David Bloor, however, has persuasively argued that this distinction does not necessarily make a whole lot of sense within a Durkheimian system, as its understanding of institutions functions in a self-referential way: that which is socially true, is so because it is collectively agreed that this is effectively the case.¹¹¹ For Durkheim, it is the practice of thinking and believing a certain thing together, which gives this thing its vitality: "it is our ideas and beliefs which give the objects of thought their vitality. Thus, an idea is true, not because it conforms to reality, but by virtue of its creative power."¹¹²

While Bloor points out that Durkheim does not seem to have fully grasped this model of self-referentiality, his lectures on pragmatism seem to suggest otherwise, as his rethinking of both pragmatist and rationalist principles centred around showing how the impersonal and the personal are *simultaneously* entirely self-sufficient as well as unable to resist outside influences. Their processes of becoming are constantly developing in every direction of its potential truth. This is because, as Durkheim himself notes, "things have a 'circular' character, and analysis can be prolonged to infinity. This is why I can accept neither the statement of the idealists, that in

[107] Ibid.
[108] Armand Cuvillier, "Preface to the French Edition of 1955", xxii.
[109] Latour, "Beyond belief", 29.
[110] Lukes, *Émile Durkheim*, 495.
[111] David Bloor, "Collective Representations as Social Institutions", in: *Durkheim and Representations*, ed. W.S.F. Pickering (London: Routledge, 2000), 159–160.
[112] Durkheim, *Pragmatism and Sociology*, 84.

the beginning there is thought, nor that of the pragmatists, that in the beginning there is action."[113] This is the full extension of the thought Durkheim posited only a few sentences earlier: "History begins nowhere and its ends nowhere."[114] We have nothing to refer to beyond ourselves, yet at the same time, this indicates that the very concept of the absolute *also* resides within us. This is an absolute which is true, not as an ontological reality per se, but as a conceptual norm collectively agreed upon, in the same way a moral ideal is normative in the guidance of our conduct; we have collectively agreed upon its normativity.[115]

So what is Durkheim doing, exactly, when he posits the existence of a society which is beyond our own means of fully knowing? What we can already clearly claim, is that he is not attempting to develop a scientific toolset for an exclusively conceptual analysis of the social. Such a program is to be found in his *Rules of Sociological Method*, and even there, Durkheim is careful to not overextend that which makes sociology scientific.[116] Rather, I would argue that what we find in his lectures on pragmatism is an elaboration of a discourse, which has as its purpose to construct a sociological language infused with duration. Sociology, in other words, is imagined here as a language with which we can live together. The dialogue between sociology and society, on an institutional level, should then be considered as a way normativity can be thought into existence in its most 'natural' form, as something that is able to accommodate individual and collective desire as well, rather than just impose obligation from any sort of subjective-dogmatic source.[117]

Here, Kant's philosophy again clearly rears its head, with Durkheim's search for a socialized and expanded scheme of the categorical imperative via the notion of collective representation a constant in his work.[118] Sociological language, again, provides the advantage that it could more easily integrate the complexity of social modernity with social mechanisms of believing, which could integrate both the increasing prominence of scientific reason as well as the developing complexity of individualized contexts of mass opinion.[119] In this way, it was the ambiguity of

---

[113] Ibid., 67.
[114] Ibid.
[115] Ibid., 98.
[116] Durkheim, *The Rules of Sociological Method*, 141.
[117] Durkheim, *Sociology and Philosophy*, 28.
[118] Ibid., 31.
[119] Tiryakian, "Durkheim and Husserl", 39.

believing—as a rational expression of human judgement as well as a particular social practice of giving shared meaning to experience—which made it possible for Durkheim to fully conceptualize the self-referential and circular nature of the social. It acted as the very foundation through which human relationality could be thought across a temporalized spectrum of reasonable becoming.

Conclusion

The standard account of Durkheim's reflexive theorization of belief has long been well-known. It constitutes an undertheorized domain of the French sociologist's methodological repertoire, with a strong dependency on neo-Kantian rationalistic views guiding the employment of the concept, courtesy of such formative figures as Charles Renouvier and Émile Boutroux. From this framework, our judgement of beliefs rests on their truthfulness, which means their correspondence to reality. Durkheim provides a clear example of this in his lectures on pragmatism, when he brings up an example in which a sane man has come to believe that evil spirits have entered his body:

> Let us suppose, for example, that a sane man has been persuaded that the physical distress he is afflicted with is due to the fact that evil spirits have entered into his body (a case which is common in certain primitive societies). He is given an unpleasant substance which, he is assured, will drive away the spirits which are tormenting him. He believes this, and is cured. The result is certainly the one expected, and is even the 'suitable' one. Nevertheless, the idea was false.[120]

Critics of Durkheimian positivist sociology have pointed out how passages like this, being founded on a conceptual distinction between our modern knowledge of medical sciences and the supposedly 'primitive', metaphysical beliefs of other civilizations, obscure our understanding of other, non-Western cultures more than enlighten them. Rather than explaining the workings of other cultures, Durkheim is seen as regurgitating the evolutionist models of the late nineteenth- and early twentieth-century moderns, who saw their own knowledge culture as a universal measuring stick for evaluating others. Inherent within these kinds of schematic

---

[120] Durkheim, *Pragmatism and Sociology*, 49.

representations of social otherness, resided, according to sociologists like Andrew Pickering, an inability to take alterity seriously, to fully understand the performative workings of non-rational beliefs.[121]

Another, contemporary critic of Durkheim, Arnold van Gennep, saw these schemes as lacking a "sense of life", with Durkheim seemingly unable to imagine the agency of historical individuals and cultures. Furthermore, such positivist obsessions with categorization and classification represented a kind of epistemic domination, according to modern-day critics, subsuming non-Western knowledge cultures to an inferior status because of their supposed non-correspondence to any kind of falsifiable truth-claim.[122] To abandon the category of belief, as often argued for by critics of Durkheim, would potentially lead to a more meaningful engagement with socio-cultural propositions defying the limits of modernist philosophical worldviews. The recent ontological turn in sociology, anthropology and history represents such an attempt at thinking otherness beyond belief, evaluating propositions only on their conditions of (in)felicity.

Returning to Durkheimian sociology, there is little reason to fundamentally contest this account on a macro-historical level, with this ontological perspective able to accommodate a number of perceptive readings of nineteenth- and twentieth-century classical sociology, such as their role in furthering the secularization-thesis, and their central part in the politics of Western epistemology and its colonization of non-Western systems of knowledge.[123] That being said, we should be careful to not confuse such a perspective for any sort of final unmasking of Durkheimian sociology, making any further creative engagements with the tradition pointless. The ontological perspective, remains, first and foremost, an interpretative reading, made possible by Durkheim's lack of obvious theorization and perhaps stimulated by positivism's long and dark political shadow, which has often clouded the ability to read modernist thought in a charitable manner, as the philosophical legacy of Auguste Comte has already made clear.[124]

---

[121] Pickering, "The Ontological Turn", 134–150.

[122] Anna Fisk, "Appropriating, romanticizing and reimagining: Pagan engagements with indigenous animism", in: *Cosmopolitanism, Nationalism, and Modern Paganism*, ed. K. Rountree (New York: Palgrave Macmillan, 2017), 21–42; Isabel Laack, "The New Animism and Its Challenges to the Study of Religion", *Method and Theory in the Study of Religion* 32 (2020): 115–147.

[123] Josephson-Storm, *The Myth of Disenchantment*; Holbraad & Pedersen, *The Ontological Turn*.

[124] Bourdeau, "Fallait-il oublier Comte?", 89–111.

While such ontological readings are stimulating in their own manner, in this chapter I have asked myself whether this is the most that can be extracted, from what is a highly complex conceptualization of sociology and its relation to languages of belief by Durkheim. Here, I have tried to approach Durkheim's philosophical problematization of belief in a more generous and charitable manner, by reconstructing his response to the pragmatist challenge, a philosophical tradition which first articulated many of the critiques still levelled at Durkheimian sociology today. By doing this, I aimed to make clear how Durkheim's theoretical engagement with the belief-category, the latter being a particularly plastic and slippery matter, was anything but a lifeless instrument of rationalist classification. Rather, the category of belief constituted a fundamental philosophical problem for pragmatism, neo-Kantianism and sociological positivism, with all of these traditions offering meaningful and convincing answers to this problem. As such, reflecting on this peculiar situation of multiple yet contradictory 'partial truths', it allowed Durkheim to further historicize the discipline of sociology as a historical institution which could make further sense of this peculiar facet of belief in modernity.

This is what Durkheim attempted to do, especially in his lectures on pragmatism and the reinvention of rationalism. What is clear is that, for Durkheim, the sociologist does not exist outside the history of belief, but is embedded thoroughly within it. Within this positivist dual science of Man, Durkheim saw the role of the sociologist, not as someone who sought to root out alterity through the conceptual classification and categorization of non-rational cultural practices, but as someone who could effectively explore the shared historical becoming of both reason and non-rational meaning, as well as their interactions.

We can further clarify this by returning to his example of the sane man with the evil spirits, reading it instead as an attempt by Durkheim of further negotiating the role of belief and otherness in the enunciation of rational-conceptual judgement. With the example appearing in his discussion on pragmatism, Durkheim wanted to show how the belief in the existence and disappearance of evil spirits undoubtedly satisfied the pragmatist conditions of truth, i.e. their experience by the sane man as true. But it is no less true, says Durkheim, that evil spirits don't exist, *rationally*. It is important to note, here, that Durkheim does not hierarchize one truth above the other. Later on, in this same lecture series, Durkheim makes the explicit point that scientific propositions are dependent on their collective representation, on their socially shared acceptance as 'true', just as much as on their objective correspondence to reality.[125] It is this very ability, the ability of sociological language to express multiple realities of belief, truth and knowledge on *a shared historical spectrum of rational becoming*, that makes sociology a crucial project for Durkheim, both as a science and as a historical institution.

So, the positivist sociological perspective proposed by Durkheim would not be to judge belief-propositions according to a single condition of veracity. This would not be able to avoid accusations of arbitrariness. Rather, its perspective would be to signal that every truth-evaluation that conforms to the real—i.e. that is either rationally or collectively true, or both—is socially productive in its own manner. The judgement of the presence of evil spirits as rationally false, then, is not just the denial of their objective existence; it is also a particular act embedded within its own history of (rational) belief, where potential solidarity between rational individuals and an impersonal truth is produced through the shared belief-in-unbelief in the existence of evil spirits.

Speculative reason, in other words, represented another valuable source of community-formation for Durkheim, one that is particularly valuable in contemporary societies marked by the division of labour, where truth for truth's sake can act as a universal, binding principle.[126] In our modern age of advanced individualism, such resources for the procurement of a social cohesion which has room for individual differentiation cannot be overlooked.[127] Furthermore, while the construction of a rational space founded on objective truth operates on an exclusionary basis, this does not mean that a sociological language that considers such a construction as historically real, like Durkheim did, necessarily succumbs to its exclusionary-rationalist principles. To speak in a sociological way, was for Durkheim to be able to move between these impersonal and personal dimensions, to be able to describe, historically, their processes of becoming autonomous (as

---

[125] Durkheim, *Pragmatism and Sociology*, 88.

[126] Durkheim, *The Elementary Forms of Religious Life* (1995), 446: "This Kant well understood, and therefore he considered speculative reason and practical reason to be two different aspects of the same faculty. According to him, what joins them is that both are oriented toward the universal. To think rationally is to think according to the laws that are self-evident to all reasonable beings; to act morally is to act according to maxims that can be extended without contradiction to all wills. In other words, both science and morality imply that the individual is capable of lifting himself above his own point of view and participating in an impersonal life."

[127] Durkheim, *Pragmatism and Sociology*, 91.

collective representations) as well as their continuous practices of transgression and relationality.

Whether Durkheim and the positivist sociology he envisioned ultimately succeeded in this ambition remains an open-ended question. The fact that so many readers of Durkheim fail to see this complex engagement with both rational beliefs and the social practice of believing, something which already surprised the sociologist after the first appearance of *The Elementary Forms of Religious Life*, would suggest that perhaps it hasn't.[128] And yet, to this day, the work of Durkheim retains an important function for present scholarship, and this as an example of the potential value to be found in a sociological exploration of the limits of the knowable and the multifaceted mechanisms of believing lying beyond those limits. Through the work of Durkheim, it becomes clear that the full reality of believing, as it was socially conceptualized as well as experienced, could not be contained to its rationalist imagination. Durkheim's honest and existential engagement with belief as both concept and its social excess experienced by the sociologist himself, as a means of self-historicization and -articulation, brought into view sociology's potential meaning as well as its inevitable limits, through dialogues with neo-Kantianism and pragmatism.

For Durkheim, the plasticity of belief made it a unique instrument for negotiating the experience of producing a socio-scientific discourse and the effects such a discourse brings into the social world. In this way, instead of prioritizing conceptual homogeneity or metaphorical alterity, Durkheim saw the real goal of the sociologist as striving towards understanding their trajectories of mutual becoming, in search for an elusive language which could allow beliefs to speak both truthfully in a conceptual manner and meaningfully in an existential manner. Classical sociology, then, does not represent a fissure in the history of believing, but its modification, its transformative continuation. To speak in a Durkheimian sociological language on belief was not merely constrictive; it added to reality as well. It is important, from an intellectual-historical perspective, that we retain the means of understanding these additions, and for this the category of belief provides an invaluable instrument.

When critics take Durkheimian notions of belief into view, they should not ask whether Durkheim took different worlds seriously. The task of the Durkheimian sociologist was not to eradicate differentiation, it was to search for a language which could satisfactorily express it. This, however,

---

[128] Durkheim, "The Dualism of Human Nature", 325–26.

does not mean that there are no questions to ask of it. Rather, they should ask whether such an institution of sociological beliefs would not lead the sociologist to eventually lose faith in society itself, as the rigidification of sociology as an institution could prevent it from transforming once more in its ongoing dialogue with a changing society. The success of the ontological turn would suggest that this is not an unimportant question to ask.

CHAPTER 10

Epilogue: Sociology and Belief Beyond Positivism

INTRODUCTION

I will begin concluding this book with an epilogue, in which I will briefly turn towards the history of social sciences in the twentieth century. Specifically, I will be looking at how Durkheim's sociological mode of existence was furthered by such students as Marcel Mauss in France and Talcott Parsons in the US through their own creative navigations of the sociological belief-language. Through Mauss and Parsons, I aim to sketch out a conceptual-historical bridge, further connecting the early sociological tradition with its contemporary post-secular iteration.

SPEAKING BELIEF SOCIOLOGICALLY, AFTER DURKHEIM: MAUSS, PARSONS AND BEYOND

In his recent book, *Durkheim and After: The Durkheimian Tradition, 1893–2020* (2020), the cultural sociologist Philip Smith discusses the afterlife of Durkheim's sociological program, showing both its many cycles of variegated revival as well as its difficulty in being coherently reproduced.[1] While Smith emphasizes this inability of the Durkheimian program to sustain itself as the dominant epistemic model of sociological

---

[1] Smith, *Durkheim and After*.

inquiry in France and beyond, citing a lack of original research and a limited, uncreative engagement with Durkheimian sociology as primary causes, my interest here lies less with the epistemological component of the Durkheimian program than its techniques of sociological self-fashioning and -historicization.[2] When approaching the sociological program from this perspective, its fragmented nature becomes less of an impediment than a crucial condition of possibility, as an extensive existential space which allowed different kinds of sociological intervention to form themselves. Or, to put it slightly differently, when looking at the Durkheimian program as an early formation of the sociological mode of existence, I would argue that this program was very successful indeed. I will touch upon this success by discussing two oppositional strands of Durkheimian sociology, the anthropological ethnography of Marcel Mauss and the structural functionalism of the American sociologist, Talcott Parsons.

As I have argued throughout this book, the availability of different historical languages of belief was central to the making of a sociological-existential space, as it served as a tool for imagining both the nature of the social relation and the role of the sociological observer itself.[3] In this section then, I will briefly elaborate on this aspect of the Durkheimian heritage, as a navigational technique of belief-languages, in order to show how the category of belief continued to function as a means of sociological self-historicization in distinctive and even contrasting ways. To show this, I look at the way 'belief' was approached by Marcel Mauss and Talcott Parsons, two sociologists who engaged with the Durkheimian tradition and its techniques of self-fashioning, but in radically different ways.

Conceptualizing the Belief-Relation in Mauss: Giving, Praying, Sacrificing

Marcel Mauss was the nephew of Durkheim and the two formed a strong intellectual bond throughout most of their lives, resulting in close collaboration and shared publications until the end of Durkheim's life in 1917.[4] Fourteen years his uncle's junior, Mauss undoubtedly stood in Durkheim's

---

[2] Ibid., 94–115.
[3] Cf. supra chapter 3.
[4] Marcel Fournier, *Marcel Mauss: A Biography*, transl. by Jane Marie Todd (Princeton & Oxford: Princeton University Press, 2006), 9.

formidable shadow, and yet, the former had the powerful ability of carving out his own scholarly style, even within the rigorously collaborative environment which was the Durkheimian School.[5] Many publications since have emphasized the numerous differences between the two: Mauss's intellectual curiosity and interdisciplinarity, his atypical pathway as a scholar, his disinterest in being the figurehead of the sociological school, his methodological openness, his ambiguity towards positivism's stringency, all of which stood in stark contrast to Durkheim's eventual legacy.[6] Here, I will echo this sentiment of Maussian originality, while simultaneously noting Mauss's debt to the Durkheimian tradition, through a discussion of Mauss's approach to the category of belief as an instrument for imagining the social and thinking the relation between the social and the religious object.

The work of Mauss built upon that of Durkheim, especially the latter's eventual interest in religious and cultural sociology. Mauss's most famous scholarly contribution, his essay *The Gift* ("Essai sur le don: forme et raison de l'échange dans les sociétés archaïques") published in 1925 in the *Année sociologique* and first translated into English in 1954, closely resembles Durkheim's *The Elementary Forms of Religious Life* in style and methodology, as he sought to extract the primitive-societal mechanisms of gift-exchange in the way they were thought of and applied in societies such as those of Kwakiutl First Nation in Northern America or the Māori and Melanesian people on the islands of the Central and Pacific Ocean.[7] His application of the belief-category closely mirrored that of the *Elementary Forms* as well: the distinction between beliefs and rites as employed by Durkheim reappears throughout the text (although used much more sparingly than in the *Elementary Forms*, with Mauss giving preference to a moral economic register rooted in the exchange/contract-distinction), as well as its understanding of the belief-category as a mental disposition towards certain propositions and its function as a symbolic representation of social phenomena.[8] Such a usage and understanding of

---

[5] Ibid., 2.
[6] Smith, *Durkheim and After*, 95–96; Steiner, *La sociologie de Durkheim*, 39; Jean-François Bert, "Priez, priez, il en restera toujours quelque chose: *La Prière* (1909) de Marcel Mauss", *Revue des sciences sociales* 64 (2020): 164–171.
[7] Marcel Mauss, *The Gift: Forms and Functions of Exchange in Archaic Societies*, transl. by Ian Cunnison, introd.by E.E. Evans-Pritchard (London: Cohen & West Ltd., 1966 [1st ed.] 1954).
[8] Mauss, *The Gift*, 14, 24, 43.

the term was consistent throughout the works of Mauss, with similar applications of the category being employed in his essays on other ritualistic phenomena, such as prayer and sacrifice (the latter being written together with regular collaborator, Henri Hubert).[9]

Same as it was for Durkheim, however, the diagnostic function of belief as an instrument of classification was only the initial engagement with the concept, one facet of the distinct ways the language of belief was made operational within the Maussian sociological operation. For example, the very act of classification itself, through the division of primitive/religious practices into ritual-physical and belief-mental components, served as a source of self-reflection, with Mauss speculating that this classificatory act has served as the main source of sociological stagnation, the socio-scientific scholars being too quickly satisfied with the explanatory value of the classification itself: "If our science seems so stalled in the face of these serious problems and others which we do not even foresee, there is probably only one cause. We had to divide in order to begin understanding. But we have done nothing but that [...] This division is too restrictive, too precise in its recitation."[10] Mauss, in this instance, articulated an early version of what would become a standard critique of classical sociology's use of categories such as belief, and its tendencies of reducing complex social phenomena to rationalistic oppositional schemes, which, in the eyes of the critics, only obscured the multi-layered, holistic and embedded nature of the practices in question.[11]

And yet, the semiotic fabric of a broader belief-language formed the very foundation of this critique as well, the employment of this classificatory category the first step to a deeper understanding, not only of the observed social phenomena, but of the sociological practice of observation as well.[12] This was ultimately the goal, for someone like Mauss, of using

---

[9] Marcel Mauss, *On Prayer*, transl. by Susan Leslie, ed. and introd. by W.S.F. Pickering (New York: Berghahn Books, 2003), 22, 49; Henri Hubert & Marcel Mauss, *Sacrifice: Its Nature and Function*, transl. by W.D. Halls, foreword by E.E. Evans-Pritchard (Chicago: Chicago University Press, 1964), 62, 77, 102.

[10] Marcel Mauss, "Divisions et proportions des divisions de la sociologie (1927)", *l'Année sociologique*, Nouvelle série, 2 (1927): 87–173. Digital edition (pages 4–55), last consulted on the 29th of May 2023, http://classiques.uqac.ca/classiques/mauss_marcel/oeuvres_3/oeuvres_3_06/divisions_sociologie.html.

[11] On this critique, cf. Good, "Belief, Anthropology Of", 1137–1141.

[12] Mauss, "Divisions et proportions des divisions de la sociologie", 23: "Elles portent donc profondément la marque de notre temps, celle de notre subjectivité."

such a language, as it functioned as a key for entering into this sociological space of interpretation and self-understanding. Such an ambition became most clearly articulated in his text on the phenomenon of prayer, its fascinating character, according to the French sociologist, lying in its ability to bring multiple facets of experience and approach—ritual and belief, act and observation, articulation and cognition—together in a single moment:

> This characteristic of prayer encourages one to study it. It is well known how difficult it is to explain a rite which is nothing but a rite, or a myth which is little else than a myth. A rite only gains its *raison d'être* when one has discovered its meaning, that is, the ideas on which it is and has been based—the beliefs to which it corresponds. A myth is not really explained until one has said to which actions and rites it is linked, what are the practices to which it gives rise. [...] We have scarcely begun to study these phenomena in which cognition (*représentation*) and action are intimately connected and whose analysis can be so fruitful. Prayer is precisely one of these phenomena where ritual is united in belief. It is full of meaning like a myth; it is often as rich in ideas and images as a religious narrative. It is full of power and efficacy like a ritual and it is often as powerfully creative as a ceremony based on sympathetic magic. At least initially, when it is composed, it is not done in a blind way: it is never something inert. So a prayer-ritual is a whole, comprising the mythical and ritual elements necessary to its understanding.[13]

The goal of a sociological belief-ritual scheme is then not necessarily to exhaustively explain the social reality of religious phenomena, in the eyes of Mauss. Rather, it has as its crucial secondary function to lay bare the physical and mental topography of such phenomena, after which the religious object can be fruitfully engaged, entered a dialogue with and witnessed, while simultaneously gaining further insight on the status of the sociological viewpoint itself.[14]

The category of 'belief' ("croyance") and its semiotic equivalents ('faith', 'trust', 'commitment', etc.) then serve as a discursive sign which is measured with its other-cultural counterparts: *potlatch, mana, dzo, nkisi, nauala, manitou*, etc.[15] The durational performativity which Mauss saw as

---

[13] Mauss, *On Prayer*, 22.

[14] Mauss, "Divisions et proportions des divisions de la sociologie", 32: "Ce qu'elle observe partout et toujours, c'est non pas l'homme divisé en compartiments psychologiques, ou même en compartiments sociologiques, c'est l'homme tout entier. *Et c'est en suivant une pareille méthode de division des faits qu'on retrouve cet élément réel et dernier* [my emphasis]."

[15] Karsenti, *L'homme total*, 170–175.

being enabled by these concrete signifiers—"By definition, a common meal, a distribution of *kava*, or a charm worn, cannot be repaid at once. Time has to pass before a counter-prestation can be made. Thus the notion of time is logically implied when one pays a visit, contracts a marriage or an alliance, makes a treaty, goes to organized games, fights or feasts of others, renders ritual and honorific service and 'shows respect', to use the Tlingit term."[16]—is, in effect, mirrored and duplicated by the sociological observer in their own practice, as the rationalistic properties of the modern language of belief are used in order to construct a new durational space between the sociological subject and the religious-cultural object, to reconstruct channels of communication and flows of 'rhythm' across all kinds of historical-conceptual boundaries and divisions.[17] The sociology of the "total social fact" is conceived by Mauss as a reconstruction of durational movement, a living instrument through which other movements—gift-giving, sacrificing, praying—can be better understood, not through propositional capture, but through discursive calibration and synchronization: "In this way, one can reveal *the 'total' in history*: the empirical, illogical and logical form of the beginning, the reasonable and positive form of the future [my emphasis and translation]."[18] In this way, the Durkheimian division of social reality in beliefs and social action does not so much represent social life, as it does present the reader with "d'un coup la réalité", a *strike of the real*.[19]

Because of this critical-reflexive attitude towards the obfuscating effects of a sociological-theoretical classification of beliefs, representations and ideals disconnected from any social action, Mauss has often been heralded as a forefather of an anti-positivist sociology and anthropology, as someone who was more sensitive to the non-translatable nature of non-Western cultural systems of meaning.[20] And yet, this problematization of a

[16] Mauss, *The Gift*, 34.
[17] Mauss, "Divisions et proportions des divisions de la sociologie", 23.
[18] Ibid., 43: "On fera ainsi apparaître le « total » dans l'histoire: l'empirique, l'illogique et le logique du début, le raisonnable et le positif du future."
[19] Ibid., 31: "Ensuite il ne faut pas se laisser arrêter par les termes abstraits que nous employons - cette division, globale cette fois, est éminemment réaliste: elle présente d'un coup la réalité."
[20] Cf. for example: Alain Caillé, *Anthropologie du don: Le tiers paradigme* (Paris: Desclée de Brouwer, 2000); Ilana F. Silber, "Gifts in Rites of Passage or gifts as rites of passage? Standing at the threshold between Van Gennep and Marcel Mauss", *Journal of Classical Sociology* 18, no. 4 (2018): 348–360; Szakolczai & Thomassen, *From Anthropology to Social Theory*, ch. 3 "Marcel Mauss: From Sacrifice to Gift-Giving or Revisiting Foundations".

sociological system of classification should, I argue, be interpreted as being rooted within the positivist language of belief itself, with such practices of critical self-historicization-via-belief already present in both *The Elementary Forms of Religious Life* as well as in Durkheim's lectures on pragmatism.[21] Similar to Durkheim, Mauss conceptualized the historical project of sociology as a civilizational product through a phenomenological perspective, considered as such as an effect of reason's progress and one which could gradually be unfolded as sociologists were able to better understand the socio-historical foundations of their own interventions.[22]

What Mauss did do, in an original fashion, was to extend this attitude, investigating the limits of positivist reason to a more rigorous extent than Durkheim, and how the sociologist could relate to such things as the historicity of foreign, historical cultures, the existence of social facts which were not rationally conditioned and the normative implications of social facts.[23] My ambition here, however, is not to resolve the question of Mauss's genuine independence from his more notorious uncle, but merely to give some examples of how Mauss was able to further cultivate a sociological space by positing his own narrative intervention into the sociological language of belief.

My aim with these brief excursions is to give a further indication of how an autonomous, sociological language of approaching belief was being continuously elaborated, and how it was becoming more and more detached from its original context as a crisis of institutional Christianity.[24] Furthermore, a second aspect that I wish to concisely highlight here is the open-ended character of this historical process of sociological self-formation through strategies of belief-narration. The Durkheimian tradition of engaging with belief provided a rich and dense conceptual fabric, through which sociologists could formulate their own sociological programs in a distinct and original fashion. Whereas Mauss delved into the question of positivism's rationalist-interpretative limits as a source of

---

[21] Cf. supra, ch. 9.

[22] Mauss, "Divisions et proportions des divisions de la sociologie", 37: "Et ces points de vue sont au fond fixés eux-mêmes par l'état historique des civilisations, des sociétés, de leurs sous-groupes, dont notre science est elle-même le produit, et de l'observation desquels elle est partie."

[23] Mauss articulates these positions more implicitly in his essays on prayer, gift-giving and sacrifice, and more explicitly throughout his methodological note in the *Année sociologique*, "Divisions et proportions des divisions de la sociologie (1927)".

[24] Cf. supra, chapters 4, 5, 6.

anthropological investigation, someone like Talcott Parsons turned instead to the Durkheimian explorations of historical institutions, societal functions, and their relation to the belief systems propagating such institutions and functions.[25]

Productive Typologies: Parsons on Systems of Belief

Like it was in the work of Mauss, the notion of 'belief' appears in multiple ways throughout the oeuvre of Parsons, allowing the reader to emphasize different meanings. There is its historical meaning, as a category which evolves alongside other conceptual tools as Parsons develops his sociology from *The Structure of Social Thought* (1937) to *The Social System* (1951) to his late collection of essays, *Action Theory and The Human Condition* (1978), the category manifesting such broader transitions in its own nuanced evolution. There is its typological meaning, which refers to the different applications of the term across Parsons's work. And there is its philosophical meaning, which concerns itself with the particular content ascribed to the concept by the American sociologist, such as in his article "Belief, Unbelief and Disbelief" (1971), which he wrote in his role as a general commentator on the symposium 'The Culture of Unbelief' organized by the Vatican.[26] Since I have insufficient space here to fully describe all three levels, I will instead focus on Parsons's philosophical reflection on the category, and how his reading of Durkheim generated his own innovative model of sociological belief systems while being profoundly distinct from the Maussian engagement with 'belief'.

The 1971 symposium on the culture of unbelief provided Parsons with the opportunity to reflect on the category, which had provided a rich if undertheorized element of his own work. He started his own paper with a brief commentary on the category itself. According to Parsons, Western culture was marked by "a strong tendency to think in terms of dichotomies", such as "rational versus irrational, heredity versus environment,

---

[25] Talcott Parsons, "Durkheim on Religion Revisited: Another Look at The Elementary Forms of Religious Life", in: Ibid., *Action Theory and the Human Condition* (New York: The Free Press, 1978), 217: "Though in the realm of the sacred there are many particularized elements, I think we can correctly say that in Durkheim's conception beliefs about the sacred are organized in their core in terms of a cultural code, which is the primary focus of the stability of the complex action system."

[26] Raf Vanderstraeten, "Talcott Parsons and the enigma of secularization", *European Journal of Social Theory* 16, no. 1 (2012): 73.

Gemeinschaft versus *Gesellschaft*", with 'belief' being yet another one of these categories characterized by its antonyms.[27] Interestingly, however, Parsons does not consider this binary form of thinking to be reductionist but rather its very opposite: such dichotomies have proven to be productive in their own right, with new variables constantly popping up and eventually creating "a larger 'family' of possible types, which differ from each other, not on one, but on several dimensions".[28] In the case of belief, for example, Parsons recounts how the oppositional pair of the believer and the disbeliever is joined by the unbeliever, someone who merely stands outside of the contentious topic. The social space of believers, in other words, is populated by a diverse host of actors, differing not only in what they believe but also in how they believe. The American sociologist draws the comparison with the history of reason, which was also marked by the historical dialectic of proliferation and differentiation, as the potential ways of 'being reasonable' was continuously expanding.[29]

According to Parsons, the same was true for belief: through a series of dichotomies and oppositions—cognitive and non-cognitive; rational and non-rational; 'belief in' and 'belief that'—all kinds of *types* could be imagined, produced and enacted by social actors, creating an increasingly complex and pluralist historical grid of different belief-compositions, with the task of the social scientist being the clarification of the nature of these types.[30] This imagination of belief as a pluralist grid also worked on multiple levels at the same time: while it primarily served as a socio-theoretical exploration on the question of religion, modernity and secularization, it simultaneously functioned as a meta-historical commentary on the historical engagement of sociology with the notion of belief. Disagreeing with the sociologist of religion Robert Bellah that standard-sociological approaches of religion contained a Western, cognitive bias through its emphasis on the category of belief, Parsons instead argued that this form of speaking and making religion was an extension of Western culture and its processes of secularization itself. Conceptualizing belief, sociologically, wasn't a form of reductionism and obfuscation, it was a facet of modern, secular religion articulating itself. Here, Parsons extends a key insight of

---

[27] Talcott Parsons, "Belief, Unbelief and Disbelief", in: Ibid., *Action Theory and the Human Condition* (New York: The Free Press, 1978), 233–234.
[28] Ibid., 234.
[29] Ibid., 234–235.
[30] Ibid.

Durkheimian sociology: that the sociological practice of classification was not just an obfuscation of reality, it added to it as well, as a symptom of the history of reason and belief.[31]

To Parsons, then, 'beliefs' function as symbolic signifiers of different types of social systems (scientific, philosophical, ideological and religious), with these systems being distinguished from each other through what he terms as their differing primary interests—cognitive, evaluative, expressive, instrumental and existential—with religious beliefs, for example, being characterized by their evaluative function as a source of meaning for social action and community-formation.[32] This categorically differentiated typology was then imposed by Parsons onto the history of religion and modernity, as a means of interpreting the varying degrees of institutionalization, with such events as the Protestant Reformation being read as both a crisis of symbolism and belief.[33] A societal process like secularization constituted for Parsons not so much a loss of belief or a victory of rationalism than a re-composition of belief systems, secularization providing an increased possibility for social actors to combine different belief systems with each other in a creative and complementary manner.[34]

Returning to the question of Parsons's reading of Durkheimian belief, it becomes apparent that this approach of what belief sociologically forms is very different from Mauss. Parsons, rather, attempted to make a synthesis of different sociological traditions and their engagement with the concept of belief, trying to bring together the main insights of Durkheim, Max Weber, Alfred Marshall and Vilfredo Pareto.[35] From Durkheim, the American sociologist mainly took his historical-evolutionary perspective, rooted in his symbiotic perspective on institutions and belief systems as a study of societal solidarity, as employed in *The Division of Labour*.[36] Belief was a means of investigating a society's value-orientation and the strength of its commitment to certain forms of social action. While Mauss and Parsons then both navigated the Durkheimian articulation of the sociological belief-category, both came up with radically different ways of

---

[31] Cf. supra ch. 9.

[32] Talcott Parsons, *The Social System* (London: The Free Press of Glencoe, 1964 [1st ed. 1951), 367–379.

[33] Parsons, "Belief, Unbelief and Disbelief", 244.

[34] Ibid., 246. Cf. also Vanderstraeten, "Talcott Parsons and the enigma of secularization", 69–84.

[35] Parsons, *The Structure of Social Action*.

[36] Cf. supra, ch. 8.

turning this articulation into something sociologically productive. To frame their different usages of the belief-category metaphorically: whereas Mauss tried to break open the black box of belief in order to reflect on the tension between thought and action, Parsons instead used the category itself as a robust object which could be used to dig, sculpt, and smash other, less robust fragments of the social space.

While Parsons's conceptual work on the belief-category was anything but simplistic, his sociological-functionalist program of a rationalist social science eventually became a symbol for the kind of overly theoretical sociology of religion which became the object of fierce critiques, critiques which would crystallize, first in the cultural turn (ethnomethodology and symbolic interactionism) and later on in a cross-disciplinary post-secular turn.[37] Whereas passages in *The Social System* distinguished between the cognitive and non-cognitive nature of religious beliefs, such distinctions were typically collapsed into singular accusations of rationalist biases, with José Casanova interpreting Parsons's modernity-narrative as a reiteration of "the seemingly perennial postmillennial visions of America as 'a City on a Hill,' 'beacon of freedom,' and redeemer nation".[38] It was in this atmosphere of scepticism towards the potential of sociological positivism that ontological philosophies, like those of Wittgenstein and Heidegger, would capture the imagination of scholars interested in religions and non-Western cultures. The category of 'belief' then would come to serve another purpose, as a tool of anti-positivist self-fashioning through the negation of the concept's validity, or at least, its illegitimacy in its positivist meaning and understanding. But this is another facet in the long and rich history of languages of belief, one which still requires further excavations.

Conclusion

What these brief explorations of the work of Mauss and Parsons have aimed to make clear is how the Durkheimian tradition, and its particular engagement with the category of belief, did not act in any sort of (necessarily) restrictive manner towards new sociological readings of non-rational practices, such as religion and gift-giving. What it offered instead was a

---

[37] Smith, *Durkheim and After*, 140–142.
[38] José Casanova, "Secularization revisited: A reply to Talal Asad", in: *Powers of the Secular Modern: Talal Asad and his Interlocutors*, eds. David Scott & Charles Hirschkind (Stanford: Stanford University Press, 2006), 21.

rich landscape for further exploration, with Mauss investigating the sociological ability to reflexively overcome some of the limitations of sociological positivism and Parsons seeking, in contrasting fashion, to push the potential of such a classificatory positivism to its fullest extent. The shared sociological language of belief provided a crucial tool for Mauss and Parsons, as it allowed them to both connect to a sociological community while also articulating their own individual contributions, emphasizing their unique voice within this community.

CHAPTER 11

Concluding Remarks: Returning to the Post-Secular

Introduction

The previous eight chapters have presented a series of impressions, tracing how several early sociologists engaged with the category of belief as a means for interpreting society. What such a history of sociological engagements ultimately demonstrates, I would argue, is that the discipline of sociology and its practitioners came into the late eighteenth and early nineteenth century in a chaotic and hostile environment. Within a maelstrom of competing discourses in the first half of the nineteenth century on the forces precisely constituting social life, the value of the belief-category could be found in its ability to function as a kind of communal language, with different individual interventions able to eventually stabilize what would come to be known as a *sociological* language of belief.

Speaking belief into being, as a sociologist, was to stamp the borders of religion, politics and science into a kind of temporary static state, after which social reality itself could be brought more clearly into view. Furthermore, it meant the articulation of a distinct sociological identity—against the theological and philosophical languages of belief—which further enabled the formation of an autonomous sociological discipline, community and mode of existence. That is why the prevalent calls in recent decades, for abandoning the category to better understand such complex phenomena as Christianity or the supernatural, carries in itself great risk. And while the employment of it has always been far from perfect, abandoning it would not, I would argue, lead to any sort of utopia of conceptual clarity on religion. Rather, I believe that its most likely result would be, in the absence of any sort of epistemological legislation, a return to a prior state, resembling the early period of nineteenth-century sociology, which was marked by a Hobbesian struggle of each against all. In this concluding section, then, I will turn more explicitly to this normative dimension present yet less articulated throughout the book, in addition to a brief recapitulation of the intellectual-historical findings brought forth throughout the previous chapters.

For this reason, throughout these concluding remarks more emphasis will be put on how the historically entangled relationship between religion and sociology—investigated through the prism of the belief-category—is still relevant to contemporary sociologists, not only in their investigations of religious phenomena but also in their understanding of themselves. Being ignorant of these entanglements, and the important role played by 'belief' as an instrument for navigating these connections, poses significant risks, as mentioned above: first of all, that sociologists lose a unique passage to tap into their history. And secondly, that they make themselves vulnerable to being manipulated by contesting disciplines who are less ignorant of the intertwined early history of sociology and religion as well as the workings of such historical languages.

These concluding remarks will be made up of two sections. The first section will consist of a broad sketch of the macro-narrative which has quietly simmered underneath the book's textual surface, carefully extracting what these different sociological techniques and interventions can tell us about the history of social sciences. Here, I articulate a number of conclusions which can be drawn from the sociological usages of the belief-category and their relation to religious objects. In the second section, I briefly touch upon some of the current critiques levelled at classical sociology from a post-secular perspective and how this impacts the more generous readings I have provided here.

Finally, I close out these concluding remarks with two claims on the current state of post-secularism, as a way of conclusion, one critical and one normative. Complementing my critique of the current post-secular debate as one devoid of a sufficient grasp on the existential components of sociological modernity, is a call for greater transparency when it comes to evaluating the relations between the social-scientific and religious domains. It is only by knowing what is at stake and by being forthright about what we are asking of our fellow occupants of this social life that we can make an informed decision on where to go next.

The Institution of Sociology and the Performativity of the Sociological Belief-Language

After these many travels, both throughout the contemporary post-secular landscape and the historical ruins of nineteenth-century sociological modernity in France, where have we exactly landed? *Où atterrir*, as Bruno Latour would ask, his own travels also thoroughly marked by this history of sociology even when reflecting on the grand narratives of ecological politics. These different historical and reflexive interventions allow me to schematically outline a number of techniques used for both navigating historical belief-languages and constructing a sociological language of belief itself. In this section then, I will give an overview of these different techniques, their performative facets and the historical trajectory they have followed from Bonald to Durkheim to our present.

While the different historical engagements with languages of belief by classical sociologists cannot be fully captured in a single, defining strategy, for reasons of clarity and argumentation we can summarize the most prominent moves enacted by these famous social theorists in an ideal-typical manner. Bonaldian mediation, Saint-Simonist poetic self-transformation, Comtean institutionalization, Durkheimian division, Maussian synchronization and Parsonian synthesization are just some of the strategies I have encountered and tried to articulate in these past chapters, not to mention the different post-secular traditions, such as ontological agnosticism, which I have also briefly discussed in the first section of the book. As such, I have tried to show how reflecting upon the notion of 'belief' was never just that for nineteenth- and twentieth-century sociologists. The sociologists, by employing the category, found themselves subsequently embedded within another *longue durée* history, that of belief-languages and their interactive mechanisms of contestation, differentiation and effectuation. The sociological participation in this history, from its earliest forms during the Enlightenment to its modern-day variant, is then shaped by both its own strategic direction *and* by the composition of the category's semiotic matrix, its space of meaning continuously evolving through the historicity and ambiguity of the different languages in action.[1]

So what were these navigational practices for the sociologists, exactly? What were they for and what did they effectively bring into being? For what purpose did they, in other words, attempt to construct their own sociological language of belief? Across these different historical eras, traditions, actors and strategies, I would argue that four distinct effects can be demarcated from the sociological speaking and writing of 'belief': (1) an epistemological technique for conducting socio-scientific research; (2) a discursive means of *making* the social object, esp. in the domains of religious and other collective-cultural phenomena; (3) an existentially overdetermined framework through which practices of self-fashioning and -historicization could be constructed; and (4) a narrative instrument through which socio-relational mentalities and forms of social action could be brought into communication.

Whereas the first effect is well-known and discussed in a range of different fields—science and technology studies, (social) epistemology, the history of social science, etc.—the other three 'performativities' are less often articulated, buried instead underneath the veils of 'theory' and 'methodology'. Exceptions to this, such as Bruno Latour's *On the Modern Cult of the Factish Gods* (2010) and his *An Inquiry into Modes of Existence* (2012), are praised for their novelty but subsequently more or less ignored or misunderstood.[2] Here, I have tried to respond to Latour's thesis of sociological modernity as a historical tool of power and obfuscation head-on, making the case that effects (2)–(4) are less instruments of domination than novel socio-historical compositions in their own right, enacting a sociological mode of existence.

Let us take a closer look at each of these four facets and how they relate to each other, before recapitulating how these different trajectories can be traced throughout the history of social sciences. First of all, to employ the category of 'belief' constituted for the sociological moderns a means of social analysis, as a category which had become an important instrument for understanding socio-mental phenomena which were distinct from falsifiable, propositional knowledge.[3] This is how sociologists like Comte and Durkheim primarily intended their usage of the concept, siding it with

---

[1] Palti, "The 'Theoretical Revolution'", 400.
[2] Cf. supra ch. 2.
[3] Shagan, *The Birth of Modern Belief*, 282.

similar concepts ('opinion', 'collective representations', 'mass sentiments', 'popular ideas', 'mentalities', ...) and distinguishing it from other signifiers—'knowledge', 'reason', 'superstition', 'ritual', 'practice', 'science', and so on—in order to classify a particular form of collective thought unique to a particular kind of action, social group or institution.[4] As I have tried to show throughout these chapters, however, this textual practice was not solely epistemological. Rather, it was also deeply existential and constitutive of the sociological operation itself as well.

How did it do this, and why was the matter of 'belief' so crucial in this regard? The answer to this question has both structural and contextual components. Structurally, the modern formality of belief was characterized by a conceptual indeterminacy: rather than signify a single, hegemonic understanding of what believing constituted, the modern regime of belief was marked, according to Ethan Shagan, by pluralism and freedom.[5] While enlightened philosophers like Kant might have argued for a single understanding of what belief truly is—the individual judgement of the state of the world as they are experienced by our internal faculties—in reality, a whole host of definitions on what it meant to believe flooded the public space, without any definition able to establish a complete hegemony.[6] Sociology, as a novel mode of theorizing belief in the social domain during the eighteenth and nineteenth centuries, was thus one such attempt at giving shape to such collective forms of thought.[7] Yet the conditions of felicity enabling such speech acts made it impossible to effectively close off its space of meaning. And while this fuelled endless discussions and disagreements on the particular nature of what sociologists meant by 'belief', resulting in a plurality of different sociological meaning-allocations to the category, at the same time this multiplicity ensured the availability of a continuous source of self-reflection and -renewal from the outside.

Contextual factors also played a key role in making the notion of 'belief' such an important framework in the history of the social sciences. The birth of sociology in France during the eighteenth century coalesced with a growing crisis of the institutional religion of the time, Catholicism. This crisis was not just one of a loss of spirituality in the everyday life of the French commoner, it was a predicament of language as well, the discourse

---

[4] Cf. for example: Fauconnet & Mauss, "La sociologie", 165–175.
[5] Shagan, *The Birth of Modern Belief*, 279.
[6] Ibid., 277–81.
[7] Cf. supra ch. 4.

of the Catholic Church (and its opposition) typically providing the instruments for reflecting on the demands and problems of the social government of the populace.[8] With this institutional structure gradually coming apart, a new space opened up which was in need of inhabitation, the new democratic nature of French civil space allowing for a more diverse range of tenants.[9] As such, the sociological terminology of 'society', 'solidarity' and 'the social' started moving into this space, articulating its own role as one between Catholicism, social philosophy and reason of State, by offering up a more scientific, measured and objective viewpoint.[10]

Yet it entered this space at a particularly tenuous point in French history, the fires of revolutionary violence still smouldering and the many ghosts of the Napoleonic Wars haunting its survivors.[11] What was crucial for the sociological viewpoint to succeed in such a historical context was a register which could tie together the many antagonistic sentiments into a new collective, without being perceived as a new hostile force, another match to light the fire. This, so I have argued throughout the book, was one of the main assets of the category of 'belief'. Through 'belief', the sociological moderns could speak on multiple levels, *at the same time*: they could enter into the space of religious believers and engage with the social-normative foundations of their conduct in a familiar tone, while simultaneously opening up this space for broader and newer ideas. This was how the earliest sociologists navigated this historical context through their applications of the category, as a means of tying together the sacred and secular domains of society.

For someone like Louis de Bonald, the pliability of belief as a category allowed him to bring together enlightened discourses on different religious worldviews and his own project of reimagining the foundations of Catholic, monotheistic belief. The French Catholic reactionary played a complex game with the concept, employing both enlightened and Catholic meanings of the term to construct a more modern, sociological theology. To reflect on 'beliefs' in a more universalizing manner then was no mere instrument of the so-called secular moderns; Catholic apologists like

---

[8] de Certeau, "The Formality of Practices", 147–205; Philippe Büttgen, "Théologie politique et pouvoir pastoral", *Annales. Histoires, Sciences Sociales* 62, no. 5 (2007): 1148–49.

[9] Pierre Rosanvallon, *Le peuple introuvable. Histoire de la représentation démocratique en France* (Paris: Gallimard, 1998), esp. 35–83.

[10] Karsenti, *D'une philosophie à l'autre*, 57–58.

[11] Brahami, *La Raison du Peuple*, 31–39; Bertran de Balanda, "Evil Raised To Its Highest Power", 52–72.

Bonald equally saw the value of such an ambiguous space as 'collective credulity', using it as both an instrument of self-legitimation as well as a means of contesting and appropriating the intellectual toolset of secularizing forces within society.

Furthermore, as the case of the proselytizing Saint-Simonists has shown, these supposed forces of secularization and modernization themselves displayed deep and reflexive engagements with the belief-category. While the movement's founder, Henri de Saint-Simon, still presupposed a more utilitarian stance towards those believing in so-called irrationalities and superstitions, his followers manifested a much greater generosity towards such practices of believing. Their own experiences in the streets, houses, workshops and factories of the workers had made it more clear how a conceptualization of such practices as belief had real value in its own right, the concept containing a theoretical density not yet foreseen by Saint-Simon himself. It meant that thinking social emancipation was not a top-down exercise but a looping mechanism of mutual transformation, the plasticity of 'belief' as a means of reflexive thought making possible such a movement across socio-economic classes.

Speaking belief in the first half of the nineteenth century, as a means of both analysing the conditions of society as well as a tool for imagining and historicizing the sociological self, was then intricately entangled with the state of Christianity and religion in the broadest sense, the collective need to explain its fate in modern society opening up an avenue for alternative interpretations on the reasons of why a society comes into existence at all.[12] This was still the case for someone like Auguste Comte, who sought to argue for the value of the sociological project as a replacement for the old religions, the positivist Religion of Humanity being more robust through its being more deeply rooted in the conditions of social reality itself. And yet, the role of belief started to become more and more pluralized, its task as an entry into spiritual authority and the soul of the collective being complemented by the increasingly internal complexity of the sociological practice itself. From signalling the broad dichotomy which existed between enlightened discourses of semi-propositional knowledge and religious forms of divine commitment, the question of belief now transformed into a matter of sociology's own historical role and existence itself. It was via the murky mirror of belief-practices that the sociologists like Comte increasingly encountered themselves, the ability of beliefs to be

---

[12] Karsenti, *Politique de l'esprit*, 9.

both knowable and intangible shining a light on the walls bordering the space of sociological reason.

I finished this historical narrative of early sociology's engagement with the different historical languages of belief with the sociologist who perhaps best articulated the peculiar relation between sociology and the history of belief, both reflexively and non-reflexively, Émile Durkheim. In contrast to previous readings, which mainly focused on Durkheim's philosophical understanding and usage of the category such as its neo-Kantian influences or its likeness to the work of Fustel de Coulanges, I have tried to show how the notion of 'belief' cut close to the bone in Durkheim's work, laying bare the limits of the positivist sociological practice as well as its many possibilities. To reflect on belief, sociologically, constituted a pathway for Durkheim to think the historical figure of the sociologist itself, as a novel and particular mode of being within the broader history of reason and belief. Beyond the positivist bravado of an objective look at the past and the present fuelled by rigorous methodology, lay another, more fragile disposition towards categories such as belief, as something encapsulating the complex nature of social reality. As such, Durkheim approached the concept of 'belief' as a rich source of sociological self-reflection, its composition as a social object with multiple potential states of being representative of how a sociological mode of existence could add value to modern society.

The sociological navigation of belief-languages then increasingly resulted in the excavation of its own autonomous, historical place—as a science, but also as an institution and mode of existence—rather than in its differentiation from its religious counterpart, as competing discourses of spiritual authority and social self-government. The question which such a statement often evokes is whether such a process should be interpreted as a form of secularization, the sociological employment of the belief-category being gradually removed from its earlier, more religious contexts of meaning. My own response to this question would be to state that, while the raising of such a question is understandable, it is destined to fall flat, and this for two reasons: the modality of speech within sociological modernity and the nature of secularization narratives themselves. First, how does the modality of sociological speech impact the question of secularization? As I have tried to show throughout this book, the sociological navigation of historical belief-languages *acts* on multiple levels at the same time.

On the one hand, we can make the argument that Durkheim secularizes the question of social government, since he distinguishes sociology from the theological class in *The Division of Labour*. For Durkheim, spiritual authority is of no concern for the sociologists, as their understanding of the workings of modern society already points to the futility of such an exercise. Whereas Comte still saw it as the task of a social science to fill up the vacuum in collective government, Durkheim, from a functionalist perspective, argued that this vacuum existed for a reason, the inexistence of collective thought constitutive of the individual freedom of conscience. On the other hand, it can be just as easily and convincingly argued, like Latour and Karsenti have done, that Durkheim simply *substituted* the principle of monotheistic divinity by calling it 'Society' instead of 'God'.[13] This is not so much a form of secularization as it is a substitution, the transcendental role played by the divine in Bonaldian sociology simply being switched around by Durkheim.

So which is it? When a possible answer to such a question is that Durkheim secularized and de-secularized a particular type of enunciation, then we must conclude that the question itself is not particularly productive in locating its respondent. Added to this is a second reason, which is the politicized nature of secularization narratives themselves, as powerful instruments employed by the different contestants within the State-Church conflict which has been flickering throughout most of our history.[14] While it is not an *a priori* necessity that each secularization narrative functions as a partial intervention within this broader conflict, any treatise which seeks to transcend this conflict needs to reflexively engage with the political and ideological mechanisms influencing these discussions, an engagement for which there is insufficient room left here. So what is the right question to ask? The question which has directed my own research problem in this book comes to mind: what does it mean to speak belief, sociologically, both in the past and the present? After summarizing the main historical findings in this past section, I will now reflect on what these findings mean for our current discussion on the post-secular and its stance towards the category of 'belief'.

[13] Latour, "Beyond belief", 27–37.
[14] Hunter, "Secularization", 1–32.

Returning to the Post-Secular and the Conditions of Sociological Modernity

The argument that I have made throughout the book is that the sociological techniques for navigating historical languages of belief represented an important tool of sociological self-fashioning, creating the conditions of a mode of existence for the sociologist. To achieve this, I argued that we need to consider the history of social sciences, not as a singular domain, but as the entanglement of multiple historical trajectories, both of forms of knowing and of forms of believing. This also impacts our potential understanding of the historical relation between sociology and religion. By moving away from a conceptual scheme dominated by the religion/secularism-distinction, and by focusing more on the textual practices of the sociological moderns rather than their self-proclaimed ambitions of "capturing social reality", we are able to achieve a more nuanced picture, one where the relation between a sociological discourse and its religious object is much more multifaceted than its epistemological self-presentation.[15] Rather, this relation, so I have argued, should more be considered as a secondary effect of multiple histories of reason and belief enacting upon each other and being enacted upon by its sociological and religious actors, at the same time.

Where does such a perspective lead to, first, historically? For one, the history of social science and its relation with religion becomes broadened, both chronologically and contextually: sociology as a practice then becomes situated, not only within the history of science and reason, but also within the history of believing. Furthermore, sociology's conditions of felicity for speaking on the social are then not only guided by epistemological factors, but by societal contexts of belief-languages as well. As a result, the success of sociology cannot be solely measured by its epistemological achievements. To think sociologically, to apply its systems of thought to an analysis of society also required the formation of a sociological community, and effective techniques of self-historicization for constructing such a community. Its ability to construct an existential space for itself—via its engagement with different languages of believing—was crucial for imagining its own role and place within the moral-intellectual culture of nineteenth-century society and beyond.

---

[15] For an example which does use this distinction, cf. Peter Harrison, "Science and secularization", *Intellectual History Review* 27, no. 1 (2017): 47–70.

At this point, my own conclusions are on a collision course with those of other scholars, specifically those who consider the sociological apparatus of modernity, and its applications of the belief-category, to be representative of a certain kind of knowledge culture, one which was marked by Cartesian philosophy and its mind-body dualism, its close association with the project of Western colonialism via a socio-philosophical discourse, and an emphasis on religion as something immaterial, individualist and limited to the private sphere.[16] When the positivist sociologists of the nineteenth and early twentieth century were to speak of 'belief', this is what they were actually imposing onto the social domain: a false Western universalism, thoroughly marked by its own Christian past and presuppositions, employed as a tool within non-Western and colonial contexts for epistemic domination and exploitation through its undermining of alternative forms of knowing, being and blessing.

While I don't mean to relativize this claim nor question its importance—it has been convincingly argued for by luminaries such as Talal Asad and Bruno Latour, as well as many others[17]—at the same time, while it succeeds in its critique of the possible effects of the modern knowledge culture, I would argue that it fails as an intellectual-historical evaluation of the practices effectuated by the sociological moderns. The sociological-modernistic understanding of belief is often seen as being representative of this aforementioned universalism, which is presented as both overly rationalist and as biased towards Christian-Protestant meanings of religiosity.[18] And while there are certainly sociological voices which echo these kinds of values (Parsons comes to mind here), it is difficult to argue that (a) there is anything like a rigorous tradition applying these categorical distinctions consistently, and (b) that this would be representative of the sociological engagement with the category. And while there are, of course, instances of such a mentality, there are equally as many instances of its opposite. Any charitable and thorough reading of the sociological moderns would lead to the conclusion that their engagement with the category of 'belief' is both highly varied and philosophically dutiful, not to mention constitutive of their own modes of existence.

---

[16] David Scott, "Appendix: The Trouble of Thinking: An Interview with Talal Asad", in: *Powers of the Secular Modern: Talal Asad and his Interlocutors*, eds. David Scott & Charles Hirschkind (Stanford: Stanford University Press, 2006), 287.

[17] Steinmetz, *The Colonial Origins of Modern Social Thought*, esp. 44–49.

[18] Asad, *Genealogies of Religion*, 46–48.

When looking at the history of (Western) social sciences and its relation to religious systems and institutions, it is, I believe, beneficial to distinguish this history in its virtual-philosophical and materialist-political dimensions. This distinction is just one of many possible distinctions, but one that is more central to the history of sociology and religion, as these are two domains with strong extensions into both dimensions. If applying this distinction to the aforementioned narrative of sociological modernity as a system that understands 'belief' as a private, mental state, I would argue that, while it neatly captures the angle of its materialist effects—its denunciations of non-rationalist beliefs, its self-exaltation through its binary mechanisms of thought (i.e. science/superstition; nature/culture, etc.)—it is less effective in understanding the sociological language of speaking and thinking belief itself, its variation, its performativity, and its function as a tool for self-government. A truly pluralist history of the social sciences and its entanglement with its religious Other would need to take this distinction into account, paradoxical as its conclusions may seem. As I have tried to show throughout this book as well, the sociological moderns were often intentionally singular and secularist in their self-presentation, yet were themselves fragmented into multiple voices by the sharp edges of the textual fabric that enveloped them.

This series of arguments eventually results in two claims on the current state of post-secularism, one critical and the other normative. The critical claim is that post-secular critiques of the sociological belief-category are insufficiently transparent on the motivations fuelling such critiques. For example, in Bruno Latour's series of critiques with regard to sociological modernity, the French philosopher remains conspicuously silent on the historical relations between early sociology and nineteenth-century religion, even though this spiritual-philosophical contest lay at the centre of sociology's burgeoning formation. Instead, his references are either personal or dug up from a deep, medieval past, far beyond the appearance of social science.[19] Reading Latour, one would imagine that religion and social science have originated from opposite corners of the cosmos, two alien civilizations who have startled upon each other in recent centuries. Rather than writing his own project of an anthropology of the moderns into the shared history of sociology and religion, Latour uses a series of alternative contexts—the so-called Science Wars, methodological discussions in social constructivism, the politics of the Anthropocene—as an

---

[19] On these references, cf. Arnold, "Believing in Belief", 245–250.

entry point into this long-term conflict, foregoing any articulation of its primordial context. When Latour faced his own sociological heritage, this was always with the latter conceptualized as a fully fledged discipline, its debates internal—i.e. on the nature of the social between Durkheim and Tarde—and its topics non-reflexive—i.e. without any historicization of the sociology-religion encounter itself.

Furthermore, I would argue that this silence is not accidental either: in a series of moves, steeped in Latourian irony, Latour uses the mechanisms of disciplinary self-obfuscation often employed by classical sociologists against them, arguing that his concerns are always merely limited to the realm of the conceptual and the epistemological.[20] Looking beyond these self-presentations, however, we can argue that other, more political-theological concerns are motivating this critique of a sociological understanding of belief.[21] Banishing this form of informational belief would make room for a return to a kind of collectively shared political spirituality, where religion would once again be transformed into a veritable mode of existence marked by its ability to tie things together.[22]

The disruption of a sovereign sociological space, fuelled by conceptual instruments such as the category of 'belief', would be a key factor for such a return, taking away the means for sociological actors to move in-between the domains of both social science and religion. The more strict dichotomies made by social theorists like Gabriel Tarde and Charles Péguy, between social science and religious forms of communication, would more easily accommodate such a political spirituality, in contrast to a Durkheimian sociology, which muddles the two domains, splitting them open in search for the social fact.[23] In other words, what Latour aims to reinstate is the agonistic space of competing discourses on 'the social' characteristic of the nineteenth century, when sociology had not yet become self-sufficient, and instead still relied upon its religious counterpart as a source of communication and inspiration. It is such a historical composition, without the possibility of secularist transgressions of the religious domain, which would come to function as a condition of possibility for a true religion's proper unfolding in the eyes of Latour.[24]

---

[20] Cf. supra, ch. 2.
[21] Howles, "The Political Theology of Bruno Latour".
[22] Ibid., 215–224; Michel Serres, *Relire le relié* (Paris: Le Pommier, 2019).
[23] Ibid., 366–367.
[24] Ibid., 238–242.

While I have focused on Latour here, similar strategies can be unearthed across, what can be called, the post-secular alliance, the different disciplines and research programs which have embraced post-secular perspectives. Whether it is via integralism (both Catholic and Protestant), Reformed Epistemology, or Taylorian hermeneutics, many of these critiques of sociological modernity and its usage of 'propositional belief' are still shrouded in a thick, historical fog, the historicity of their own philosophical reflections and their ties to particular self-interests (philosophical, institutional, ideological) within the sociology/religion-conflict insufficiently problematized and brought to the surface.[25] As Joan Stavo-Debauge has already argued, while such argumentative procedures are not uncommon as scholarly techniques, the polarizing nature of the discussions on the state of religion and secularism in the current public space makes these techniques susceptible for their arguments to be interpreted as being made in bad faith.[26]

Again, my argument is not to reject such post-secular theses nor is it to defend the project of sociological modernity. Although I would argue that the latter's engagement with languages of belief has been insufficiently understood, at the same time, the sociological moderns can just as easily be accused of hiding behind their epistemological discourses of science and objectivity, obscuring their own transgressions into the religious domain. Both parties, in other words, are guilty of playing such shrewd language games. And yet, this pseudo-egalitarian nature of mistrust and deception might hold the key for a way out of the conflict. My own position would be to advocate—and here lies my conclusive normative claim— for a greater deal of transparency on what it means to speak of 'belief' in a sociological context, to take into account the way these discourses are existential in their historical constitution, and how discussing these categories go beyond mere matters of methodological clarification (which is not to say that methodological clarification isn't very important in its own

---

[25] Cf. for example: Joan Stavo-Debauge, *Le loup dans la bergerie: le fondamentalisme chrétien à l'assaut de l'espace public* (Geneva: Labor et fides, 2012); Arnold, "Believing in Belief", 250n38; Charles Turner, "Review of On The Modern Cult of the Factish Gods by Bruno Latour" (Durham, Duke University Press, 2010), *European Journal of Sociology* 53, no. 3 (2012): 423–428.

[26] Joan Stavo-Debauge, "Mauvaise foi. Du revival de la philosophie analytique de la religion à l'introduction de l'objection intégraliste en théorie politique", in: *Quel âge post-séculier? Religions, démocraties, sciences*, eds. Joan Stavo-Debauge, Philippe Gonzalez & Roberto Frega (Paris: Éditions de l'EHESS, 2015), 151–182.

right). It is only by mapping out the full range of sociological and religious performativities in their own attempted constructions of a belief-language that we can make a proper evaluation of what can be gained through secular and/or sociological views on religious phenomena, and what is lost.

To consider the value of what can be allowed to be lost in civil society is something that should not only concern political philosophers, but all scholars active in these fields. My conclusion, in other words, is that we need to properly know what sociological modernity is and does within our contemporary system of thought, before we can effectively reflect on whether it is an institution worth conserving or not. With this book, I have tried to show some of the things it is capable of doing: constructing a number of different techniques for imagining a disposition towards the domain of the social and erecting a habitable space within which the social can be communally thought and institutionalized. Returning to a more agonistic dimension—in which different registers of negotiating the social are given equal footing, in an *a priori* manner—is a scenario which requires careful deliberation. It is yet another moment in history at which we can choose to give honesty and reciprocity a chance. It is yet another moment in history at which the mechanisms of violence and obfuscation are tirelessly at work.

Bibliography

Jacques Alibert, *Les triangles d'or d'une société catholique. Louis de Bonald théoricien de la Contre-Révolution* (Paris: Téqui, 2002).

Véronique Altglas & Matthew Wood, "Introduction: An Epistemology for the Sociology of Religion", in: *Bringing Back the Social into the Sociology of Religion*, eds. Véronique Altglas & Matthew Wood (Leiden: Brill, 2018), 1–34.

Kwame Anthony Appiah, "Liberalism and the Plurality of Identity", in: *Knowledge, Identity and Curriculum Transformation in Africa*, eds. N. Cloete, M.W. Makgoba and D. Ekong (Johannesburg: Maskew Miller Longman, 1997): 79–99.

Giorgi Areshidze, "Taking Religion Seriously? Habermas on Religious Translation and Cooperative Learning in Post-secular Society", *American Political Science Review* 111, no. 4 (2017): 724–737.

Carolina Armenteros, "The Counterrevolutionary Comte: Theorist of the Two Powers and Enthusiastic Medievalist", in: *The Anthem Companion to Auguste Comte*, ed. Andrew Wernick (London: Anthem Press, 2017), 91–115.

William Arnal & Russell T. McCutcheon, *The Sacred is the Profane: The Political Nature of "Religion"* (Oxford: Oxford University Press, 2013).

John H. Arnold, *Belief and Unbelief in the Middle Ages* (London: Hodder Arnold, 2005).

John H. Arnold, "Believing in Belief: Gibbon, Latour, and the Social History of Religion", *Past & Present* 260, no. 1 (2023): 236–268.

Talal Asad, "Anthropology and the Colonial Encounter", in: *The Politics of Anthropology: From Colonialism and Sexism Toward a View from Below*, eds. Gerrit Huizer & Bruce Mannheim (Berlin: De Gruyter, 1973), 85–94.

Talal Asad, *Formations of the Secular: Christianity, Islam, Modernity* (Stanford: Stanford University Press, 2003).

Talal Asad, *Genealogies of Religion: Discipline and Reasons of Power in Christianity and Islam* (Baltimore: The Johns Hopkins University Press, 1993).

Keith M. Ashman & Philip S. Baringer (eds.), *After the Science Wars* (London/ New York: Routledge, 2001).

Audran Aulanier & Joan Stavo-Debauge, "La phénoménologie: méthode pour la sociologie ? Entretien avec Joan Stavo-Debauge", *Implications Philosophiques*, https://www.implications-philosophiques.org/la-phenomenologie-methode-pour-la-sociologie-entretien-avec-joan-stavo-debauge-propos-recueillis-par-audran-aulanier-2/.

J.L. Austin, *How To Do Things with Words: The William James Lectures delivered at Harvard University in 1955* (Oxford: Clarendon Press, 1962).

Stéphane Bachiocchi and Jean-Louis Fabiani, "Durkheim's Lost Argument (1895–1955): Critical Moves on Method and Truth", *Durkheimian Studies* 18 (2012): 19–40.

Bosco Byungeun Bae, "The Textures of 'Belief': An interdisciplinary study towards a social scientific epistemology" (PhD diss., Durham University, 2015).

Keith Michael Baker, "Closing the French Revolution: Saint-Simon and Comte", in: *The Transformation of Political Culture 1789–1848*, edited by François Furet and Mona Ozouf. (Oxford: Pergamon, 1989), 323–39.

Keith Michael Baker, *Inventing the French Revolution* (Cambridge: Cambridge University Press, 1990).

Étienne Balibar, *Secularism and Cosmopolitanism: Critical Hypotheses on Religion and Politics* (New York: Columbia University Press, 2018).

Giorgio Barberis, *Louis de Bonald. Ordre et pouvoir entre subversion et providence* (Paris: Desclée de Brouwer, 2016).

Émile Barrault, "Au Père Enfantin", in: *Religion Saint-Simonienne. Recueil de prédications*, Vol. I (Paris: Au bureau du Globe, 1832a), i–ii.

Emile Barrault, "Dégout du présent, besoin d'avenir", *Religion Saint-Simonienne. Recueil de prédications*, Vol. I (Paris: Au bureau du Globe, 1832b), 469–489.

Emile Barrault, "La Hiérarchie", *Religion Saint-Simonienne. Recueil de prédications*, Vol. I (Paris: Au bureau du Globe, 1832c), 179–203.

Emile Barrault, "Le Sacerdoce", *Religion Saint-Simonienne. Recueil de prédications*, Vol. I (Paris: Au bureau du Globe, 1832d), 205–230.

Albert Bastenier, "Le croire et le cru: Les appartenances religieuses au sein du christianisme européen revisitées à partir des travaux de Michel de Certeau", *Social Compass* 54, no. 1 (2007): 13–32.

Saint-Amand Bazard & Barthélemy Prosper Enfantin, *Doctrine Saint-Simonienne: Exposition* (Paris: Librairie Nouvelle, 1854 [1st ed. 1829–30]).
Justin Beaumont (ed.), *The Routledge Handbook of Postsecularity* (Abingdon: Routledge, 2019).
Justin Beaumont & Klaus Eder, "Concepts, processes, and antagonisms of postsecularity", in: *The Routledge Handbook of Postsecularity*, ed. Justin Beaumont (Abingdon: Routledge, 2019), 3–24.
Irene Becci, "Religious Superdiversity and Gray Zones in Public Total Institutions", *Journal of Religion in Europe* 11, no. 2–3 (2018): 123–137.
Ulrich Beck, Anthony Giddens, and Scott Lash, *Reflexive Modernization: Politics, Tradition and Aesthetics in the Modern Social Order* (Oxford: Polity Press, 1994).
David A. Bell, "Nation et patrie, société et civilisation: Transformations du vocabulaire social français, 1700–1789", in: *L'invention de la société. Nominalisme politique et science sociale au XVIII*^{e} *siècle*, eds. Laurence Kaufmann & Jacques Guilhaumou (Paris: Éditions de l'École des hautes études en sciences sociales, 2003), 99–122.
Robert N. Bellah, "Durkheim and History", *American Sociological Review* 24, no. 4 (1959): 447–461.
Michel Bellet, "On the Utilitarian Roots of Saint-Simonism: From Bentham to Saint-Simon", *History of Economic Ideas* 17, no. 2 (2009): 41–63.
Carlos Belvedere, "Durkheim as the Founder of Phenomenological Sociology", *Human Studies* 38, no. 3 (2015): 369–390.
Paul Bénichou, *Le Temps des Prophètes: Doctrines de l'Âge Romantique* (Paris: Gallimard, 1977).
Nicole Dhombres & Jean Dhombres, *Naissance d'un pouvoir: sciences et savants en France (1793–1824)* (Paris: Payot, 1986).
Peter L. Berger, "The Desecularization of the World: A Global Overview", in: *The Desecularization of the World: Resurgent Religion and World Politics*, ed. Peter L. Berger (Grand Rapids, MI: William B. Eerdmans Publishing Company, 1999).
Louis Bergeron, François Furet & Reinhart Koselleck (eds.), *Das Zeitalter der europäischen Revolution 1780–1848* (Frankfurt am Main: Fischer Bücherei, 1969).
Henri Bergson, *Essai sur les données immédiates de la conscience* (Paris: Félix Alcan, 1889).
Christopher J. Berry, *Essays on Hume, Smith and the Scottish Enlightenment* (Edinburgh: Edinburgh University Press, 2018).
Christopher J. Berry, *Social Theory of the Scottish Enlightenment* (Edinburgh: Edinburgh University Press, 1997).
Jean-François Bert, *Le corps qui pense: Une anthropologie historique des pratiques savantes* (Basel: Schwabe Verlag, 2023).
Jean-François Bert, *Le courage de comparer. L'anthropologie subversive de Marcel Mauss* (Genève: Labor et fides, 2021).

Jean-François Bert, "Priez, priez, il en restera toujours quelque chose: *La Prière* (1909) de Marcel Mauss", *Revue des sciences sociales* 64 (2020): 164–171.

Jean-François Bert, "Relire "les techniques du corps". Les enjeux d'un programme de recherche", in: *Lire Les techniques du corps. Relire Marcel Mauss*, ed. Jean-François Bert (Paris: Éditions de la Sorbonne, 2022), 5–43.

Jean-François Bert & Jérôme Lamy, *Voir les savoirs: Lieux, objets et gestes de la science* (Paris: Anamosa, 2021).

David Bloor, "Collective Representations as Social Institutions", in: *Durkheim and Representations*, ed. W.S.F. Pickering (London: Routledge, 2000), 157–166.

Inigo Bocken, "Nomad and Layman: Spiritual Spaces in Modernity – Mysticism and Everyday Life in Michel de Certeau", in: *Spiritual Spaces: History and Mysticism in Michel de Certeau*, ed. Inigo Bocken (Leuven: Peeters, 2013), 111–123.

Massimo Borlandi, "Lacombe, Durkheim et le groupe de L'Année sociologique", in: *Histoire et anthropologie de la parenté. Autour de Paul Lacombe (1834–1919)*, ed. A. Fine & N. Adell (Paris: Éditions du CTHS, 2012), 257–268.

Maarten Boudry, Michael Vlerick & Taner Edis, "The end of science? On human cognitive limitations and how to overcome them", *Biology & Philosophy* 35, 18 (2020): 1–16.

Maarten Boudry, Michael Vlerick & Taner Edis, "Demystifying Mysteries. How Metaphors and Analogies Extend the Reach of the Human Mind", in: *Metaphors and Analogies in Sciences and Humanities: Words and Worlds*, eds. Shyam Wuppuluri & A.C. Grayling (Cham: Springer, 2022), 65–83.

Michel Bourdeau, "Auguste Comte et la religion positiviste: présentation", *Revue des sciences philosophiques et théologiques* 87, no. 1 (2003): 5–21.

Michel Bourdeau, "Fallait-il oublier Comte? Retour sur The Counter-Revolution of Science", *Revue européenne des sciences sociales* 54, no. 2 (2016): 89–111.

Michel Bourdeau, "Pouvoir spirituel et fixation des croyances", *Commentaire* 136, no. 4 (2011): 1095–1104.

Pierre Bourdieu, "Sociologues de la croyance et croyances de sociologues", *Archives de sciences sociales des religions* 32, no. 63.1 (1987): 151–161.

Pierre Bourdieu and Loïc Wacquant, *An Invitation to Reflexive Sociology* (Chicago: University of Chicago Press, 1992).

Alain Boureau, "Croire et croyances", in: *Michel de Certeau: Les chemins de l'histoire*, eds. Christian Delacroix, François Dosse, Patrick Garcia & Michel Trebitsch (Paris: Éditions Complexe, 2002), 125–140.

Alain Boureau, *L'Événement sans fin: Récit et christianisme au Moyen Âge* (Paris: Les Belles Lettres, 2004).

Frédéric Brahami, "De la nécessité du pouvoir spirituel chez les modernes: Comte, critique de l'âge critique", *Archives de sciences sociales de la religion* 190 (2020): 127–141.

Frédéric Brahami, "Individu, pouvoir, société dans la pensée contre-révolutionnaire", in: *Le libéralisme au miroir du droit. L'État, la personne, la propriété*, ed. Blaise Bachofen (Lyon: ENS Éditions, 2008), 145–163.

Frédéric Brahami, *La Raison du Peuple: Un héritage de la Révolution française (1789–1848)*(Paris: Les Belles Lettres, 2016).

Frédéric Brahami, "Sortir du cercle Auguste Comte, la critique et les rétrogrades", *Archives de Philosophie* 70, no. 1 (2007): 41–55.

Jean-François Braunstein, "La religion des morts-vivants. Le culte des morts chez Auguste Comte", *Revue des sciences philosophiques et théologiques* 87, no. 1 (2003): 59–73.

Stewart J. Brown, "Movements of Christian awakening in revolutionary Europe, 1790–1815", in: *The Cambridge History of Christianity, Vol. VII: Enlightenment, Reawakening and Revolution 1660–1815*, eds. Stewart J. Brown & Timothy Tackett (Cambridge: Cambridge University Press, 2008), 575–595.

Jeffrey D. Burson, "Nicolas-Sylvestre Bergier (1718–1790): An Enlightened Anti-Philosophe", in: *Enlightenment and Catholicism in Europe: A Transnational History*, eds. Jeffrey D. Burson & Ulrich L. Lehner (Notre Dame, IN: University of Notre Dame Press, 2014), 63–88.

Philippe Büttgen, "Le contraire des pratiques: Commentaires sur la doctrine de Michel de Certeau", in: *Lire Michel de Certeau. La formalité des pratiques*, eds. Philippe Büttgen & Christian Jouhaud (Frankfurt Am Main: Vittorio Klostermann, 2008), 69–97.

Philippe Büttgen, "Théologie politique et pouvoir pastoral", *Annales. Histoires, Sciences Sociales* 62, no. 5 (2007): 1129–1154.

Alain Caillé, *Anthropologie du don: Le tiers paradigme* (Paris: Desclée de Brouwer, 2000).

Jean-Pierre Callot, "Les polytechniciens et l'aventure saint-simonienne", *Bulletin de la Sabix* 42 (2008): https://journals.openedition.org/sabix/131.

Craig Calhoun, "Classical Social Theory and the French Revolution of 1848", *Sociological Theory* 7, no. 2 (1989): 210–225.

Euan Cameron, *Enchanted Europe: Superstition, Reason, and Religion 1250–1750* (Oxford: Oxford University Press, 2010).

Jeremy L. Caradonna, *The Enlightenment in Practice: Academic Prize Contests and Intellectual Culture in France, 1670–1794* (Ithaca: Cornell University Press, 2012).

José Casanova, *Public Religions in the Modern World* (Chicago: University of Chicago Press, 1994).

José Casanova, "Secularization revisited: A reply to Talal Asad", in: *Powers of the Secular Modern: Talal Asad and his Interlocutors*, eds. David Scott & Charles Hirschkind (Stanford: Stanford University Press, 2006), 12–30.

Jean-Pierre Cavaillé, "Libertinage, irréligion, incroyance, athéisme dans l'Europe de la première modernité (xvie–xviie siècles). Une approche critique des tendances actuelles de la recherche (1998–2002)", *Les Dossiers du Grihl* [En ligne], 1–2 | 2007: http://journals.openedition.org/dossiersgrihl/279.

Dipesh Chakrabarty, *Provincializing Europe: Postcolonial Thought and Historical Difference* (Princeton: Princeton University Press, 2000).

Jacques M. Chevalier & Daniel J. Buckles, *Participatory Action Research: Theory and Methods for Engaged Inquiry* (London: Routledge, 2013).

Sandro Chignola, *Società e costituzione. Teologia e politica nel sistema di Bonald* (Milan: Franco Angeli, 1993).

Mark S. Cladis, "Introduction", in: Émile Durkheim, *The Elementary Forms of Religious Life*, transl. by Carol Cosman, introduction by Mark S. Cladis (Oxford: Oxford University Press, 2001), vii–xxxv.

Paul Cloke & Justin Beaumont, "Geographies of postsecular rapprochement in the city", *Progress in Human Geography* 37, no. 1 (2012): 27–51.

Paul Cloke, Christopher Baker, Callum Sutherland, & Andrew Williams (eds.), *Geographies of Postsecularity: Re-envisioning Politics, Subjectivity and Ethics* (London: Routledge, 2019).

Elizabeth F. Cohen, *The Political Value of Time: Citizenship, Duration, and Democratic Justice* (Cambridge: Cambridge University Press, 2018).

Auguste Comte, *Catéchisme positiviste, ou Sommaire exposition de la religion universelle, en onze entretiens systématiques entre une Femme et un Prêtre de l'Humanité* (Paris: Chez Carilian-Goeury et V^{or} Dalmont, 1852).

Auguste Comte, "Considérations sur le pouvoir spirituel (Mars 1826)", in: Auguste Comte, *Système de politique positive, ou Traité de sociologie, Instituant la Religion de l'Humanité*, Vol. IV: Appendice général du système de politique positive (Paris: Chez Carilian-Goeury et V^{or} Dalmont, 1854a), 177–216.

Auguste Comte, *Cours de philosophie positive* (Paris: Rouen Frères & Bachelier, 1830–42), 6 vol.

Auguste Comte, *Plan des travaux scientifiques nécessaires pour réorganiser la société* (Paris: Les Éditions Aubier-Montaigne, 1970 [1st ed., 1822]).

Auguste Comte, "Sommaire appréciation de l'ensemble du passé moderne (avril 1820)", in: Auguste Comte, *Système de politique positive, ou Traité de sociologie, Instituant la Religion de l'Humanité*, Vol. IV: Appendice général du système de politique positive (Paris: Chez Carilian-Goeury et V^{or} Dalmont, 1854b), 4–46.

Auguste Comte, *Système de politique positive, ou Traité de sociologie, Instituant la Religion de l'Humanité* (Paris: Chez Carilian-Goeury et V^{or} Dalmont, 1851–1854c), 4 vol.

Auguste Comte, *Système de politique positive, ou Traité de sociologie, instituant la Religion de l'Humanité*, Vol. I (Osnabrück: Otto Zeller, 1967 [1st ed., 1851]).

Monique Cottret, *Jansénismes et lumières: pour une autre XVIIIe siècle* (Paris: Albin Michel, 1998).

Guillaume Cuchet, *Les voix d'outre-tombe. Tables tournantes, spiritisme et société au XIXe siècle* (Paris: Éditions du Seuil, 2013).

Guillaume Cuchet, *Une histoire du sentiment religieux au XIXe siècle. Religion, culture et société en France, 1830–1880* (Paris: Les Éditions du Cerf, 2020).
Armand Cuvillier, "Preface to the French Edition of 1955", in: Émile Durkheim, *Pragmatism and Sociology*, ed. John B. Allcock, transl. by J.C. Whitehouse (Cambridge: Cambridge University Press, 1983), xi–xxii.
Douglas J. Davies & Michael J. Thate (eds.), *Religion and the Individual: Belief, Practice, and Identity* (Basel: MDPI, 2017).
Flavien Bertran de Balanda, "Deux sciences de l'homme. Idéologie et Contre-Révolution dans le débat anthropologique du premier XIXe siècle", *Cahiers de philosophie de l'Université de Caen*, « Lecture de Cabanis au XIXe siècle », 57 (2020a): 71–84.
Flavien Bertran de Balanda, "Evil Raised To Its Highest Power. The Philosophy of the Counter-Enlightenment, a Project of Intellectual Management of the Revolutionary Violence", *The Philosophical Journal of Conflict and Violence* IV, no. 1 (2020b): 52–72.
Flavien Bertran de Balanda, "La Théorie du pouvoir de Louis de Bonald (1796) ou l'édification d'une métaphysique sociale de la royauté", *Annales historiques de la Révolution française* 403, no. 1 (2021a): 45–62.
Flavien Bertran de Balanda, "Louis de Bonald et la question du divorce, de la rédaction du Code Civil à la loi du 8 mai 1816", *Histoire, économie & société* 36, no. 3 (2017): 72–86.
Flavien Bertran de Balanda, *Louis de Bonald. Philosophe et homme politique. Une tradition dans la modernité, une modernité dans la tradition 1754–1840* (Paris: CNRS Éditions, 2021b).
Louis de Bonald, *De la Chrétienté et du Christianisme* (Paris: impr. de Lachevardière fils, 1825).
Louis de Bonald, *Démonstration philosophique du principe constitutif de la société* (Brussels: La société nationale, 1845a [1st ed. 1830]).
Louis de Bonald, *Œuvres complètes de M. de Bonald* (Brussels: La Société Nationale, 1845b), 8 vol.
Louis de Bonald, *Théorie du pouvoir politique et religieux, dans la société civile, démontrée par le raisonnement & par l'histoire* (S.l.: s.n., 1796), 3 vol.
Michel de Certeau, *La faiblesse de croire*, ed. Luce Giard (Paris: Seuil, 1987a).
Michel de Certeau, *La prise de parole, et autres écrits politiques* (Paris: Seuil, 1994).
Michel de Certeau, "Le noir soleil du langage: Michel Foucault", in: Michel de Certeau, *Histoire et psychanalyse: entre science et fiction*, ed. Luce Giard (Paris: Gallimard, 2002, 2nd ed. [1st ed., 1987b]), 152–173.
Michel de Certeau, "Les révolutions du « croyable »", in: Michel de Certeau, *La culture au pluriel* (Paris: Seuil, 1993 [1st ed. 1974]), 17–32.
Michel de Certeau, "L'institution du croire. Note de travail", *Recherches de science religieuse* 71 (1983): 61–80.

Michel de Certeau, "The Formality of Practices: From Religious Systems to the Ethics of Enlightenment", in: Michel de Certeau, *The Writing of History*, transl. by Tom Conley (New York: Columbia University Press, 1988), 147–205.

Michel de Certeau, *The Practice of Everyday Life*, transl. by Steven Rendall (Berkeley: University of California Press, 1984).

Michel de Certeau, "Une pratique sociale de la différence: croire", *Faire croire. Modalités de la diffusion et de la réception des messages religieux du xiie au xve siècle*, École française de Rome, no. 303 (1981): 363–383.

Michel de Certeau, "What We Do When We Believe", in: *On Signs*, ed. Marshall Blonsky (Baltimore: Johns Hopkins University Press, 1985), 192–202.

Michel de Certeau & Jean-Marie Domenach, *Le christianisme éclaté* (Paris: Éditions du Seuil, 1974).

Michel de Certeau, Dominique Julia & Jacques Revel, *Une politique de la langue* (Paris: Gallimard, 2002 [first published 1975]).

François-René de Chateaubriand, *Génie du christianisme, ou Beautés de la religion chrétienne* (Paris: chez Migneret, 1802).

Mary Jo Deegan, "Jane Addams, the Hull-House School of Sociology, and Social Justice, 1892 to 1935", *Humanity & Society* 37, no. 3 (2013): 199–278.

Felicité de la Mennais, *Essai sur l'indifférence en matière de religion* (Paris: Tournachon-Molin et H. Seguin, 1817).

De la religion Saint-Simonienne. *Aux élèves de l'École polytechnique* (Brussels: Laurent Frères, 1831).

Henri de Lubac, *Corpus Mysticum: The Eucharist and the Church in the Middle Ages*, trans. Gemma Simmonds, with Richard Price and Christopher Stephens (Notre Dame, IN: Notre Dame Press, 2007 [1944]).

Joseph de Maistre, *Du Pape* (Lyon: Chez Rusand, 1819), 2 vol.

Jacques Donzelot, *L'invention du social. Essai sur le déclin des passions politiques* (Paris: Fayard, 1984).

François Dosse, *Michel de Certeau: le marcheur blessé* (Paris: La Découverte, 2002).

Michael Drolet, "A nineteenth-century Mediterranean union: Michel Chevalier's *Système de la Méditerranée*", *Mediterranean Historical Review* 30, no. 2 (2015): 147–168.

Daniel Dubuisson, *The Invention of Religions*, transl. by Martha Cunningham (Sheffield: Equinox Publishing Limited, 2019).

Émile Durkheim, *Les formes élémentaires de la vie religieuse: le système totémique en Australie* (Paris: Félix Alcan, 1912).

Émile Durkheim, "Marxism and Sociology: The Materialist Conception of History (1897)", in: Durkheim, *The Rules of Sociological Method*, 123–129.

Émile Durkheim, *Moral Education: A Study in the Theory and Application of the Sociology of Education*, ed. Everett K. Wilson, transl. by Everett K. Wilson & Herman Schnurer (New York: The Free Press, 1961).

Émile Durkheim, *On Morality and Society*, ed. Robert Bellah (Chicago: Chicago University Press, 1973).
Émile Durkheim, *Pragmatism and Sociology*, ed. John B. Allcock, transl. by J.C. Whitehouse (Cambridge: Cambridge University Press, 1983).
Emile Durkheim, *Socialism and Saint Simon*, ed. Alvin W. Gouldner, transl. by Charlotte Sattler (London: Routledge & Kegan Paul Ltd, 2009).
Émile Durkheim, *Sociology and Philosophy*, transl. by D.F. Pocock (Abingdon, Oxon: Routledge, 2010).
Émile Durkheim, *Suicide: A Study in Sociology*, ed. George Simpson, transl. by John A. Spaulding & George Simpson (London & New York: Routledge, 2002).
Émile Durkheim, *The Division of Labour in Society*, intro. by Lewis Coser, transl. by W.D. Halls (London: Macmillan, 1984).
Émile Durkheim, "The Dualism of Human Nature and its Social Conditions", in: Émile Durkheim, *Essays on Sociology and Philosophy*, ed. Kurt H. Wolff (New York: Harper & Row, Publishers, Inc., 1964), 325–340.
Émile Durkheim, *The Elementary Forms of Religious Life*, transl. and with an introduction by Karen E. Fields (New York: The Free Press, 1995).
Émile Durkheim, *The Elementary Forms of Religious Life*, transl. by Carol Cosman, introduction by Mark S. Cladis (Oxford: Oxford University Press, 2001).
Émile Durkheim, *The Rules of Sociological Method, And Selected Texts on Sociology and its Method*, ed. Steven Lukes, transl. by W.D. Halls (Basingstoke, Hampshire: Palgrave Macmillan, 2013).
Émile Durkheim & Marcel Mauss, *Primitive Classification*, ed. and transl. by Rodney Needham (London: Cohen & West, 1963).
Émile Durkheim & Gabriel Tarde, "The debate", in: *"The Social after Gabriel Tarde: Debates and assessments*, ed. Matei Candea (London & New York: Routledge, 2010), 27–43.
Dan Edelstein, *The Enlightenment: A Genealogy* (Chicago: University of Chicago Press, 2010).
Dan Edelstein, *The Terror of Natural Right: Republicanism, the Cult of Nature, and the French Revolution* (Chicago: University of Chicago Press, 2009).
Barthélemy Prosper Enfantin, "Deuxième enseignement (20 novembre 1831): l'histoire", in: *Œuvres de Saint-Simon et d'Enfantin*, vol. XIV (Paris: E. Dentu, 1868), 45–75.
Gilbert Faccarello, "A dance teacher for paralysed people? Charles de Coux and the dream of a Christian political economy", *The European Journal of the History of Economic Thought* 24, no. 4 (2017a): 828–875.
Gilbert Faccarello, "Saeculum", *European Journal for the History of Economic Thought* 24, no. 4 (2017b): 625–639.
Paul Fauconnet and Marcel Mauss, "La sociologie: objet et méthode", *Grande Encyclopédie* 30 (1901): http://classiques.uqac.ca/classiques/mauss_marcel/essais_de_socio/T1_la_sociologie/la_sociologie.html.

Jeanne Favret-Saada, *Désorceler* (Paris: L'Olivier, 2009).
Jeanne Favret-Saada, *Les Mots, la Mort, les Sorts: la sorcellerie dans le bocage* (Paris: Gallimard, 1977).
Stefania Ferrando, "Le "détournement" de la révolution. Continuité historique et conflit social chez Saint-Simon", *Archives de Philosophie* 80, no. 1 (2017): 33–54.
Jonathan S. Fish, "Religion and the Changing Intensity of Emotional Solidarities in Durkheim's *The Division of Labour in Society* (1983)", *Journal of Classical Sociology* 2, no. 2 (2002): 203–223.
Anna Fisk, "Appropriating, romanticizing and reimagining: Pagan engagements with indigenous animism", in: *Cosmopolitanism, Nationalism, and Modern Paganism*, ed. K. Rountree (New York: Palgrave Macmillan, 2017), 21–42.
Timothy Fitzgerald, "Introduction", in: *Religion and the Secular: Historical and Colonial Formations*, ed. Timothy Fitzgerald (London: Equinox, 2007a), 1–24.
Timothy Fitzgerald (ed.), *Religion and the Secular: Historical and Colonial Formations* (London: Equinox, 2007b).
Michel Foucault, *Il faut défendre la société: Cours au Collège de France (1976)*, ed. François Ewald and Alessandro Fontana (Paris: Gallimard/Seuil, 1997).
Michel Foucault, *L'archéologie du savoir* (Paris: Gallimard, 1969).
Michel Foucault, "Nietzsche, Genealogy, History", in: *Language, Counter-Memory, Practice: Selected Essays and Interviews*, ed. D.F. Bouchard (Ithaca: Cornell University Press, 1977), 139–164.
Michel Foucault, "Qu'est-ce que les Lumières?", in: *Michel Foucault, Dits et Écrits, vol. II: 1976–1988*, eds. Daniel Defert & François Ewald (Paris: Gallimard, 2001), 1381–1397.
Marcel Fournier, *Marcel Mauss: A Biography*, transl. by Jane Marie Todd (Princeton & Oxford: Princeton University Press, 2006).
Agustín Fuentes, *Why We Believe: Evolution and the Human Way of Being* (New Haven: Yale University Press, 2019).
Steve Fuller, *Social Epistemology* (Bloomington and Indianapolis: Indiana University Press, 2002).
François Furet & Mona Ozouf (eds.), *The French Revolution and the Creation of Modern Political Culture, vol. 3: The Transformation of Political Culture 1789–1848* (New York: Pergamon Press, 1987).
Numa Denis Fustel de Coulanges, *The Ancient City: A Study on the Religion, Laws, and Institutions of Greece and Rome* (Kitchener: Batoche Books, 2001 [1864]).
Mike Gane, "Comte and his Liberal Critics: From Spencer to Hayek", in: *The Anthem Companion to Auguste Comte*, ed. Andrew Wernick (London: Anthem Press, 2017), 205–225.
Gérard Gengembre, "Les concepts et l'Histoire" (PhD diss., Université de Paris IV, 1983).
Anthony Giddens, *Capitalism and Modern Social Theory* (Cambridge: Cambridge University Press, 1971).

Philippe Gonzalez & Laurence Kaufmann, "The Social Scientist, the Public and the Pragmatist Gaze: Exploring the Critical Conditions of Sociological Inquiry", *European Journal of Pragmatism and American Philosophy* 4, no. 1 (2012): 1–30.

B.J. Good, "Belief, Anthropology Of", in: *International Encyclopedia of the Social & Behavioral Sciences*, eds. Neil J. Smelser & Paul B. Baltes (Amsterdam: Elsevier, 2001), 1137–1141.

Philip S. Gorski, David Kyuman Kim, John Torpey, and Jonathan VanAntwerpen, "The Post-Secular in Question", in: *The Post-Secular in Question: Religion in Contemporary Society*, eds. Philip S. Gorski, David Kyuman Kim, John Torpey, and Jonathan VanAntwerpen (New York & London: Social Science Research Council/New York University Press, 2012), 1–22.

Anthony Grafton, "The History of Ideas: Precept and Practice, 1950–2000 and Beyond", *Journal of the History of Ideas* 67, no. 1 (2006): 1–32.

Neil Gross, "Durkheim's Pragmatism Lectures: A Contextual Interpretation", *Sociological Theory* 15, no. 2 (1997): 126–149.

Charles Guignon, "Philosophy after Heidegger and Wittgenstein", *Philosophy and Phenomenological Research* 50, no. 4 (1990): 649–672.

Vincent Guillin, "Comte and Social Science", in: *Love, Order, & Progress: The Science, Philosophy, & Politics of Auguste Comte*, eds. Michel Bourdeau, Mary Pickering, & Warren Schmaus (Pittsburgh: University of Pittsburgh Press, 2018), 128–160.

Jürgen Habermas, "Notes on Post-Secular Society", *New Perspectives Quarterly* 25, no. 4 (2008): 17–29.

Jürgen Habermas & Charles Taylor, "Dialogue: Jürgen Habermas and Charles Taylor", in: *The Power of Religion in the Public Sphere*, eds. Eduardo Mendieta and Jonathan VanAntwerpen (New York: Columbia University Press, 2011), 60–69.

Ian Hacking, "L'ontologie historique", in: *L'invention de la société. Nominalisme politique et science sociale au XVIIIe siècle*, eds. Laurence Kaufmann & Jacques Guilhaumou (Paris: Éditions de l'École des hautes études en sciences sociales, 2003), 287–310.

Ian Hacking, "Making Up People", in: *Forms of Desire: Sexual Orientation and the Social Constructionist Controversy*, ed. Edward Stein (New York: Routledge, 1992), 69–88.

Ian Hacking, *The Social Construction of What?* (Cambridge, MA: Harvard University Press, 1999).

Graham Harman, "Entanglement and Relation: A Response to Bruno Latour and Ian Hodder", *New Literary History* 45, no. 1 (2014): 37–49.

Graham Harman, *Heidegger Explained: From Phenomenon to Thing* (Chicago & La Salle: Open Court Publishing, 2007).

Graham Harman, *Tool-Being: Heidegger and the Metaphysics of Objects* (Chicago & La Salle: Open Court Publishing, 2002).
Peter Harrison, "Introduction: Narratives of secularization", *Intellectual History Review* 27, no. 1 (2017a): 1–6.
Peter Harrison, "Science and secularization", *Intellectual History Review* 27, no. 1 (2017b): 47–70.
Peter Harrison, *The Territories of Science and Religion* (Chicago: University of Chicago Press, 2015).
Friedrich Hayek, *The Counter-Revolution of Science: Studies on the Abuse of Reason* (Glencoe: The Free Press, 1952).
Jack Hayward, *After the French Revolution: Six Critics of Democracy and Nationalism* (New York: New York University Press, 1991).
Paul Hazard, *La crise de la conscience européenne (1680–1715)* (Paris: Boivin, 1935).
Johan Heilbron, "Auguste Comte and historical epistemology: a reply to Dick Pels", *History of the Human Sciences* 9, no. 2 (1996): 153–159.
Johan Heilbron, "Auguste Comte and the Second Scientific Revolution", in: *The Anthem Companion to Auguste Comte*, ed. Andrew Wernick (London: Anthem Press, 2017), 23–41.
Johan Heilbron, *French Sociology* (Ithaca: Cornell University Press, 2015).
Johan Heilbron, "Intellectuele geschiedenis als sociologisch probleem", *Amsterdams Sociologisch Tijdschrift* 18, no. 1 (1991): 140–160.
Johan Heilbron, "The Emergence of Social Theory", in: *The Cambridge Handbook of Social Theory, vol. I: A Contested Canon*, ed. Peter Kivisto (Cambridge: Cambridge University Press, 2021), 1–23.
Johan Heilbron, *The Rise of Social Theory*, transl. by Sheila Gogol (Minneapolis, MN: University of Minnesota Press, 1995).
Johan Heilbron, Lars Magnusson & Björn Wittrock (eds.), *The Rise of the Social Sciences and the Formation of Modernity: Conceptual Change in Context, 1750–1850* (Dordrecht: Kluwer Academic Publishers, 1998).
Nora M. Heimann, *Joan of Arc in French Art and Culture (1700–1855): From Satire to Sanctity* (Aldershot: Ashgate, 2005).
François Héran, "De la Cité Antique à la sociologie des institutions", *Revue de synthèse* 4 (1989): 363–390.
François Héran, "Le rite et la croyance", *Revue française de la sociologie* 27, no. 2 (1986): 231–263.
François Héran, "L'institution démotivée de Fustel de Coulanges à Durkheim et au-delà", *Revue française de sociologie* 28, no. 1 (1987): 67–97.
David Herbert & Josh Bullock, "The Diversity of Nonreligion: Meaning-Making, Activism and Towards a Theory of Nonreligious Identity and Group Formation", in: *Non-Religion in Late Modern Societies: Institutional and Legal Perspectives*, eds. Anne-Laure Zwilling & Helge Årsheim (Cham: Springer, 2022), 151–171.

Danièle Hervieu-Léger, "La religion, mode de croire", *Revue du Mauss* 22, no. 2 (2003): 144–158.

Danièle Hervieu-Léger, "Le partage du croire religieux dans des sociétés d'individus", *L'année sociologique* 60, no. 1 (2010): 41–62.

Danièle Hervieu-Léger, *Le Pèlerin et le Converti* (Paris: Flammarion, 1999).

Martin Holbraad & Morten Axel Pedersen, *The Ontological Turn: An Anthropological Exposition* (Cambridge: Cambridge University Press, 2017).

Mitsutoshi Horii, "Historicizing the category of "religion" in sociological theories: Max Weber and Emile Durkheim", *Critical Research on Religion* 7, no. 1 (2019): 24–37.

Mitsutoshii Horii, *'Religion' and 'Secular' Categories in Sociology: Decolonizing the Modern Myth* (Cham: Palgrave Macmillan, 2021).

Tim Howles, "The Political Theology of Bruno Latour" (PhD diss., University of Oxford, 2018).

Henri Hubert & Marcel Mauss, *Sacrifice: Its Nature and Function*, transl. by W.D. Halls, foreword by E.E. Evans-Pritchard (Chicago: Chicago University Press, 1964).

Florence Hulak, "Sociologie et théorie socialiste de l'histoire. La trame saint-simonienne chez Durkheim et Marx", *Incidence. Revue de philosophie, littérature, sciences humaines et sociales 11* (2015): 83–106.

Lynn Hunt, Margaret C. Jacob & Wijnand Mijnhardt, *The Book That Changed Europe: Picart & Bernard's Religious Ceremonies of the World* (Cambridge, MA: Harvard University Press, 2010).

Ian Hunter, "Secularization: The Birth of a Modern Combat Concept", *Modern Intellectual History* 12, no. 1 (2015): 1–32.

Edmund Hüsserl, *The Crisis of European Sciences and Transcendental Phenomenology: An Introduction to Phenomenological Philosophy*, transl. by David Carr (Evanston: Northwestern University Press, 1989).

Georg G. Iggers, *The Cult of Authority: The Political Philosophy of the Saint-Simonians* (The Hague: Martinus Nijhoff, 1970 [1st. ed., 1958]).

Tim Ingold, *Perception of the Environment: Essays on Livelihood, Dwelling, and Skill* (London: Routledge, 2000).

Dominique Iogna-Prat & Alain Rauwel, "Introduction: Reconfigurations socio-religieuses post-révolutionnaires", *Archives de sciences sociales des religions* 190 (2020): 11–26.

François-André Isambert, "The early days of French sociology of religion", *Social Compass* 16, no. 4 (1969): 435–452.

Christian Jacob, *Des mondes lettrés aux lieux de savoir* (Paris: Les Belles Lettres, 2018).

Christian Jacob, *Qu'est-ce qu'un lieu de savoir?* (S.l.: Open Edition Press, 2014).

William James, *The Varieties of Religious Experience: A Study in Human Nature* (London and Glasgow: Collins, 1960).

William James, *Writings 1902–1910: The Varieties of Religious Experience. Pragmatism. A Pluralistic Universe. The Meaning of Truth. Some Problems of Philosophy. Essays* (New York: Literary Classics of the United States, Inc., 1987).

Paul Janet, "Le socialisme moderne: l'école Saint-Simonienne – Bazard et Enfantin", *Revue des Deux Mondes* 17, no. 3 (1876): 587–618.

Marc Joly, *La révolution sociologique. De la naissance d'un régime de pensée scientifique à la crise de la philosophie (XIXe-XXe siècle)* (Paris: Éditions La Découverte, 2017).

Jason Ā. Josephson-Storm, *The Myth of Disenchantment: Magic, Modernity, and The Birth of The Human Sciences* (Chicago and London: University of Chicago Press, 2017).

Jason Ā. Josephson-Storm, "The Superstition, Secularism, and Religion Trinary: Or Re-Theorizing Secularism", *Method and Theory in the Study of Religion* 30 (2018): 1–20.

Joseph Karbowski, "Complexity and Progression in Aristotle's Treatment of *Endoxa* in the *Topics*", *Ancient Philosophy* 35, no. 1 (2015): 75–96.

Bruno Karsenti, "Autorité, société, pouvoir: le science sociale selon Bonald", in: *L'invention de la société: nominalisme politique et science sociale au XVIIIe siècle*, ed. Laurence Kaufmann & Jacques Guilhaumou (Paris: Éditions de l'École des Hautes Études en Sciences Sociales, 2003), 261–286.

Bruno Karsenti, "Destin du culte des morts", *Incidence* 2 (2009): 136–154.

Bruno Karsenti, *D'une philosophie à l'autre. Les sciences sociales et la politique des Modernes* (Paris: Gallimard, 2013).

Bruno Karsenti, *La place de Dieu. Religion et politique chez les modernes* (Paris: Fayard, 2023).

Bruno Karsenti, *La société en personnes. Études durkheimiennes* (Paris: Economica, 2006a).

Bruno Karsenti, "La sociologie à l'épreuve du pragmatisme. Réaction durkheimienne", in: *La croyance et l'enquête. Aux sources du pragmatisme*, eds. Bruno Karsenti & Louis Queré (Paris: Éditions de l'École des Hautes Études en Sciences Sociales, 2004), 317–349.

Bruno Karsenti, "Le problème des sciences humaines. Comte, Durkheim, Lévi-Strauss", *Archives de Philosophie* 63, no. 3 (2000): 445–465.

Bruno Karsenti, *L'homme total: sociologie, anthropologie et philosophie chez Marcel Mauss* (Paris: Presses Universitaires de France, 1997).

Bruno Karsenti, *Politique de l'esprit: Auguste Comte et la naissance de la science sociale* (Paris: Hermann Éditeurs, 2006b).

Laurence Kaufmann, "Aux sources de la sociologie. Science et politique de la « société » au 18e siècle", *L'Année Sociologique* 67, no. 2 (2017): 333–366.

Laurence Kaufmann & Jacques Guilhaumou, "Présentation", in: *L'invention de la société. Nominalisme politique et science sociale au XVIIIe siècle*, eds. Laurence

Kaufmann & Jacques Guilhaumou (Paris: Éditions de l'École des hautes études en sciences sociales, 2003), 9–20.

Webb Keane, *Christian Moderns: Freedom and Fetish in the Mission Encounter* (Berkeley: University of California Press, 2007).

Thomas Kemple, "Comte's Civic Comedy: Secular Religion and Modern Morality in the Age of Classical Sociology", in: *The Anthem Companion to Auguste Comte*, ed. Andrew Wernick (London: Anthem Press, 2017), 159–174.

Lily Kong, "Global shifts, theoretical shifts: Changing geographies of religion", *Progress in Human Geography* 34, no. 6 (2010): 755–776.

Reinhart Koselleck, *Futures Past. On the Semantics of Historical Time*, transl. by Keith Tribe (New York: Columbia University Press, 2004).

Alexandre Koyré, Leonora Cohen-Rosenfield (transl.), "Louis de Bonald", *Journal of the History of Ideas* 7, no. 1 (1946): 56–73.

Thomas Kselman, *Conscience and Conversion: Religious Liberty in Post-Revolutionary France* (New Haven: Yale University Press, 2018).

Isabel Laack, "The New Animism and Its Challenges to the Study of Religion", *Method and Theory in the Study of Religion* 32 (2020): 115–147.

Jérôme Lamy, *Faire de la sociologie historique des sciences et des techniques* (Paris: Hermann, 2018).

Charles V. Langlois & Charles Seignobos, *Introduction to the Study of History*, transl. by G.G. Berry. New York: Henry Holt and Company, 1904).

Timothy Larsen, *The Slain God: Anthropologists and the Christian Faith* (Oxford: Oxford University Press, 2014).

Bruno Latour, *An Inquiry into Modes of Existence: An Anthropology of the Moderns*, transl. by Catherine Porter (Cambridge, MA: Harvard University Press, 2013a).

Bruno Latour, "Beyond belief: Religion as the 'dynamite of the people'", in: *The Routledge Handbook of Postsecularity*, ed. Justin Beaumont (Abingdon: Routledge, 2019), 27–37.

Bruno Latour, "Comment redistribuer le Grand Partage?", *Revue de synthèse* 110 (1983): 203–236.

Bruno Latour, *Down to Earth: Politics in the New Climatic Regime*, transl. by Catherine Porter (Cambridge, MA: Polity Press, 2018).

Bruno Latour, "Formes élémentaires de la sociologie: Formes avancées de la théologie", *Archives de sciences sociales des religions* 167, juillet–septembre (2014): http://journals.openedition.org/assr/26199.

Bruno Latour, "Gabriel Tarde and the End of the Social", in: *The Social in Question. New Bearings in History and the Social Sciences*, ed. Patrick Joyce (London: Routledge, 2002), 117–132.

Bruno Latour, *On the Modern Cult of the Factish Gods*, transl. by Catherine Porter and Heather MacLean (Durham: Duke University Press, 2010).

Bruno Latour, *Pandora's Hope: Essays on the Reality of Science Studies* (Cambridge, MA: Harvard University Press, 1999).

Bruno Latour, *Reassembling the Social: An Introduction to Actor-Network Theory* (Oxford: Oxford University Press, 2005).
Bruno Latour, *Rejoicing, Or the Torments of Religious Speech*, transl. by Julia Rose (Malden, MA: Polity Press, 2013b).
Bruno Latour, *We Have Never Been Modern*, transl. by Catherine Porter (Cambridge, MA: Harvard University Press, 1993).
Bruno Latour & Tim Howles, "Charles Péguy: Time, Space, and le Monde Moderne", *New Literary History* 46, no. 1 (2015): 41–62.
Robert Leroux, *History and Sociology in France: From Scientific History to the Durkheimian School* (New York & London: Routledge, 2018a).
Robert Leroux, "Tarde and Durkheimian Sociology", in: *The Anthem Companion to Gabriel Tarde*, ed. Robert Leroux (London: Anthem Press, 2018b), 119–134.
Neil Levy, *Bad Beliefs: Why they happen to good people* (Oxford: Oxford University Press, 2022).
David Lockwood, *Solidarity and Schism: 'The Problem of Disorder' in Durkheimian and Marxist Sociology* (Oxford: Clarendon Press, 1992).
Matthijs Lok, "François-Xavier de Feller (1735–1802) et l'élaboration des Contre-Lumières européennes", in: *Rhétorique et politisation: De la fin des Lumières au printemps des peuples*, eds. S.-A. Leterrier & O. Tort (Arras: Artois Presses Université, 2021), 119–128.
Matthijs Lok, Friedemann Pestel & Juliette Reboul (eds.), *Cosmopolitan Conservatisms: Countering Revolution in Transnational Networks, Ideas and Movements (c. 1700–1930)* (Leiden: Brill, 2021).
Donald Lopez, "Belief", in: *Critical Terms for Religious Studies*, ed. Mark C. Taylor (Chicago: University of Chicago Press, 1998), 21–35.
Arthur O. Lovejoy, *The Great Chain of Being: A Study of the History of An Idea* (Cambridge, MA: Harvard University Press, 1936).
Steven Lukes, *Émile Durkheim: His Life and Work. A Historical and Critical Study* (New York: Harper & Row, Publishers, 1972).
Steven Lukes, "Introduction to this Edition", in: Émile Durkheim, *The Rules of Sociological Method, And Selected Texts on Sociology and its Method*, ed. Steven Lukes, transl. by W.D. Halls (Basingstoke, Hampshire: Palgrave Macmillan, 2013), xi–xxxv.
Steven Lukes, "Sociology's inescapable past", *Journal of Classical Sociology* 21, no. 3–4 (2021): 283–288.
Pierre Macherey, "Aux sources des rapports sociaux. Bonald, Saint-Simon, Guizot", *Genèses* 9 (1992): 25–43.
Arvind-Pal S. Mandair and Markus Dressler, "Introduction: Modernity, Religion-Making, and the Post-Secular", in: *Secularism and Religion-Making*, eds. Markus Dressler & Arvind-Pal S. Mandair (Oxford: Oxford University Press, 2011), 3–36.

Didier Masseau, *Les ennemis des philosophes. L'antiphilosophie au temps des Lumières* (Paris: Albin Michel, 2000).

Didier Masseau, "L'idée et la pratique de la retraite dans le combat antiphilosophique", *Dix-huitième siècle* 48, no. 1 (2016): 41–56.

Anton M. Matytsin, *The Specter of Skepticism in the Age of Enlightenment* (Baltimore: Johns Hopkins University Press, 2016).

Marcel Mauss, "Divisions et proportions des divisions de la sociologie (1927)", *l'Année sociologique*, Nouvelle série, 2 (1927): 87–173. Digital edition (pages 4–55): http://classiques.uqac.ca/classiques/mauss_marcel/oeuvres_3/oeuvres_3_06/divisions_sociologie.html.

Marcel Mauss, "Métier d'ethnographe, méthode sociologique", Extrait de la "Leçon d'ouverture à l'enseignement de l'histoire des religions des peuples non civilisés". *Revue de l'histoire des religions* 45 (1902): 42–54. Digital edition (pages 3–9): http://classiques.uqac.ca/classiques/mauss_marcel/oeuvres_3/oeuvres_3_09/metier_ethnographe.html

Marcel Mauss, *On Prayer*, transl. by Susan Leslie, ed. and introd. by W.S.F. Pickering (New York: Berghahn Books, 2003).

Marcel Mauss, *The Gift: Forms and Functions of Exchange in Archaic Societies*, transl. by Ian Cunnison, introd. by E.E. Evans-Pritchard (London: Cohen & West Ltd., 1966 [1st ed. 1954]).

Michael C. McCarthy, S.J., "Modalities of Belief in Ancient Christian Debate", *Journal of Early Christian Studies* 17, no. 4 (2009): 605–634.

Gregor McLennan, "The Postsecular Turn", *Theory, Culture & Society* 27, no. 4 (2010): 3–20.

Eduardo Mendieta, "The postsecular condition and the genealogy of postmetaphysical thinking", in: *The Routledge Handbook of Postsecularity*, ed. Justin Beaumont (Abingdon: Routledge, 2019), 51–58.

Patrick Michel, "La « religion », objet sociologique pertinent?", *Revue du Mauss* 22, no. 2 (2003): 159–70.

Patrick Michel, "Pour une sociologie des itinéraires des sens: Une lecture politique du rapport entre croire et institution", *Archives de sciences sociales des religions* 38, no. 82 (1993): 223–38.

John Milbank, *Theology and Social Theory: Beyond Secular Reason* (Malden, MA: Blackwell Publishing, 2006, 2nd ed. [1st ed., 1990]).

Jean-Claude Monod, "Inversion du pensable et transits de croyance: la trajectoire de sécularisation et ses écarts selon Michel de Certeau", *Revue de Théologie et de Philosophie* 136, no. 4 (2004): 333–346.

Erwan Moreau, "À propos de Louis de Bonald et de sa sociologie", *Sociétés* 150, no. 4 (2020): 139–150.

Nico Mouton, "An Apologia for Arthur Lovejoy's Long-Range Approach to the History of Ideas", *History & Theory* 62, no. 2 (2023): 272–295.

Laurent Mucchielli, "Aux origines de la Nouvelle Histoire en France: l'évolution intellectuelle et la formation du champ des sciences sociales (1880–1930)", *Revue de synthèse* 116 (1995a): 55–98.

Laurent Mucchielli, "Une lecture de Langlois et de Seignobos", *Espaces Temps* 59–61 (1995b): 130–136.

Pierre Musso, *La religion industrielle. Monastère, manufacture, usine. Une généalogie de l'entreprise* (Paris: Fayard, 2017a).

Pierre Musso, "Religion and political economy in Saint-Simon", *The European Journal of the History of Economic Thought 24*, no. 4 (2017b): 809–827.

Frederick Neuhouser, "Conceptions of Society in Nineteenth-Century Social Thought", in: *The Cambridge History of Philosophy in the Nineteenth Century (1790–1870)*, eds. Allen W. Wood & Songsuk Susan Hahn (Cambridge: Cambridge University Press, 2012), 651–675.

Robert A. Nisbet, "Conservatism and Sociology", *American Journal of Sociology* 58, no. 2 (1952): 167–175.

Robert A. Nisbet, "De Bonald and the Concept of the Social Group", *Journal of the History of Ideas* 5 (1944): 315–331.

Robert A. Nisbet, "The French Revolution and the Rise of Sociology in France", *The American Journal of Sociology* 49, no. 2 (1943): 156–164.

Robert A. Nisbet, *The Sociological Tradition* (New Brunswick: Transaction Publishers, 1993 [1st ed. 1966]).

Robert A. Orsi, "Belief", *Material Religion* 7, no. 1 (2011): 10–16.

Robert A. Orsi, *History and Presence* (Cambridge, MA: The Belknap Press of Harvard University Press, 2016).

Tomas Orylski, "L'itinéraire du croire dans la démarche de Michel de Certeau", *Revue des sciences religieuses* 82, no. 2 (2008): 245–251.

Elías José Palti, "The "Theoretical Revolution" in Intellectual History: From the History of Political Ideas to the History of Political Languages", *History and Theory* 53 (October 2014): 387–405.

Louis Panier, "Pour une anthropologie du croire. Aspects de la problématique chez Michel de Certeau", in: *Michel de Certeau ou la différence chrétienne*, ed. Claude Geffré (Paris: Les Éditions du Cerf, 1991) 37–59.

Giovanni Paoletti, "Representation and belief: Durkheim's rationalism and the Kantian tradition", in: *Durkheim and Representations*, ed. W.S.F. Pickering (London: Routledge, 2000), 118–135.

Giovanni Paoletti, "Solidarity as a social relation: history of Durkheim's project. Some remarks about solidarity and "lien social" in Durkheim's works", *Europeana* 3 (2014): 115–130.

Talcott Parsons, "Belief, Unbelief and Disbelief", in: Talcott Parsons, *Action Theory and the Human Condition* (New York: The Free Press, 1978a), 233–263.

Talcott Parsons, "Durkheim on Religion Revisited: Another Look at The Elementary Forms of Religious Life", in: Talcott Parsons, *Action Theory and the Human Condition* (New York: The Free Press, 1978b), 213–232.

Talcott Parsons, "Durkheim's Contribution to the Theory of Integration of Social Systems", in: *Essays on Sociology and Philosophy*, ed. Kurt H. Wolff (New York: Harper & Row, 1960), 118–153.

Talcott Parsons, *Societies: Evolutionary and Comparative Perspectives* (Englewood Cliffs: Prentice-Hall, 1966).

Talcott Parsons, *The Social System* (London: The Free Press of Glencoe, 1964 [1st ed. 1951).

Talcott Parsons, *The Structure of Social Action* (Glencoe: Free Press, 1949 [1st ed., 1937]).

Julien Pasteur, *Les héritiers contrariés. Essai sur le spirituel républicain au XIXe siècle* (Paris: Les Belles Lettres, 2018).

Charles Sanders Peirce, "Philosophy and the Conduct of Life (1898)", in: *The Essential Peirce: Selected Philosophical Writings, Volume 2 (1893–1913)*, ed. The Peirce Edition Project (Bloomington and Indianapolis: Indiana University Press, 1998), 27–41.

Dick Pels, "Dupliek. Nogmaals: Heilbron's Comte", *Amsterdams Sociologisch Tijdschrift* 18, no. 1 (1991a): 161–164.

Dick Pels, "Historisch positivisme", *Amsterdams Sociologisch Tijdschrift* 18, no. 1 (1991b): 118–139.

Dick Pels, "Reviews: Johan Heilbron, The Rise of Social Theory. Cambridge: Polity Press, 1995", *History of the Human Sciences* 9, no. 1 (1996): 113–131.

Peter Pels, "Classification revisited: On time, methodology and position in decolonizing anthropology", *Anthropological Theory* 22, no. 1 (2022): 78–101.

Sanja Perovic, *The Calendar in Revolutionary France: Perceptions of Time in Literature, Culture, Politics* (Cambridge: Cambridge University Press, 2012).

Olivier Pétré-Grenouilleau, *Saint-Simon. L'utopie ou la raison en actes* (Paris: Biographie Payot, 2001).

Richard Pettigrew, *Epistemic Risk and the Demands of Rationality* (Oxford: Oxford University Press, 2022).

Alvin Plantinga & Nicholas Wolterstorff, *Faith and Rationality: Reason and Belief in God* (Notre Dame: Notre Dame University Press, 1983).

Andrew Pickering, "The Ontological Turn: Taking Different Worlds Seriously", *Social Analysis* 61, no. 2 (2017): 134–150.

Mary Pickering, "Auguste Comte and the Saint-Simonians", *French Historical Studies* 18, no. 1 (1993a): 211–236.

Mary Pickering, *Auguste Comte: An Intellectual Biography*, Vol. I (Cambridge: Cambridge University Press, 1993b).

Mary Pickering, "Conclusion: The Legacy of Auguste Comte", in: *Love, Order, & Progress: The Science, Philosophy, & Politics of Auguste Comte*, eds. Michel

Bourdeau, Mary Pickering, & Warren Schmaus (Pittsburgh: University of Pittsburgh Press, 2018), 250–304.

Antoine Picon, "La religion Saint-Simonienne", *Revue des sciences philosophiques et théologiques* 87, no. 1 (2003): 23–37.

Pamela M. Pilbeam, *Saint-Simonians in Nineteenth-Century France: From Free Love to Algeria* (Basingstoke: Palgrave Macmillan, 2014).

J.G.A. Pocock, "Enlightenment and Counter-Enlightenment, Revolution and Counter-Revolution: A Eurosceptical Inquiry", *History of Political Thought* 20, no. 1 (1999): 125–139.

J.G.A. Pocock, "Historiography and Enlightenment: A View of Their History", *Modern Intellectual History* 5, no. 1 (2008): 83–96.

J.G.A. Pocock, *Political Thought and History: Essays on Theory and Method* (Cambridge: Cambridge University Press, 2009).

Richard H. Popkin, *The History of Scepticism: From Erasmus to Descartes* (Assen: Van Gorcum & Comp. N.V., 1960).

Jean-Yves Pranchère, "The Social Bond in Maistre and Bonald", in: *Joseph De Maistre's Life, Thought, and Influence: Selected Studies*, ed. Richard Lebrun (Montreal: McGill-Queens University Press, 2001), 190–219.

Jean-Yves Pranchère, "Totalité sociale et hiérarchie: La sociologie théologique de Louis de Bonald", *Revue européenne des sciences sociale* 49, no. 2 (2011): 145–167.

Michael Puett, "Wittgenstein on Frazer", ", in: *The Mythology in Our Language: Remarks on Frazer's Golden Bough*, transl. by Stephan Palmié, preface by Giovanni da Col, ed. by Giovanni da Col & Stephan Palmié (Chicago: Hau Books, 2018), 137–153.

W. V. Quine & J. S. Ullian, *The Web of Belief* (New York: Random House, 1970).

Jacques Rancière, *Proletarian Nights: The Workers' Dream in Nineteenth-Century France*, transl. by John Drury (London: Verso, 2012).

Anne Warfield Rawls, *Epistemology and Practice: Durkheim's The Elementary Forms of Religious Life* (Cambridge: Cambridge University Press, 2004).

W. Jay Reedy, "The historical imaginary of social science in post-Revolutionary France: Bonald, Saint-Simon, Comte", *History of the Human Sciences* 7, no. 1 (1994): 1–26.

W. Jay Reedy, "The Traditionalist Critique of Individualism in Post-Revolutionary France: The Case of Louis de Bonald", *History of Political Thought* 16, no. 1 (1995): 49–75.

Philippe Regnier, "Du Saint-Simonisme comme science et des Saint-Simoniens comme scientifiques: généralités, panorama et repères", *Bulletin de la Sabix* 44 (2009): http://journals.openedition.org/sabix/626.

Philippe Regnier, "Entre politique et mystique, sécularisation et resacralisation. Pour une nouvelle approche de la religion saint-simonienne", *Archives de sciences sociales des religions* 190, no. 3 (2020): 87–108.

Philippe Regnier, "L'institution et son en-dehors: la théorie littéraire des saint-simoniens", in: *Philologiques I. Contribution à l'histoire des disciplines littéraires en France et en Allemagne au xixe siècle*, eds. M. Espagne & M. Werner (Paris: Éditions de la Maison des Sciences de l'Homme, 1990), 211–237.

Jacques Revel, "Forms of Expertise: Intellectuals and "Popular" Culture in France (1650–1800)", in: *Understanding Popular Culture. Europe from the Middle Ages to the Nineteenth Century*, ed. Steven Kaplan (Berlin: Mouton Publishers, 1984), 255–273.

Judith Revel, *Dictionnaire Foucault* (Paris: Ellipses, 2008).

Judith Revel, "'What Are We at the Present Time?' Foucault and the Question of the Present", in: *Foucault and the History of Our Present*, eds. Sophie Fuggle, Yari Lanci, & Martina Tazzioli (New York: Palgrave Macmillan, 2015), 13–25.

Melvin Richter, "Reconstructing the History of Political Languages: Pocock, Skinner, and the Geschichtliche Grundbegriffe", *History and Theory* 29, no. 1 (1990): 38–70.

Paul Ricoeur, *La Mémoire, l'histoire, l'oubli* (Paris: Seuil, 2003).

Paul Ricoeur, *Temps et récit* (Paris: Seuil, 1983–1985), 3 vol.

Mark Risjord, "Anthropology Without Belief: An Anti-representationalist Ontological Turn", *Philosophy of the Social Sciences* 50, no. 5 (2020): 586–609.

Scott B. Ritner, "Simone Weil's Heterodox Marxism: Revolutionary Pessimism and the Politics of Resistance", in: *Simone Weil, Beyond Ideology?*, eds. Sophie Bourgault & Julie Daigle (Cham: Palgrave Macmillan, 2020), 185–205.

Pierre Rosanvallon, *Le peuple introuvable. Histoire de la représentation démocratique en France* (Paris: Gallimard, 1998).

Patrick Royannais, "Michel de Certeau: l'anthropologie du croire et la théologie de la faiblesse de croire", *Recherches de Science Religieuse* 91, no. 4 (2003): 499–533.

Claude-Henri de Saint-Simon, "Le Nouveau Christianisme (1825)", in: *Œuvres choisies de C.-H. de Saint-Simon, précédées d'un essai sur sa doctrine*, vol. III (Brussels: Fr. Van Meenen et Cie, 1859a), 315–382.

Claude-Henri de Saint-Simon, "Introduction aux travaux scientifiques du dix-neuvième siècle (1808)", in: *Œuvres choisies de C.-H. de Saint-Simon, précédées d'un essai sur sa doctrine*, vol. I (Brussels: Fr. Van Meenen et Cie, 1859b), 43–260.

Claude-Henri de Saint-Simon, *Œuvres choisies de C.-H. de Saint-Simon, précédées d'un essai sur sa doctrine* (Brussels: Fr. Van Meenen et Cie, 1859c), 3 vol.

Matteo Santerelli, "Concepts, habitudes et le pragmatisme mal entendu. Une lecture des Principles of Psychology à partir de Durkheim", *Revue philosophique de la France et de l'étranger* 147, no. 4 (2022): 491–508.

Richard Schaefer, "Program for a New Catholic *Wissenschaft*: Devotional Activism and Catholic Modernity in the Nineteenth Century", *Modern Intellectual History* 4 (2007): 433–462.

Heinz Schilling, "Confessional Europe", in: *Handbook of European History 1400–1600: Latin Middle Ages, Renaissance and Reformation, vol. 2, Visions, Programs and Outcomes*, eds. T. A. J. Brady, H. A. Oberman, and J. D. Tracy (Leiden: Brill, 1995), 641–82.

Eric Schliesser, "Philosophical Prophecy", in: *Philosophy and its History: Aims and Methods in the Study of Early Modern Philosophy*, eds. Mogens Lærke, Justin E. H. Smith, Eric Schliesser (Oxford: Oxford University Press, 2013), 209–235.

Warren Schmaus, Mary Pickering, & Michel Bourdeau, "Introduction: The Significance of Auguste Comte", in: *Love, Order, & Progress: The Science, Philosophy, & Politics of Auguste Comte*, eds. Michel Bourdeau, Mary Pickering, & Warren Schmaus (Pittsburgh: University of Pittsburgh Press, 2018), 3–24.

Henning Schmidgen, *Bruno Latour in Pieces: An Intellectual Biography*, transl. by Gloria Custance (New York: Fordham University Press, 2015).

James Schmidt, "Misunderstanding the Question: 'What is Enlightenment?': Venturi, Habermas and Foucault", *History of European Ideas* 37, no. 1 (2011): 43–52.

James Schmidt, "The Counter-Enlightenment: Notes on a Concept Historians Should Avoid", *Eighteenth-Century Studies* 49, no. 1 (2015): 83–86.

David Scott, "Appendix: The Trouble of Thinking: An Interview with Talal Asad", in: *Powers of the Secular Modern: Talal Asad and his Interlocutors*, eds. David Scott & Charles Hirschkind (Stanford: Stanford University Press, 2006), 243–303.

Charles Seignobos, *History of Ancient Civilization* (London: T. Fisher Unwin, 1907).

Charles Seignobos, "L'inconnu et l'inconscient en histoire," *Bulletin de la Société Française de Philosophie* 8 no. 6 (1908): 217–247.

Michel Serres, *Petite Poucette* (Paris: Le Pommier, 2012).

Michel Serres, *Relire le relié* (Paris: Le Pommier, 2019).

Francisco Sevillano, "La controversia finisecular sobre el método histórico en Alemania y Francia (1883–1908)", *Hispania* 78 (2018): 193–217.

William H. Sewell, Jr., *Logics of History: Social Theory and Social Transformation* (Chicago: University of Chicago Press, 2005).

William H. Sewell, Jr., *Work and Revolution in France: the Language of Labor from the Old Regime to 1848* (Cambridge: Cambridge University Press, 1980).

Ethan H. Shagan, *The Birth of Modern Belief: Faith and Judgment from the Middle Ages to the Enlightenment* (Princeton: Princeton University Press, 2018).

Lynn L. Sharp, *Secular Spirituality: Reincarnation and Spiritism in Nineteenth-Century France* (Lanham/Boulder: Lexington Books, 2006).

Philip Sheldrake, *Explorations in Spirituality: History, Theology and Social Practice* (New York: Paulist Press, 2010).

Ilana F. Silber, "Gifts in Rites of Passage or gifts as rites of passage? Standing at the threshold between Van Gennep and Marcel Mauss", *Journal of Classical Sociology* 18, no. 4 (2018): 348–360.
Quentin Skinner, "Meaning and Understanding in the History of Ideas", *History and Theory* 8, no. 1 (1969): 3–53.
Quentin Skinner, *Visions of Politics, Vol. I: Regarding Method* (Cambridge: Cambridge University Press, 2002).
David Smilde and Matthew May, "The Emerging Strong Program in the Sociology of Religion", *SSRC Working Papers*: https://tif.ssrc.org/wp-content/uploads/2010/02/Emerging-Strong-Program-TIF.pdf.
Christian Smith, *The Sacred Project of American Sociology* (Oxford: Oxford University Press, 2014).
Jonathan Z. Smith, "A Twice-Told Tale: The History of the History of Religion's History", in: Jonathan Z. Smith, *Relating Religion: Essays in the Study of Religion* (Chicago: Chicago University Press, 2004), 362–374.
Philip Smith, *Durkheim and After: The Durkheimian Tradition, 1893–2020* (Cambridge: Polity Press, 2020).
W.C. Smith, *Belief and History* (Charlottesville: University of Virginia Press, 1977).
W.C. Smith, *Faith and Belief* (Princeton: Princeton University Press, 1987).
Robert Spaemann, *Der Ursprung der Soziologie aus dem Geist der Restauration: Studien über L.G.A. de Bonald* (München: Kösel, 1959).
Robert Sparling, "Theory and Praxis: Simone Weil and Marx on the Dignity of Labor", *The Review of Politics* 74, no. 1 (2012): 87–107.
Dan Sperber, "Apparently Irrational Beliefs", in: *Rationality and Relativism*, eds. Martin Hollis & Steven Lukes (Cambridge, MA: MIT Press, 1982), 149–180.
Dan Sperber, "Culturally transmitted misbeliefs", *Behavioral and Brain Sciences* 32, no. 6 (2009): 534–535.
Dan Sperber, *Explaining Culture: A Naturalistic Approach* (Oxford: Blackwell Publishing, 1996).
Dan Sperber, "Intuitive and Reflective Beliefs", *Mind & Language* 12, no. 1 (1997): 67–83.
Timothy Stacey, "Imagining solidarity in the twenty-first century: towards a performative postsecularism", *Religion, State and Society* 45, no. 2 (2017): 141–158.
Timothy Stacey, *Myth and Solidarity in the Modern World: Beyond Religious and Political Division* (Abingdon, Oxon: Routledge, 2018).
Trevor Stack, Naomi Goldenberg & Timothy Fitzgerald (eds.) *Religion as a Category of Governance and Sovereignty* (Leiden: Brill, 2015).
Joan Stavo-Debauge, *Le loup dans la bergerie: le fondamentalisme chrétien à l'assaut de l'espace public* (Geneva: Labor et fides, 2012).

Joan Stavo-Debauge, "Mauvaise foi. Du revival de la philosophie analytique de la religion à l'introduction de l'objection intégraliste en théorie politique", in: *Quel âge post-séculier? Religions, démocraties, sciences*, eds. Joan Stavo-Debauge, Philippe Gonzalez & Roberto Frega (Paris: Éditions de l'EHESS, 2015), 151–182.

Sue Stedman Jones, "Representations in Durkheim's Masters: Kant and Renouvier. I. Representation reality and the question of science", in: *Durkheim and Representations*, ed. W.S.F. Pickering (London: Routledge, 2000), 37–58.

Philippe Steiner, "Altruism, sociology and the history of economic thought", *European Journal for the History of Economic Thought* 26, no. 6 (2019): 1252–1274.

Philippe Steiner, "French political economy, industrialism, and social change (1815–1830)", in: *Economic Development and Social Change. Historical Roots and Modern Perspectives*, eds. Yiorgos Stathakis & Gianni Vaggi (London: Routledge, 2006), 232–256.

Philippe Steiner, *La sociologie de Durkheim* (Paris: La Découverte, 2005, [4th ed.; 1st ed., 1994]).

Philippe Steiner, "Religion and the sociological critique of political economy: Altruism and gift", *European Journal for the History of Economic Thought* 24, no. 4 (2017): 876–906.

George Steinmetz, *The Colonial Origins of Modern Social Thought: French Sociology and the Overseas Empire* (Princeton: Princeton University Press, 2023).

Phyllis Stock-Morton, *Moral Education for a Secular Society: The Development of Moral Laïque in Nineteenth Century France* (New York: SUNY Press, 1988).

Julian Strube, "Socialist religion and the emergence of occultism: a genealogical approach to socialism and secularization in 19th-century France", *Religion* 46, no. 3 (2016): 359–388.

Arpad Szakolczai & Bjørn Thomassen, *From Anthropology to Social Theory: Rethinking the Social Sciences* (Cambridge: Cambridge University Press, 2018).

Piotr Sztompka, "Modernization as Social Becoming: Ten Theses on Modernization", in: *The Art and Science of Sociology: Essays in Honor of Edward A. Tiryakian*, eds. Roland Robertson & John Simpson (London: Anthem Press, 2016), 163–171.

Timothy Tackett, *The Coming of the Terror in the French Revolution* (Cambridge, MA: The Belknap Press of Harvard University Press, 2015).

Joseph J. Tanke, "On the Powers of the False: Foucault's Engagements with the Arts", in: *A Companion to Foucault*, eds. Christopher Falzon, Timothy O'Leary & Jana Sawicki (Malden, MA: Wiley-Blackwell, 2013), 122–136.

Gabriel Tarde, *The Laws of Imitation*, transl. by Elsie Clews Parsons (New York: Henry Holt and Company, 1903).

Charles Taylor, "A Catholic Modernity?", in: *A Catholic Modernity? Charles Taylor's Marianist Award Lecture*, ed. James L. Heft, S.M. (Oxford: Oxford University Press, 1999), 13–37.

Charles Taylor, "Heidegger on Language", in: *A Companion to Heidegger*, ed. Hubert L. Dreyfus and Mark Wrathall (Oxford: Blackwell, 2007), 433–455.

Charles Taylor, *The Language Animal: The Full Shape of the Human Linguistic Capacity* (Cambridge, MA: The Belknap Press of Harvard University Press, 2016).

Alfredo Teixeira, "Pour une anthropologie de l' « habitat institutionnel » catholique dans le sillage de Michel de Certeau", *Revue d'histoire des sciences humaines* 23, no. 2 (2010): 117–139.

Bjørn Thomassen, "The hidden battle that shaped the history of sociology: Arnold van Gennep contra Emile Durkheim", *Journal of Classical Sociology* 16, no. 2 (2016): 173–195.

E.P. Thompson, *The Making of the English Working Class* (London: Victor Gollancz, 1963).

Edward A. Tiryakian, "Durkheim and Hüsserl: A Comparison of the Spirit of Positivism and the Spirit of Phenomenology", in: *Phenomenology and The Social Sciences: A Dialogue*, ed. Joseph Bien (The Hague: Martinus Nijhoff, 1978), 20–43.

Edward A. Tiryakian, *Sociologism and Existentialism: Two Perspectives on the Individual and Society* (Englewood Cliffs, NJ: Prentice Hall, 1962).

Edward A. Tiryakian, *The Phenomenon of Sociology: A Reader in the Sociology of Knowledge* (New York: Appleton – Century – Crofts, 1971).

Briana Toole, "Recent Work in Standpoint Epistemology", *Analysis* 81, no. 2 (2021): 338–350.

Abel Transon, "Morale du monde", in: *Religion Saint-Simonienne. Recueil de prédications*, Vol. I (Paris: Au bureau du Globe, 1832), 417–429.

Charles Turner, "Review of On The Modern Cult Of The Factish Gods by Bruno Latour (Durham, Duke University Press, 2010)", *European Journal of Sociology* 53, no. 3 (2012): 423–428.

Stefania Tutino, *The Many Faces of* Credulitas*: Credibility, Credulity, and Belief in Post-Reformation Catholicism* (Oxford: Oxford University Press, 2022).

Raf Vanderstraeten, "Talcott Parsons and the enigma of secularization", *European Journal of Social Theory* 16, no. 1 (2012): 69–84.

Dale K. Van Kley, *Reform Catholicism and the International Suppression of the Jesuits in Enlightenment Europe* (New Haven & London: Yale University Press, 2018).

Manuel A. Vásquez, "Grappling with the Legacy of Modernity: Implications for the Sociology of Religion", in: *Religion on the Edge: De-centering and Re-centering the Sociology of Religion*, eds. Courtney Bender, Wendy Cadge, Peggy Levitt, & David Smilde (Oxford: Oxford University Press, 2013), 23–42.

Sebastiano Vecchio, "Modi e questioni del credere", *Rivista Italiana di Filosofia del linguaggio* 14, no. 1 (2020): 181–193.
Paul Veyne, *Did the Greeks Believe in their Myths? An Essay on the Constitutive Imagination*, transl. by Paula Wissing (Chicago: University of Chicago Press, 1988).
Paul Veyne, *Foucault: His Thought, His Character*, transl. by Janet Lloyd (Malden, MA: Polity Press, 2010).
Paul Veyne, "Foucault Revolutionizes History" in: *Foucault and his Interlocutors*, ed. A. Davidson (Chicago: University of Chicago Press, 1997), 146–182.
Eduardo Viveiros de Castro, *The Inconstancy of the Indian Soul: The Encounter of Catholics and Cannibals in Sixteenth-century Brazil*, transl. by Gregory Duff Morton (Chicago: Prickly Paradigm Press, 2011).
Paul W. Vogt, "Un durkheimien ambivalent: Célestin Bouglé, 1870–1940)", *Revue française de sociologie* 20, no. 1 (1979): 123–139.
Sophie Wahnich, "Désordre social et émotions publiques pendant la période révolutionnaire", in: *L'invention de la société. Nominalisme politique et science sociale au XVIIIe siècle*, eds. Laurence Kaufmann & Jacques Guilhaumou (Paris: Éditions de l'École des Hautes Études en Sciences Sociales, 2003), 227–259.
Ernest Wallwork, *Durkheim: Morality and Milieu* (Cambridge, MA: Harvard University Press, 1972).
Ernest Wallwork, "Religion and Social Structure in *The Division of Labour*", *The American Anthropologist* 86, no. 1 (1984): 43–64.
Simone Weil, *La condition ouvrière* (Paris: Gallimard, 1951).
Simone Weil, *L'Enracinement, prélude à une déclaration des devoirs envers l'être humain* (Paris: Gallimard, 1949).
Andrew Wernick, *Auguste Comte and the Religion of Humanity: The Post-Theistic Program of French Social Theory* (Cambridge: Cambridge University Press, 2001).
Andrew Wernick, "Introduction", in: *The Anthem Companion to Auguste Comte*, ed. Andrew Wernick (London: Anthem Press, 2017a), 1–22.
Andrew Wernick, "The "Great Crisis": Comte, Nietzsche, and the Religion Question", in: *The Anthem Companion to Auguste Comte*, ed. Andrew Wernick (London: Anthem Press, 2017b), 117–141.
Andrew Wernick, "The Religion of Humanity and Positive Morality", in: *Love, Order, & Progress: The Science, Philosophy, & Politics of Auguste Comte*, eds. Michel Bourdeau, Mary Pickering, & Warren Schmaus (Pittsburgh: University of Pittsburgh Press, 2018), 217–249.
Ludwig Wittgenstein, "Remarks on Frazer's *The Golden Bough*", in: *The Mythology in Our Language: Remarks on Frazer's Golden Bough*, transl. by Stephan Palmié, preface by Giovanni da Col, ed. by Giovanni da Col & Stephan Palmié (Chicago: Hau Books, 2018), 29–75.

Björn Wittrock, Johan Heilbron & Lars Magnusson, "The Rise of the Social Sciences and the Formation of Modernity", in: *The Rise of the Social Sciences and the Formation of Modernity: Conceptual Change in Context, 1750–1850*, eds. Johan Heilbron, Lars Magnusson, & Björn Wittrock (Dordrecht: Springer Dordrecht, 1998), 1–33.

Robert Wokler, "From the Moral and Political Sciences to the Sciences of Society by Way of the French Revolution", *Jahrbuch fur Recht und Ethik* 33 (2000): 33–46.

Robert Wokler, "The Enlightenment and the French Revolutionary Birth Pangs of Modernity", in: *The Rise of the Social Sciences and the Formation of Modernity: Conceptual Change in Context, 1750–1850*, eds. Johan Heilbron, Lars Magnusson, & Björn Wittrock (Dordrecht: Springer Dordrecht, 1998), 35–76.

Johannes Zachhuber, "Individual and Community in Modern Debates about Religion and Secularism", in: *Religious Responses to Modernity*, eds. Yohanan Friedmann & Christoph Markschies (Berlin: Walter de Gruyter, 2021), 11–32.

Tarcisio Zandonade, "Social Epistemology from Jesse Shera to Steve Fuller", *Library Trends* 52, no. 4 (2004): 810–832.

Andrew Zimmerman, "German sociology and empire: From internal colonization to overseas colonization and back again", in: *Sociology & Empire: The Imperial Entanglement of a Discipline*, ed. George Steinmetz (London: Duke University Press, 2013), 166–187.

Index[1]

A

Altruism, 4, 12, 58, 178, 179, 189, 191, 193, 197n117
Archaeology, 25, 26
Aristotle, 108n39, 182, 185–190, 193, 194
Arnold, John H., 54, 54n80, 54n81, 57n92, 66, 66n13, 67n14, 91n36, 236n2, 292n19, 294n25
Asad, Talal, 2n4, 41, 41n17, 43, 51n66, 279n38, 291, 291n16, 291n18

B

Barrault, Émile, 138, 157, 157n77, 158n83, 158n85, 159n89, 160n91, 161n93, 162, 165n104
Bazard, Saint-Amand, 138, 143, 144n34, 157n80
Belief/knowledge-composition, 37, 54, 164, 187n74, 236

Bellah, Robert N., 206n6, 219n52, 277
Berger, Peter L., 1n1
Bergson, Henri, 33, 70, 70n28, 249
Bert, Jean-François, 27, 28, 28n92, 28n93, 28n94, 28n95, 31, 31n102, 271n6
Bossuet, M., 121, 145, 145n41
Bourdeau, Michel, 59n102, 84n4, 176n21, 178, 178n33, 178n35, 179, 179n37, 179n38, 179n39, 180n42, 184n58, 184n59, 185n62, 185n63, 186n65, 186n67, 187n72, 187n73, 188n79, 189n81, 193n103, 263n124
Bourdieu, Pierre, 23n76, 32, 37, 54n82, 58, 59n99, 62, 64, 77–80, 78n63
Boureau, Alain, 66n10, 69n24, 70n25, 73, 74n45, 76n59, 80n71, 87n15, 125n112

[1] Note: Page numbers followed by 'n' refer to notes.

Brahami, Frédéric, 87n14, 92n42, 94n49, 95n52, 171n1, 172n4, 178, 179, 179n38, 183n56, 183n57, 185n64, 196n111, 286n11

C

Casanova, José, 35n1, 44, 44n34, 279, 279n38
Chateaubriand, François-René de, 57, 57n93, 142, 180
Comte, Auguste, 1, 33, 36, 54, 59, 59n100, 83, 83n1, 83n2, 84, 84n3, 84n4, 84n6, 92, 92n42, 99, 107, 129, 135–137, 135n4, 136n10, 140n24, 173n8, 175–201, 176n18, 176n19, 176n21, 176n22, 176n23, 176n24, 177n30, 178n31, 178n32, 178n33, 178n34, 178n35, 179n37, 179n38, 179n39, 180n40, 180n42, 180n43, 181n44, 181n46, 181n49, 182n50, 183n55, 184n58, 184n61, 185n62, 186n65, 186n66, 187n70, 187n73, 188n75, 188n80, 189n84, 189n85, 190n87, 190n88, 190n90, 191n92, 191n93, 191n96, 192n97, 192n98, 192n99, 193n101, 193n102, 193n105, 194n108, 196n110, 196n112, 197n115, 197n117, 198n118, 199n123, 217–224, 223n68, 224n71, 224n72, 226, 227n88, 229, 230, 232, 235, 258, 263, 263n124, 284, 287, 289
Nicolas de Condorcet, 12, 168
Critical religion, 21, 175

Cuvillier, Albert, 260
Cuvillier, Armand, 247n45, 260n108

D

De Bonald, Louis, 32, 57, 57n93, 92, 99, 99n2, 100n3, 100n7, 101–115, 101n11, 102n13, 102n14, 103n18, 103n19, 103n20, 105n30, 106n31, 106n33, 106n34, 107n35, 116n70, 117n77, 128n126, 129, 133, 136, 141, 172, 172n6, 180, 182, 286
De Certeau, Michel, 4, 4n7, 11n31, 12n36, 15, 15n45, 16n49, 17n51, 25n82, 26, 26n88, 27, 27n91, 32, 56n88, 58n95, 58n96, 61n104, 62, 64, 65, 65n6, 65n7, 66n9, 66n10, 66n11, 69–75, 69n22, 69n23, 69n24, 70n25, 70n26, 70n27, 70n28, 71n30, 71n31, 71n32, 71n33, 71n34, 72n37, 72n38, 72n39, 73n41, 73n42, 73n44, 74n47, 74n49, 75n50, 75n51, 75n52, 76n55, 77, 78, 80, 85, 85n7, 86, 86n9, 87n12, 89n23, 92n41, 93n45, 103n22, 112n55, 160n92, 209n18, 248n50, 251, 253, 253n72, 253n75, 254n79, 259, 259n105, 286n8
De la Mennais, Felicité, 57, 57n93, 102
De Maistre, Joseph, 21n66, 57, 57n93, 99, 102, 180
Derrida, Jacques, 7
Dewey, John, 240
Division of labour, 125, 177, 184, 187, 220, 222–224, 226–228, 229n92, 265

Durkheim, Émile, 1, 12n35, 29, 29n96, 29n97, 29n99, 30, 30n100, 32, 33, 36, 54, 77n60, 79, 99, 107, 129, 135, 135n5, 136n9, 137, 138n13, 149n52, 150n55, 162, 172, 173n8, 173n12, 175, 203–211, 205n3, 205n4, 206n6, 206n7, 206n8, 207n9, 208n11, 209n14, 210n20, 211n21, 212n25, 213–215, 213n30, 213n31, 214n32, 214n33, 214n34, 215n36, 215n39, 216n41, 217–233, 217n47, 218n50, 219n51, 219n52, 219n53, 220n55, 220n56, 221n60, 222n62, 222n64, 223n65, 223n66, 223n67, 223n68, 223n69, 224n72, 224n73, 224n74, 226n79, 229n95, 235–252, 236n2, 237n4, 238n6, 238n7, 239n10, 239n11, 239n13, 239n14, 241n22, 241n24, 242n27, 243n31, 243n32, 244n33, 245n34, 246n38, 246n39, 246n40, 246n41, 246n42, 247n43, 247n44, 247n45, 248n47, 249n52, 249n55, 251n64, 252n69, 253n71, 253n76, 254–266, 254n80, 254n83, 255n84, 256n90, 256n91, 259n104, 259n106, 260n110, 260n111, 260n112, 261n116, 261n117, 261n119, 262n120, 265n125, 265n126, 265n127, 266n128, 269–272, 269n1, 271n6, 275, 276, 276n25, 278, 279n37, 283, 284, 288, 289, 293

E

Enfantin, Barthélemy Prosper, 138, 140, 143, 144n34, 151, 152n63, 153, 157n80, 158, 159n89, 176
Enlightenment, 6n15, 12n32, 14, 17, 20n62, 20n64, 32, 43, 67, 72, 72n38, 84n6, 85–88, 86n10, 86n11, 88n17, 88n21, 89n22, 89n23, 91–94, 92n43, 95n57, 96, 99n1, 100, 100n6, 101, 105, 111, 111n53, 117, 125, 128, 129, 146, 197n117, 200, 207n10, 283

F

Fauconnet, Paul, 247n46, 285n4
Favret-Saada, Jeanne, 166, 167n112
Fitzgerald, Timothy, 21, 22n69, 22n70, 175n16
Foucault, Michel, 7, 21n67, 24, 25n79, 25n80, 25n83, 26n84, 26n85, 26n86, 27, 28, 89n22, 90n30, 95n53, 96n59
French Revolution, 83, 83n1, 87, 87n13, 93n44, 99n3, 100, 104n25, 133, 135, 136n10, 141, 145n41, 171, 171n2, 172n3, 176
Fustel de Coulanges, Numa Denis, 218–224, 221n60, 222n63, 223n66, 223n67, 229, 232, 235, 240, 240n20, 288

G

Gall, Franz Joseph, 190, 200

H

Habermas, Jürgen, 2n2, 38, 39, 39n13, 39n14, 40n15, 44, 44n34, 50, 89n22
Hacking, Ian, 5n9, 55n83
Hayek, Friedrich, 184n59, 193n101
Heidegger, Martin, 42, 42n24, 43, 43n31, 48, 279
Heilbron, Johan, 6, 6n12, 6n14, 19n58, 20n60, 20n62, 20n63, 23n74, 93n43, 172n4, 172n5, 173, 173n9, 176n18, 177, 177n25, 177n29, 177n30
Hervieu-Léger, Danièle, 66, 66n12, 73, 73n43
Historical belief-languages, 4, 200, 232, 283, 288
Hubert, Henri, 272, 272n9
Hume, David, 12, 12n32, 20, 20n64, 41, 54, 91, 197n117
Hunter, Ian, 89, 89n24, 89n26, 90, 90n28, 90n29, 90n32, 94n50, 103, 104n24, 289n14
Hüsserl, Edmund, 246, 246n41

I

Identity, 17, 96, 111, 199, 243, 250, 281

J

James, William, 65, 70, 240, 245, 248, 251, 252
Joly, Marc, 6, 6n14, 174n14

K

Kant, Immanuel, 54, 182, 213, 225, 238n7, 240, 261, 265n126, 285
Karsenti, Bruno, 34, 34n104, 55n85, 84n3, 91n36, 95n53, 95n54, 104n26, 117n79, 118n84, 129n129, 173n8, 181n48, 183n53, 185n62, 186n69, 189n83, 190n91, 197n113, 198n119, 199n122, 199n124, 217n49, 238n8, 240n21, 256n90, 273n15, 286n10, 287n12, 289
Kaufmann, Laurence, 5n8, 5n9, 5n11, 18n55, 93, 93n46, 95n56, 103n23, 104n26
Koyré, Alexandre, 102, 102n13

L

Lamy, Jérôme, 27, 28n92, 31, 31n102
Languages of belief, 4, 6, 16–18, 30–34, 30n100, 37, 38, 55, 58, 59, 62, 63, 68, 77, 78, 80, 82, 85, 104, 129–131, 134, 136, 139, 169, 190, 199, 203, 204, 210, 217–218, 223, 244, 251, 264, 270, 279, 281, 283, 288, 290, 294
Latour, Bruno, 3, 13, 32, 35n2, 37, 40, 41n20, 44–57, 44n33, 44n36, 44n37, 45n38, 45n39, 45n42, 46n45, 47n47, 47n48, 47n50, 48n52, 48n54, 48n55, 49n57, 49n60, 50n63, 51n67, 51n68, 52n69, 52n70, 52n71, 52n73, 52n74, 54n80, 54n81, 56n86, 56n87, 57n90, 57n91, 60, 61, 63, 65, 72, 72n37, 75, 75n51, 167, 167n113, 168n115, 174, 174n15, 216, 216n43, 216n46, 217, 236n1, 242n28, 260, 260n109, 283, 284, 289, 289n13, 291–294, 293n21, 294n25
Locke, John, 41, 91
Lovejoy, Arthur O., 7, 7n17, 7n18

M

Mauss, Marcel, 28, 28n93, 28n94, 28n95, 36, 55n85, 66n12, 73n42, 174n13, 213n31, 216n41, 238n6, 247n46, 269–276, 270n4, 271n6, 271n7, 271n8, 272n9, 272n10, 272n12, 273n13, 273n14, 274n16, 274n17, 274n20, 275n22, 275n23, 278, 279, 285n4

Mental state, 11, 15, 16, 179n39, 240, 292

Mill, John Stuart, 94, 178, 193n102

Mode of existence, 18, 30, 33, 48, 49, 54, 55, 57, 59, 90, 129, 134, 203, 221, 233, 269, 270, 281, 284, 288, 290, 293

Montesquieu, 12, 20, 116

N

Needham, Rodney, 43, 213n31

Neo-Kantianism, 233, 235, 254, 255, 264, 266

Nisbet, Robert, 6, 6n14, 19n59, 20n65, 99, 99n3, 100n4, 142

P

Palti, Elias Jose, 8–11, 8n21, 14, 14n43, 16, 16n50, 58n97, 284n1

Parsons, Talcott, 33, 219, 219n52, 239n12, 269–270, 276–279, 276n25, 276n26, 277n27, 278n32, 278n33, 278n34, 278n35, 291

Peirce, Charles Sanders, 65, 70, 70n29, 193, 240, 245n36, 246, 250, 251n63

Performativity, 40, 47, 117, 218, 223, 273, 283–289, 292

Pickering, Andrew, 263n121

Pickering, Mary, 83n2, 84n4, 84n6, 135n4, 176n19, 176n21, 176n22, 176n23, 178, 178n32, 178n34, 178n35, 179n39, 180n41, 180n42, 184n58, 186n65, 190n87, 192n98, 193n102

Pickering, W.S.F., 215n36, 238n7, 260n111, 272n9

Picon, Antoine, 83n2, 138n16, 139, 139n18, 140n21, 150n56, 159, 159n88

Positivism, 171–175, 178, 182, 183, 188, 197, 199, 210, 211, 213–215, 232, 233, 236, 242, 251–264, 271, 275, 279, 280

Post-secular, 1–3, 17, 18, 31, 35, 37–40, 43–50, 55, 60, 61, 81, 236, 269, 279, 282, 283, 289–295

Post-secular critique of belief, 44–49, 55

Post-secularism, 21, 38, 44, 44n34, 48, 50, 51, 282, 292

Pragmatism, 233, 235, 237, 240, 241, 244–257, 260–262, 264, 266, 275

Prayer, 12, 48, 195–199, 198n121, 201, 272, 273, 275n23

Pseudoscience, 58, 71, 74

Public opinion, 2, 161, 206

R

Rancière, Jacques, 84n2, 153–155, 153n66, 154n69, 156n73, 163n97, 163n98, 165, 165n105

Regnier, Philippe, 136n9, 139, 139n17, 139n20, 140, 158, 158n86, 159n87

330   INDEX

Religion of Humanity, 83n1, 129, 178, 180n42, 184, 189–191, 189n82, 193, 197, 217, 287
Representation, 43, 47, 52, 60, 65, 67, 84, 103, 165, 206, 218, 221, 225, 249, 251, 261, 264, 271
Reynaud, Jean, 138, 151, 162
Rodrigues, Eugene, 138, 150
Rosanvallon, Pierre, 10, 286n9
Rousseau, Jean-Jacques, 12, 20, 111

S

Sacrifice, 12, 109, 109n46, 111, 118, 119, 121, 122, 122n103, 127, 130, 272, 275n23
Saint-Simon, Henri de, 1, 32, 33, 83, 83n2, 84, 84n6, 92, 100n3, 135–151, 136n10, 138n15, 138n16, 139n19, 140n24, 142n25, 143n30, 143n31, 143n33, 145n39, 145n41, 147n45, 148n46, 148n47, 149n54, 150n57, 152n63, 153, 153n65, 155–157, 156n75, 161–165, 164n101, 164n103, 167–170, 167n114, 172–174, 172n5, 176, 178n31, 180, 182, 184, 287
Schiller, F.C.S., 240, 249
Secularity, 1–4, 17, 22
Secularization, 1, 3, 23, 24, 26, 32, 35, 39, 67, 68, 80, 84, 84n5, 89–91, 89n25, 94, 97, 175, 219, 263, 276n26, 277, 278, 278n34, 287–289, 290n15
Seignobos, Charles, 204–214, 206n5, 208n13, 211n23, 212n26, 212n28, 217, 230, 232
Self-historicization, 4, 18, 33, 58, 60, 61, 68, 85, 102, 104, 115–128, 193, 203, 207, 221, 238, 266, 270, 275, 292
Shagan, Ethan H., 6n15, 12n32, 64, 66–68, 66n13, 67n15, 67n17, 91n38, 96n58, 108n41, 112n59, 113n62, 133, 133n1, 214n35, 285, 285n5
Smith, Adam, 12, 20
Smith, Christian, 13, 22
Sociological community, 13, 80, 104, 280, 290
Sociological language of belief, 31, 32, 68, 81, 203, 281, 283, 284
Solidarity, 2, 2n3, 4, 57, 70, 79, 105–115, 128, 128n126, 129, 131, 154, 158, 191, 204, 213, 214, 218–220, 222–233, 222n65, 237, 237n4, 265, 278, 286
Sperber, Dan, 15, 15n46, 15n47, 74n48, 80n72, 103n21, 200n125
Spinoza, Baruch, 157
Spinozist, 256n90
Spiritual authority, 143–145, 168, 179–181, 185, 186, 188, 192, 193, 195, 199, 223, 224, 224n71, 226, 228, 287–289
Stavo-Debauge, Joan, 31, 31n103, 294, 294n25
Steinmetz, George, 21, 21n68, 44n35, 291n17
St. Paul, 143, 185–190, 193
Superstition, 58, 74, 93, 121, 285, 292

T

Tarde, Gabriel, 32, 33, 204, 214–217, 214n33, 216n46, 217n47, 232, 239, 239n12, 242n27, 293

Taylor, Charles, 38,
    39n11, 40, 40n15, 43,
    44, 44n34
Tiryakian, Edward A., 77n61, 77n62,
    219n52, 246n41,
    259n104, 261n119
Transon, Abel, 154,
    155n72, 156n74, 160,
    160n90, 162

V

Van Gennep, Arnold, 236, 236n2,
    242, 250, 263

Vecchio, Sebastiano, 63–65, 64n1,
    65n6, 65n8, 67, 68
Veyne, Paul, 6n13, 26, 26n86, 27

W

Weber, Max, 1, 20n65, 54, 172,
    173n12, 175, 278
Weil, Simone, 165, 165n107, 166,
    166n108, 166n109
Wittgenstein, Ludwig, 42, 42n24,
    42n25, 42n27, 43, 49, 279
Wokler, Robert, 92n43, 93n44, 94,
    95n57, 99n1, 164n100